Bill Cowher (signature)

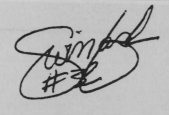

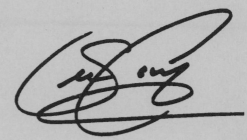

Jack Ham (signature)

(signature)

Josh 1:9

(signature)

(signature)

GLORY YEARS

A Century of Excellence in Sports

By Jim O'Brien

"Sports stories can be memories and daydreams by which we measure our growth, like a parent's strokes inching up the unseen insides of a doorway."

—Scott Simon
Home and Away
Copyright, 2000

Books By Jim O'Brien

COMPLETE HANDBOOK OF PRO BASKETBALL 1970-1971

COMPLETE HANDBOOK OF PRO BASKETBALL 1971-1972

ABA ALL-STARS

PITTSBURGH: THE STORY OF THE CITY OF CHAMPIONS

HAIL TO PITT: A SPORTS HISTORY OF
THE UNIVERSITY OF PITTSBURGH

DOING IT RIGHT

WHATEVER IT TAKES

MAZ AND THE '60 BUCS

REMEMBER ROBERTO

PENGUIN PROFILES

DARE TO DREAM

KEEP THE FAITH

WE HAD 'EM ALL THE WAY

HOMETOWN HEROES

GLORY YEARS

To order copies of these titles directly from the publisher, send $26.95 for hardcover edition. Please send $3.50 to cover shipping and handling costs per book. Pennsylvania residents add 6% sales tax to price of book only. Allegheny County residents add an additional 1% sales tax for a total of 7% sales tax. Copies will be signed by author at your request. Discounts available for large orders. Contact publisher regarding availability and prices of all books in Pittsburgh Proud series, or to request an order form. Several of them are sold out and no longer available. *Doing It Right* and *Dare to Dream* are available in hardcover and softcover editions. E-mail address: jpobrien@stargate.net

---

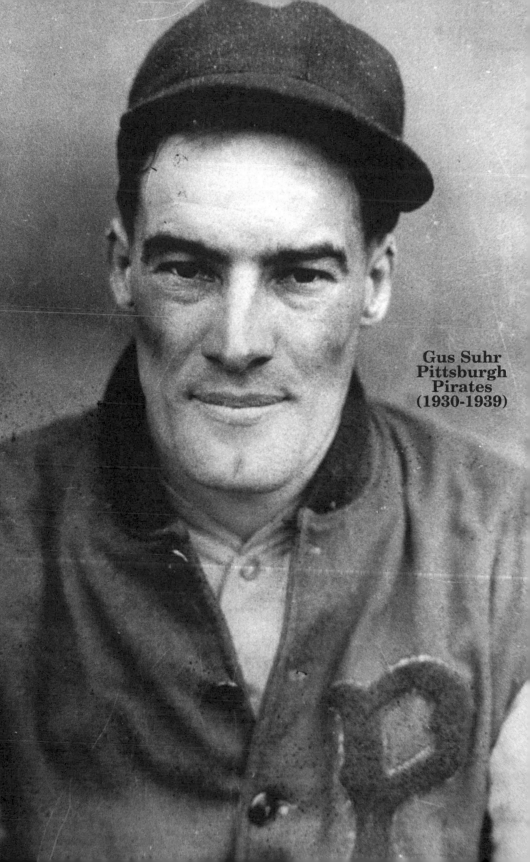

Gus Suhr
Pittsburgh
Pirates
(1930-1939)

Jim O'Brien

Olympic gold medalist John Woodruff speaks to children in his hometown of Connellsville in July of 1999.

This book is dedicated to my daughters, Sarah and Rebecca, for their outstanding achievements in their college careers. Their mother, Kathleen, and I are proud of them and optimistic about their future.

James P. O'Brien — Publishing
P.O. Box 12580
Pittsburgh PA 15241
Phone: (412) 221-3580
E-mail: jpobrien@stargate.net

First printing: September, 2000

Manufactured in the United States of America

Printed by Geyer Printing Company, Inc.
3700 Bigelow Boulevard
Pittsburgh PA 15213

Typography by Cold-Comp
810 Penn Avenue
Pittsburgh PA 15222

ISBN 1-886348-05-7

Contents

> *"When you read a Jim O'Brien book,*
> *you swear you've been there with him."*
> —Bob Pompeani, KDKA-TV

Acknowledgments

Everyone needs help to get anything worthwhile accomplished. I have been privileged to have a great support team in my efforts to write and publish my "Pittsburgh Proud" sports book series. It would not be possible to do this without the broad-based support I have enjoyed the past 20 years.

Special thanks are offered to Robert G. Navarro and Bob Czerniewski of Stevens Painton Corporation and Tom Snyder of Continental Design & Management Group for their loyal support.

Other loyal patrons include John Rigas and Anthony W. Accamando, Jr. of Adelphia Cable Communications; Louis Astorino and Dennis Astorino of LD Astorino Associates, Ltd.; Pat McDonnell and Allison Hoffman of Atria's Restaurant & Tavern; Ronald B. Livingston Sr. of Babb, Inc.; Bill Baierl of Baierl Automotive Group; Rich Barcelona of Bailey Engineers, Inc.; Paul Lang of Bayer Corp.; Andrew F. Komer of Bowne of Pittsburgh; Miles Bryan of Bryan Mechanical Inc.; Charles L. Cost of Cost Company.

Don Carlucci of Carlucci Construction Co.; Tom Sweeney of Compucom, Inc.; James T. Davis of Davis & Davis Law Offices, Armand Dellovade of A.C. Dellovade, Inc.; Walter Sapp of Daniel-Sapp-Born Associates, Inc.; Don DeBlasio of DeBlasio's Restaurant; Jim and Susie Broadhurst of Eat'n Park Restaurants; Everett Burns of E-Z Overhead Door & Window Co.

John E. McGinley Jr. of Grogan, Graffan, McGinley & Luccino, P.C.; Frank B.Fuhrer of Fuhrer Wholesale Co.; Joe Faccenda of Giant Eagle, Inc.; John M. Kish and Todd Cover of Great American Federal Savings & Loan; Frank Gustine Jr. of The Gustine Company; Jeffrey Berger of Heinz, U.S.A.; Jack Shaw of Highmark Blue Cross Blue Shield; Mike Hagan of Iron & Glass Bank; William V. Campbell of Intuit; Larry Werner of Kechum Public Relations; Jack Mascaro of Mascaro Construction Company; Joseph A. Massaro, Jr. of The Massaro Company, Charles N. Becker, Jr. of Marsh & McClennan.

F. James McCarl, Robert Santillo and Danny Rains of McCarl's, Inc.; Clem Gigliotti of Merit Contracting, Inc.; David B. Jancisin of Merrill Lynch; Jack B. Piatt of Millcraft Industries, Inc.; John C. Williams Jr. and Angela Longo of National City Bank of Pennsylvania; Louis Grippo of The Oyster House; Jack Perkins of Mr. P's in Greensburg; Dan R. Lackner of Paper Products Company, Inc.; A. Robert Scott of *Point*; Joe Browne Sr. of National Football League.

Lloyd Gibson and John Schultz of NorthSide Bank; Pat Rooney of Palm Beach Kennel Club; Patrick J. Santelli of Pfizer Labs; Thomas H. O'Brien, James E. Rohr and Sy Holzer of PNC Bank Corp.; Joseph Costanzo, Jr. of The Primadonna Restaurant; Fred B. Sargent and Ed Prebor of Sargent Electric Co., Sam Sciullo of *Inside Panther Sports*, Joseph Piccirilli of Pittsburgh Brewing Company; John D. Gamble of Pitt Systems Inc.

Jim Roddey and Michael J. Fetchko of SportsWave, Inc. (International Sports Marketing); Daniel A. Goetz of Stylette, Inc.; Dick Swanson of Swanson Group Ltd.; Robert J. Taylor of Taylor & Hladio Law Offices; Barbara and Ted Frantz of Tedco Construction Corp.; W. Harrison Vail of Three Rivers Bank.

John Paul of University of Pittsburgh Medical Center; John Lucey and Alex J. Pociask of USFilter; Thomas J. Usher of USX Corporation; Clark Nicklas of Vista Resources, Inc.; Charles and Stephen Previs of Waddell & Reed Financial Services; Ray Conaway of Zimmer Kunz; John Williamson of J.C. Williamson Company.

Friends who have been boosters include Jon C. Botula, John Bruno, Beano Cook, Bob Friend of Babb, Inc., Ralph Cindrich, Darrell Hess of DJ Hess Advertising, Harvey Hess, Mrs. Elsie Hillman, Tommy Kehoe, Joey David, Jim Meston, George Morris, Andy Ondrey, Arthur J. Rooney Jr., George Schoeppner and Freddie Lewis.

Friends who have offered special encouragement and prayer and those who have opened up doors for our endeavors include Bill Priatko, Rudy Celigoi, Ron Temple, Bob Shearer, Jim Kriek, Dennis Meteny, Foge Fazio, Stan Goldmann, Ed Lutz, Pete Mervosh, Mike Ference, Bob Wissman, Kenneth E. Ball, Bob Lovett and Art Stroyd of Reed Smith Shaw & McClay, Bob Harper and Art Rooney II of Klett Lieber Rooney & Schorling, Herb Douglas of Schiefferlin & Somerset, Sally O'Leary of the Pirates' Black & Gold Alumni Newsletter, Chuck Klausing, Nellie Briles of Pittsburgh Pirates, John Longo of WCNS Radio in Latrobe, Rob Pratte of KDKA Radio and Jack Bogut of WJAS Radio. My heartfelt thanks to Mavis Trasp, my "Christmas angel" and her daughter, Sherry Kisic, and their friends at Century III Mall for all their kindnesses.

I do all my work with Pittsburgh firms. All of my books have been produced at Geyer Printing. Bruce McGough, Tom Samuels, Charlie Stage and Keith Maiden are great to work with each year. Denise Maiden and Cathy Pawlowski of Cold-Comp Typographers did their usual outstanding job. The cover design was done by Guiseppi Francioni and Christopher Longo of Prisma, Inc.

The *Almanac* newspaper in the South Hills, for which I have been writing a man-about-town column for the past decade, has promoted my book signing appearances through the years, as has *The Valley Mirror* in Homestead-Munhall.

I have always appreciated the fine efforts of Pittsburgh photographers David Arrigo, Michael F. Fabus, Jack A. Wolf, Matt Polk and George Gojkovich.

Sports publicists who merit thanks are Ron Wahl of the Steelers, Jim Trdinich and Dan Hart of the Pirates, Tom McMillan and Brian Coe of the Penguins, Harvey Greene and Seth Levit of the Miami Dolphins, E.J. Borghetti and Patti Shirk of the University of Pittsburgh, Shelly Poe of West Virginia University, Joe Horrigan of the Pro Football Hall of Fame, Robin Deutsch of the Basketball Hall of Fame, Tim Tolokan, Annmarie Person and staff at University of Connecticut sports information office.

7

Bill Feniello of Connellsville has provided me with great photos of Johnny Lujack and John Woodruff for my last two books. Photographs were provided by Jerry Malarkey, Helen Rusnica, Mickey Furfari, John C. Veasey of *Times West Virginian* in Fairmont, Doug Huff of the *Wheeling Intelligencer*, Tom Hathaway of University of Cincinnati sports information office, and Jim Lembo.

My support team begins with my wife of 33 years, Kathleen Churchman O'Brien, and our daughters, Dr. Sarah O'Brien-Zirwas and Rebecca O'Brien. They make it all worthwhile.

Author Jim O'Brien paid one last visit to what remained of Pitt Stadium.

Introduction
John Woodruff showed the way

"He's done so much for me."
—Roger Kingdom

It was inspirational stuff. The University of Pittsburgh was paying tribute to its track & field and cross-country athletes of the 20th Century. Seated at the dais at one end of the ballroom of the Masonic Temple were four former Olympians. They were, left to right, John Woodruff, Herb Douglas, Roger Kingdom and Arnie Sowell. It was a distinguished foursome in so many ways.

There was a large white screen behind them. It was used to show a documentary film about the school's history in those sports. It was narrated by Dick Schaap of ESPN Sports. It showed each of the four Olympians in action, along with some footage showing Lee McCrae, once an NCAA record holder as an indoor sprinter, who was also present at the celebration dinner.

From a front row seat, those four Olympians were silhouetted against the bottom of that screen during the showing of the film.

It was stirring stuff. Woodruff had won the 800-meter run in the 1936 Olympic Games at Berlin, Germany. Douglas had won the bronze medal by finishing third in the long jump in the 1948 Olympic Games in London, England.

Kingdom had won the 110-meter high hurdles in 1984 and 1988 at Los Angeles and at Seoul, South Korea, respectively. Sowell had entered the 1956 Olympic Games in Melbourne, Australia as the favorite in the 800-meter run, but finished fourth and did not earn a medal.

I had never seen Woodruff's triumphant run in its entirety. He was boxed in midway through the race and nearly came to a full stop to step outside and get away from the traffic. He was spiked on his heel while doing so. He gained the lead, lost it, regained the lead and won going away. He had such a long, magnificent stride. He actually slowed just before breaking the tape. The crowd at the Masonic Temple burst into applause at the race's conclusion.

It was a history lesson for the young members of the contemporary track & field and cross-country teams of Coach Steve Lewis. "This is awesome," allowed Lewis when he came to the microphone.

There had never been a night quite like this in Pitt's rich sports history. This was Friday night, June 16, 2000. When Woodruff went over his historic victory, detailing what he'd done to win the gold medal, you could have heard a menu drop in the ballroom. He had everyone's attention. A huge banner from the Berlin Olympics hung from a nearby balcony to enhance the setting. The U.S. Olympic Committee had provided the banner for this special occasion.

9

Kingdom disclosed that after watching the film of Woodruff's run at Berlin Stadium, during Kingdom's student days at Pitt, that he was determined to become an Olympic champion. "He's done so much for me," Kingdom said. "Not necessarily by personally contributing to what I've done. But just following his path has been such an inspiration for me.

"When I got to Pitt, I was so much like a fruit fly. I had so much talent and I was here on a football scholarship. But just to see the videotape of his competition back in the 1936 Olympics made me want to win a medal. I knew if I worked hard, I could do it."

And, of course, he did.

Douglas, who spearheaded and coordinated the dinner in Woodruff's honor, called him "one of my heroes, one of my mentors."

Jesse Owens, who won four gold medals in those 1936 Olympic Games, had been one of Douglas' boyhood heroes and had similarly motivated him. In turn, Douglas developed an international award and annual dinner at New York's Waldorf-Astoria Hotel to honor Owens and the outstanding Olympic athletes of the world.

Pittsburgh attorney Jerry Richey, Pitt's only sub-4 minute miler, told me at the dinner that he had learned something striking about those 1936 Olympic Games while doing research at the Mt. Lebanon Library where his wife, Cynthia, is the head librarian. "There were 10 African-Americans on the U.S. track & field team in 1936," related Richey. "Those ten blacks accounted for enough points to have won the team championship in track & field on their own."

Hitler was espousing his Aryan supremacy theories at that time. He considered blacks and Jews and gypsies to be inferior. So Hitler had to hate what Owens, Woodruff and the other African-Americans had achieved before his glaring eyes.

Douglas was from my hometown of Hazelwood and was someone I have greatly admired since I was 12 years old. I passed his home on the way to special shop classes at Gladstone Junior High School when I was a student at nearby St. Stephen's Grade School. I met him for the first time when he was honored as a Letterman of Distinction at an awards dinner held at Webster Hall, a few blocks east of the Masonic Temple on Fifth Avenue, at Homecoming on October 1, 1980.

Douglas was sitting on the dais near Rev. Jimmy Joe Robinson, a former teammate on the Pitt football team. Robinson was the first black football player to put on a blue and gold uniform at the University, back in 1945. Douglas joined the squad a few days later. Robinson came from Connellsville, where he had been a teammate of Johnny Lujack and Dave Hart on some champion Coker football teams in the early '40s. He has long been active in the civil rights movement in Pittsburgh. He has long been an admirer of Woodruff who grew up on a farm on the outskirts of Connellsville.

I was pleased to see and shake hands with Sowell. We had spoken on the telephone several times through the years. He has lived and worked near San Francisco since retiring in 1979 as a lieutenant colonel in the U.S. Army.

John Woodruff enjoys reunion with another top athlete from Connellsville, Rev. Jimmy Joe Robinson, Pitt's first black football player in 1945, and meets former NCAA indoor sprint champion Lee McCrae at dinner to honor Pitt's track & field performers of 20th Century.

He had come out of the Terrace Village projects and Schenley High School that surrounded Pitt Stadium to become an NCAA champion at Pitt. *Sport* magazine named him the outstanding American track & field performer in 1956. Just before the Olympic Games.

Sowell injured his leg playing basketball two weeks before he went to Australia. He simply wasn't at his best at Melbourne. He sagged in the stretch run after battling Tom Courtney of Fordham for the lead most of the race. I mentioned to Sowell that Courtney was now living in Pittsburgh, in the suburb of Sewickley, and had been working here as a counselor for Federated Investors. "I'd heard that," said Sowell with a thin smile.

Reflecting on what might have been, Sowell said, "I'm somewhat disappointed in not going as far as I had hoped to go. My goal was to become the Olympic champion; to be what Tom Courtney became. But we can only have one of them and he won.

"I'm glad I went to Pitt, and I'm glad I was on the track team here, even though it never got the attention that I thought it should have. Under Coach Carl Olson, at the University of Pittsburgh, I was required to get an education. To me, that's the bottom line.

"Olson always told me that fame is fleeting, that they forget. He told me you can be a great athlete, and that was nice, but he asked, 'What are you going to do afterward?' That's what gives me the most pleasure about my Pitt experience."

Seeing Sowell reminded me of how I got into sports writing in the first place. I was 14-years-old when Sowell competed in the 1956 Olympic Games. For some reason, I loved to read stories about Olympic athletes in *Sport* magazine. I clipped the stories and kept them in a scrapbook. I formed my own track & field team on the street where I lived. Two years later, as a student at Allderdice High School in Squirrel Hill, I often went to the school library to read a book about the Olympic Games.

When Woodruff was a student-athlete at Pitt he could not rent housing in the central Oakland area. The students of color had to live and eat at the Centre Avenue YMCA ("the colored Y") in the Hill District, a mile away from Pitt Stadium. While training, John carried his dinner, generally sandwiches, with him in a paper bag, because the YMCA cafeteria would be closed by the time he completed his training. As a freshman, he won the first Olympic gold medal in the school's history.

He would come back from Berlin to win gold medals in the half-mile run three years running in the IC4A and NCAA meets. Douglas said that Woodruff would have been the favorite in the 800-meters if they had an Olympic Games in 1940, but they were cancelled because of international hostilities that would lead to World War II. The Games wouldn't resume until 1948.

Woodruff earned a bachelor's degree in sociology from Pitt, and a master's degree in the same field from New York University. Woodruff earned a Bronze Star Medal with the 8th U.S. Army in

Huge banner from 1936 Olympic Games in Berlin served as backdrop for dinner to honor four former Olympians who competed for Pitt, left to right, Herb Douglas, who organized the event, John Woodruff, Arnie Sowell and Roger Kingdom.

Korea, and retired from the U.S. Army Reserves in 1975, with the rank of lieutenant colonel.

This dinner in his honor was held in a building that once belonged to the Masonic fraternal organization. Non-members could not enter the building until recent years. The blacks at this dinner would not have been welcome. The building is located on Fifth Avenue, just across the street from Pitt's Cathedral of Learning. Pitt had purchased the building the year before and refurbished it. It had been transformed from a bleak mausoleum-like building into a beautiful addition to the campus complex. The Student Admissions and Financial Aid office was one of the departments housed there. So was the Pitt Alumni office. It was next door to the Pittsburgh Athletic Association (PAA), which did not accept blacks for membership until 1986. Women were first extended membership privileges at the PAA in 1983. Progress comes slow in some places.

Douglas, who is a member of the New York Athletic Club, had taken me to lunch at the PAA on several occasions in recent years, as these private clubs had a reciprocal arrangement with each other for use of their facilities. So things had changed.

This dinner at the Masonic Temple was held the day after Pitt officials had broken ground for a new 12,500-seat Convocation Center where the men's and women's basketball teams would play, and where a recreation complex for students would be located. The Convocation Center was being built on the site where Pitt Stadium once stood.

I had attended the groundbreaking and found it to be a heartbreaking experience. I was excited about what Pitt was planning to do there, but only wished they had done it somewhere else on the campus. I would miss Pitt Stadium. The hole in the ground was as big as the hole in my heart. Pitt was still searching for a site to build facilities for the track & field team, the soccer team and the student band, which had all lost their home with the leveling of Pitt Stadium. During the dinner, Allison Williams, a Big East champion, challenged Chancellor Mark Nordenberg and Athletic Director Steve Pederson to speed up the process so that they might soon be attending a groundbreaking for a new track & field complex. She did so in a dignified and restrained way, but was firm in her message.

The former Olympians had to be proud of her. She was standing up and being counted. She didn't want those who followed her to settle for second best. Some thought she was out of line.

Woodruff said he would be 85 years old come July 5, 2000. I had seen him a year earlier to interview him for this book. He was having a more difficult time getting around than he had then. He seemed to be even more stooped. One year had taken its toll. Woodruff couldn't run anywhere anymore. He had been using a cane when I visited him the previous summer in his hometown of Connellsville, but he was leaning on it a lot more now.

I had driven to Connellsville several times in recent years, to see Woodruff and, before that, to interview Johnny Lujack, who had won

14

the Heisman Trophy as a quarterback of a national championship team at Notre Dame in 1947.

I had traveled other roads to visit some of the people I have profiled in this book, a sequel to *Hometown Heroes*. I had traveled on three different occasions to visit with Mace Brown in Greensboro, North Carolina. Brown had been a top-notch pitcher for the Pittsburgh Pirates in the '30s. He was at Forbes Field as a rookie on May 25, 1935 when Babe Ruth, playing for the Boston Braves in the National League, hit three home runs, the final three home runs of his amazing career. Woodruff had no recollection of Ruth's big day. "I didn't follow baseball much then," he confessed.

John Woodruff had come from Connellsville to Oakland that same year to enroll as a student at the University of Pittsburgh. So 1935 was quite a year in Pittsburgh, and at the University of Pittsburgh. Sam Parks Jr., one of the first members of the golf team at Pitt, made history that same summer.

Five years out of college and the head professional at the South Hills Country Club, Parks won the U.S. Open Golf Championship with a record 299 at Oakmont in 1935. He was regarded as a rank outsider, someone who was not considered a contender for the title.

During the same weekend that Pitt was honoring Woodruff & Co., Tiger Woods was running away with the U.S. Open at Pebble Beach, California. He won by a record 15-stroke margin over Ernie Els, a blond from South Africa. How ironic. Woods was 24 years old and already had 20 PGA Tour victories to his credit, including the Masters. Tiger was the biggest name in sports since Michael Jordan. The biggest companies in the country —make that the world — wanted to employ their services to help promote their product.

I enjoy talking to these people to find out what made them special, and how they succeeded in sports and in life.

In late October of 1999, my wife Kathie and I took to the road for five days for some rest and recreation. We visited her brother and sister-in-law, Harvey and Diane Churchman, in Raleigh, North Carolina. We left there to visit our daughter, Rebecca, at Ohio University in Athens, Ohio. We had to drive across the width of West Virginia to get there.

We entered West Virginia at the southeastern tip and stopped in Princeton, the hometown of Rod Thorn, who had been an All-American basketball player at West Virginia University. I said we had to stop and check out the town. From there, we went west on Interstate 77. Later, I spotted a sign for Cabin Creek, hailing it as the hometown of Jerry West, another All-American at West Virginia. Since I was a teenager and had read a story in *Sport* magazine about West, entitled "The Zeke from Cabin Creek," I had wondered where Cabin Creek was located. We got off the main road to check out the community. I felt West's presence. Then we arrived at our destination for that night, Charleston, the hometown of "Hot Rod" Hundley, also an All-American at West Virginia. Thorn, West and Hundley had all gone on to play in the NBA.

15

"Do you realize," I said to Kathie as we entered a hotel in Charleston, "that today we were in the hometowns of three of the greatest players in West Virginia University basketball history?"

"I know," Kathie came back. "That's why it's so much fun to travel with you."

West Virginia highways lead to hometowns of some of state's all-time greatest basketball players.

Photos by Jim O'Brien

Sean Casey
A good kid comes through

"He's the best person I've met in sports."
—Marty Brennaman,
Reds' broadcaster

A four-game series in late April of 2000 between the Pirates and Cincinnati Reds was expected to lure large crowds to Three Rivers Stadium. The main attraction was the first visit as a National Leaguer by Ken Griffey, Jr., a home run hitting sensation with roots in Donora, Pennsylvania.

Others were just as excited by the return of another hometown hero, Sean Casey of Upper St. Clair, a suburban community just south of Pittsburgh, who was an All-Star first baseman for the Reds during the 1999 season. That was certainly true for Jim and Joan Casey, proud parents of the popular ballplayer.

Casey was so popular they should have called him "The Cincinnati Kid." That was before Junior came back to the Queen City where he grew up. His father, Ken Griffey Sr., was a fine outfielder for the Reds back then and was now a coach with the club. Three Rivers Stadium has not been kind to Casey, perhaps because he's too busy or distracted by all the people seeking his time and attention.

During the Reds' visit to Pittsburgh, Casey had eight of his teammates and some of his close friends — does he have any other kind? — out to his parents' home for a cookout after a Sunday afternoon game.

I was coming out of Columbus, Ohio on Wednesday, April 19, 2000, scanning the car radio for an oldies station when I stumbled upon the pre-game shows prior to a Reds' home game with the San Francisco Giants. They were talking about Sean Casey.

The Reds had activated Casey from their disabled list that day, much earlier than expected. Casey, out since the end of spring training with a broken thumb, had been scheduled to play a couple of rehab games at Class AAA Louisville before rejoining the major-league club.

Reds general manager Jim Bowden, who got his start as a front-office staff worker in the days when Syd Thrift was responsible for the Pirates' operation, was the first at bat in the pre-game lineup. Bowden explained his decision to activate Casey. "I'm not concerned about him not being ready to play," observed Bowden. "Sean Casey can roll out of bed and hit the ball."

Birdie Tebbetts once said something like that about Smoky Burgess when Tebbetts was the manager of the Reds, before the Reds swapped Burgess, Don Hoak and Harvey Haddix to the Pirates on January 30, 1959. It was a trade that helped boost the Bucs to becoming World Series champions the following season.

"Sean Casey can hit a baseball the way Tony Gwynn can hit a baseball," continued Bowden. "He's a natural hitter."

Jack McKeon, the present-day manager of the Reds, followed Bowden with his own pre-game show. "It'll be a boost to have him back," McKeon said of Casey. "He's always in the middle of something. He'll find a way to get something going. He'll get on base."

My wife, Kathie, and I had been to Columbus to visit our younger daughter, Rebecca, who was in a management-training program there with Red Lobster Restaurants. Casey was a classmate of our older daughter, Sarah, at Upper St. Clair High School. Plus, Barry Bonds, one of the best ever to wear a Pirates' uniform, was playing for the Giants. So there were lots of reasons to stay with the Reds' radio broadcast. The game was on ESPN that night as well.

Marty Brennaman, the "Voice of the Reds," was an old friend, too, going back to my days covering the American Basketball Association. Brennaman, who had been with the Reds for 27 years, two years longer than Lanny Frattare has been with the Pirates, was the "Voice of the Virginia Squires" when Julius (Dr. J) Erving starred for the Squires in the early '70s.

Brennaman would be inducted into the broadcasters' wing of the Baseball Hall of Fame in Cooperstown in the summer of 2000. I bumped into Brennaman at "Dad's Weekend" at Ohio U. in the fall of 1999. He has had two daughters go to school there. He was raving about Casey.

"He's the nicest guy I've met in sports since Dr. J," he said. "He's the most popular ballplayer in Cincinnati since Pete Rose."

It was good to hear Brennaman talking once again about Casey on the radio. When Casey came to bat in the bottom of the second inning, the Reds were trailing by 3-0. He was batting fifth in the lineup. It was his first time up in a regular season game in the 2000 season.

"The crowd is giving him quite a welcome back," Brennaman said. "They love Sean Casey here in Cincinnati."

Casey had two strikes after two pitches, fouled off a pitch and then drew a walk. He later scored from third on an infield hit, drawing praise from Brennaman for his hustling style. The Reds scored four runs in the second to take the lead, and won, 5-4.

Casey fielded a grounder at first base and threw a runner out at home early in the game, drawing praise for a fine play. Casey hit two doubles in three more at bats, not bad for his 2000 debut. He committed an error just to show he wasn't perfect.

It was fun catching Casey's comeback on the radio and knowing he was resuming a successful career in the big leagues. It couldn't happen to a nicer kid.

He drew walks in the late going of the second and third games of the series with the Pirates, scoring runs that helped turn the games in favor of the Reds.

SEAN CASEY
"It's a thrill just to wear the uniform"

Jim O'Brien

"He has a gift for life."
—Aaron Boone

A huge smile creased the cherubic face of Sean Casey as he approached the visitors' clubhouse at Three Rivers Stadium on a Sunday, August 8, 1999. "Keep smiling, Sean," shouted Marty Brennaman, the veteran broadcaster of the Cincinnati Reds. "Show him all those pearly white teeth."

Sean Casey kept smiling. He can't help himself. He doesn't know any other way to face the world. His smile, and his genuine enthusiasm for the game and everybody he meets, is his signature as well as his left-handed batting stroke as the Reds' first baseman. He was carrying a white coat bag over his round shoulders, as it was getaway day for the Reds after a three-game series here.

He stopped and spoke to me for a moment, as we had met behind the batting cage the night before. He said he'd be right back after he put his stuff in the clubhouse. "They call him the mayor," said Brennaman. "That's how popular he is in Cincinnati. He's the nicest kid I've ever met in sports. He's one of the best people I've ever met. I hope he doesn't change.

"We deal in a world where there are so many jerks, so he's a helluva change for the better. I know how he went to Dayton on a day off to help out this family with a serious health issue. He did this unobtrusively. He wouldn't want me telling you too many of the details. The family didn't have much money and Sean helped raise funds. We heard about it and we wanted to do an interview with Sean about it. He refused to do an interview. He said it wasn't done to get favorable publicity. He was upset that anyone knew. It wasn't easy for Sean to say 'no' to anybody about anything, but he wanted to keep this quiet."

It felt good to hear that about Casey, then 25. "Sean Casey was nice to everybody," my daughter, Sarah, told me when I passed along Brennaman's observation. "That wasn't true with all the varsity athletes." Sean signed a baseball for Sarah with a kind congratulatory message.

"Dr. J and Tony Perez are the two classiest ballplayers I've been around," explained Brennaman. "But Sean Casey is the nicest person."

A week after the Reds' visit to Pittsburgh, the Pirates returned the favor and traveled to Cincinnati for a weekend series. On Thursday, August 19, Casey hit a home run in the 8th inning off Kris Benson to beat the Bucs, 1-0.

Casey couldn't believe the life he was living. Anybody who watched the 1999 All-Star Game at Boston's Fenway Park will never forget the introductions of some of the All-Century Players, especially Ted Williams. They may also remember the sight of Casey, carrying a videocam with him around the field, shooting film of all the stars. "I never had more fun," said Casey.

Former Pirates pitcher and present-day broadcaster Steve Blass and Sean Casey both call Upper St. Clair home.

Sean Casey's smile and left-handed hitting stroke draw praise from Reds' Hall of Fame broadcaster Marty Brennaman, seen below.

Photos by Jim O'Brien

Added Brennaman, "I thought he was working for MGM the way he was going around filming everything."

Despite his youth, Casey could appreciate seeing the likes of Willie Mays, Henry Aaron, Tom Seaver, Carl Yastrzemski, Stan Musial, Warren Spahn, Brooks Robinson and Frank Robinson, Yogi Berra and Johnny Bench. Casey would have gotten all their autographs if they had let him. Casey liked the company he was keeping.

He was also in a game, playing right alongside the likes of Mark McGwire, Sammy Sosa, Ken Griffey, Roberto Alomar, Randy Johnson, Jim Thome, Mike Piazza and Tony Gwynn.

"You had to be at Fenway to understand how I felt," claimed Casey. "You had to hear the crowd. Just to be in their company was a highlight for me. Every time I ran into another Hall of Famer I felt like a little kid again."

He would learn the hard way just a year later how difficult it can be to get back to the All-Star Game. It's not something that should be taken for granted. When Danny Marino got to the Super Bowl early in his career, he figured he'd be back soon for another crack at a championship. It never happened.

"He was so excited," Casey's mother Joan said of her son's All-Star Game appearance. "He went out and bought a video camera so he could tape the game from the bench. He couldn't believe he was playing with all those guys. Actually, he couldn't believe he was going, but that's as it should be."

Everybody I spoke to in the visitors' dugout that night in August of 1999 at Three Rivers raved about Sean Casey, including manager Jack McKeon and one of his coaches, Harry Dunlop, who both started out in the Pirates' organization in the early '50s.

Aaron Boone, a 27-year-old infielder for the Reds whose dad and grandfather were both major leaguers, is a throwback to ballplayers of another era, just like Casey. They roomed together at spring training. "At first, you wonder if Sean Casey is for real, or where he comes from," said Boone. "He's too good to be true. He's like Forrest Gump. He has a gift for life.

"I lived with him in the spring at Sarasota, and I'm around him all the time. I've never caught him in a bad mood. You see him in the locker room and he's always talking so enthusiastically. We have watched baseball highlight films from the past, and he's quite a student of the game. I like that stuff, too, because of my family's baseball history."

Harry Dunlop, an instructor with the Reds, said of Casey, "He loves people and he loves life. He treats everybody the same. I don't know how many times he says, 'I want you to meet my good friend' and he's not trying to impress anyone, either."

Dunlop's pale blue eyes brighten when he talks about Casey. "We have some good guys on our team here," declared Dunlop, "but they don't come any better than this kid Casey."

Sean Casey is a favorite of Reds' manager Jack McKeon, at left above, and teammate Aaron Boone and instructor Harry Dunlop in visitors' dugout at Three Rivers Stadium.

Photos by Jim O'Brien

To which Boone interjected, "If he doesn't remember somebody's name he'll lose sleep over it. After he had his eye surgery, he heard about a kid who got hit by a pitched baseball. Sean calls the guy like he's a long-lost friend. He tried to give the guy his moral support. It's not an effort for him. He's different on the field, though. He's an intense, fiery guy between the lines. At the end of the day, however, the game is not important to him."

It's comforting to know that the South Hills has turned out a young man who everybody raves about. His parents, Jim and Joan, who traveled to Cincinnati at season's end to see him play against the Mets in a one-game playoff for the NL's wildcard spot, can take pride in him. "Isn't he great?" said his mother a week later. "I don't know where he comes from, either." Jerry Malarkey, his high school baseball coach, and Frank Porco of North Strabane, who helped him as a hitting instructor, can smile, too. They all go to see Casey when he comes to Pittsburgh to play against the Pirates.

They helped Casey develop as a ballplayer, and he has demonstrated his gratitude at every opportunity.

"I've never seen a kid work harder to develop his skills," said Malarkey. "It's disappointing to see some of my kids get cut when they have similar major league ambitions. Anyone who is cut should remember Sean Casey and be motivated by his example.

"From one level to the next, his work ethic and competitiveness pushed him to improve his skills to the point where he was ready to move on. He did what he needed to do to make him the best he could be at that particular level.

"I'm not surprised by anything he accomplishes because of the way he works. All that Sean gets is because he earned it. Making the all-star team is a great reward for someone who has worked very hard to make himself the player that he is. You must look at the kind of young man that he is. Sean always has been a leader because of his dynamic personality."

Casey had been a .200 hitter on Malarkey's junior varsity team in his sophomore season at Upper St. Clair High School. He was on the pudgy side back then and slow-footed around the bases. "Other than the fact that he worked so hard, you wouldn't think he had a chance to be a professional baseball player," said Malarkey.

As a 14-year-old, Casey went to Porco, who was providing hitting instruction at the Family Sports Complex in Bethel Park. "He was coming off a horrible sophomore year," said Porco. "He came to me and told me he wanted to be a major leaguer. Here's this little pudgy kid asking me if I can help him become a major leaguer. He was 5-feet, 8-inches tall and on the heavy side. But I learned that this kid had a head for the game and a huge heart."

Casey continued to work with Porco in high school, during his days at the University of Richmond, in the minors and, when he's in town, he checks in with him even now. "Frank was the greatest influence on me as a hitter," said Casey. "He taught me that nothing comes easy."

24

Sean Casey first made his mark with WPIAL champion Upper St. Clair High School where Coach Jerry Malarkey, at right above, and teammate Mike Junko became two of his closest friends and biggest boosters.

Casey became a starter as a junior and senior on some good teams.

"All he could do was hit the ball," said veteran scout Elmer Gray of Dormont, who watched Casey many times during his scholastic days, and on local sandlots during Sean's University of Richmond days.

Casey finished the 1999 season as one of the Top Ten hitters in all of baseball with a .332 batting average, fourth best in the National League. He had 197 hits, 42 doubles, 25 home runs and 99 RBIs to his credit. He was hitting .371 at the All-Star break. He slumped in the second half; although he hit .313 with four home runs in September to help the Reds make up four games on the Mets and force that 163rd game.

He was married to Mandi Kanka of Cleveland on November 6, 1999 and they couldn't find a reception hall big enough to invite all their close friends. Mike Junko, a former high school teammate and long-time friend, had introduced him to Mandi. Mandi was a volleyball player at Akron University where Mike played football. His dad, Bob Junko, was an assistant coach there at the time, but had since returned to coach at the University of Pittsburgh. Sean and Mandi met when he was playing in the Indians' farm team at Class AA Akron. Mike Junko was the best man at the wedding.

"I'm going to be there someday."

Sean Casey and his dad, Jim Casey, used to go to Pirates' games at Three Rivers Stadium. They liked to sit on the third base side, so Sean could get the best possible look at the left-handed batters. Andy Van Slyke, the Pirates' centerfielder, was one of his favorites.

"Dad, I'm going to be here someday," Sean kept saying.

Casey had quite a career at Upper St. Clair High School and was one of the stars when Jerry Malarkey's club won the WPIAL Class AAA title. Casey had carried a high batting average. Even so, the only college that called to express interest in Casey coming to their campus was John Carroll University, a Division III athletic program in suburban Cleveland.

Jim Casey suggested his son write letters to schools he'd like to attend to see if he could get them interested in his services. He wrote to Penn State, Clemson, Notre Dame and about 30 others. The only school that responded was the University of Richmond. They offered him a $1,000-a-year scholarship to a $22,000-a-year school. Casey said he was coming.

"It just about paid for my books," cracked Casey, recalling how Richmond recruited him. "My parents had to get all kinds of loans, and we got some student aid."

Family is uppermost in Sean Casey's mind, especially wife Mandi Kanka from Cleveland, and his father and mother, Jim and Joan Casey of Pittsburgh.

From the Casey family photo album

It turned out to be a good deal for Richmond, and for Casey. He grew to be six feet four inches at Richmond and kept hitting the ball. He was the NCAA batting champion in 1995 with a .461 batting average. He gained All-American honors.

Kasey McKeon, a scout for the Cleveland Indians, liked what he saw of Casey at Richmond and recommended him to his bosses. They selected him in the draft. Kasey McKeon and Sean Casey had become good friends in the meantime.

It's funny how things work out. Casey would eventually get traded to the Cincinnati Reds to play for Kasey's dad, Jack McKeon. He was traded the day before the 1998 opener. Then, in that same season, Kasey went to work for the Reds. "Sean stopped at our house a few times to see Kasey when he was coming back and forth from Pittsburgh to Richmond and Charlotte," said the senior McKeon. "I know him better than most of my players. We traded our opening day pitcher to get him, and it's been a good deal for both clubs.

"He's a great kid. He's the nicest Reds' player you'll ever run across in this game. He's a beautiful person. He's hard-working. He has a very positive tremendous makeup. He really enjoys playing the game. That's one of the keys to his success, plus he has a great work ethic. He's a very coachable young man. He makes adjustments real good. He's very fan friendly, sometimes too much.

"I feel fortunate to be able to say I managed Sean Casey. He's one of the best hitters in baseball, right up there with Tony Gwynn and those guys. He's right in that category. I introduced him to Al Kaline at the ballpark, and Sean came over to me and said, 'Do you think he'd sign a ball for me?' Just give me 12 Caseys, 12 Alomars, 12 Larkins and we wouldn't need anybody else. We've had him over our house a few times. I have some things on display there in my game room that were signed by Joe DiMaggio and Ted Williams, President Nixon and President Bush. He enjoyed that. He was thrilled. My son had told me in advance, 'Dad, you'll never meet a guy like this. He's the greatest kid I ever met.' I've met his parents. They think my son is part of their family."

Three days after Casey came to the Reds, he suffered a serious injury during infield practice. He was blindsided in the right eye by a throw by Damian Jackson. The impact broke four bones around Casey's eye. There was concern about Casey's sight and his baseball career.

He was admitted to Cincinnati's Good Samaritan Hospital. That's the same hospital where Maurice Stokes, an NBA All-Star player from Pittsburgh, was cared for over a 12-year-period when he was stricken with encephalitis, a crippling brain disease when he was in his third pro season. Stokes was never able to walk again and died 12 years later, at age 36, of a heart attack.

Two surgeons performed a four-hour surgical procedure to repair the damage to Casey's face. They inserted five screws and a titanium plate around Casey's eye, working from underneath Casey's upper lip.

He had suffered an orbital fracture of the eye and lacerations that required 20 stitches to close.

Casey was sent to the minors for rehabilitation. He came back briefly to the Reds, was still struggling, including a difficult stand in Pittsburgh before about 60 friends and relatives, and returned to the minors for a month-long stint. He came back to the Reds after the All-Star break and hit all seven of his rookie season home runs and batted .300 to finish his first full season at .272.

Tests disclosed that his injury and surgery had, strangely enough, improved the vision in his right eye. His hospital stay and a sermon from his soccer-playing sister, Beth, made Sean more sensitive to the needs of youngsters in hospitals. He got involved with more youth-related hospital programs and fund-raising projects.

Casey came back to become a vital part of a push by the Reds that nearly got them into the playoffs. They were one of the low-budget baseball teams and they had a lot of people rooting for them.

They won 96 games with a $33 million payroll. That was about half of what the Mets were playing their players. The Mets beat the Reds, 5-0, in an October 4, 1999 game in a one-game playoff for the wild-card spot. The Reds' payroll was $40 million less than the Atlanta Braves.

"It's so hard," Casey said after that heart-breaking setback. "It's hard because all of a sudden it's just over. For eight months, we were together every day. We were like a family. Then, suddenly, it's over. We needed one more win, but it didn't happen. That doesn't mean that 96 wins isn't a wonderful, wonderful year. I'll always remember this as a magical year for the Cincinnati Reds."

Casey was certainly part of the magic mix. "I'm probably most proud that I was able to fight through the tough times and finish strong," said Casey. "That's what makes a good player. You can't get down on yourself because it is such a long season."

Casey was a real bargain for the Reds at $220,000 per year, but better things lie ahead.

"You can't help but think about the opportunity you have,' Casey said. "I look at some of my peers and think, 'Wow! That's a lot of money for playing a game.' I know I'm truly blessed. Not so much because of the money, but because I get to put on a uniform every day and play a game."

Casey had to keep those thoughts in mind when he returned to Pittsburgh during the next season, the summer of 2000. He was struggling. He had missed the first two weeks of the season because of a hand injury on the final day of spring training.

It was the second time in three years that Casey had to overcome an early-season injury. The previous one, the eye injury, was much worse, of course. "This was no comparison, it wasn't career-threatening," said Casey. "There's a lot worse things that could have happened. It really wasn't that big a deal."

Casey was pleased with his performance during the previous season, his second in Cincinnati.

"I just feel more comfortable and more confident, and was able to be more focused every day. That's the most important thing in this game. You have 162 games and sometimes you wander out there and just try to stay locked in every day."

Asked about the attraction of coming back home to play at Three Rivers Stadium, Casey said, "The first couple of times it was a real neat experience to come back home and stay with my family. Now it's getting to seem like old hat. The nicest part of coming back to Pittsburgh is getting to stay at my house and see my family."

At the end of this series, however, he was six-for-46 (.130) at Three Rivers Stadium, certainly nothing to write home about. He's hoping that the new PNC Park will be kinder to him.

"I think it will be exciting to see the new stadium," said Casey. "Hopefully, it will rejuvenate the city."

Asked what it's been like to have Ken Griffey Jr. in the Reds' lineup, Casey said, "Before he came over, it was like wow, Ken Griffey, Jr., a larger-than-life character. When you get to meet him, he's a regular guy, just another piece of the puzzle who just happens to be one of the best players in baseball."

"It's a game of failure."

Sean Casey called me, as he had promised, at 11:30 a.m. on Thursday, June 22, 2000, from his apartment in Montgomery, Ohio, a suburb about 20 minutes north of Cincinnati. His wife, Mandi, had just gone out for awhile, and it would be a few hours before he'd be leaving for the ballpark. The Reds were closing out a series with the Colorado Rockies. Casey had one hit, a double, in three at-bats the night before, but the Reds had lost a tough one to the Rockies. He had struggled at the plate in April and May, batting about .210 or .215, and he was coming around in June, batting about .310 or .315. He said he knew he would start hitting again. He would get up to .270 by mid-July.

Talking to Casey is an uplifting experience. He is upbeat and so honest. He giggles in the middle of something he's saying, and is deferential and respectful in the way he talks to the father of a former high school classmate.

He went to Covington, just across the Ohio River, after the game the night before with one of his high school buddies, Dean Astorino. They had something to eat at TGI Fridays. Dean had been a soccer star at Upper St. Clair High School and at the University of Pittsburgh. "My friends come out to see me from time to time," said Casey. "It's a four-hour drive from Pittsburgh to here. Mike Junko, my best friend in the world, was out to see me two weeks ago."

Working his way up the ladder, Sean Casey's stops included Brewster Whitecaps of Cape Cod League, where his grandmother, Ruth Casey, came to see him play in 1996, the Buffalo Bisons in 1997, the Cleveland Indians at spring training in 1998.

TGI Friday's is in the same complex as Applebee's, where my daughter, Sarah, and I had dinner when we visited Cincinnati a few months earlier. I suggested to Casey that the view across the river reminded one of Pittsburgh. There was a football stadium and a baseball ballpark being built near the existing stadium used by both the Bengals and Reds.

"I think about that all the time," said Casey. "When I drive into the city here it really resembles Pittsburgh. It's unbelievable. You've got the Ohio River, the bridges, and the skyline. They're so much alike. Their old stadium looks the same as ours. It's pretty funny. It's hard to get homesick."

His parents, Jim and Joan Casey, make the trip often. They are the source of their son's constant smile, he claims.

"My parents are everything I am today," he said. "My mom is my best friend in the world. My dad is my role model. They wanted me to experience everything, but they didn't push me into anything. My mom wanted me to take piano lessons, but I just couldn't. They'd bought a piano and my sister, Beth, had taken lessons. Now I wish I could play the piano. That would be cool.

"My parents were always encouraging me to do whatever I enjoyed. I really enjoyed hitting a baseball, and my parents approved of the time I spent doing just that. God and spirituality were important in our home. My parents were my guiding influence."

I told him that only two nights earlier I had driven past the Family Sports Complex in Bethel Park where he had spent so much time as a teenager getting batting instruction from Frank Porco. "I spent a lot of hours there," he said.

The 2000 Major League All-Star Game would be held July 11, nine days after his 26th birthday. He knew he would not be going this time around, but he was confident he could get back to meriting inclusion in the near future. The injuries he incurred, the slumps he experienced, all made him realize how fragile his status was as a professional ballplayer.

He had been there the year before, at Boston's Fenway Park, and nobody could ever take that experience away from him. Nobody looked like they were having a better time than Casey, who kept showing up on the network telecast of the contest and all the All-Star window dressing.

"I felt like I had just won a contest," Casey said. "It's a time I'll never forget. Being ten feet away from Mark McGwire when he was smashing the ball out of the park in the home run derby. It was the end of the century, and it was the greatest experience I'd ever had in my life. I couldn't stop smiling. It was just so amazing.

"My dad is big on history so I learned a lot about baseball at an early age. I always thought to appreciate the game today you had to know about what came before. I know there were a lot of guys who got this going, who paid their dues and set the standards for the rest of us to live and play by. I always thought I had an obligation to learn the history of the game.

32

"So I knew about Stan Musial and Warren Spahn and Pete Rose, and it was unreal to see them all up close like that. I saw Rollie Fingers, Nolan Ryan and Johnny Bench. All those legends. I got chills. When Ted Williams came out in the golf cart I got the ultimate chill. The history of the sport was right there on the field. It was one of the most amazing experiences."

Being a part of that show was a validation that Sean Casey had made it big in the big leagues. Injuries and batting slumps are a part of the process, according to Casey.

"If everyone could do it then everyone else would be up here," said Casey. "I know I have a special gift. I thank God for that every day. It's a game of failure. Even the biggest stars fail seven out of ten times at bat. Those difficult times you have to get through make you a better ballplayer. Even those great players on the field at Fenway Park all went through a few slumps each season, and a ton of them in their careers.

"I read a statistic that only six to seven percent of professional baseball players even make it to the big leagues, and only four percent make a career of it. I intend to have a long career, and I will do whatever it takes to realize that goal. You have to keep battling. You're going to struggle from time to time, in life and in sports.

"When you go through a tough time right in the beginning of the season, as I did this year, it's magnified. I had to keep telling myself earlier this season that there were still 100 games to go."

When I told Casey that I had heard a radio broadcast of his first game of the season, when he had two hits, he said, "That's been my history. When I came back from my eye injury, I went three-for-four in my first game. Then I think I went 0-for-27 right after that. It's all so much a part of the game.

"If you can't accept and deal with failure this isn't the game for you. Even when you hit the ball well you might hit four liners in a row right at somebody. It doesn't show up in the box score but you have to tell yourself you had a pretty good game. That happens.

"Anyone can be a great player when things are going well. It's tougher to be a great player when you're not. That's the true test."

I asked Casey where his smile and friendly spirit originated. "I attribute that to my family," he said. "My folks are both outgoing. They're always positive. That was fed into me when I was growing up. My faith in God helps. I sit down with him every day when I say my prayers. It's tough at times. I'm not immune from that. Sometimes I get down, too. It's easy to harp on the negative.

"They say life's ten percent of what happens and 90 percent of how you react to it. If you have the hope, things will take care of themselves. If you don't mind, I'd like to mention that there's a lesson in the Bible about that. Check out Romans. 5:3-5."

Here's the excerpt from the Bible that Casey was referring to:

"We also boast of our troubles, because we know that trouble produces endurance, endurance brings God's approval, and his approval creates hope. This hope does not disappoint us, for God has poured out his love into our hearts by means of the Holy Spirit, who is God's gift to us."

Casey continued, "I'm going to keep working through the tough times. I'm not going to let baseball dictate the kind of person I am. There have been times I've come home to Mandi, and started feeling sorry for myself. I was bringing my job home with me. But I don't want to do that.

"I'm going to continue to lift weights, and work at my hitting and fielding drills, and I'll care what I'm doing on the baseball field. But I'll still be the same person I've been.

"There aren't any guarantees. So you can't take this for granted."

Casey mentioned the deaths in auto accidents of several famous athletes in recent months, such as Malik Sealy of the Minnesota Timberwolves and Derrick Thomas of the Kansas City Chiefs. "Those tragedies point up how temporary this can all be," said Casey.

"Yeah, I get down. I'm not always smiling. But I work at getting out of a funk as fast as possible. You have to work your way through adversity and, as that passage in the Bible says, you have to have hope. There are times I get down on myself and feel sorry for myself. I'll be miserable. But I can't be a baseball player every hour of the day. I'm also a husband, a son, a brother, and a friend. I have to keep that in mind.

"So don't let things keep you down. Hang in there, Jim. Keep your spirits up. Keep smiling."

From the Casey family photo album

Sean Casey, at age 8

Mario and Michael
Top celebrity field at Nevillewood

"A lot of people showed up."
—Mario Lemieux

A galaxy of good memories remains from the 2000 Mellon Mario Lemieux Celebrity Invitational. Anyone who participated in or attended the third annual star-studded golf outing June 8-11, 2000 at The Club at Nevillewood shared stories for weeks afterward about some celebrity they saw, spoke to, overheard saying something, or had sign something they treasure as a memento of the occasion. It's up close and personal for 18 holes. Those with a light or flexible work schedule can follow the stars for four days.

Some schedule their vacations so they can volunteer to work the entire event. That way they gain an insider's involvement in this celebrity roundup and it's for a good cause. Anyone who enjoys sports and stargazing, with some pretty impressive and some pretty poor golf thrown in for good measure, would enjoy this gathering.

Mario is a tremendous magnet in attracting an outstanding field of Hall of Fame caliber competitors from the sports, entertainment and media worlds, and a seasoned and enthusiastic volunteer corps as well. They come to a marvelous patch of green in the neighboring communities of Collier and Presto in the suburbs just south of Pittsburgh. It's only four miles from my house, taking the backroads through Bridgeville, but it's a trip to a different world. It's like going to the Magic Kingdom at Walt Disney World. The Mellon Lemieux Invitational has become a rite of summer, one of the most enjoyable events on the Pittsburgh sports or social calendar. It's a fun place to be. It's a place to see and be seen.

The folks at Ketchum, the city's top public relations agency, do an outstanding job in calling attention to the promotion. It gets great national and local coverage.

Mario and Michael Jordan, Dan Marino, John Elway, Charles Barkley and Bryant Gumbel were the biggest names this time around, but wherever one looked Thursday through Sunday they saw someone they recognized who had done something special in sports, showbiz or television. Hey, even Marino's caddy, Emil Boures, was a pretty fair offensive lineman with Pitt and the Steelers in the '80s. Wayne Gretzky and Johnny Bench had been in the celebrity lineup the year before, but had schedule conflicts this time around that prevented them from playing. They have promised to return for future outings.

Mario was the main man, drawing the biggest applause from the adoring crowds and corporate sponsors who helped raise more than a million dollars for cancer research. "Mario, thanks for the Pens!" hollered someone in the gallery as Mario left the No. 1 tee on the final day of the competition.

35

It's important to remember that Lemieux's career with the Penguins was interrupted and shortened by his battle with Hodgkin's Disease, a form of cancer. So his concern for this cause is quite genuine. He is also the father of four children, one of whom was considerably challenged by a premature birth. So Mario and his wife, Nathalie, lend their names, time and fund-raising talents to several related causes to help children and their families.

"It was a great week," allowed Lemieux. "The purpose of the week is to raise a lot of money for a good cause. We're gonna beat cancer yet. It was a great event. A lot of people showed up."

In addition to contributions from major sponsors, revenue for the Mario Lemieux Foundation is generated by tournament ticket sales, a two-day golf pro-am that matches three amateur golfers with one celebrity, hospitality tent and skybox sales, program advertising, oncourse advertising and a celebrity/auction party that was held this time under a tent at Three Rivers Station.

Bob Pompeani, the sports broadcaster from KDKA TV, emceed the auction and told a story about Danny Marino in the media room the next day. "To mark his retirement, Danny was presented with a black and gold Steelers jersey with No. 13 and his name on the back of it," said Pompeani. "It was signed by Mario Lemieux, Michael Jordan, John Elway and some of the other guys here. Danny was really taken aback. There aren't many things you can give Danny Marino that he doesn't already have. He was moved by this gesture."

Lemieux and his staff of volunteers run a first-class program in nearly every respect. Here's a handsome young man who brought two Stanley Cup championships to town in the early '90s, beat cancer and saved the Penguins for Pittsburgh. No wonder he is the most popular athletic figure in these parts. He's not one to play to the crowd, as some of the celebrities do so easily, but a mere smile from Mario seems to satisfy his fans.

When he raises his right arm to acknowledge their cheers, the sight looks familiar. That's the way he acknowledged their cheering when the Penguins won their first Stanley Cup in 1991. Mario gets more mileage out of a slight smile than some get out of a sparkling speech. When he holds his Penguins ballcap overhead it brings to mind another image of a local icon: Roberto Clemente standing on second base after getting his 3000th hit.

We were lucky to have the likes of Lemieux and Clemente and oh so many others come to our city to play their respective games. To have so many stars that represent other cities come to Pittsburgh each June is just icing on the celebrity cake.

> **Mario Lemieux:**
> *"The purpose of the week is to raise a lot of money for a good cause. We're gonna beat cancer yet."*

JOHN ELWAY and MARIO LEMIEUX
Two of biggest draws

ANGIE HARMON
Assistant D.A. on "Law and Order"

RICK RHODEN
Former Pirates pitcher

MARIO LEMIEUX
Meets the press

Lemieux Celebrity Invitational photos by Jim O'Brien

"Michael Jordan is like a little kid."
—Dan Quinn

Michael Jordan jumped out of a golf cart when he arrived at the practice tee on Thursday and hugged Mario and shook hands with Dan Quinn, one of Mario's former Penguin teammates and best friends.

"Welcome to my world," quipped Quinn, which was a tip-off as to what lie ahead for Jordan and all the other visitors to Mr. Quinn's Neighborhood at Nevillewood. Quinn had carded a course record 65 in a practice round earlier in the week.

Eyes follow Jordan's every move. Many of the other celebrities clamor for his attention, an exchange or pat on the shoulder suffices. He's always animated and seldom disappoints anyone with his antics or acknowledgments. Jordan was jubilant and on the hustle from the get-go.

"We got a gin game tonight?" asked Jordan for openers.

"I'm sure we can get something going," allowed the lower-key Lemieux, with a slight smile.

"How many strokes you guys going to give me?" said Jordan.

"How's your golf game?" said Mario.

"Terrible," Jordan came back. "I'm working, you know."

"I'm working, too," said Lemieux.

"Yeah, but you got a coach," said Jordan, now an exec with the NBA's Washington Wizards. "I still need to get a coach. I'd get you, but you don't come cheap."

Such exchanges are the sort of special moments that stay with you after the Lemieux event has come and gone. "Michael Jordan is like a little kid," said Quinn. "He just wants to play. He loves to play any game. He loves being with the guys."

As it turned out, Quinn could have given Jordan 37 strokes and Lemieux 22 strokes and still taken their money. The 14-year-NHL veteran buried everybody on his home course with a record 202 score, a 14-under showing for three rounds. He had scores of 66-67-69 on a par 72 course. So there was no suspense regarding who was going to win when they teed off the final day.

Quinn won by 14 strokes over runner-up Al Del Greco, a place-kicker for the Tennessee Titans, to take home a $40,000 first prize out of a total purse of $125,000. In a classy gesture, Quinn gave half the money back to the Lemieux Cancer Foundation. No one ever won by a bigger margin on the celebrity tour.

Lemieux and Quinn once roomed together when they were playing for the Penguins and have remained close friends. No one was more congenial and respectful of the crowds at Nevillewood than Quinn. A handsome blond under his Ben Hogan cream-colored golf cap, he looked like he owned the place and talked as if he were trying to sell real estate to the visitors.

Basketball superstar
Michael Jordan drew
attention from
Mario Lemieux and
eventual winner
Dan Quinn at
Lemieux Celebrity
Invitational.

Judge Ralph Cappy, who played with Jordan's foursome on the first day, said as he walked down the fairway of the No. 1 hole. "I've never felt more pressure on a tee shot than that one in my life," Judge Cappy confessed. He had a strong shot that slipped into a sand trap to the right of the fairway, but he made a nice recovery on his second shot onto the green.

"I can't keep this up too long," said Judge Cappy. "I'll wear out, I know."

"I'm still excited about meeting all the celebrities."
—Rick Rhoden

Rick Rhoden, the former pitcher for the two-time National League champion Dodgers and for the '79 World Series champion Pirates, had won the previous two Lemieux Invitationals, and was in the running until the last day for the third title as well.

Rhoden, at 47, is honing his game so that he might be good enough to qualify for the PGA Senior Tour when he turns 50. He knows that's a much more demanding kind of competition, but he is confident that if he continues to work at his game that he can do it. He's won more than $1.5 million in golf earnings since 1990 as one of the leaders on the celebrity golf tour. Quinn, who is second only to Rhoden in celebrity tour victories, has similar ambitions.

"I wish they had some thing like this tournament when I was a kid," related Rhoden. "I still get excited about meeting all the celebrities. I feel like a part of a team again when I get together with the guys at these tournaments. It's not unusual for ten or fifteen of us to go out together, with wives, to dinner.

"The crowds are great. Our guys know the gig: be nice to the corporate people on Thursday and Friday. I think the corporate people get a bang for their buck with us. This is a great event to entertain customers, either playing or watching and enjoying all the social activity. This is a great setting.

"I first met Mario when he was 18 and I was playing for the Pirates. They had just drafted him, and someone brought him to the locker room to meet the guys. We were told he was going to be a great one. You hear that a lot about a hot prospect, but this one turned out to be the real thing. He's had a great career. Mario does a great job pulling this all together.

"Michael Jordan is the Pied Piper here. Everyone follows him around. Everyone wants a piece of him. It can't be easy to concentrate on your golf game when you get that kind of crowd chasing after you. I think he enjoys the locker room and the men's grill the best, when he can get in out of the sun and sit and have fun with guys who'll give him his space.

There were sports superstars on the sidelines as well as on the golf course at Mario Lemieux Celebrity Invitational, like former Hopewell High School teammates Danny Rains, left above, and Tony Dorsett, who won Super Bowl rings with Chicago Bears and Dallas Cowboys, respectively, and former Steelers linebackers Jack Ham, left below, and Andy Russell.

"He likes hanging out with the guys. He can play gin and be one of the guys. He doesn't need to be here. He can play at Augusta and no one will bother him," Rhoden related.

Rhoden was one of the golfers who said the course was in great shape. That was a tribute to Ken Flisek and Isaac Farabaugh and their course maintenance staff.

While Rhoden was in Pittsburgh, he took advantage of the opportunity to visit with some former teammates like Phil Garner and Bill Madlock, who are looking after the Detroit Tigers, in town for a series with the Bucs. "I came here in 1979 to be a part of a championship team," related Rhoden. "And I'd been with good teams with the Dodgers; we were always fighting with Cincinnati for the National League title. I stayed in Pittsburgh through the early '80s. We had some great teams. We had Willie Stargell and Dave Parker. They can say what they want about Dave Parker, but he played as hard as anybody did. I thought Parker always gave you his all. He was OK with me. He and Willie were the two best ballplayers I ever played with.

"The Pirates were closer than the Dodgers. If you went into the hotel restaurant for breakfast with the Dodgers there'd be eight guys at eight different tables. With the Pirates, there'd be eight guys sitting together. Willie was a good influence on everybody in that respect. Our manager, Chuck Tanner, was the kind of guy who didn't have a lot of rules. If you hustled on the field, he didn't care what you did otherwise. Tanner's still a great guy. Getting together with the guys here is the kind of spirit we had when I was playing with the Pirates."

Many of the sports celebrities came up and introduced themselves to Jordan. "I just wanted to say hello to you," said Steelers' head coach Bill Cowher. "You talk about poise under pressure, and I use you as an example of that when I'm talking to my guys."

Cowher also embraced Marino. "Retiring wasn't easy, I know," Cowher told him. "It's probably the hardest decision you've ever had to make."

Charles Barkley wanted to meet Cowher. "I like the way you coach," the recently retired NBA player told the Steelers' sideline leader. "You've got passion."

"Who was Digger Phelps?"

There isn't a better bargain in sports than this tournament. The price is right, $10 a ticket for adults, and $5 for youngsters, free parking and free shuttle service. The concession stand prices are twice what they ought to be, which is par for the course at all sports venues.

Seeing what one person on a shuttle bus nearing Nevillewood described as "monster houses" is another attraction of touring the elite golf community. Checking out the cars in the parking lot near the clubhouse is worth the walk. You won't find any jalopies there.

Michael Jordan gets a pep talk at practice tee from Steelers coach Bill Cowher, above, while Cowher's close friend Marty Schottenheimer, from nearby McDonald, pairs up with former Ohio State and NBA great Jerry Lucas at Mario Lemieux Celebrity Invitational.

Quinn lives alongside the 13th hole at the Jack Nicklaus-designed course. Many of the homeowners at Nevillewood host their own backyard parties during the tournament. Some who come to the event, the high rollers anyhow, like what they see and buy land to build homes there, or buy existing properties. It's great exposure for Nevillewood, one of the newest and fastest-growing communities of its kind in the tri-state area.

The young autograph seekers chase after the five or six headliners each year and those, naturally, are the toughest to get. The top stars are usually flanked by security guards and they keep the fans at a distance until they have completed their round. Jordan had four personal guards, Elway, Mario and Marino three apiece.

There are about 50 former and current outstanding athletes at Nevillewood who would gladly sign autographs for anyone who asked.

The field for the 2000 event included the following football players: Donny Anderson, Steve Bartkowski, Jerome Bettis, John Brodie, Keith Byars, Chuck Cecil, Chris Chandler, John Congemi, Randy Cross, Trent Dilfer, Bill Fralic, Roy Green, Jack Ham, John Kidd, Brian Kinchen, Mark Malone, Mark May, Jim McMahon, Andy Russell, Mark Rypien, Marty Schottenheimer, Jason Sehorn, Emmitt Smith, Kordell Stewart, Lynn Swann and Joe Theismann.

Representing the basketball world were Vinny Del Negro, Bill Laimbeer, Jerry Lucas, Digger Phelps and Truck Robinson.

"Who was Digger Phelps?" one onlooker asked at the 10th hole. He was the basketball coach at Fordham and Notre Dame and is now an analyst for ESPN. It said so in the tournament program. He got his nickname, I knew, from his father who was in the funeral business.

Some of baseball's best were Kurt Bevacqua, Gary Carter, Rollie Fingers, Carlton Fisk, Jim Leyland, Kevin McClatchy, Joe Morgan, Shane Rawley, Mike Schmidt and Andy Van Slyke.

Former NHL players at Nevillewood were Jay Caufield, John Cullen, Bob Errey, Mike Eruzione, Grant Fuhr, Clark Gillies, Bobby Hull, Eddie Johnston, Pierre Larouche, Stan Mikita, Jean Potvin, Mark Recchi, Dale Tallon, John Vanbiesbrouck and Darren Veitch. Judy Merz, a member of the U.S. women's hockey team, was the lone woman entry.

Former tennis great, Ivan Lendl, who won eight Grand Slam titles, is one of the best golfers on the celebrity tour. They say he plays six days a week and takes a lesson on the seventh day.

From the television and showbiz world were Dan Cortese, Tom Dreesen, Bryant Gumbel, Joe Kernen, Matt Lauer and Bob Pompeani.

The best place to check them out is the practice tee. The lineups, from left to right, are often impressive when one considers the accomplishments of these people. There are placards identifying each of the celebrity entries.

The men's grill at The Club at Nevillewood is an exclusive retreat for the celebrities during the tournament. That's where they go to get away from the madding crowd. That's where they have go to cool off, have a few drinks, play cards or simply to swap stories. I was

NHL Hall of Famers and former Chicago Black Hawks teammates, Bobby Hull and Stan Mikita, were reunited at Nevillewood golf event, while two former Pittsburgh sports performers, baseball's Jim Leyland and hockey's Mark Recchi, get together at the No. 10 hole.

standing outside the guarded doors from time to time to pick off players as they passed. You could hear them trying to outshout one another from time to time. It sounded like any clubhouse in sports. No one talked more or louder than Charles Barkley. He was always holding court. He's a terrible golfer — with a weird hitch or halt in his swing — but he was fun for all.

"Don't let him play in the foursome ahead of us," Jordan told Lemieux on opening day. "We'll never get done. Can't you switch him now?"

There was somebody who outbarked Barkley at the Invitational. One of the sideshows was a trick shot exhibition by Dennis Walters of Fort Lauderdale. He also brought along his trained dog, Benjy Hogan.

Walters said his dog knew Michael Jordan's jersey number — 23. He asked his dog what the first number was on Jordan's jersey. The dog barked twice. Asked for the next number, the dog barked three times. Asked how many championship rings Michael had, the dog barked six times.

Jordan just smiled as he looked on. "How many rings does Charles Barkley have?" Jordan asked the dog. The dog didn't bark. Everybody laughed.

Nevillewood continues to grow as a golf community. Stunning homes, most of them mansions that cost several million dollars to build, surround the course. There are some $250,000 to $300,000 carriage houses on the outskirts of the plan as well. This land was just an open field ten years earlier, left vacant when a state mental hospital was closed down. It has become a picturesque residential and recreation complex.

The weather was perfect the first two days, and a tad too hot and too humid on Saturday and Sunday, with temperatures hovering around the 90 degrees mark. There was no rain, however, which spoiled one of the earlier editions of this event. The rain held off till the action was concluded.

The highlight for me was meeting Angie Harmon, who plays the role of Abbie Carmichael, the assistant district attorney, on NBC-TV's "Law and Order" show. That's one of my favorite shows. Miss Harmon was on "Baywatch" before that. I never saw her in that show.

"I was always fully clothed," said Miss Harmon, rather defensively. "No nudity."

She was so slender, so sweet and personable with everyone she met. She couldn't have been nicer to those who approached her. She signed autographs, posed for photos and exchanged pleasantries. She strolled the fairways with her fiancé, New York Giants defensive back Jason Sehorn. She wore a pink short-sleeved jersey and snug black Capri pants, quite a contrast to the gray or dark blue business suits she always wears in her television show. "I wear big clothes on TV," she said with a smile. She seldom smiles in her TV role, always having an edge about her.

Sehorn turned in the worst scorecard, with 311, but who cared? Everyone was happy he came. They were even happier that his girl friend tagged along. Hey, it was all for a good cause.

"Do I look Italian to you?"
—Michael Jordan

Michael Jordan signed autographs for anyone with an affliction who was called to his attention along the ropes that lined the course. It was that way everywhere he went in his NBA playing days. Danny Marino and most of the top sports stars are great in that regard. A young man in a wheelchair from East Liverpool, Ohio thanked Jordan for his signature and said he hoped he wasn't too much of a bother.

"No problem," said Jordan. "This is what I do for a living."

A caddie tossed an Italian coin Jordan's way, telling him it would bring him good luck. Jordan tossed it back. "Do I look Italian to you?" he asked.

Jordan showed up the first day wearing a black shirt and black and white striped slacks, an unlit cigar with the band still on it in the corner of his mouth.

Phil Collier, a retired businessman from Moon Township, announces the celebrities when they begin play at the No. 1 tee. He carries bio sketches on all of them, and alters them from one day to the next, and sometimes has difficulty finding the right notes when the golfers are ready to go. He gets teased a lot by the players.

Jordan has jousted with Collier every time he has come by his station the two years he has played in the tournament. Jordan listens carefully to the introduction and always corrects Collier about something he says.

"Michael Jordan — *probably* the greatest basketball player in the world," called out Collier.

"I don't like that *probably* stuff," said Jordan with a snort as he came over to Collier after hitting his tee shot.

In succeeding rounds, Collier called Jordan "the greatest basketball player in the world."

"Last year I said he *was* the greatest basketball player in the world," recalled Collier. He came over and said, 'What's this *was* business? I've only been retired one year. You should say *is* the greatest player in the world.' No matter what I say he gives me a hard time."

Upon further reflection, Collier continued, "He's the friendliest fellow you'd want to meet."

The volunteer staff doesn't say that about everybody. They whisper about who gave them a hard time, too. A few of the celebrities behave like jerks at times. Some of the old ballplayers have a chip on their shoulders. Most of them are cordial, cooperative and recognize that it's in their best interest to be kind to everyone they meet along the way. Some of them just don't get it. They never will. As someone once said of Ted Williams, "He never learned how to say hello until it was time to say goodbye."

Collier cautioned the crowd not to click their cameras when the players were swinging their clubs and to be quiet during play. Dead silence followed.

"Hey, this is like a morgue," hollered Andy Van Slyke, the former ace outfielder for the Pirates, Cardinals and Phillies. "You can talk now! I'd be better off if you were hollering when I'm hitting."

Jim McMahon, the former Bears quarterback, played golf in his bare feet the first day, before the more serious competition got underway. He also wore some false monster teeth. He warned the corporate guys in his foursome, "Hey, I just want to tell you guys that I swear a lot. Is that OK with you?"

Joe Theismann, the former Redskins quarterback and TV analyst, never stopped talking. He can't help himself. He's like Barkley in that respect. Anyone who played with them, or watched them play, got some laughs for their money.

I introduced myself to Jordan, and reminded him that I had interviewed him one-on-one on two different occasions as the editor of *Street & Smith's Basketball Yearbook*.

I mentioned a story he had told me about how, before his senior year in high school, he had gone to an Eckerd's Drug Store in Wilmington, North Carolina with his mother to get the newest *Street & Smith's Basketball Yearbook*. He thought his name would be on the high school All-America listing. It was nowhere to be found in the yearbook. The prep expert from his area had never seen him play in person, so he left him off his recommended list.

Jordan made a face. Yes, he remembered. "That really ticked me off," he said. "Do you think I should have been on that list now? But I know you wrote some nice stuff about me later on."

"You can't win alone."
—Mario Lemieux

A letter from Mario Lemieux that appeared in the tournament program puts the whole thing in its proper light:

"When I first moved to Pittsburgh from Montreal 14 years ago, I didn't know much about the city of Pittsburgh or what people called its 'winning tradition.'

"It didn't take Nat (his wife, Nathalie) and me long to embrace the city's friendly people, open attitude and unique affinity for striving for the best in every aspect of our lives.

"The theme of the third tournament, the 2000 Mellon Mario Lemieux Celebrity Invitational, is winning. Over the past year, winning

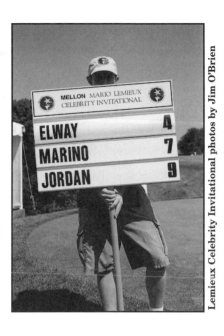

Lemieux Celebrity Invitational photos by Jim O'Brien

Michael Jordan signed autographs for young fans at Mario Lemieux's golf tournament.

for Team Lemieux has been embodied through our uphill battle to purchase our hometown Pittsburgh Penguins and the Pens' remarkable run in the Stanley Cup playoffs.

"Personally, winning for me is waking up each morning confident that I am cancer free. Through this tournament and the Mario Lemieux Foundation, our goal is to help other Western Pennsylvanians win the battle against cancer and other life-threatening diseases. But we all know you can't win alone. The million dollars we will raise for medical research through this year's tournament can be directly credited to our magnificent sponsors — including Mellon Financial Corporation, UPMC Health System, Toyota, SmithKline Beecham and Marconi Communications and over 50 others. Special thanks, also, to our celebrities, volunteers, executive committee and the staff of the event who have worked tirelessly for an entire year to make this event shine beyond all expectations.

"I hope everyone enjoys the tournament. By helping us in our quest to make cancer an affliction of the past, each and every one of us is a winner."

The Mario Lemieux Foundation funds cancer and other important medical research at the University of Pittsburgh Cancer Institute and Magee Womens Hospital. John Paul, the executive vice president of UPMC, is one of the event's most enthusiastic patrons and participants. The key movers-and-shakers that do the critical behind-the-scenes work and planning for this event include Gail Balph, Tom Grealish, Nancy Angus and Michael Dixon.

"Mario's personal involvement and his commitment to the event go a long way in helping us assemble such a first-class field," said Miss Balph, the tournament's executive director. "There's no question people come to Nevillewood to see the stars. Once we get them here, however, our job is to make the invitational fun, affordable and entertaining for the entire family. We want them to come back and, judging from our attendance, they are."

"The tournament is able to raise so much money because of Mario's vision, our sponsors and the hundreds of volunteers who devote their time to the tournament," said Grealish, chairman of the tournament executive committee. "We have people from all walks of life who give both their time and their talents for the tournament. Through everyone's hard work, we've been able to hopefully make a difference in the lives of many cancer patients and their families."

Bill Clinton, U.S. President:
"There are no bastions that any child of any background can't scale. Tiger Woods does a lot of good just by going out and playing great golf. Just being there and exhilarating those kids and making them imagine they can do that or something else is a very powerful thing. Just by proceding with dignity and strength — who knows how many people watch him on television and it changes an attitude they have toward people who are different from them when they go to work the next day."

Snapshot:

John Congemi, Former Pitt and Canadian Football League quarterback:

"Jack Nicklaus was my first hero. I liked golf early because my grandfather and father liked it so much. Football-wise, it was probably Fran Tarkenton. I always wanted to watch Jack Nicklaus in a golf tournament. He was from Ohio and he was the best. I got to meet him when I was in high school. I was in a high school golf tournament and his son, Gary, was playing in it, too. He was in eighth grade, but good enough to play with high school kids. I was a senior. We both ended up in the rough in the same area. He was shooting one way and I was shooting the other way. He had about 30 people, including his father, following him around the course. He hit first. I figured they'd all leave, but they stayed to see me hit. I was so nervous by the attention that I just wanted to make contact. I hit an eight-iron on the green just a few inches from the hole. Jack came over and patted me on the back. He said, 'Nice shot.' That meant so much to me. Suddenly, I was in seventh heaven."

Former Pitt and Canadian Football League star John Congemi, left, compares quarterback notes with Steelers' signal-caller Kordell Stewart.

Mary Lou Retton
Perfect 10 from Fairmont

"You give up your childhood."

Mary Lou Retton came from Fairmont, West Virginia and captured an Olympic gold medal in gymnastics and the hearts of people everywhere in the world in the summer of 1984. She put Fairmont on the map, and created the kind of excitement the Marion County community hasn't known since she vaulted into the international spotlight. Anyone traveling the highways through wild and wonderful West Virginia thinks of her immediately when they see the road signs for Fairmont.

She was the most popular performer in the Olympic Games in Los Angeles because she came through under the most intense pressure and she never stopped smiling. She turned Pauley Pavilion at the University of Southern California into a personal showcase with her stunning moves and explosive power. The 9,000-seat facility was filled to the brim with enthusiastic spectators, and there were record ratings for the international TV audience.

She stood only 4 feet 8¾ inches tall on her tiptoes, and weighed 95 pounds, yet she was the biggest star in the most commercially successful Olympic Games in history. She was a product of that corporate sponsorship explosion and prime time TV coverage of the Games. She turned the gymnastics world upside down with her style and smile.

Bob Ottom wrote in *Sports Illustrated* before the Games, "If there were such a thing as the Official Pixie of the 1984 Olympic Games, this girl would be it. The story is that she was born in a small West Virginia town, and you can believe it if you want to, but there's better reason to suspect that she simply stepped out from under a toadstool one day in 1968. Scale-model leotards and all."

Mary Lou Retton gained the kind of instant fame and fortune that no one in her sport had ever known. She didn't have the staying power of an Arnold Palmer or Michael Jordan, but she was BIG and she still pops up in national ads, and she came out with another book on her success story, *Gateways to Happiness*, in early 2000. Sales were solid everywhere and especially strong at the Waldenbooks outlet in her hometown. She is still in demand as a motivational speaker. She is married and the mother of two daughters.

Fairmont is located 88 miles south of Pittsburgh, at the mouth of the Monongahela River. There's now a Mary Lou Retton Youth Park there to honor the most famous athlete ever to come out of the area. Fairmont is known as "The Friendly City," and Mary Lou Retton has certainly epitomized that with her natural public relations skills.

One sports commentator described her as a "jalapeño pepper with the smile of an angel."

MARY LOU RETTON
Captured five medals at 1984 Olympic Games

Her timing was perfect in executing her routines and in taking advantage of a once-in-a-lifetime opportunity. That's how she gained one of the highest honors an American athlete can achieve when her image appeared on a Wheaties box.

The world's top political powers at the time were feuding and the Cold War led to a Soviet protest and boycott of the 1984 Olympic Games, just as the U.S. had boycotted the 1980 Olympic Games. The Russians had won the team combined gold medal and many individual medals at the previous eight Olympic Games and their absence opened the way for other countries and competitors to take advantage of their absence. No one did this more than Mary Lou Retton.

No American woman had ever won an individual gymnastics medal — let alone a gold medal — before 1984. The American team figured to do well, and might have given the Soviets a strong run for the medals in any case, but this made it easier for the breakthrough.

She won five medals at the LA Games, a gold medal in the all-around, silver medals in the vault and the team, bronze medals in the uneven bars and floor exercise. She won more medals than any other American athlete did at the 1984 Games. She was fourth in the balance beam, just missing out on a six-medal performance.

Having the coaching services of Romanian Bela Karolyi, who had been Nadia Comaneci's mentor when she amazed everyone with her seven perfect 10s at the 1976 Olympic Games, had to be beneficial to Mary Lou as well. Talking about Mary Lou, Karolyi commented, "She became the No. 1 representative of a new trend in gymnastics, a trend of high difficulty and very athletic stunts."

It's unreal on reflection that Retton had little experience in major gymnastic competition outside the U.S. before the 1984 Olympic Games. A wrist injury kept her from competing in the 1983 World Championships. She was virtually unknown on the international as well as the American sports scene before the hoopla that preceded and accompanied the Olympic Games.

Her family had made its mark in West Virginia. Her Uncle Joe Retton had been a highly successful basketball coach for a long tenure at Fairmont State College. The Falcons were an NAIA powerhouse. Her father, Ronnie, had been co-captain along with the great Jerry West of the West Virginia University basketball team that lost to California by 71-70 in the 1959 NCAA championship, and he played shortstop in the New York Yankees farm system until 1963.

Mary Lou Retton suffered a knee injury that threatened her presence in the 1984 Olympic Games, but she underwent successful arthroscopic surgery to remove torn cartilage and was ready to compete.

Often forgotten is the fact that Retton was not the top performer in women's gymnastics at the 1984 Olympics. Romanian Kati Szabo won five medals, with four gold medals and one silver medal. She finished second in the all-around competition to Retton and that turned out to be the focal point of the gymnastics aspect of the Olympic program.

Teenager Mary Lou Retton was happy to be home with parents, Lois and Ron, in Fairmont, West Virginia.

Retton photos provided by John C. Veasey, *Times West Virginian*

The all-around competition was made up of performances on the vault, uneven bars, balance beam and the floor exercise. It was like the decathlon event for gymnasts. With two rotations to go, Retton trailed Szabo by .15 of a point. That's when Retton reached back and showed her true stuff, earning perfect 10s on both the floor exercise and the vault to win the gold medal.

Those of us who watched it on TV would not forget the thrill we felt rooting for Retton and seeing her come through in the clutch. It was electrifying stuff.

People who pay little attention, if any, to sports endeavors like gymnastics, diving and synchronized swimming any other time do get caught up in the TV coverage of the Olympic Games.

She landed on the cover of *Sports Illustrated* and was named Female Athlete of the Year by the *Associated Press*. In 1985, she won the McDonald's American Cup all-around title for the third year in a row.

"The biggest celebration here since World War II ended."

John C. Veasey, editor of the *Times West Virginian* in Fairmont, followed the Mary Lou Retton story and offered some interesting insights on a hometown hero when I contacted him in the summer of 2000.

"The Mary Lou Retton Era, in looking back, was a glorious period for Fairmont and Marion County," he said. "I had known her father, Ronnie, since our days at WVU, but only knew what I read in the newspapers about Mary Lou. That was until one night when she was 11 or 12 and was participating with the local Aerial-Port gymnastics team during the halftime of a Fairmont State College basketball game. There was one girl who, although very small in stature, was head and shoulders above all the other girls that night, drawing many oohs and aahs from the crowd during the exhibition of tumbling and things like that. That, of course, was Mary Lou.

"I think that we all realized, as time went on, that Mary Lou was special. But we didn't realize just how special until one week when we received word that she was competing in China or Russia or some far-off land. At least that's when I personally realized that this young lady was quite a star.

"I remember seeing her at a high school basketball game several days before she departed for Houston to live and work with Bela Karolyi's stable of young gymnasts. She was so tiny and it was difficult for me to believe the publicity she had already received regarding her gymnastic skills.

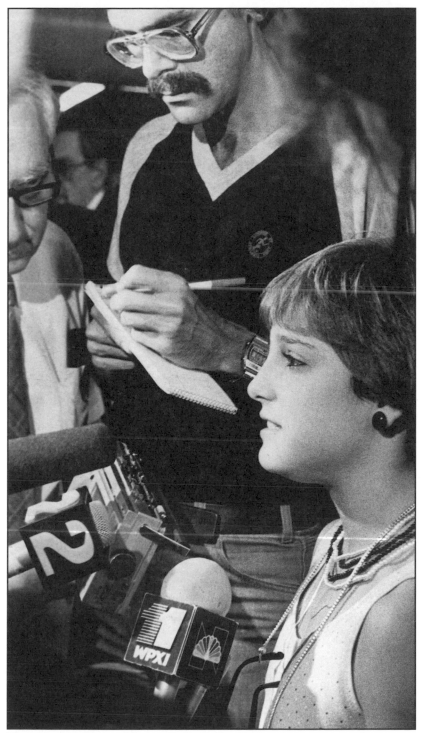

Mary Lou Retton was in spotlight during impromptu press conference at Pittsburgh International Airport upon return from 1984 Olympic Games in Los Angeles.

"I was the sports editor here at the time. I recall vividly telling my staff, before leaving on a two-week vacation just prior to the 1984 Olympics, that if Mary Lou won the gold the acclaim that would come to her would be even bigger than they could ever imagine. And, as things turned out, the national hoopla that surrounded Mary Lou was even bigger than I imagined.

"She came back to Fairmont for a spontaneous celebration the Monday after she made her famous vault that enshrined her forever with gymnastics' best. I wasn't here, but from all accounts, that was the biggest celebration here since World War II ended. When she returned home, West Virginia Governor Jay Rockefeller greeted her. Her admirers lined the street for five miles to welcome her. A street in Fairmont was named for her.

"Then, in September, she returned for a scheduled appearance at Fairmont's East-West Stadium — the local high school stadium that seats about 6,000 people. Despite a thunderstorm that struck the area in late afternoon and lasted until about 7:30, there was an overflow crowd at the stadium. Many of them had stayed through the storm to keep their seats. I think there may have been a few hard feelings in the years that followed when people had to go through her agent to get her. And the fact she couldn't or didn't return to Fairmont for a few dinners and events held here in her honor didn't go unnoticed.

"But I think most of that is past and she remains a darling of most of the people who followed her outstanding success in 1984. There certainly has been no one like Mary Lou to pass this way since then. She provided Fairmont and Marion County with some outstanding things that will never be forgotten."

"I want to be like Nadia."

Mary Lou Retton looked like she was having the time of her life. She thrived on the competition. We were captivated by her close-cropped brown hair and blazing brown eyes. She couldn't have been cuter, and kids wanted to get their hair cut like Mary Lou Retton, the way they once wanted their hair cut like Dorothy Hamill or Peggy Fleming, Olympic ice skating champions.

Mary Lou said the darndest things, whatever came to her mind, and she made people smile the way she did. Her effervescence was contagious. She was stronger looking, more athletic, than any of the girl gymnasts who had captured our attention at earlier Olympic Games. They were lithe little girls who got sidetracked at dancing school. Mary Lou Retton was an athlete, all the way. And she was one of ours. This powerful Italian-American represented a new breed of female gymnast.

As much as we enjoyed and exalted in the earlier successes of Olga Korbut of Russia and Nadia Comaneci of Romania, we were

Day-long rain couldn't keep fans in Fairmont from coming out to welcome hometown hero Mary Lou Retton for parade and stadium appearance.

more excited about an American amazing us this way. In my days as a sports writer for *The New York Post*, I had participated in press conferences in New York City that were hosted by ABC-TV's "Wide World of Sports" at which Korbut and, later on, Comaneci came to meet the American media. They were so little in person, not nearly as big as they appeared on TV.

Roone Arledge, the president of ABC Sports at the time, believed in telling us in-depth stories about the athletes at the Olympic Games or any other competition covered by his ABC-TV crew. "Up close and personal" was a phrase popularized by Arledge and his troops. By the time the competition commenced, you knew these guys and gals. Or, at least, you thought you did.

ABC Sports started covering sports that way beginning in 1964 at the Winter Olympics in Innsbruck.

To appreciate the rise in popularity of gymnastics, and what brought Mary Lou Retton to the forefront as an American icon, you must go back to the Olympic Games in Munich, Germany in 1972 when Olga Korbut burst onto the scene. The 17-year-old Soviet girl captured the hearts of all that saw her in those memorable games. She was hailed as the "Munchkin of Munich," however, and she had real star appeal, the way Shirley Temple did as a child actor in so many of those mushy movies we loved so much. Her gestures, wide smile and charm won her extra points. Gymnastics was a ridiculously obscure aspect of the Olympic Games until Olga Korbut came along. She grew up in Grodno and would change the way we looked at gymnastics forever.

Like Retton, she was not the greatest gymnast in the competition. She was not even the best gymnast on the Soviet squad.

Korbut, in fact, finished seventh in the all-around competition. She made mistakes and had misses that left her in tears. She was 4-11 and 85 pounds, so fragile, so vulnerable. She wore red bows in her pigtails. We felt her pain and disappointment. She bounced back to win the gold medal in both the balance beam and the floor exercise. Lyudmila Tourischeva, the true Soviet star, claimed the gold medal for the all-around competition. She simply lacked the charisma of Korbut.

Then along came Comaneci. In 1976 in Montreal, Comaneci made Olympic history by receiving the first perfect score of ten for her performance on the uneven bars and the balance beam. She had seven 10s throughout the competition. She won gold medals in the all-around, the uneven bars and the balance beam. She didn't have the charisma of Korbut, either, but she was striking enough and so perfect in her performances that she won us over, too. Hers was not always a happy story and it was disappointing to learn the year after her Montreal triumph that, at age 15, she attempted to commit suicide.

Before Nadia and Olga caught the public attention, no one outside of true gymnastic aficionados paid any attention to the sport. Everyone paid attention to Nadia and Olga. Before those two came along, there were about 7,000 American gymnasts competing once or twice a year. After they made their big splash, about 60,000 Americans were performing in gymnastics competitions of one kind or another. Women gymnasts outnumbered the men, 7 to 1. It was estimated that there were about 3.5 million children participating in gymnastics every day.

Comaneci certainly inspired Retton. "I want to be like Nadia," said Mary Lou, as an eight-year-old girl stretched out on the floor in front of the TV set.

The parents of Mary Lou allowed her to leave home at age 14 and move to Houston to train with Bela Karolyi, thought to be the greatest women's gymnastics coach in the world. He was a controversial coach as well, called "The Mad Transylvanian."

He had built the strong Romanian team that ended the USSR domination of the sport. He had met Mary Lou at a competition in Reno, Nevada and told her and her parents that he could make her a champion. He said she had so much potential.

Asked what it took to be a gymnast, Mary Lou Retton had this advice:

"It takes imagination, hard work and persistence," she said. "Persistence means continuing to try, even when you fail. Every gymnast starts out as a rookie. Every gymnast has fallen out on hand stands or toppled over trying to do a cartwheel. The key is to get up and try again."

She once answered questions in a magazine called *USA Gymnastics*.

An aspiring gymnast asked her if she ever got frustrated.

"Yes, I get very frustrated during practice," she wrote in reply. "Every gymnast, at one time or another, gets frustrated. When I would get upset and angry, I would talk to myself and calm myself down. I'd say, 'Mary Lou, just calm down and think about what you're doing. You can do this. Really concentrate.' And believe me, this worked for me. Try it."

In Los Angeles, the battle for the all-around gold medal developed into a tight contest between Retton and the Romanian champion, Katie Szabo. With two rotations to go, Szabo led by .15 of a point. But Retton rose to the occasion, earning 10s for the floor exercise and the vault, and ensuring her place in sports history books. Aspiring gymnasts, or athletes of all kinds, can take heart from the story of Retton's first competition as a little girl.

Like so many other girls around the world, Mary Lou had watched Nadia Comaneci score her history making 10s in 1976. Retton noticed that the scoreboard, unprepared for Comaneci's skill level, had registered 1.0 rather than 10.0. It lacked enough digits to carry a 10.0 score.

After performing in the first competition — on the uneven bars — Mary Lou jumped for joy when the scoreboard flashed 1.0. Alas, it really was a 1.0. That was a real kick in the pants. But she persisted.

She refused to give up on gymnastics until her 1.0 turned to a genuine 10.0.

Peter Ueberroth, a one-time travel agent, was hired to oversee and market the 1984 Olympic Games. He succeeded in a fashion never previously thought possible. He transformed the entire Olympics with his marketing strategies and the corporate support he and his staff were able to develop.

Roone Arledge and his staff had some new techniques and new ideas about how best to cover the Olympic Games. ABC Sports spent $225 million for the TV rights. Arledge used more cameras than before. He set out to get the audience emotionally involved with the athletes and their agendas. It was stirring stuff. We loved the close-ups.

This turned out to be the last Olympic Games done by ABC Sports. It was an artistic success, but ABC Sports lost $75 million in the process.

Mary Lou Retton wasn't the only star in those 1984 Games.

The Romanian gymnast Ecaterina Szabo was the most successful competitor in Los Angeles. The 17-year-old whiz kid won four gold medals and a silver medal — the judges awarded her a perfect 10 in one round of the floor exercise event. The U. S. men's gymnastics team, led by Tim Daggett, won the team gold medal.

Bart Conner, a gold medal gymnast and three-time U.S. Olympic team member, said of the improved showing by our men and women, said, "I hope this changes things. For a sport to get a following, it has to have heroes. Look what Nadia did for gymnastics. Who ever knew where Romania was before she came along," he said. "Now we have Americans who have had success."

Carl Lewis won four gold medals in track & field competition at the 1984 Olympic Games. He followed in the footsteps of Jesse Owens 48 years after Owens' triumph in Berlin. Lewis emulated his achievements exactly — winning gold medals in the 100- and 200-meters, the 4x100-meter relay and the long jump. Edwin Moses won the 400-meter hurdles race to keep his winning streak intact, and Pitt's Roger Kingdom won the 110-meter hurdles. Kingdom, who made his home in Monroeville, just east of Pittsburgh, would repeat four years later at Seoul, South Korea.

Britain's Daley Thompson successfully defended the decathlon title, becoming only the second man to do so. The first was Bob Mathias, who came out of Kiski Prep in Saltsburg, Pennsylvania and Stanford University in his home state of California to do it in 1948 and 1952.

The U.S. teams won the men's and women's basketball gold medals, with Patrick Ewing leading the men and Cheryl Miller leading the women to victory.

Yes, 1984 was quite a year. It was the year that Geraldine Ferraro became the first woman to run for vice president on a major party ticket. Vanessa Williams had to relinquish her Miss America title after nude photos of her were published in *Penthouse* magazine.

Mary Lou Retton shows off her USA Gymnastics uniform and collection of medals and ribbons at her home in Fairmont, West Virginia.

Indira Gandhi was assassinated in India. Ronald Reagan defeated Walter Mondale for the U.S. Presidency.

And Mary Lou Retton ruled the world.

"I'm still just Mary Lou."

In her latest book, *Gateways To Happiness: 7 Ways to a More Peaceful, More Prosperous, More Satisfying Life*, written with David Bender, Mary Lou Retton stresses the importance of her family in her development and ultimate success. It's a worthwhile read for anyone seeking ways to improve their position and approach to daily challenges. There's a strong spiritual message as well.

In reflecting on her family and upbringing in Fairmont, Mary Lou talks about their love, unselfishness, support and understanding of all she attempted to do. She was the youngest of five children. She has three brothers, Ronnie, Donnie and Jerry, and a sister, Shari. There's a seven-year age gap between Mary Lou and her brother Ronnie.

Ronnie and Donnie both played college baseball. At the time of the Olympics, her youngest brother, Terry, had lettered in three sports in high school. Shari was an All-American gymnast in college. So sports competition was part of the regimen in the Retton household.

Mary Lou started training at age 7. Her parents sent her to ballet and acrobatics classes to direct some of her boundless energy. She began competing on an international basis in gymnastics at the age of 14.

"I firmly believe that everything I've achieved in my life thus far is due, in no small part, to the fact that I was born into a strong, stable family," Mary Lou relates in her book. "They have been there, offering love and encouragement, in my darkest hours and my brightest. They have been a constant source of strength."

When she came out of Fairmont in 1983, Mary Lou was a straight A student with pierced ears and size three shoes. She had tremendous raw gymnastic talent. From Coach Gary Rafalowski she had acquired a solid foundation in gymnastics and advanced to the elite level. She was scared on the one hand, but confident that she could succeed if she got the best possible coaching. She believed in Bela Karolyi.

After having coached 14 girls to Olympic medals, in 1981 he defected to the United States with his wife, Marta, and one suitcase, leaving his Mercedes Benz behind. In organizing the Sundance Athletic Club in Houston, he showed how a male gymnastics coach often seems to emerge, sometimes controversially, as a father figure for the young girls under his guidance. He scolds them and he hugs them.

In early 1983, Retton left West Virginia for Houston to train with Karolyi. She dropped out of public school and switched to correspondence courses after her freshman year. She was determined to become a great gymnast, and was driven by a desire for an Olympic medal. Yes, like Nadia. She and Diane Durham, a black girl from Gary, Indiana, developed a friendly rivalry at the Karolyi camp. "If she does well, I have to do well, too," remarked Retton.

"Bela's girls were prepared," Retton said after competing against Karolyi's teams early in her career. "He had them psyched up. They were there with such obvious self-confidence. His whole body says, 'C'mon, let's go.'

"When I got to Houston, we had two workouts a day, one at eight in the morning and another at six in the evening. If you missed even one day, you noticed it. Monday was our day off. We had only one workout then."

Retton responded quickly to Karolyi's training regimen. He taught her how to use her tremendous power and together they perfected certain routines. Karolyi's methods were intense, demanding and repetitious.

Mary Lou's break in gymnastics came when she substituted for Durham, who had been injured, at the 1983 McDonald's American Cup in New York City's Madison Square Garden. Retton was not well known at the time. She dominated the meet. She won the all-around title and took gold medals as well in the floor exercise, the vault, and uneven bars.

"It was the greatest performance of 1983," recalled Kayolyi. "A complete unknown in the American Cup beating everyone else in the world."

The next competition was in the 1983 World Championships in Budapest, Hungary, but Mary Lou had to miss it because of an injury.

In March 1984, Retton repeated her McDonald's American Cup victory by winning the all-around title again, and received perfect 10s in both the floor exercise and uneven bars.

When the Soviets boycotted the 1984 Summer Olympics — the way the U.S. had boycotted the 1980 Games — she emerged as America's sweetheart. Before Retton, the best-known American woman gymnast had been Cathy Rigby, and she had never won a gold medal in either the Olympic or World Championships. In the 1970 World Championships, Cathy won a silver medal on the beam, the first medal ever won by an American woman gymnast in international competition.

Mary Lou won more than medals with her outspoken manner.

In explaining the balletic tiptoe steps gymnasts use onstage, Mary Lou Retton remarked, "That stuff's just for show, to make us look classier than we really are. Ordinarily, we all walk like little bitty football players."

Explaining her success, she said, "It's all in the training. I work at this seven days a week — two long, hard sessions a day, drilling myself. Constantly. And at night sometimes I dream gymnastic dreams. I'll be lying there quietly, sound asleep, and suddenly my whole body will give a great big jump and practically throw me out of bed.

"Here's what it takes to be a complete gymnast: Someone should be able to sneak up and drag you out at midnight and push you out on some strange floor, and you should be able to do your entire routine sound asleep in your pajamas. Without one mistake."

When she performed her last-chance execution of a full-twisting layout Tsukahara vault in LA, she cried out, "I stuck it!" Following her victory, as she was leaving the Olympic Village, she couldn't get over the response to what she'd done. "I mean, there were mobs of people," said Retton. "They said things like, 'Mary Lou, you've been in our home. You've been in our living room. We feel like we know you, Mary Lou.' I mean, I'd understand people recognizing me if I had purple hair or something, but I'm just a normal teenager. I'm still just Mary Lou."

Companies seeking someone to sell their products came calling on Mary Lou Retton.

She signed contracts with ten different corporations, each paying an estimated $100,000 to $200,000 a year, including McDonald's, Vidal Sassoon, Wheaties, Super Juice frozen juice bars and Energizer batteries. She did her own exercise video, published an autobiography and appeared in a series of exercise spots called Funfit.

Retton retired from competition in 1986, but returned to serious training again in 1989 to prepare for a U.S. tour with Olga Korbut. Before long, she started thinking about the idea of competing in the 1992 Games. Then she realized that was a crazy idea. "I just can't do it," she said. "My body's strong enough, but I don't have the discipline. The girl who won those medals was a machine.

"You give up your childhood. You miss proms and games and high school events, and people say it's awful. I don't know. I mean, I walked on top of the Great Wall of China when I was in eighth grade. I rode the bullet train in Japan. I met Gorbachev. I met Michael Jackson. I say it was a good trade. You miss something, but I think I gained more than I lost."

Jim O'Brien

The Sentinel of Second Avenue
Memorial Days were important

"He didn't want people to forget."

Memorial Day meant a great deal to Frank Rakaczky. He had been a soldier in the U.S. Army in World War II, a combat veteran of the Pacific as a member of a howitzer team in the Philippines. His country, his flag, his fellow soldiers, sailors and nurses were important in his world. He wanted us to remember those who served their country.

As a kid, I can remember Frank marching in the Memorial Day parades in my hometown of Hazelwood, a milltown in the southeast end of Pittsburgh. He always looked so spiffy and so serious.

I looked for Frank Rakaczky (Ra-kaz-ky) because he was one of my first bosses. He and Michael Michaliszyn — I still have to look up their names to spell them properly — owned a print shop and they published a tabloid community newspaper every two weeks. That's where I got my start at age 14, serving as the sports editor of *The Hazelwood Envoy*.

They haven't had any parades or local newspapers in Hazelwood for a long time. It's not that kind of community anymore. Frank kept the spirit of Memorial Day alive by coordinating tributes at Calvary Cemetery. Then, when attendance for that dwindled, he started having services at the two war memorials in the heart of the community, closer to everyone's doorstep.

"He didn't want people to forget," recalled his son, Tom, a staff worker in the Court of Common Pleas the past 39 years. Tom and his wife, Gail, live in West Mifflin. Their son, Timothy, a loan officer at National City Bank, lives two streets away. Their daughter, Veronica Rakaczky Smith, lives in Munhall. She graduated with a perfect 4.0 grade point average from nursing school at the University of Pittsburgh. She's a registered nurse at Mon Valley Hospital. Her grandfather would be boasting about her academic achievements.

"I was born before my dad left to go overseas in 1942," said Tom, "and by the time he came back home 2½ years later I didn't know who he was. He didn't talk much about what happened over there, but I respected him a great deal."

Frank was an officer in the Veterans of Foreign Wars (VFW), American Legion and Hungarian Club in Hazelwood. Such military and ethnic clubs have fallen on hard times throughout this area and the rest of the country. Many of the old-timers who cared about being identified that way have died off; the younger generation has other places to go.

Change didn't wear well with Frank Rakaczky. Frank found things to complain about in the best of times. He was a difficult man with a difficult name. "I think he relished being cantankerous,"

67

offered David O'Connor, who looks after his family's funeral parlor on Second Avenue, the main street in town.

Yes, Frank Rakaczky was cantankerous, but he cared. He cared deeply.

On Labor Day, 1999, everybody left our home near noon to do something. Left alone, I decided to take a drive, and I ended up in Hazelwood. I don't know why.

I was sitting in my car at the corner of Hazelwood and Second Avenues, looking at a vacant lot where the Hazelwood Bank once stood. It had been torn down the week before. I had gone there many times with my mom as a child. It meant something to me, the people who worked there were always nice to us. There was something sacred about the bank. The only building in the town with more marble in it was our church. I took one of the bricks with me, the way I did when they tore down Forbes Field.

I spotted a familiar face in my rearview mirror. It was Frank Rakaczky. He had come to open up the VFW Hall. That building had been a Kroger Super Market in my youth. This was a chance to thank Frank for getting me started.

I asked Frank if he'd let me take a look at the VFW.

A large room was filled, for the most part, with flea market items spread across many tables. Nothing caught my eye. The bar had about a dozen well-worn stools and all the ambience of a bomb shelter. I wondered why anyone would want to spend any time there. Frank said it was open only one or two days a week. Membership had fallen off. "It's tough to get seven members here for a quorum to decide any-thing," offered Frank.

There were two walls covered with framed photographs of soldiers and sailors from the community who had served in different wars. Some were badly faded, discolored, chipped or splintered. I recognized some of the faces. I had seen them while growing up in Hazelwood.

Frank grumbled about this and that, the changing face of the community, the government looking after certain interests but ignoring the needs of old soldiers and clubs like the VFW. His grievances were great in number. He smoked several cigarettes.

He thanked me for attending the funeral of his wife, Catherine, who had died three years earlier. He was alone in his home on nearby Sylvan Avenue. "I'm glad you're here," he said. "I was feeling kinda down this morning, but you've brightened my day."

He placed a metal chair in the doorway and sat there, smoking another cigarette, looking from the dark into a sun-drenched street. He was the last soldier in town, I thought, a silhouette of a sentinel on Second Avenue. He was 84, he told me, and holding down the fort.

That was September 6. On September 22, Frank Rakaczky died. They played taps at his funeral. The vets in attendance offered a final salute to a good soldier. Hopefully, they will remember him next Memorial Day.

Frank Rakaczky stands guard in front of corner lot where Hazelwood Bank once stood on Second Avenue, just across the street from the VFW Hall where he served since returning home from World War II.

Jack Twyman
The Good Samaritan

"I just happened to be there. Somebody had to help him."

J ack Twyman is a good story. It's a story that has stood the test of time. It's a parable, really, an adaptation of The Good Samaritan story in the Bible. Twyman has been successful on several fronts: sports, television, business, family, community, church, you name it. He was driven to succeed, but he always took time out to look after others. That's the real charm of Jack Twyman.

He comes from Pittsburgh, but he has spent most of his adult life in Cincinnati. There is more than the Ohio River that links these two cities, as far as Twyman is concerned. He values his association with both cities, learned much of lasting value in both places, and is honored that each claims him as a favorite son.

Most of us have heard the inspiring story of how Michael Jordan was cut the first time he tried out for his high school basketball team in Wilmington, North Carolina, and came back and made the most of a second opportunity. Well, Twyman was even more persistent in that regard. He wouldn't take "no" for an answer, not once, but three times. Twyman was cut from the squad three straight seasons before he made the team as a senior at Pittsburgh's Central Catholic High School. It set the tone and an attitude that has served him well ever since.

"Pittsburgh was not the most pleasant time of my life," said Twyman. "It was a hard lesson that I learned. From that I formed the basis of what Jack Twyman is all about."

He left his home in the Sheraden section of the city in 1951 to attend the University of Cincinnati where he gained second team All-American honors as a senior. He was the first basketball All-American at Cincinnati. He set scoring and rebounding records that required the great Oscar Robertson to eclipse them.

Twyman was a second round draft pick of the NBA's Rochester Royals in 1955. There were only eight teams in the league at the time, the NBA's 10th year of existence, so he was the ninth player picked from the college ranks. He played a significant role in convincing club owner Lester Harrison to sell his team to a Cincinnati group a year after he shifted the franchise to Cincinnati. This move to the Queen City changed the course of Twyman's life.

Twyman, a 6-6 forward, starred for the Royals for 11 seasons, averaging 18.3 points and playing in six NBA All-Star Games. A terrific shooter and competitor, Twyman was one of the league's premier ballplayers. He was good enough to finish second in the NBA scoring race to Bob Pettit of the St. Louis Hawks in the 1958-59 season, with 25.8 points per game compared to Pettit's 29.2 mark. The

following season, Twyman finished second to Wilt Chamberlain, with 31.2 points per game compared to Chamberlain's 37.6 mark. That's keeping some pretty impressive company.

"I would've been the first player in the NBA ever to average over 30 a game," said Twyman with a chuckle, "except that Wilt comes along as a rookie to steal the spotlight from me."

Twyman gained attention and praise for his dedication in looking after teammate Maurice Stokes, another Pittsburgh-born NBA All-Star, for 12 long years after Stokes was stricken with encephalitis in 1958. The crippling brain disease left Stokes an invalid in a wheelchair. Stokes can still provide all the details of what happened to sideline Stokes.

Stokes was able to learn how to do various tasks for himself, but he never walked again. They even made a movie, "Maurie," about their special relationship. Stokes died of a heart attack at age 36 on April 6, 1970. His funeral was held at his alma mater, St. Francis of Loretto College. Seven days after his death, Stokes' twin sister, Clarice, died of a heart attack, too. Now that's eerie.

"I got more out of my experience with Maurice," said Twyman, "than he got out of me. I learned not to think about yesterday, but to worry more about tomorrow. We can't do anything about yesterday. I'm proud of what I've accomplished."

During his days with the Royals, Twyman teamed with Stokes, who went from Westinghouse High School to put St. Francis of Loretto on the national map. Stokes was the first player picked in the 1955 NBA draft and won Rookie of the Year honors. He was the first black player picked to play in the league's All-Star Game. Chuck Cooper of Pittsburgh, a standout at Duquesne University, was the first black taken in the NBA draft, selected on the second round of the 1950 draft by the Boston Celtics. So Pittsburghers have played a significant role in the early history of the NBA. The Pittsburgh Ironmen played in the pro league's first season.

Twyman is proud of his relationship with Stokes. Stokes first gained national attention when he was named the MVP in the 1955 NIT, even though his team finished fourth. Stokes averaged 17.3 rebounds per game in his three NBA seasons and he led the league in rebounding (17.4) in 1956-1957. A totally unselfish player, the powerful 6-8, 260-pound forward averaged 5.3 assists per game and he finished third in the NBA in assists on two different occasions. His career scoring average was 16.4 points. He played in three All-Star games and was second-team All-NBA each of those years.

Here's a disheartening history lesson:

Both Duquesne University and Pitt passed up the opportunity to offer a scholarship to Stokes in his senior year at Westinghouse because Duquesne had a limit on how many blacks could be on their basketball team, and Pitt picked another black ballplayer when it decided to break the color line.

72

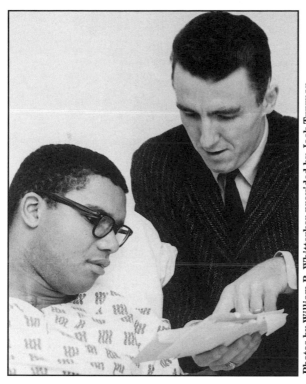

Jack Twyman served as guardian for Cincinnati Royals teammate Maurice Stokes after NBA All-Star was stricken with crippling disease.

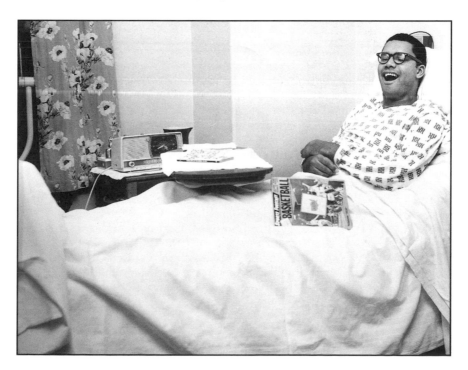

They both missed out on a wonderful basketball player and, from all reports, an even more wonderful person. I learned from one of Stokes' high school teammates, ace sports photographer Ralph Echols, that Pete Dimperio, the Westinghouse High football coach, was responsible for opening a pipeline to St. Francis of Loretto for Westinghouse athletes the year before Stokes went there. Others followed.

This was 1951, mind you, four years after Jackie Robinson broke the color line in baseball.

Bob Cousy, the former Boston Celtics' flashy guard, said Stokes "was the first great athletic power forward. He was Karl Malone with more finesse." Cousy's coach, Red Auerbach, drew comparisons between Stokes and Magic Johnson. That's how good he was.

Twyman later teamed with Oscar Robertson and then Jerry Lucas in his long career with the Cincinnati Royals. Going back to their days in Rochester, the Royals always had a strong offensive punch. "I was glad to see Oscar come to the Royals," said Twyman. "I thought he was the one who could lift us to the next level. He brought a lot of additional fan support for us. I always got along with Oscar."

I bumped into Lucas, once a prep phenom at Middleton, Ohio at the Mellon Mario Lemieux Celebrity Invitational Golf Tournament on June 10, 2000. I had gotten to know Lucas when he finished up his NBA career with three seasons with the New York Knicks. He had played six seasons with the Cincinnati Royals, three of them (1963-64 to 1965-1966) as a teammate of Twyman.

"He was a good man, a caring individual who gave of himself," Lucas said of Twyman. "He was quite a man, smart and resourceful." Never passing up an opportunity to have some fun, Lucas added, "I'd get a rebound and throw it out to Oscar and Jack would be at the other end of the court for a lay-up."

After Twyman retired, he worked as analyst to the play-by-play call of Chris Schenkel on ABC-TV's coverage of the NBA from 1966 to 1971. He succeeded Cousy and gave way to Bill Russell as color man. Auerbach may have had something to do with that change. He once complained to Twyman's boss, Roone Arledge, that Twyman had talked on the air about the presence of "dead spots" on the famous parquet floor at Boston Garden. "Well, isn't that true?" Arledge said to Auerbach. That was the end of that argument.

Actually, Twyman gave up the TV assignment and the travel demands after five years so he could spend more time with his family.

Twyman was elected to the Basketball Hall of Fame in 1983, being inducted in the same class as two former New York Knicks stars, Bill Bradley and Dave DeBusschere.

Twyman was successful in business, first as an insurance salesman for the A.W. Shell Insurance Co. of Cincinnati during and after his playing days with the Royals, and as the president and chairman of the board of Super Food Service, Inc., a national wholesale food company based in Dayton. "We're a food wholesaler," said Twyman.

Photos from University of Cincinnati sports information

Oscar Robertson could score and rebound and make plays with the best of them in college days.

Jack Twyman scrapped for loose ball with Centenary competitor.

Jack Twyman sweeps past Indiana All-America Don Schlundt in opening game at Cincinnati's Armory Field House in 1954-55 season.

"We deal with everything your wife would buy in a supermarket."
Twyman drove to and from work each day from suburban Cincinnati,
about a 45-minute commute. "I wrote insurance for this company,"
said Twyman. "That's how I got to know them in the first place." Once
again, he moved among giants in the game, like Anthony O'Reilly of
Pittsburgh-based H.J. Heinz. They could talk at national food shows
and meetings with equal enthusiasm about the sports scene in
Pittsburgh as well as about pickles and ketchup.

During his early days with the Royals in Cincinnati, Twyman
shared a nightly sports show with Ted Kluszewski, the muscular first
baseman for the Reds and later the Pirates. "When I played here in
Cincinnati, I had no idea in the early days what I would do after I was
finished playing," said Twyman. "But doing that show with Big Klu
gave me exposure, and it taught me how to talk under pressure. That
helped me later with ABC Sports. I was always the first to volunteer
when someone needed a speaker. I still get asked by colleges to come
in to talk to their basketball players. Skip Prosser, the coach at
Xavier, comes from Carnegie, and he has me talk to his players. That's
a little touchy because Xavier and Cincinnati are rivals. But I do it for
the kids. I just talk about my life."

He served six months of active duty as a lieutenant in the U.S.
Army, followed by seven years of reserve duty. His hobbies included
tennis, golf and walking ("I try to keep my joints moving."). His
Roman Catholic faith remained an important part of his life ("God's
been good to me").

"I parlayed a professional sports career into a successful business career," said Twyman. "I transferred my competitiveness and
enthusiasm for sports into the business world, and it worked. I think
it's important to promote yourself in a proper way. I think Michael
Jordan is a perfect example of this. He made a lot of money playing
basketball, but he had a good business sense, too. He's the epitome of
what a role model should be today."

I hadn't seen Twyman in a long time, since we used to see each
other on occasion in New York back in the '70s. So I was excited when
I spotted him, the white-white hair and square jaw were the give-
aways, as he pulled up in front of The Vernon Manor Hotel on
Monday, January 10, 2000. Twyman tooled into the circular driveway
in a shiny 1998 Cadillac that appeared to be black, at first glance, but
upon closer inspection turned out to be forest green. Whether he's
"The Pittsburgh Kid" or "The Cincinnati Kid," Twyman had definitely
arrived. A kid from Sheraden always wanted to be rich enough to
afford to drive a Cadillac. I enjoyed riding shotgun with him around
town later on.

When we were talking to each other at lunch in one of the dining
rooms at The Vernon Manor Hotel, Twyman told me he was well
acquainted with the place because, by coincidence, it was the site of
his wedding reception. "That was on May 15, 1956," said Twyman,
with more than a hint of pride. The place was as special to him as any
of the arenas where he once strutted his stuff.

Seeing a Pittsburgher who cared about basketball brought back a lot of memories for Twyman. He mentioned Pittsburghers from his days there, asking me if I knew them. We had a lot of mutual friends and acquaintances. We talked about Gene Farrell, Jack Barrett, Billy Conn and Joey Diven. Twyman mentioned that Diven, a lifetime friend of Conn who was called "the world's greatest street-fighter," came from Sheraden and ended up in Oakland and then Brookline. "Tommy Smith was a teammate of mine at Central, and he was a nephew of 'Greenfield Jimmy' Smith, who was Billy Conn's father-in-law," said Twyman. It went on like that for an hour. It was a warm time, helped perhaps by our luncheon offering of steaming chicken rice soup and a grilled chicken sandwich. Twyman wore a green windbreaker over a white knit golf shirt, and he appeared quite comfortable .

Twyman said he had lived at 3100 Sacramento Avenue in Sheraden, just a block away from a hilltop that overlooked McKees Rocks. He spent time as a teen in both communities.

Twyman still points to the experience of being disappointed three straight years at tryout camps for the Central Catholic High School basketball team and what he did to see that it would never happen again as the basis for all that has been good in his life since those formative years. "I've learned that hardship is good," he said.

Jack Kennedy Twyman was looking good. He was 65 years of age and would be 66 on May 11, 2000. He retired two years earlier from the business world and a more relaxed pace appeared to agree with him. He said he had taken his daily walk around a golf course near his home before coming to the hotel. It was great to see him.

"It's great not worrying about how I'm going to make a living," he said. "I worked hard to get to this position. Now I get to spend more time with my family, and helping other people."

"I'm a goal person and I just kept taking it one step at a time."

Jack Twyman was one of the last players to be inducted into the building that formerly housed the Basketball Hall of Fame in Springfield, Massachusetts. The new building opened in late 1984. Twyman was thrilled by being so honored. I was working at *The Pittsburgh Press* at the time and talked to him for a Sunday magazine (*Roto*) story in his hometown newspaper.

"Being elected to the Hall of Fame means a great deal to me," Twyman told me at the time. He was then 48. "I don't think anybody can play a sport as long as I played basketball and not be thrilled about being recognized this way.

"I was determined to make it to the pros. I worked hard to get there and I set goals all along. I'm a goal person, and I take it one step at a time."

Lee Williams, who was the director of the Basketball Hall of Fame at the time, was happy to have Twyman in the fold. "Football has a wonderful brotherhood story in Gale Sayers and Brian Piccolo, and basketball has its with Stokes and Twyman," said Williams. "It's a point of pride to all of us who have been involved in the sport."

The original Hall of Fame was located on the campus of Springfield College, where the sport started in 1891 when Dr. James A. Naismith hung a peach basket on the wall of a gymnasium at the school, then the YMCA Training Center, to give future physical education instructors something to do between football and baseball.

Peach baskets were hanging from opposite ends of a circular balcony in the Basketball Hall of Fame, and a miniature playing court was drawn on the floor below, at the time Twyman was inducted. Next to the baskets were life-size photos of Twyman, Bradley, DeBusschere and Dean Smith, the University of North Carolina coach.

Twyman's likeness had been on display in the same room for many years, on a bubble gum card, sharing space with the likes of Bill Russell, Bob Cousy, George Mikan and Wilt Chamberlain. Back then, each of the honored players was pictured in separate stained glass windows. Those stained-glass windows were removed when the new building went up, and the ones of Twyman and Oscar Robertson, for instance, are now on display in the University of Cincinnati's Sports Hall of Fame. Twyman showed them to me during a personal tour of the athletic facilities at Cincinnati during my visit.

Twyman and Stokes broke into the NBA together as rookies with the Rochester Royals. Ed Fleming, from Westinghouse High School and Niagara University, and Dick Ricketts of Duquesne University were also rookies with the Royals in 1955. Twyman recalled that they reported to Rochester together.

"Stokes and Fleming met me at my place," recalled Twyman, "and we drove up to Rochester together. Stokes was the first pick in the country and he made $8,000 that year. I was the ninth player picked and I made $7,500. By 1957, our third year, we were both making $10,000 a year."

Stokes' first impression was a lasting one. In his professional debut at the Rochester War Memorial on November 5, 1955, Stokes scored 32 points, grabbed 20 rebounds and assisted on eight other baskets.

Stokes finished eighth in the league in scoring as a rookie with 16.8 points per game, while Twyman was tenth with 14.4 points per game. Stokes was first in rebounding, with 16.3 per game compared to Bob Pettit's 16.2 average. Almost incredibly, Stokes was eighth in playmaking with 4.9 assists per game.

"Pettit had a lot of respect for Stokes," said Twyman. "Speaking of Pettit, now there was a classy guy. He epitomized a great athlete."

Any basketball buff in Pittsburgh back then had to relate to the Royals as far as rooting for an NBA team. Especially when Sihugo Green of Duquesne University and Dave Piontek, of Bethel Park High School and Xavier University, joined that cast the following season. In Stokes' third season, he grabbed 38 rebounds in a single game.

"In my mind, he would have been one of the five best all-time," said Twyman. "He could play every position, and do it all. He could start the fast break and finish it, too. No one had seen a guy with that combination of strength and speed and size before. There were nights he was unstoppable."

Stokes and Green died young, Ricketts in his 50s. "I talked to Piontek over the holidays," said Twyman, "and he's had some tough times. He's being challenged with several health problems."

I was 14 years old during that second season Twyman was with the Royals in Rochester and had formed a three-man team league to play at the basket I had put up on a telephone pole in front of our home in Hazelwood. All the teams in our league had NBA nicknames. My team was called the Royals. I kept statistics on our league, wrote stories about our games, and that's how I broke in to become the sports editor of *The Hazelwood Envoy*. That's how I began my newspaper writing stint.

In 1991, while attending the NBA All-Star Weekend in Miami with my then teenage daughter, Sarah, I spotted Lester Harrison in the lobby. I went over to the man who once owned the Royals, one of the real pioneers in pro basketball, and introduced myself. I told him about the Royals of Sunnyside Street. Talking to him was a real treat. I was 14 again.

Pittsburgh has never produced as many pro basketball players as it did back then. Those individuals were all important to Twyman's early development. The only comparable period was in the '70s when a new breed of local basketball talent — Billy Knight, Maurice Lucas, Kenny Durrett, Mickey and Brad Davis and Sam Clancy — came along, as well as a super import from Macon, Georgia named Norm Nixon, maybe the best ballplayer in Duquesne University history.

"I could never figure it out."

It's hard to believe that Jack Twyman took four tries to make the Central Catholic team. It took Twyman that long to convince Joe Penzelik, the coach at the Oakland school, he belonged on his ballclub. Penzelik had lettered in basketball at Duquesne University in 1947-48. Twyman was a year younger than most of the boys in his class.

"I didn't know why I wasn't regarded as good enough," said Twyman. "I could never figure it out. Between my junior and senior season, I told Penzelik he wouldn't be able to cut me again. I lived at Mellon Park that summer."

That's a recreation complex on a triangular slice of ground where Oakland says hello to East Liberty, Point Breeze and Homewood. There are two basketball courts and three or four tennis courts there. The great boxer Billy Conn came out of that same neighborhood to nearly wrest the world heavyweight boxing title from the even greater Joe Louis back in the '40s. That's where Twyman played basketball every day in the summer before his senior year at Central Catholic.

"Stokes, Green, Fleming and all the Duquesne players were out there on the court every day," recalled Twyman. "It was the kind of thing where the losers sat down and the winners stayed on. I'd get there early, and play from dawn to dusk.

"I started playing sports when I was at Holy Innocents Grade School in Sheraden. I never played basketball then, but I played football and baseball. I was also an altar boy when I was in grade school. My dad, they called him 'Sky,' was good at everything he tried. He was a terrific bowler all his life, a pool player of some reputation, and he played Triple A baseball at Birmingham. He played on the Original Allentown Turners who played against the original Celtics.

"I have a younger brother, Ned, who played at Central Catholic, and then at Notre Dame and Duquesne (1959-61) and for a brief stint with the ABA. He also did some basketball broadcasting work as a color man. So we had an athletic family."

Kenneth "Sky" Twyman, for the record, was well known on the Pittsburgh sports circuit. He worked at J&L Steel on the South Side, and was involved in many sports activities. He played for several top independent basketball teams and was a star sandlot baseball pitcher. He left the St. Louis Cardinals organization after a brief try at big league baseball. He later gained respect as a baseball umpire in the Greater Pittsburgh League, a top-notch bowler and an outstanding pocket billiards player. He once ran 65 balls to beat Irving Crane, the world champion, in an exhibition. In his 50s, "Sky" Twyman captained the Brannan's Bowl teams in the fast Central and Greater Pittsburgh Duckpin Leagues, where he sported a 170 average.

"My dad was always off somewhere; he was out a lot," said Twyman. "My mother — her name was Teresa — was the driving force in our family. She made sure we went to mass at Holy Innocents every morning when we were in grade school.

"When I went to Central," continued Twyman, "I was getting fairly tall and I thought I'd like to try out for the basketball team. I didn't make the team, but there was a teacher (a Christian Brother) named Brother Matthew, and he had an independent team called the Apaches. I played with them for three years and we played everywhere in the city. One of the fellows on our team was Jack Barrett. He was a good guy and we send our regards to each other when we meet mutual friends.

"Brother Matthew gave me an opportunity to play basketball. He's dead now, but I'd seen him through the years and had a chance to thank him. As a freshman and sophomore, I was also the manager

Duquesne U. All-America Sihugo Green gets ride on Jack Twyman's back in mid-50s.

of the varsity basketball team, so I had a heavy schedule. It gave me a goal: to make the varsity. And I succeeded.

"I not only made the team my senior year, but I made All-State with people like Tom Gola.

"I worked out at Duquesne during the Easter vacation, and I could have gone there on a basketball scholarship. In fact, I had my fall schedule made out at Duquesne. That's what I wanted to do. Dudey Moore was the coach, and he was highly respected. I had gone to their games as often as I could. Nick Skorich was the football coach at Central Catholic at the time, and he had graduated from the University of Cincinnati. Skorich asked me to visit Cincinnati, as a favor to him. I went down and I loved it. The rest is fairly well known. I played as a freshman, and I just kept trying to improve."

During each off-season, he worked out four days a week. "Every session, I'd shoot 100 foul shots, 200 jump shots and between 150 and 200 set shots. I'd shoot about 500 shots a day. I would do sets of 10 from the same spot. I wanted to make 50 in a row. I'd make 48 in a row and miss and I'd start all over again."

"Twyman has more determination than any player I've ever seen."
—Bobby Wanzer

In his day, Twyman was regarded as a gunner, but it was said with respect. He hit 48 per cent of his shots in his best seasons, and nobody was more accurate back then with the exception of Chamberlain, who scored most of his points in close, and scored half of his points on dunks. Twyman led the league in field goal percentage (45.2 per cent) in the 1957-58 season.

"I took my share of shots," said Twyman. "Yes, I was a gunner. I admit it. I believed I could put the ball in the hole. I wasn't shy about it. It came from hours and hours of practice. It came from valuable lessons I had learned at an early age. I always had to prove that I belonged. There wasn't anybody who was going to stop me."

Indeed, he became one of the greatest shooting forwards in the NBA. Bobby Wanzer, his coach at Rochester, said, "Twyman has more determination than any player I've ever seen. He's the kind of guy who can key himself into things."

Asked to pick a few highlights in his career, Twyman said, "There was the 59-point game against the Minneapolis Lakers one night (January 15, 1960)." He had 50 points against the St. Louis Hawks in another high-scoring effort. He had 14 games in which he scored 40 or more points.

The hoop looked bigger than ever and the ball seemed smaller than ever, according to Twyman when he had one of those big games players dream about. "You can feel it when you're hot," he said. "You feel like everything you throw up there at the basket is going to drop through."

He scored 15,840 points in his career, more than such stars as Bill Russell, Walt Frazier, Sam Jones, Jerry Lucas, Maurice Lucas, Cliff Hagan, Willis Reed and George Mikan. "None of those points came on dunks, either," said Twyman. "I couldn't dunk the ball when I was playing."

Asked to recall some of his best memories of his career, Twyman offered, "I remember the All-Star Games I played in, and the all-league teams I made. I had worked hard to become a pro, and that was the culmination. I tried to play every game as hard as I could, and I enjoyed those years very much. When you go through a pro career, it's the people you meet and the accomplishments. Money can't buy these things or this recognition."

"It was only natural that I took over."

Red Auerbach of the Boston Celtics raved about Twyman. "Show him a little daylight and it's up and in," said Auerbach.

"I'd have liked to have played for Auerbach," said Twyman. "I think that would have worked out fine."

Auerbach was along those who got to know Twyman even better after Stokes was hauled, helpless and comatose, into Good Samaritan Hospital in Cincinnati. Stokes had been jarred in a headfirst fall a few days earlier, in the final game of the season. "That was on March 15, 1958," said Twyman, the date still on the tip of his tongue. "He died 12 years later, on April 6, 1970."

Stokes was stricken with encephalitis, a disease that damaged that part of his brain controlling voluntary actions. He spent the rest of his life in a hospital bed or wheelchair.

Twyman cited two doctors for helping Stokes a great deal, namely Dr. Howard Rusk of the Rusk Institute and Dr. Emily Hess, who came to Good Samaritan Hospital in 1960. "She was the best in her field," said Twyman, "and the timing was perfect for Maurice.

"I had heard about the great work Dr. Rusk was doing at the Rusk Institute in New York," explained Twyman. "He had looked after Roy Campanella when he was injured in an auto accident, and Ted Kennedy when he broke his back. I went up there to see if Maurice might be moved there to get better treatment. Dr. Rusk told me that his top assistant for 30 years, Dr. Emily Hess, was going to Good Samaritan in Cincinnati — she was from that area — to set up a physical rehabilitation center there. He assured me that Maurice couldn't get better care anywhere. That was a stroke of good fortune for all of us. She looked after Maurice the rest of his life."

Twyman and Stokes had known each other casually as high schoolers, playing in those pickup games at Mellon Park. They played against each other in the 1955 NIT when Cincinnati beat St. Francis, and as teammates with the Royals. But they were not close friends. Not until Stokes needed Twyman.

"Everybody else had left town at the end of the season," recalled Twyman, making light of his Good Samaritan role. "It was only natural that I'd take over. He needed to stay in Cincinnati, and he needed some one to look after his affairs. There wasn't anything heroic about my role. Maurice couldn't be his own advocate. He needed someone to speak on his behalf, and help him in time of need. It was Maurice who was the hero."

Twyman and Auerbach and other people in basketball, like Haskell Cohen, a Duquesne grad who was then the NBA's director of publicity, talked Milton Kutsher of Kutsher's Country Club in Monticello, New York, into hosting a summer pro all-star game to raise funds for Stokes, who required expensive and constant care. The Maurice Stokes Memorial Basketball Game was played there even after his death, when funds were used to help former NBA players in need.

Kutsher fed and housed the players who competed. They raised over $400,000, which really helped defray expenses not taken care of by Ohio worker's compensation.

Twyman felt he gained much more from his relationship with Stokes than Stokes did from knowing him.

"Being exposed to him did so much for me," Twyman told me. "I was exposed to an amazing person, and this has exposed me to so many great people, people who are sincerely charitable. He gave me a concept of life, a sense of direction as to where I wanted to go.

"He was a fantastic, loving person, utterly unselfish. When I would get down in the dumps, over problems, or business — when things weren't going right — I could go to Maurice and discover I had no problems at all. He could always cheer me up.

"I never saw him in a bad mood. This terrible thing happened to him, but Maurice never felt unfortunate at all. He was just happy to be alive."

It was critical to keep Stokes in Ohio so he would be covered by worker's compensation. His parents were elderly and living in Pittsburgh. Dorothy Parsons, his fiance, was a publishing executive in New York. They all agreed that Twyman would be Maurice's legal guardian.

Stokes' story was inspirational for others, according to Twyman. He recalled a Cincinnati youngster who had been paralyzed after diving into the shallow end of a swimming pool. The kid was so depressed by what happened to him that he contemplated suicide. Talks with psychiatrists and priests couldn't pull him out of his funk.

His parents arranged for him to meet Maurice Stokes at Good Samaritan Hospital. Stokes met with him on several occasions.

"About ten years later," said Twyman, "I went to Purcell High School to speak to the kids there. One of the teachers told me, 'There's somebody here who wants to meet you.' It was the kid who had spoken to Stokes after he was hurt. We shook hands and he told me, 'I wouldn't be alive if it weren't for Maurice Stokes.' "

Twyman wanted to tell me another story that shows how things were so much different in those days. "When Harrison decided to sell the team in 1958, his asking price was $225,000 if Stokes was part of the team," said Twyman, "and the team would go for $200,000 without Stokes."

Twyman has been honored on many occasions for his achievements as an athlete and for community service. Among his many credits, he has served as chairman of the Cincinnati Multiple Sclerosis and Cancer Society drives, as a member of the Executive Board of Boy Scouts of America, the Newman Club of Cincinnati. He raised $160,000 as chairman of the Cincinnati Knothole Baseball Committee, and was chairman of the Cincinnati United Appeal Drive.

"I've had four careers," said Twyman. "There was professional basketball, television, the insurance business and the food business. I'm retired now, but I'm busy enough. I'm working with the Archdiocese of Cincinnati to raise money to help underprivileged kids in the inner-city school system. I'm involved with a couple of foundations in a similar role."

"My dad is an extraordinary man."
—Lisa Twyman Bessone

His wife, the former Carole Frey, and their four children are a source of great pride to Twyman. The children (with their ages at the time of our get-together) are Lisa, 42; Jay, 40; Julie, 37; and Michele, 32.

"Things are fine for a guy who left Pittsburgh in 1951," he said. "I have a wonderful wife and a wonderful family. I met Carole at the University of Cincinnati. We were in the same class and graduated together in 1955. We met in 1952. She's the best thing that ever happened to me. We've been married for 44 years.

"We raised four children and I was gone a lot. My wife and I made a deal. We were a team. We had different roles and responsibilities. I'm so excited about what's ahead of us. My concern is that we stay healthy, so we can go visit our kids as often as we'd like, and as often as they'd like us to. I try to stay physically fit. To see them grow up and make their own way is a thrill. There's nothing that tops that.

"Things couldn't have worked out better. I'm not the smartest guy in the world, but I'll work harder than anyone else. It all goes back to the experience I had at Central Catholic High School. Getting cut three years in a row, and how I responded to that challenge, was the most valuable experience of my life. I convinced myself at the age of 15 that I could have anything I wanted in the world if I worked at it.

"Getting cut three years in a row was a horrible experience, and I hated it at the time. Some bad things happened to me in Pittsburgh.

85

But it served me well throughout my life. My persistence, whether I was right or wrong, worked well for me. If I put forth an extra effort I could succeed. I was willing to work harder than anyone else. I never forget that lesson. We're going to outwork everyone.

"My children have my work ethic. That's what parents are supposed to do, provide a role model for their children. I married a saint and she has shown our children how to do it, too. I have ten grandchildren and, hopefully, they'll be like that.

"My dad was a great athlete and I inherited his genes. I had a great mother and she had high expectations for me. I had one brother, Ned, and a sister, Judy, and they were terrific, too."

His daughter, Lisa, became a writer for *Sports Illustrated*. She gained the basketball beat in 1982. She has written about her early memories of tagging along with her father. "The thing I remember best is Dad retiring," related Lisa. "He jumped through one of those stupid paper hoops with a 27 on it. And they gave him, among other things, a dog. It was a beagle, and it came with a little doghouse. I stayed home from school for a week to be with that dog. They also gave Dad a year's supply of popcorn; I think I ate all of it."

Her dad remembered that he scored 39 points against the Knicks that night.

"The best part of his basketball career for us was when he was broadcasting for ABC," he said. "When he was playing, he got a pre-game steak and we got tuna. But when he was broadcasting, he took me to a game in Boston and we had room service at the Ritz."

She was 11 years old when Maurice Stokes died, but she learned a lot about him and what that period was all about for her parents. She regarded her father as "an extraordinary man" for his efforts on behalf of a teammate. She wrote about it in the NBA's *Hoop* magazine.

"Dad says he had no idea the responsibility he was taking on would span 12 years. Everybody thought Maurice would get better someday. My Dad is of the mind that when you make a commitment, you live up to your obligations. He did, mightily. In doing so, Dad found a friend. And this friendship was a powerful one, certainly because of the situation, but more so because of the men involved.

"Two forceful personalities came together and the result was a mutual and heart-felt affection and respect. Dad is white. Maurice was black. In those more segregated times, such friendships weren't common and people could be cruel. But it didn't matter. Dad had made a commitment. So had Maurice.

"Finally, there was sadness. The first time I ever saw Dad cry was the day Maurice died. I opened the door to the study and Dad was sitting on a couch sobbing. He held his face in his hands and his shoulders shook. Mom finally took him in her arms to comfort him. I had never seen such grief. To lose a friend, a really great friend who touches your soul and pushes you to be more than you otherwise might have been, is devastating."

When I checked with Twyman about the death of Stokes, he said, "I remember that it was Opening Day for the Cincinnati Reds. I was at the game when I was called with the news. That I remember."

"Please don't say anything sappy."
—Sarah O'Brien

My trip to Cincinnati to see Jack Twyman was special on several levels. My older daughter, Sarah, midway through her fourth and final year as a student in the School of Medicine at the University of Pittsburgh, asked me if I would accompany her to Cincinnati for a job interview. Her husband, Matthew, had a commitment at Pitt that prevented him from going to Cincinnati. Sarah was interested in checking out Children's Hospital there for a possible residency in pediatrics. She asked me about three weeks before she planned to make the trip. I jumped at the chance. I thought it would be great to spend nearly two days in her company, just the two of us, like we once did when we went to New York or Miami for basketball games or tournaments. They were special times. After I told Sarah I'd chauffeur her to Cincinnati, I considered what I might do to occupy myself while she was doing a long series of interviews.

I wondered whether I might be able to talk to Jack Twyman. When I think of Cincinnati, his name is one that still comes to mind.

I called George Von Benko to see if he could get me a telephone number for Jack Twyman. Von Benko, a good friend from his days as a Pittsburgh sports talk show host, was broadcasting University of Cincinnati football and basketball games. He was commuting from his home in Connellsville to Cincinnati to do the games. He checked with Tom Hathaway, the sports information director at Cincinnati, and got me the number. Twyman answered on the second ring. He told me his number was in the Cincinnati telephone book. I told Twyman I'd like to see him on Monday, January 10. Sarah's interview and tour would last from 8 a.m. to 3 p.m., so we had to work within that time frame.

It's about 220 miles from Pittsburgh to Cincinnati. We listened to an NFL playoff game between the Vikings and Cowboys on the radio en route. I was rooting for the Vikings because of Foge Fazio, an old friend from Pittsburgh who was serving as the defensive coordinator on the Vikings staff. We got to the hotel a few minutes before the start of the Dolphins-Seahawks playoff game. I had covered the Dolphins in Miami back in 1969 and had remained interested in the team. Plus, the Dolphins were led by quarterback Danny Marino, a former Pitt All-American from the Oakland section of the city, and I always liked him.

Sarah and I had some cold soft drinks and some snacks and settled in to watch the game. It was great to be with her. The Vikings won and so did the Dolphins.

We went out to dinner later that night. We traveled across the Ohio River to Covington, Kentucky and dined at a waterfront Applebee's Neighborhood Grill & Bar. Our view at the window was a preview of what's to come in Cincinnati, as well as in Pittsburgh. We could see the skeletal outlines of the football and baseball stadiums that were being built along the river, near Riverfront Stadium which the Reds and Bengals have been sharing. Riverfront Stadium is a similar in design to Three Rivers Stadium, so the view across the river was a familiar one. It was like dining at LeMont on Mount Washington.

Seeing the silhouette of Riverfront Stadium brought back some memorable times I had spent there as a sportswriter. I was there, as a reporter for *The New York Post*, on October 11, 1972 when Bob Moose, a pitcher for the Pirates from Export, Pennsylvania, threw a wild pitch in the ninth inning. The ball bounced past catcher Manny Sanguillen and enabled George Foster to score from third with the winning run in a 4-3 victory by the Reds in the fifth and deciding game of the National League playoffs. That hurt just as much as a fifth game loss to the Atlanta Braves 20 years later at Three Rivers Stadium. Remember Francisco Cabrera? I remembered the games I had covered at Riverfront Stadium between the Steelers and the Bengals, and how so many Steelers fans came to Cincinnati to root for their favorite team in those days. Even more so, I remember being there on January 10, 1982 — I had to look up the date and details — when the Bengals beat the San Diego Chargers, 27-7, in the AFC championship to advance to the Super Bowl. More than the details of the game, I remember the weather was so brutal. The temperature was 9 degrees below zero. There were wind gusts up to 35 miles an hour out of the northwest. The wind chill factor was 59 degrees below zero. The Chargers had no chance. Everybody in the Chargers' travel party had to go out and buy winter gear just to survive the Arctic-like weekend in Cincinnati.

Back in 1980, when Sarah was 7 years old, she had stayed overnight with me in a dorm room at St. Vincent College when I was covering the Steelers. Players like Joe Greene, Rocky Bleier and L.C. Greenwood and team officials fussed over her during her stay. When we were returning home, we stopped for breakfast at a Howard Johnson's Restaurant at the intersection of Route 70 and Route 51. When I asked her what she liked best about her stay at the Steelers' training camp, Sarah said, "Having you all to myself."

As we were returning from our overnight stay in Cincinnati, I asked Sarah, "What do you think I enjoyed the most about these two days?" She smiled knowingly and said, "Please don't say anything sappy like 'having you all to myself.' " I smiled back, but didn't say anything. Those were my sentiments, indeed.

Jack Twyman:
"I'm not the smartest guy in the world, but I'll work harder than anyone else."

"Jack Twyman has a special place in our hearts."
—James P. Kelly

I had asked Jack Twyman to pick me up at 11 a.m, and he appeared on schedule. As we warmed up to each other, talking about things we'd done the night before, he said he had also been rooting for Marino and the Dolphins in the televised game. "Us Central Catholic guys have got to root for one another," said Twyman.

"I'm also rooting for Bill Bradley in the Presidential race. I'd vote for him, and I'm a Republican. We went into the Hall of Fame together and I've always been an admirer of his."

I had decided that morning to go to the athletic department at the University of Cincinnati. I thought I could take a picture of Twyman at the Sports Hall of Fame. I'm glad I thought of this. Touring the campus sparked many memories for Twyman, and I had a chance to meet some special people.

When we arrived, there were three students lying on the concrete area by the doors of the athletic department. They were in sleeping bags.

Twyman was curious. "What's this all about?" he asked the students.

We learned that they were there to get tickets for upcoming basketball games with Ohio U. and Memphis. When we left, there were four more students getting settled in for the day.

There were front-page stories that same day in the *Cincinnati Inquirer* and *USA Today* saluting Cincinnati for being chosen the No. 1 basketball team in the nation. The Bearcats had beaten Marquette over the weekend and had a 14 1 record. The story about their No. 1 ranking that appeared in the *Inquirer* was written by Mike DeCourcy. He was originally from Pittsburgh and, by coincidence, had taken my place on the sports staff of *The Pittsburgh Press* when I left to go to work at Pitt in 1982. When *The Press* went out of business, DeCourcy moved to Memphis and later Cincinnati.

As soon as Twyman and I entered the lobby of the athletic department, someone called out to Twyman. The gray-haired man was wearing a UC baseball cap and a big smile. It was James P. Kelly, a former administrator from Twyman's days at the school. Kelly had been a receiver on the UC football team prior to Twyman's student days and had stayed on to assist a series of athletic directors. Twyman and Kelly were happy to see each other.

"Jack Twyman has a special place in our hearts," commented Kelly. "We talk about Jack all the time."

By coincidence, we were there to check out what is called the James P. Kelly UC Athletic Hall of Fame, a display on a wall about 25 yards ahead. I recognized some of the names of the basketball players represented, Lloyd Batts, Ron Bonham, Pat Cummings, Derrek

Dickey, Connie Dierking, Paul Hogue, Ed Jucker, Rick Roberson, George Smith, Tom Thacker, George Wilson and Tony Yates. There were some other sports stars I recognized, like Greg Cook, Elbie Nickel, Tony Trabert and a personal friend, Danny Rains. Rains, an executive responsible for business development with McCarl Inc. in Beaver Falls, was an outstanding linebacker for the Bearcats and later the Super Bowl winning Chicago Bears of Mike Ditka.

Kelly complimented Rains for being a good guy as well as a former standout football player on a college and pro level. Rains had played on the same team as Tony Dorsett for Butch Ross at Hopewell High School in the early '70s. Coincidentally, I had spoken to Rains at a Pitt vs. University of Connecticut Big East basketball game at the Pitt Field House just two nights earlier and had told him I was going to Cincinnati to talk to Twyman.

"Rains ran interference for Dorsett so he could set all sorts of rushing records," commented Kelly, proving he was a genuine booster of Rains.

I saw a plaque recognizing Rains as a member of the school's sports Hall of Fame. There was a cleaning lady running a vacuum sweeper on a red carpet behind a rope. When he went behind the rope to pose for a photo by his Pro Basketball Hall of Fame stained glass likeness, Twyman apologized to the woman, "We don't want to mess up what you've done," he said.

Twyman wanted me to see that his larger-than-life replica of his jersey and Oscar's jersey were on display at Shoemaker Center, the current venue for UC's basketball team.

Twyman's name was still evident in the Cincinnati basketball guide. He was the team's scoring leader each of his three varsity seasons, averaging 15, 21.8 and 24.6 points a game. Robertson came along two years after Twyman was gone, and he led the team in scoring all three of his varsity seasons, averaging better than 32 points a game in each of those campaigns.

Twyman was one of the best free throw shooters in Cincy history and, somewhat surprisingly, he was second in career rebounds with 1,242 to Robertson's 1,338. Robertson averaged 15.2 rebounds and Twyman averaged 13.8 rebounds for his career. As a senior, Twyman averaged 16.5 rebounds.

Twyman went to a receptionist to ask if we could see Bob Goin, the school's athletic director.

The receptionist told us where Goin's office was located. As it turned out, Kelly escorted us there. Goin came out to his reception area and invited us into his office. Twyman kept apologizing all the way. "We don't want to take up your time," Twyman said more than once. Goin insisted he had time to talk to us. I felt good when I spotted a copy of my latest book, *Hometown Heroes*, resting on a table behind Goin's desk. I knew I had signed a copy for Goin as well as basketball coach Bob Huggins only the week before at the request of George Von Benko. A half hour into our visit, Von Benko stopped by to say hello.

Jack Twyman visits with University of Cincinnati director of athletics Bob Goin on January 10, 2000 and points out his plaque in school's Hall of Fame.

I knew a little about Goin's background because he had grown up in Penn Hills, a suburb just east of Pittsburgh, and was a graduate of Bethany College. He was a good friend of Andy Urbanic, a former Penn Hills High School and Pitt football coach who was on Goin's administrative staff when he served as athletic director previously at Florida State University.

Twyman asked Goin about his daughter. It had been reported in the local papers, I was informed, that Goin was ready to be a kidney donor for his ailing daughter. Twyman mentioned that Oscar Robertson had done the same thing for his daughter. Goin spoke about his daughter Janice and her challenges. "She's got a very rare problem," said Goin, "It's like winning a lottery of bad luck. She's got too many antibodies in her system. They're competing with each other. They've ruined her lungs and kidneys. The chemotherapy treatments have weakened her. She has to get stronger before we can do a transplant."

Goin gave us a little background that showed how much he appreciated the Twyman-Stokes story. "I grew up in Gary, Indiana," began Goin, age 62 at the time. "But my parents divorced and I ended up, at age 12, in Pittsburgh, out in Penn Hills. My step-dad had two sons who were classmates of Maurice Stokes at Westinghouse High School. Maurice Stokes was a hero of mine. That was 50 years ago, so we're talking about 1950. Later on, I used to sneak into Duquesne Gardens. Jack Twyman was going to school across the street from the Gardens at Central Catholic at the time. I saw some pretty good Duquesne University basketball teams then. I remember when teams like Cincinnati and Dayton came in every year to play the Dukes.

"Duquesne University had a good basketball team in 1951. They had all their best players back," said Twyman. "They had a group of recruits at their campus gym. The recruits included Ed Fleming, Maurice Stokes, Dick Ricketts and me. They had us play against the varsity in a series of scrimmages that weekend. We won every game by 15 or more points. We swept the Duquesne team in four games."

I checked the record books when I got back to Pittsburgh. The 1950-51 Dukes had a 17-10 record. The 1951-51 team went to the NIT and NCAA Tournament and posted a 23-4 record.

Goin showed Twyman what was on the drawing board at the University of Cincinnati. He showed an artist's rendering for a village to house the athletes.

When Goin talked about plans for student housing it made Twyman shake his head. "I remember living with seven other guys in a room under the stadium when I was here," said Twyman. "We were all in bunkbeds."

Later, when we checked out Nippert Stadium, Twyman pointed to an area of the stands where he had resided in his student days.

Seeing Nippert Stadium sparked some memories for me as well. I went there the first time in the fall of 1969 — it was hard to believe that 31 years had passed since then — when I was working as a sportswriter for *The Miami News*. I was covering the Miami Dolphins in the final year of the American Football League. The Dolphins were there to play the Cincinnati Bengals, the team founded by Paul Brown. The Bengals had a great young quarterback, Greg Cook, a red-headed hometown hero. Cook was the leading passer in the AFL that season. Cook came before Ken Anderson and he was tall and talented. His career would be cut short of its expected greatness by injuries. The Dolphins were quarterbacked by Bob Griese, a former Purdue passer. Griese was having a tough time finding his way that same season. No one then would have bet that Griese would be coming back to Ohio some day to be inducted into the Pro Football Hall of Fame in Canton. The Dolphins' fullback was Larry Csonka of Stowe, Ohio, another future Hall of Fame inductee.

No one knew better than Twyman that some times it takes a while for an athlete to establish himself and realize his or her potential. No one knew where Twyman's talent would take him when he first came to Cincinnati in 1951. That was even longer ago — 49 years! — but it was all coming back to Twyman as he toured his old college campus. Some things had changed a great deal, some things were still the same. The memories would always be there, waiting to jump out from behind a row of hedges or from behind a pillar.

Twyman was paying attention to what was going on at his alma mater. When he spotted a photo of Kenyon Martin on the wall in the athletic director's office complex, he turned to Goin, and said, "I think Martin made a wise decision to come back this year. He's really improved his game. It's helped your program and it will help him in the long run. Now it appears he's really ready to play pro ball."

When we left Goin's office, we went to the Armory Field House. That's where Twyman had played his varsity games as a senior. The Armory Field House was now used for practice and for intramural activity for several sports.

We entered the dimly lit Armory Field House. It was a shell of its old self, like a neglected giant airport hangar. Twyman explained where the seats came out from the walls to courtside. He looked up at the ceiling. The paint was peeling in places. It was tough to make out what was up there in the rafters. Some students were shooting baskets. Twyman talked about his training regimen back in those days, how many shots he took each day in his personal practice workout. Twyman could see more in that old building than anybody else that afternoon. He could see the crowds, his teammates, his coaches, his teachers, the students, certain shots, exciting scenes. He smiled as they rolled through his mind like an old newsreel.

The Armory Field House opened for the 1954-55 basketball season, Twyman's senior year. Before that, the Bearcats had played in another campus gym and mostly at Cincinnati Gardens. Twyman had played center his first three seasons and switched to forward in his final season.

"I remember our first game there," Twyman said with more than a twinkle in his eyes. "We played against Indiana. They had been the No. 1 team in the polls the previous two seasons. They'd won the NCAA tournament in 1953. Branch McCracken was the coach at

Indiana, and Don Schlundt, an All-American, was their star player. I still have the ball at home from that first game. It was a high-scoring game (97-65 on December 18). I know we beat them by 30 or so points. I had 37 points in that game. Schlundt had 16. They had basically the same team back from the year before, so we felt pretty good about beating them the way we did. It was a great way to break in a new building." Shoemaker Center opened in 1989. Before that, the Bearcats home court was Riverfront Coliseum. Goin said the program had improved and gotten better when the team again had a campus court to call its own.

"This guy is making me work," Twyman complained to Von Benko as we moved back and forth between the buildings that made up the athletic complex at the University of Cincinnati. "I thought we were just going to stop by." He was having fun seeing his old haunts, but he was also having difficulty going up and down steps. You could smell the chlorine as we went through a hallway near the natatorium. The tiled hallways were those of an old-fashioned college athletic plant. There was a mix of old and new.

The University of Cincinnati had moved its home football games to Riverfront Stadium for a few years, but that didn't work and they came back to the campus and an improved Nippert Stadium. Goin thought it best to keep the games on campus. He thought the University of Pittsburgh was making a big mistake by abandoning and leveling Pitt Stadium in favor of new facilities on the North Side and South Side that it would share with the Steelers. "We tried it and it didn't work for us," said Goin. "Our students and alumni like it better here."

We visited with Tom Hathaway, the Cincinnati sports information director, and flipped through some photographs from Twyman's playing days. It had been a long time since Twyman had been in the building. Cincinnati's basketball team had regained the No. 1 ranking in the *USA Today/ESPN* poll that same day, so spirits were high in the department. The season would come to a premature stop when Martin was hurt as the NCAA Tournament was getting underway. Without Martin in the lineup, the Bearcats simply weren't up to challenging for the national championship. Martin did end up being the first player picked in the pro draft.

"There's a restaurant that's a big favorite with sports fans here in town," said Twyman. "It's called the Montgomery Inn. It's a ribs place. It's very famous here. I gave the owner my uniform from my last year with the Royals. A guy called me and wanted to know if I had still had one of my uniforms. I didn't keep much, I told him. The guy was in the collectors' business. He said one of my Royals uniforms would be worth $10,000.

"When I first came here the coach was John Wiethe. He had played football for the Chicago Bears. Coaching was a sideline for him. He was an attorney in town. Then George Smith became my coach in my sophomore season. With him, it was a full time job.

Checking out the University of Cincinnati athletic complex brought back a lot of great memories for Jack Twyman as he revisited the Armory Field House where he once starred for the Bearcats, a stained-glass honor from the Basketball Hall of Fame and Nippert Stadium where he resided during his student days.

"Growing up in Pittsburgh, I was a Duquesne fan. Everybody who grew up in Pittsburgh wanted to play at Duquesne. I was honored that they wanted me. But I wanted to get away from Pittsburgh; I wanted to be independent. Cincinnati is the greatest town I've ever been in. I've been here 50 years and it's been a wonderful town. I love this town. I love the University. It's my home."

I asked Twyman how he got the Royals to leave Rochester in favor of Cincinnati. "In 1957, I convinced Les Harrison to bring one game to Cincinnati," recalled Twyman. "Our attendance had dipped badly the year before in Rochester, so Harrison was eager to test the waters someplace else. We played the Pistons in a TV game in Cincinnati. We sold out the building. Les said, 'I'm coming next year to Cincinnati.' Then, a year later, Harrison sold out to Cincinnati interests."

The Pistons moved from Fort Wayne to Detroit for that same 1957-58 season. Both moves were thought to be upgrading the NBA as a real major league. The NBA had adopted the 24-second shot clock for the 1954-55 season, so it was a period where the league was improving its product. It still had a long way to go. "I think it's terrific how the league has grown," said Twyman, "and I'm proud of the part I played in it.

"I'm proud of my Pittsburgh roots, too. It all started in Sheraden. My mother was persistent. She wanted me to go to Central Catholic. She thought it was the best prep school in the city. It was not easy. I took the streetcar from Sheraden to downtown. I remember the streetcar stop was in front of Kappel's Jewelers. My routine was to walk through the old Jenkins Arcade to Kappel's. It would take 40 minutes to get downtown. Then it was another 30 minutes to Central. It was a little longer to get to Mellon Park in the summer because that was another dozen blocks past Central Catholic. Between my junior and senior year I lived at Mellon Park. I was there from 8 a.m. to 9 p.m. I'd get up at 6 a.m. to get to Mellon on time. I took the streetcar from Sheraden each day. I went four or five stops past Central Catholic High School on Fifth Avenue. It was at Mellon Park that I first met Maurice Stokes and Ed Fleming. Once in a while Chuck Cooper would come by and play. Everybody came there to test his game.

"I worked hard to become a good basketball player. We had a lot of good athletes at Central Catholic when I was there. Eddie Vereb was a halfback on our football team and he went on to play as an All-American for Maryland when they won the national championship. Don Schaefer went to Notre Dame. Don Bailey went to Penn State. Ray DiPasquale and Fred Glatz went on to play at Pitt. Steve Zappalla went on to become a judge. Now his son's the D.A. in Pittsburgh. Jack O'Malley came a little later from Morningside. He went to St. Francis of Loretto, and was good enough to be drafted by the Detroit Pistons. But he wanted to become a priest. And he did. He's worked at a lot of parishes in Pittsburgh. He's a good man. I hear he still goes to all the Pitt and Duquesne basketball games. He was a tough competitor. You can't believe how combative he was on a basketball court."

I knew all those names. Vereb was from my hometown of Hazelwood. He played with the Washington Redskins. Schaeffer, who grew up in neighboring Greenfield, played for the Philadelphia Eagles. I often see Father O'Malley and always enjoy his company.

"I was brimming with confidence when I tried out for the basketball team in my senior year at Central Catholic," recalled Twyman. "I had played that summer with Stokes, Ricketts and Fleming. Who was going to keep me off the team? I had told our coach, Joe Penzelik, the year before, 'I'll be back and I'm going to make this team, whatever it takes. You won't be able to cut me.' I wanted to make the team and I wasn't going to be denied. I've told my children that story, and now I tell my grandchildren that story."

Talking about the summers at Mellon Park made Twyman think about later summers at Kutsher's Country Club in the Catskill Mountains north of New York City. "Wilt Chamberlain was the key to the success of the Maurice Stokes fund-raising games at Kutsher's," said Twyman. "He was the star. I coordinated things, but it was Wilt who was the big draw. In the summer of 1958 Chamberlain worked at Kutsher's, so he knew his way around the place. Milton Kutsher came to see me in New York. He talked about hosting a summer basketball game for the top pros at his place. He said, 'You won't have to spend a dime. All you have to do is get there.' We had so many guys show up. Wilt had left Kansas before his senior season, and was with the Harlem Globetrotters. He was touring Europe during the 1958-59 season.

"I asked Wilt if he would come to help us help Maurice. He said, 'I'll be there.' He came at his own expense. He took a flight from Paris to Kennedy Airport in New York. He chartered a helicopter from there to Kutsher's. He returned to Paris after the game. He only missed one day with the Globetrotters. Wilt came up every year. He would tell me, 'I'll bet I can do more.' He was unbelievable the way he supported the game. Wilt never missed a game at Kutsher's."

I mentioned to Twyman that it was at the Stokes Game at Kutsher's that I first got to meet Chamberlain up close and personal and what a wonderful experience it had been. "I'm in my room one day," I told Twyman, "and there was a knock at my door. I opened the door and there was Wilt in the doorway. Then he was in my room. He filled the room. It was unreal. And he was so personable. It left a lasting impression."

Always the competitor, Twyman had one to top that.

"My daughter Lisa worked for *Sports Illustrated* for ten years as a writer. She wanted to do a piece on Wilt Chamberlain. One day Wilt was announcing that he was forming a volleyball league. All the media were there in New York. He took three questions and said that's it. My daughter goes up to him and introduces herself. 'Mr. Chamberlain, I'm Lisa Twyman with *Sports Illustrated*. Jack

Twyman is my father.' He took her down to a coffee shop and he spent three hours with her. That's the way Wilt was. He looked after my Lisa, and he never missed one game for Maurice. That's why I'll always be grateful to Wilt."

"I don't know anybody who didn't like Jack Twyman."
—Gale Catlett

On May 18, 2000, Jack Twyman served as a pallbearer for a gentleman who had been a significant patron of the basketball program during its glory days. Walter Paul, a retired Cincinnati businessman who had been the head of the boosters group when the Bearcats won national championships (1961 and 1962), had died in Florida.

His body was returned to Cincinnati for funeral services. Twyman was joined in carrying Paul to his final resting place by Oscar Robertson and former Cincinnati coach, Gale Catlett, who had left Cincinnati to coach at his alma mater, West Virginia University. Catlett related this story in a telephone conversation from his office in Morgantown on June 7.

"It was good to see Oscar and Jack again," said Catlett. "Walter Paul was one of the main reasons Cincinnati won a national championship. He supported that program in every way. It was a great program (Catlett's record was 126-44 in six seasons, 1972-1978) and my wife and I loved Cincinnati. I would have left there only for Kentucky or West Virginia. Oscar told me Walter Paul was the reason he went to Cincinnati and the reason he stayed there. I have always admired Jack Twyman. He's done well for himself. We used to do some things together. I don't know anybody who didn't like Jack Twyman. That's the best tribute a man could have."

Twyman has another thought on that subject. Going to friends' funerals more often reminds him of his own mortality. Asked what words he might like to have cut into his tombstone someday, Twyman told me, "He got more out of what God gave him than he should have."

**Bill Bradley,
Former U.S. Senator:**
"I have long known that the nurturing provided by Crystal City, Missouri, my hometown, gave me a solid foundation from which to launch many a journey.
But only now, in the worsening crisis that has overtaken America's children, have I fully realized how lucky I was to have been raised by two loving parents and in such a caring community."

Jim O'Brien

Snapshot:

Lynn Swann, Former Steelers star receiver, ABC-TV college football sideline reporter:

"I didn't have any sports heroes when I was a kid. Sammy Davis Jr. was my favorite performer. I loved the way he danced and played the drums. He could sing and act, and do it all. He had such great enthusiasm. Fred Astaire might have been second. Keep in mind, I was going to dancing school at the time. I went to see him perform on stage. Sammy Davis Jr. came to Pittsburgh on business once, and Franco Harris invited him to come to the Steelers' locker room and meet the guys. Franco knew one of his people, or something like that. So I got to meet him. I didn't tell him about how I'd once felt about him, not there, anyhow. Later on, I told him."

Pitt Stadium
They closed it down in grand style

*"I understand how some of the long-time
Pitt fans and alumni feel about this."*
— Walt Harris

The students couldn't wait for the final football game at Pitt Stadium to end. With five or six minutes remaining in the exciting contest with traditional rival Notre Dame, and the outcome rather obvious in favor of the home team, the students started to move. It was some movement.

They started to seep out onto the near sideline. Yes, seep, that's the only way to describe the scene. The security guards gave way slowly. They didn't want to confront or challenge the students. They had been told to contain but not confront the students. Not this day. It wasn't necessary. The security guards were content to keep the students under control, so the game could be completed without incident. The students kept moving forward. It was some sight. The bleacher seats and gray concrete started to show at the top of the student section. It revealed itself one row at a time.

In weeks to come, that same concrete would be broken into bits by bulldozers moving in the opposite direction, from bottom to top. Watching that destruction was even more of an emotional strain on a Pitt man.

The student section, only minutes before, had taken part in the final "wave" at Pitt Stadium. It seemed to signify a celebration, a party to end Pitt Stadium, something to smile about, something to enjoy about this bittersweet experience. The students came down out of the stand, moving like lava from an erupting volcano. There was a lot of energy and emotion unleashed at Pitt Stadium on this final Saturday — November 13, 1999 — on Cardiac Hill.

Pitt was going to get the ball back with nine seconds showing on the stadium scoreboard clock, but the students had seen enough. It was time to go crazy. They swarmed the field, and couldn't be stopped, despite feeble protests from the officials, and the public address announcer to get off the field. It was too late. It was party time. They stormed the goal posts and weighed them down to the turf. Some tore up some of the turf for souvenirs. Pitt officials had hoped against hope this wouldn't happen, yet it wasn't that bad. It was controlled mayhem, student madness that somehow seemed appropriate for the occasion and the 37-27 victory to end an era.

"I think everybody just got caught up in the emotion," said senior safety D.J. Dinkins, who went to nearby Schenley High School and was more familiar with Pitt Stadium than most of his teammates. "They were just enjoying themselves. It was a one-time event. They were just living in the moment."

100

Fireworks went up and goal posts came down after final football game at Pitt Stadium as students celebrated the closing.

Sophomore defensive end Bryan Knight was pleased by the response. "I've dreamed about that all my life," he said. "Just pandemonium, the fans rushing the field."

Somehow, they were able to clear the field for a planned post-game event to mark the closing of Pitt Stadium. Marshall Goldberg, one of the grand old names in Pitt football lore, was at midfield with a treasure chest of sorts. It was a receptacle in which to symbolically store the spirit of Pitt Stadium, to be loosed into the air when the Panthers play their first game in the new stadium on the North Side in 2001.

Neither Notre Dame nor Pitt has a football team that lives up to the standards of their glory days, but they were not that bad, either. The presence of Goldberg and some of Pitt's finest from the past gave the game a special aura, and the finality of it all made it an emotional evening under the lights.

I had moved myself toward the end of the game. I left the press box where emotions are, understandably, to be kept in check. There is no cheering in the press box. There is no tearing in the press box. So I went to the wooden bridge that abuts the press box, and stood there with others similarly moved by the moment. I compared notes with Larry Eldridge, who had succeeded me as sports information director at Pitt in 1985 and was now doing public relations work with Pittsburgh's Fox Sports. That press box bridge was like a widow's walk high above a seaport. I had a great view of the students spilling out of their seats and onto the field. I could feel the vibes, smell the smells, take it all in. One last time. I wondered why I cared so much about Pitt Stadium. I wished that I didn't care so much. Going to Pitt as a student in 1960 opened up so many doors for me in my life. It changed my life. I will be forever grateful for the experience and the people I was lucky to meet. I learned so much on those hallowed grounds. I didn't want to let go of Pitt Stadium. I always feel better when I am on the Pitt campus. I am a student forever. The new stadium on the North Side will be special, too. But it's the Steelers stadium. It will never be Pitt Stadium. I hope it works out well, that it helps improve the Pitt football program. But something significant was happening before my eyes. Something was lost, something was gained. History was being made.

The students understood the story less than the faithful alumni, and less than the more than 400 football letter-winners present for the finale. Yet in some way their loss was the greatest.

It will be interesting to see if the students follow the team to the North Side. Students prefer to be able to drift in and out of a stadium on game day to suit their own schedule, to walk from their campus dorm or fraternity house, to eat and drink and party as they please. It will be different in the new setting across town.

The young adjust to change better than the old, however, and maybe the transition will be easier for the students. Some day, three or four years hence, the new stadium would be all the students have ever known. They won't live in the past.

This was a real happening, a memorable moment in Pittsburgh sports history, not appreciated perhaps by those in the press box who didn't have a vested interest in the University of Pittsburgh.

"We'll have something special to show them."
— Walt Harris

I had been at a sports luncheon earlier in the week at Three Rivers Stadium where Walt Harris, the Pitt football coach, was the featured speaker. As he spoke, he glanced over his shoulder through an expansive wrap-around window to where the new football stadium was being built, and talked about what it was going to be like, and why it would be a plus for Pitt.

He promised his best effort and his team's best effort for the Pitt Stadium finale with Notre Dame. He felt challenged to deliver because he recognized what was about to unfold. "This is a historic game going in," he explained. "Usually, you don't know until after a game that it's going to be remembered. Our coaching staff has to coach its best game, our players have to play their best game."

He mentioned some special games in his first season at Pitt, exciting victories over Miami, Virginia Tech and West Virginia that would be long remembered.

"This is all about the University of Pittsburgh being able to recruit the best students and some of the best football players," Harris told the Pittsburgh business people assembled at the Allegheny Club.

He was marking his 53rd birthday, by coincidence, and it prompted him to add, "This is not about us anymore. It's about our young people. We have to do things to make Pittsburgh more attractive to our young people, to be able to provide them with opportunity here. We want to keep our young people in Pittsburgh.

"I think it will make a big difference when I have a new stadium and a new setting to sell to prospective student athletes. We'll have something special to show them: the new stadium and the city skyline in the background. I think it will be impressive. I understand how some of the long-time Pitt fans and alumni feel about Pitt Stadium. They're giving up something that's been significant in their lives, and I can appreciate that. But it hasn't been working in recent years, and we have to be competitive with the schools we play. We have to look to the future."

> ## "The greatest tragedy in life is that most people spend their entire lives preparing to live."

103

"Just imagine the turnout you'd get by tearing down the Cathedral of Learning."
— Bill Baierl

The weekend of November 12-13, 1999 was a look back at the past. It drew a sellout crowd, first to a Varsity Letter Club dinner at the downtown Doubletree Hotel on Friday night, and then to Pitt Stadium, for one last time, on Saturday evening. One of the largest crowds in the history of the school, 60,190, showed up, many so they could always boast that they were there. There was a time when this game was going to be played at Three Rivers Stadium, as a transitional step to the change of venue, but that wouldn't have been right.

If Pitt Stadium was going to be leveled before its 75th birthday, there had to be an appropriate sendoff. Some stayed away. They wanted no part of it, and were offended by the attempt at putting a positive spin on what they viewed as a bum decision. It was their final protest. They thought Pitt Stadium was significant and worth preserving. They said they were finished with Pitt football.

Some came with mixed emotions. Bill Baierl, the North Hills automobile magnate who has been so generous to the Pitt athletic program through the years, had played basketball for Doc Carlson at the Pavilion in the bowels of Pitt Stadium. In his student days, he used to commute to Pitt by streetcars. He loved being on the campus, modest as it might have been by comparison to some college campuses. He had been for the move to his native North Side in the beginning, but changed his mind in recent months and was now opposed to the plan. He continued to support Pitt programs because he still bled Blue and Gold.

"I told Chancellor Nordenberg," said Baierl at the banquet Friday night, "that if you can get a crowd like this by tearing down Pitt Stadium, just imagine the turnout you could get by tearing down the Cathedral of Learning."

They came to pay their last respects to Pitt Stadium. After 74 years, the concrete bowl that sits above the campus of the University of Pittsburgh was to be leveled after one last game with Notre Dame. Some came with heavy hearts, disappointed by the decision to move the football program off campus to new facilities on the city's North Side and South Side, but with high hopes that all would work out well for the Blue and Gold. Many attended the weekend festivities convinced that the move to new facilities would be in the best interest of the University, no question about it. Some came just to see old friends.

Pitt not only prevailed, 37-27, in a classic back-and-forth contest, full of exciting plays, but there were parades and fireworks and presentations that made for quite a show. The goalposts and some tears came down at the end.

Those who were there witnessed an emotional and energy-charged event that should rate right up there with Maz's home run

Bill Baierl, Dick and Nancy Mills and Rick Leeson toasted each other at Pitt Varsity Letter Club dinner at Doubletree Hotel on eve of Pitt Stadium finale.

John Maczuzak and Ernie Borghetti were both fifth-year linemen on Pitt's 9-1 team in 1963 season. Maczuzak became a top administrator at U.S. Steel and Borghetti became a dentist in his hometown of Youngstown.

that won the World Series in 1960, Franco's "Immaculate Reception" to beat the Oakland Raiders in the 1972 AFC playoffs, and the Penguins' first Stanley Cup championship in 1991.

Marshall Goldberg

"It was a great weekend."
— Dave Jancisin

I spotted lots of familiar faces over the weekend. If you were there, you have your own faces and names to store in your memory bag.

Judge Emil Narick of Upper St. Clair and his good friend and former teammate Ernie Bonelli of Mt. Lebanon led the letter-winners from the decade of the 1940s across the field in a halftime parade. They had played with Marshall Goldberg and for Jock Sutherland, two of the legendary names in Pitt history.

The presence of Goldberg, 1976 Heisman Trophy winner Tony Dorsett and Hall of Famers Bill Fralic and Joe Schmidt among the letter-winners brought a special aura to the atmosphere.

At the dinner, I sat across the table from Dr. John "Jock" Beachler, who was named by his father after the legendary figure who coached Pitt and the Steelers. Eddie Beachler had been a sportswriter on *The Pitt News*, and later with *The Pittsburgh Press*. He was an editor at KDKA-TV and the original Pittsburgh correspondent for *Sports Illustrated*. "My dad started taking me to games at Pitt Stadium when I was about five or six years old," recalled Dr. Beachler, an orthopedic physician who remained in his hometown of Mt. Lebanon and had offices in Scott. I had gone to him once after injuring my knee in a pick-up basketball game, and thought I benefited greatly from his care. "I grew up with Pitt football and was honored to have a chance to play football there," Dr. Beachler added. "Pitt Stadium is special to me, but I guess we have to move on."

Also seated at our table were Dr. Brian Generalovich, Dr. Robert Bazylak, Ed Gallin and Dr. Carl Peterson. It didn't get any better.

The dinner was a special reunion. It was organized and coordinated by Walt Bielich of Bethel Park, who delivered a stirring pep talk and closed by leading the singing of the alma mater.

John Guzik, who grew up as the son of a coal miner in Cecil Township, was there with his kid brother, Bob. Both played for the Panthers. John, who went on to play with the Los Angeles Rams and was now a big success in the recycling business, was honored at the dinner as a letter-winner of distinction along with the likes of NFL coaches Mike Ditka, Dave Wannstedt and Foge Fazio, and Donna DeMarino Sanft and Dr. Dave Blandino.

Armand Dellovade, a Pitt booster in the construction business in Canonsburg, told Guzik he remembered the big block he threw to

Judge John G. Brosky, Dr. Woody Haser and Judge Emil Narick

**Boys of Donora: Rudy Andabaker, Tony Romantino, Nick DeRosa and
Lou "Bimbo" Cecconi**

spring quarterback Bill Kaliden loose for a late game-winning touch-down in a 29-26 victory over Notre Dame in 1958. It was that kind of get-together.

Soon after I arrived at the Doubletree Hotel, I saw some old friends. John Maczuzak and Ernie Borghetti, both outstanding fifth-year offensive linemen on the 1963 9-1 team of our senior year at Pitt, came up the escalator together.

I was approached by three players who were on the football team in the 1980s, back when I was working as the assistant athletic director for sports information. They were Barry Pettyjohn, Marc Bailey and Tony Magnelli. They weren't great players, but they were great kids. "My mom said to be sure to say hello to you," said Pettyjohn. That remark points up the kind of relationship I had with some of them in their student days at Pitt.

Everywhere one looked there were Pitt people, from every decade. Four Pitt men from Donora were together: Lou "Bimbo" Cecconi, Rudy Andabaker and Nick DeRosa from the late '40s, and Tony Romantino from the early '50s.

Beano Cook, the irrepressible publicist from the '50s and '60s, cornered Foge Fazio to reflect on some recruiting stories. Nobody knows more about Pitt football or cares more about it than Beano Cook. He was for the new stadium, anything that might return Pitt to national contention again. He hoped that, before he died, Pitt would win again. Priscilla and Bill Zito and Roz and Bill Kaliden came by. I saw and spoke to Sue Michelosen Mazurek, the daughter of the late football coach, John Michelosen. She married Pitt quarterback Fred Mazurek, who became an attorney in California.

Seen in the crowd were Joe "Tippy" Pohl, Emil Boures, Glenn Lehner, Ken Montanari, John Telesky, Ray Popp, Dennis Atiyeh, Lee Baierl, Mickey Depp, Al Romano, Andy Beamon, Peter Billey, Nick Bolkovac, Tom Brown, Lloyd Weston, John Wiley, Jack Wiley, Randy Reutershan, Tony Brown, Bob Buczkowski, Eric "Snuffy" Schubert, Gary Burley, Joe Curtin, Merle DeLuca, Ivan Toncic, Ray Conway, Ray Tarasi, Dr. Darrell Lewis, Gordon Jones, Gordon Oliver, Haywood "Woody" Haser, Pete Gonzalez, Dr. Richard Gradisek, Dick Haley, Gary Burley, Bob Sorochak, Tom Ricketts, Davey Havern, Craig Heyward, Troy Hill, Randy Holloway, Dave Janasek, Paul Killian, Roger Kingdom, Bob Kuziel, Andy Kuzneski, Dr. Rick Leeson, Bill Lindner, Roman Matusz, Larry Vignali, Rege Coustillac, Paul Martha, Rudy Mattioli, Chuck Brueckman, Joe Wall, Bob Rosborough, Bob Ostrosky, John Pelusi, Tony Recchia, Dean Caliguire, Dave Havern, Corky Cost, Dick Mills and Bill Wallace,

Representing other sports were Olympian Herb Douglas, a member of Pitt's board of trustees, Dr. Bill Sulkowski, Ray Capelli, George Schoeppner, Kirk Bruce, Judge John G. Brosky, Tom Bigley, Bob Lovett, Jerry Matulevic, and Laverne Lewis, wife of the late baseball coach Bobby Lewis.

Dr. Joe McCain, Bill Lindner, Jim Zanos and Ken Montanari

Bill Kaliden, Foge Fazio and Beano Cook

Others seen at the dinner and game were Jon Botula, Ralph Cindrich, Ralph Jelic, Jim Zanos, Dave Jancisin, Frank Gustine, Jr., Henry Suffoletta, Don DeBlasio, Dr. Dick Deitrick, Dr. Edwin Assid, Dr. Barry McKnight, Dr. Rod Fedorchak, Dr. Ron Linaburg, Caesar Aldisert, John Rees, Joe Moore, Ron Sams and John Nicolella.

"This weekend made me even more proud to be a Pitt man," said Cindrich, now a respected sports attorney with offices in Carnegie.

"It couldn't have been more perfect," said Jancisin, an executive officer with Merrill Lynch. "It's tough to say goodbye to Pitt Stadium, but I'm sure this is the right thing."

Jancisin hosted many of the players at a party at his home in Mt. Lebanon after the game. Gary Burley stayed at his home. "I came to Pitt from West Mifflin and I wasn't a great player," said Jancisin. "But I was a three-year starter. I was there when we went 1-10 under Carl DePasqua, and I was there the next year when John Majors came in and turned it around and we went 6-4-1 and went to the Fiesta Bowl. I survived that transition somehow and I'm proud of that. It was a great weekend. I saw people I hadn't seen in over 20 or 25 years, and I may never see again. If I could relive that weekend every so often it would be great."

Alex Pociask

Final tailgate party at Pitt Stadium was bittersweet time for Darrell Hess, Bill Fralic, Jim O'Brien and Dave Jancisin.

Two former Pitt running backs Charles "Corky" Cost of Wilkinsburg and Dr. Rick Leeson of Scott Township

Two former all-around athletes Frank Gustine Jr. of Canevin and Dr. Brian Generalovich of Farrell

Pitt Stadium as it appeared before they began to level the 74-year-old campus

The last remaining section was behind Gate 1 of Pitt Stadium.

Former manager John Nicolella and NFL standouts Joe Schmidt and Dick Haley get together at tailgate party prior to Notre Dame game.

Stars of the '60s included, left to right, Dr. Peter Billey, Ray Conway, Jerry Matulevic and Dr. Bob Ostrosky.

Jackie Sherrill
Still proud of Pitt record

"The best thing you can say about me is that I'm a player's coach."

Jackie Sherrill is still the most successful football coach in the history of the University of Pittsburgh. When this accolade was tossed his way at a breakfast meeting in Pittsburgh in early February, 2000, Sherrill smiled that trademark thin smile of his, and refined it by interjecting, "The best winning percentage anyway."

Yet Sherrill is seldom mentioned when anyone talks about the great football coaches in Pitt's glory days. Pop Warner and Jock Sutherland get the most attention, of course, with John Majors and John Michelosen mentioned as well. The Sherrill oversight is difficult to understand.

It may have something to do with image. Sherrill must not have stroked enough backs when he was working in Pittsburgh. Some still get a sourpuss look on their face at the mere mention of his name. "Do you like Sherrill?" they ask.

Even Sherrill admits he wasn't a complete college coach when he was at Pitt, and may not have understood his role as well as he did in later years. He knows he stubbed some toes, and wasn't always politically correct. He wasn't trying to win any popularity contests, just football games. He cuts corners, according to his critics.

Even so, Sherrill's numbers are simply better than anybody else who has ever coached the football team at the University of Pittsburgh. You could look it up. Sherrill sits at the top of the all-time coaching records by winning percentage at .833 with an overall record for five years (1977-1981) of 50-9-1. He guided the Panthers to a post-season bowl game every one of those five years. Warner is next at .800 with a record for nine years (1915-1923) of 60-11-4, followed by Sutherland at .776 for 15 years (1924-1938) with a record of 111-20-12.

There is still a place in Sherrill's heart for Pitt and Pittsburgh, even though he believes now that he will conclude his coaching career at Mississippi State where he would start his ninth season in the fall of 2000. "I'll retire where I am now," he said. His team posted a 10-2 record, and finished No. 12 in the nation in 1999, showing that Sherrill still had the magic touch.

Sherrill led Mississippi State to five bowl games in eight seasons in Starkville. His overall record for 22 seasons as a collegiate head coach was 163-87-6, a .637 winning percentage.

He was visiting Pittsburgh for two days, February 4-5, 2000, as a guest speaker at the 38th Annual Nike Coach of the Year Clinic hosted by Pete Dimperio Jr., son of the late legendary football coach who ruled the City League while working at Westinghouse High School. The weekend clinic was held at the Radisson Hotel in Green Tree, a few miles south of downtown Pittsburgh. Sherrill submitted to an interview that lasted nearly three hours.

He had the time because he wasn't working the crowd like he would at a clinic closer to Starkville. He had successfully recruited a kid out of New Jersey the year before, but he doesn't normally recruit in the East because Mississippi State is a tough sell in these parts.

Sherrill was conducting a special teams clinic for area coaches, most of them on the high school level. He was wearing a burnt orange golf shirt buttoned to the Adam's apple and a burnt orange and brown herringbone sport jacket. His 57th birthday was fast approaching, and he looked good.

He stood in front of a hotel directory that was evidence of a sense of the city's history. Meeting rooms at the hotel, formerly the Green Tree Marriott, are named after Heinz, Carnegie, Mellon, Frick, Cather, Salk, Foster, Westinghouse, Thompson, familiar names who helped put Pittsburgh on the national and even international map through their accomplishments.

Being in the lobby, talking to Pete Dimperio Jr., reminded Sherrill of an earlier edition of the Dimperio-coordinated clinic, one he had attended in 1974 in Pittsburgh with John Majors. Two of the headliners at that clinic were John McKay of Southern Cal and Charlie McClendon of LSU.

"McKay was talking about why USC was so good," said Sherrill. "He drew circles on a chalkboard to indicate his offensive players in a certain set. Then he drew circles to indicate the opposing defensive players. The circles for his team were much larger than the ones for the opposing team. 'That's one of the reasons we're so good,' said McKay. 'We have bigger people than the people we play. That helps.' I can still remember that."

Sherrill smiled at his own story. Dimperio did the same. He appreciated a good story when he heard one. His father, who came from the same hometown as I did — Hazelwood — was one of the funniest after-dinner speakers on the sports banquet circuit for so many years.

Sherrill recognized old friends in the lobby. He still knew his way around Pittsburgh.

He left Pitt twice. In doing so, he missed out on the national championship season of 1976, and he believes that if he had stayed the second time around he could have coached the Panthers to a national championship in 1982. He wanted to come back a third time — Pitt was like an old girl friend you can't forget — but he never got the chance.

He left the staff of John Majors after the 1975 season to become head coach at Washington State for one season. When Majors departed Pittsburgh after winning Coach of the Year honors for the second time in four years and a national title in 1976 to go home to

116

Jackie Sherrill returned to Pittsburgh in February of 2000 as guest speaker at Nike Coach of the Year Football Clinic hosted by Pete Dimperio Jr.

The Posh Look
Telephones
Chats Lounge
Conference Center
 Board
 Linc
 PPG
 Interstate
 Allegheny
 Monongahela
 Salk
 Ohio
 Brockett
 Foster
 Westing...
 Carnegie
 Thompson
 Frick
 Heinz
 Mellon
 Cather
 Bartrooms

Tennessee, Sherrill came back to Pittsburgh. He had an escape clause in his contract at Washington State should there be an opening at Pittsburgh.

His five-year stay as head coach produced spectacular results, especially the last three years when his teams posted three straight 11-1 records. Considering the opposition and number of schools in the nation fielding big-time football teams at the time this may have been the best span ever for Pitt football.

Pop Warner had three straight undefeated teams (26-0 overall) during three seasons (1915-1917), and won the first four games of the 1918 schedule to post a 30-game winning streak at the start of his Pitt stay.

As he picked at a western omelet, Sherrill sprinkled his conversation with observations as meaty and colorful as the ingredients in his three-egg entrée.

He joins John Majors in second-guessing his decision to leave Pitt. Sherrill left in favor of Texas A&M before the 1982 season. "If I had stayed for Dan Marino's senior season," he said, "I think we would've won a national championship. We had something special going here. I could discipline Dan and keep him in line. He was never a real problem, but he had this sense of himself and his importance to the program that needed to be kept in check."

At the time, though, Sherrill had several reasons to leave Pittsburgh for College Station, Texas. The contract offer at Texas A&M was so superior to what Pitt was willing to pay, plus he was at odds with his boss, Pitt Athletic Director Dr. Edward Bozik. The Aggies offered Sherrill a six-year rollover contract, valued at approximately $250,000 a year, that renewed itself after every season.

"It's the plum job in the country," Sherrill said at the time in explaining his decision. "I'm going to miss Pittsburgh. The city has been good to me."

"You just cost us a million dollars!"
—Dr. Edward E. Bozik

Pitt was No. 1 in the national rankings going into the final regular season game of the 1981 season when they were destroyed, 48-14, by Penn State at Pitt Stadium. The Panthers plunged to eighth in the rankings. "Dr. Bozik comes after me in the locker room after the game and he's screaming at me," said Sherrill. "He's saying I cost Pitt a million dollars by losing the game. I couldn't believe him. I lose one game the whole season and that's how I'm treated."

Sherrill says he wouldn't have allowed his problems with Bozik to enter into the equation these days, believing he's matured.

"I wasn't a good football coach until 1987," said Sherrill in a surprising revelation. "Before that, I'd won a lot of games, but I wasn't a good college coach. I had the ability to recruit, evaluate talent and motivate them, but I didn't understand the whole picture of being a head coach. That's only part of it. The other part is what you're doing with the fans, the students, the athletic director and the school administration. They're as important in winning as the players. You've got to get all those entities moving in the same direction. At some schools the administration doesn't allow them to win.

"You have to have that all going for you to win consistently. Notre Dame has earned that. Penn State has. Florida State has. Those schools should win all the time. You can win at Pittsburgh, too. It's been done before. Pitt has something else in its favor. The media here is fair. They don't attack the kids. That's not the case in a lot of markets."

Sherrill has so many great memories from his days at Pitt. He was interested in coming back when Pitt fired Paul Hackett after the 1992 season. Oval Jaynes, the athletic director at the time, wanted to hire Sherrill. Pitt's chancellor at the time, Dr. J. Dennis O'Connor, rejected Sherrill as a candidate. Instead, Pitt turned to John Majors once more. That didn't work out and, after four mostly frustrating years, Majors gave way to Walt Harris as head coach.

"I like Walt Harris and think the program is in good hands," said Sherrill. "I don't think it's a good idea for them to tear down Pitt Stadium and play in the new Steelers Stadium, but I think the football team keeps getting better."

"You get a key on a kid when you go into his home."
—Jackie Sherrill

Sherrill was a contributor to winning programs at Pitt as a top assistant and as the head coach. It began with being one of the key figures in the recruitment of Tony Dorsett out of Hopewell High School in 1973. "Tony's family lived in a project," said Sherrill, "but it had to have the cleanest, most spotless kitchen in the entire project. You get a key on a kid when you go into his home and meet his family. I can learn all I need to know in five minutes."

I have heard so many people take credit for being the prime player in the recruitment of Dorsett. I bumped into Butch Ross at the Steelers' offices during the 2000 college draft, and asked him who was the most important person in that recruiting process.

"It was Foge Fazio," said Ross. "He was the first to contact Tony. He brought Majors to meet him. Foge didn't stay on with Majors, but went to Cincinnati. He took Danny Rains from our team with him.

119

Rains is now in Cincinnati's Hall of Fame, and he was a member of Mike Ditka's Super Bowl championship team in Chicago. Majors always said he made a mistake in not taking Danny Rains along with Tony Dorsett. After Foge left town, Sherrill stayed close with Tony. He was at our school so often the principal said he was going to include his name when we took the class roll in the morning. So Sherrill deserves a lot of credit for his recruitment. He stayed after Tony. Dr. Mickey Zernich of Aliquippa had an influence on him going to Pitt, too."

Sherrill says he never tries to pressure a prep player into coming to his school. "That goes back to the way I was treated by Bear Bryant when he recruited me to Alabama," said Sherrill. "He wanted you to come because you wanted to come and play for him. I was with Coach Bryant for two hours and he never asked me to come to Alabama. I'm a professional salesman and I don't want to sell a 17 or 18 year old kid on coming to my program because I'm pressuring him to do so."

Some of Sherrill's critics will, no doubt, smile at that claim, but he insists it's a true assessment of his recruiting methods.

Sherrill was certainly a successful recruiter in his Pitt days, right from the start. His 1977 recruiting class might have been the best in school history, and one of the best at any school in the country, and Dan Marino signed two years later.

A kid from Mississippi named Hugh Green led the pack. From upstate New York they landed Mark May. From the South came Lynn Thomas, Carlton Williamson and Terry White, who formed the nucleus of a great defensive backfield, and Rickey Jackson, who was to almost match Green, an all-time great, as a player at Pitt, and may have surpassed him in the pros.

Green, Jackson and May all visited Pitt on the same weekend. Dorsett was one of their hosts. Imagine getting those three in the same weekend.

Locally, there were Benjie Pryor, Greg Meisner, Steve Fedell, Russ Grimm and Dave Trout. From the other side of the state came Bill Neill and Jerry Boyarsky. And from Ohio came Rick Trocano and Mark Reichard.

"I think 11 of those players were drafted in the first five rounds of the NFL draft," said Sherrill, "and I think about 18 of them played pro ball."

He noted that three linemen, Neill, Boyarsky and Meisner were not heavily-recruited high school prospects. "Boyarsky had one other big-time scholarship offer, from Syracuse," said Sherrill.

He singled out Meisner as a recruiting coup. "He was tremendously intelligent," said Sherrill. "He could have been a doctor or something like that. I think he had a 3.9 QPA in his first year. His dad looked like his brother; that's what great shape he was in. It was between West Virginia and us. Meisner calls me from his high school coach's office one day to tell me he's going to West Virginia. Joe Pendry was an assistant coach at West Virginia at the time, and he

Pitt wins 1979 Fiesta Bowl with 16-10 victory over Arizona and Coach Jackie Sherrill is carried off the field by, left to right, Jerry Boyarsky, Dave Trout and Greg Meisner, all Western Pennsylvania recruits.

The Pitt football coaching staff for 1979 season included, left to right front row, Foge Fazio, head coach Jackie Sherrill and Wally English, back row, Joe Daniels, Joe Moore, Joe Naunchik, Ron Dickerson, Bob Matey and Ray Zingler.

was in the coach's office with Meisner. Joe Naunchik was his high school coach.

"I told Meisner I hadn't talked to his mom and dad about his decision. I asked him to prove his courage by telling Coach Pendry that he needed more time to make up his mind. I'm trying to think of something to say to get him to go home and talk to his mom and dad. Then his dad told West Virginia and us that he didn't want anyone calling his son for a week so he could make up his own mind. I didn't call him. Penn State came in at the end, but we still didn't call him. Then the dad calls me. I think it was after the signing date. He said, 'My son wants to go to Pitt. Do you still have a scholarship left?' We had one left. Meisner was as tough a kid as we had on the team back then."

"I respect Joe Paterno in a lot of different ways."

Sherrill knows he has had his critics throughout his coaching career. Penn State's Joe Paterno once said he was staying in the game because "I don't want to turn college football over to the Barry Switzers and Jackie Sherrills of the world." Ouch. That had to hurt.

Sherrill can sweet talk with the best of them, so the mention of Paterno no longer throws him off stride. "Joe Paterno is a good football coach," said Sherrill at the Radisson session. "He's done a lot for college football. I respect Joe Paterno in a lot of different ways. That didn't keep me from competing against him when I was at Pitt. Penn State was smart to extend Joe's contract by five years. They wouldn't get as many good kids if there was any question about whether Joe was going to be there or not.

"Joe has earned his place in college football. The same can be said for LaVelle Edwards at Brigham Young and Bobby Bowden at Florida State. My hat's off to them. The best thing you can say about me is that Jackie Sherrill is a player's coach. A player's coach is not putting your arm around them and making them happy, or saying what they want to hear. A player's coach is about discipline. And you're there and available to them if it's two or three in the morning. You're going to be there when they need you.

"The reason people don't like me is because I don't play games. I'm the most non-political coach there is. I know what you have to do to win. When I sat down with Chancellor (Wesley) Posvar at Pitt and the administration and we did the schedules, I told them what we needed to do. 'Here's the kind of schedule you must have, whether I'm here or not,' I said. You have to have six teams on your schedule you're going to beat. You should have two or three teams you should beat because you're going to out-recruit them. That leaves two games that

Curbstone Coaches lineup in fall of 1980 included, left to right, Dan McCann, Bob Prince, Jackie Sherrill, Bill Smith, John Troan and Joe Paterno. Paterno and Sherrill put on a playful tug of war for services of Penn Hills High School prospect Bill Fralic, one of the most sought after prospects in the country.

you can flip a coin to see which one is best. I told them that is the for-
mula for going to bowl games on a regular basis.

"If I had done a better job of coaching, we could have won the
national championship twice when I was there. Everybody has players. There are a lot of good coaches out there. Recruiting doesn't win
the big games. If that was the case Notre Dame would never lose a
game.

"In my career, I wish I could change some things. I didn't always
do the smartest thing. I hurt myself with some of the stuff I did. But
it's probably why I was successful, too. When schools considered me as
a candidate, they didn't ask if I could coach. They were more concerned about if they could handle me.

"I try to give my players choices. The more mature your football
team is the more games you're going to win. We all want affirmation
that we made the right choices. I have never applied for a job and I
won't start now. It's just one of those stubborn things.

"During my stay at Pitt, we did things as a football team that
won't be matched. I wasn't here when we won the national championship in 1976, but I had recruited and coached a lot of those guys. I
knew I was going to go to Washington State before we beat Kansas in
the Sun Bowl. I knew this football team was going to win a national
championship the next year. I told them that after I told them I was
taking the job at Washington State. Tony (Dorsett) wasn't happy I
was leaving.

"Caz Myslinski, our athletic director at the time, tried to talk me
out of going to Washington State. There'd been some talk that John
Majors might go back to Tennessee at some time. I called Coach
Bryant and asked him what I should do. Bear said, 'I can't tell you
what to do.' I went to my father-in-law. He said, 'If they want you now
they'll want you later.' And he was right."

"Danny Marino was the most
focused player I ever had."

Jackie Sherrill saw Dan Marino throwing a football one day at practice and asked him who had taught him to throw a ball like that — up
and out. "His dad had showed him how to throw a football," said
Sherrill. "I told him to never let anyone fool around with his motion,
or attempt to change it. The way he did it worked for him, that was
easy to see.

"When he went to the pros, he went to the best place. Don Shula
could see right away that he was something special, and gave him
early opportunities to play. He couldn't have been in a better
situation.

124

Jackie Sherrill of Pitt, Franco Harris of the Steelers and Bruce Atkins of Wilkinsburg and Duquesne University were among featured guests who signed autographs for youngsters attending sports banquet at the Press Club.

Pittsburgh Curbstone Coaches luncheon program featured local football representatives, seated left to right, Jackie Sherrill of Pitt, Dick Bowen of Serra High School, Dick Hoak of Steelers; and standing, Jack Ham of Steelers, Jeff Petrucci of California State University and Sal Sunseri of Pitt.

"Danny Marino was the most focused player I ever had. We'd come out of the tunnel at Pitt Stadium, and everyone was looking at the students in the stands, checking out the crowd, the cheerleaders, you name it. Not Dan. His mind was on the field. He was thinking about what he had to do, how we were going to win the game.

"He was a true family man. His mom and dad and sisters were important to him. He wanted to have them around. His dad often came to practice and would be the only one sitting in the stands. He came from a real working class family. His mother was a crossing guard, and his dad drove a truck during the night shift, delivering the morning newspaper (*Post-Gazette*) to stores and for home delivery. Dan was always respectful of his parents. He was raised right; that was a key to his success, I'm sure. I'm not surprised to hear that Dan has his family living near him in Florida.

"The expectations were great for Dan, right from the start. The media in Miami set him up to fail, saying he was the best quarterback since Y.A. Tittle and Johnny Unitas, stuff like that. He lost his cool sometimes and threw his helmet around to express his unhappiness. But he grew up fast, and he's been a real success story. He's never been in one bit of trouble in Miami. I'm proud to say I was his college coach."

**Tony Dorsett, Pro Football Hall of Fame,
Pitt and Dallas Cowboys:**
"Jackie Sherrill worked hard to get me to come to Pitt. He was at my school and home all the time. He knew how to get to my mom. She loved pecan pie and he was always bringing her some pecan pie. Jackie and I made a pact that he would stay at Pitt for four years if I went there. So I was upset when he went to Washington State to be the head coach before my senior season. We talked about that. I owe a lot to him. He helped me learn the mental toughness part of the game. I only weighed 155 pounds when I went to Pitt, and I was getting pounded pretty good. Those big defensive linemen were waxing me. I came to the sideline and I told him, 'Man, I ain't gonna go out there.' He looked me in my eyes and he said, 'Hawk, we need you.' And I went back in."

Steve Volk
He served his country

"I'm 110 percent."

A light rain fell all weekend on the fresh grave at St. Joseph's Cemetery in West Mifflin. It soaked a small American flag that had been stuck in the mound so that the flag soon stopped flapping in the breeze.

The flag signified that the deceased man was a military veteran, one of those we ought to remember and pay tribute to on Memorial Day.

A larger American flag was folded in a triangle at the top of the casket, and had caught my eye, during the viewing earlier in the week at the Gregris Funeral Home in Duquesne. It's the favored funeral home for Croatian Catholics in the community, across the street from the high school, up the steep hill from where the U.S. Steel Works once dominated the landscape.

Steve Volk, my wife's uncle, had lived most of his 84 years in Duquesne, and once owned an automotive repair shop there. He later managed an automotive repair unit of J.C. Penney's. He died in May of 1999.

During World War II, Volk trained airplane mechanics for the U.S. Army at an airfield near Chicago. Like most men and women who were in the military service, he was not a decorated war hero. He simply served his country as best he could and when he came back home he got a job and raised a family.

Steve Volk was no big shot, just a simple man. He was about 5-7, but walked tall and was a sociable fellow. I didn't know him that well, but every time I saw him at a family get-together he wore a hat and a smile. When anyone asked how he was doing, he would reply, "I'm 110 percent."

He was the sort of man NBC newscaster Tom Brokaw wrote about in his best-selling book, "The Greatest Generation."

It dealt with individual men and women who came of age during the Great Depression and World War II and went on to build modern America. "This generation was united not only by a common purpose," wrote Brokaw, "but also by common values — duty, honor, economy, courage, service, love of family and country and, above all, responsibility for oneself."

Steve was the oldest of eight children. He was survived by his sisters, Helen Volk and Peggy Rusnica, and his brothers, Gary and Joseph. He was preceded in death by his brothers, John, Henry and Michael.

Volk did a great job of raising his sons, Steve and Jimmy, now in their mid-40s. Young Steve was just 14 and Jimmy 12 when their mother, Mildred Volk, died. They've always been good kids, and now they have wonderful families of their own. Their dad taught them how to do that.

Steve has been a big success in the insurance business, and Jimmy has done just as well in the retail business.

They have fond memories of their father. He was a simple man who enjoyed hunting, fishing, golfing and smiling.

Memorial Day always reminds me of earlier Memorial Days and Memorial Day parades I attended with my father and brother in my youth.

As I get older, I take greater pride in having served in our Armed Forces. I was in the U.S. Army during the Vietnam War, but never went overseas and was never in harm's way. Unless you count basic military training at Fort Knox near Louisville, Kentucky, where I was always fearful that some awkward recruit might stumble and fall and fire off a few rounds in my back as we participated in advance firing movements.

I spent ten months at the U.S. Army Home Town News Center, located in Kasas City, Missouri, writing stories about the activities of men and women in the military service for their hometown newspapers. I spent ten more months editing a weekly camp newspaper at Fort Greely, Alaska.

My stories were always calling positive attention to those who were serving their country. Like most of my fellow students in college, I was not too keen on going into the military service when I was called in the draft. I'm glad I went, though. Every day seemed demanding in a way, but it was nothing compared to what others were experiencing on the battlefront.

Seeing a movie like "Saving Private Ryan" makes one realize how lucky they were not to have been in combat. It's the combat veterans who really rate our admiration. But people like Steve Volk did their best in a supportive way.

His sons are real sports fans, but their favorite hero has always been their dad.

Bill Cowher has high regard for another "Pittsburgh guy," retired Miami Dolphins quarterback Dan Marino.

Snapshot:

Bill Cowher, Head Coach, Pittsburgh Steelers:
"My first football hero was Dick Butkus. I loved the way he played the game. He was such a force on the field, and he tackled people from sideline to sideline. They knew it when he hit them. I was playing linebacker so I wanted to play like Dick Butkus. He and Ray Nitschke. Butkus was the leader of the Chicago Bears' defense, and Nitschke was the leader of the great Green Bay Packers defensive team. I met Ray about four years ago at a golf tournament in Cleveland and that was a big thrill. When I was playing at North Carolina State, coming from Crafton, I was a big Pittsburgh Steelers fan. So I liked Jack Lambert. They all brought a lot of intensity to the game."

Pitt Stadium
Home to many heroes

"You can't put the campus someplace else for six games a year."
— Bill Fralic

I strongly believed that there were compelling reasons why the University of Pittsburgh should have kept its home football games at Pitt Stadium, and reversed its decision to move its home schedule to a new stadium on the city's North Side.

I have no problem with Pitt playing West Virginia or Penn State in showcase contests once a year or every so often at Three Rivers Stadium or the new football stadium to be built for the Steelers, but I wanted a refurbished Pitt Stadium to remain its home field.

After all, the new stadium is always referred to as the Steelers stadium. Why should Pitt play in the Steelers stadium?

It was good to have my feelings reaffirmed by Bill Fralic and Harbaugh Miller, the honorary chairmen for Homecoming Weekend, when they appeared at the Pitt Varsity Letter Club dinner at Fitzgerald Field House on the eve of the Pitt-Rutgers football game in mid-October, 1998.

The feelings they expressed, however, which were seconded by many others with similar attachments, were ignored by Pitt officials who went ahead and finalized plans to raze Pitt Stadium and shift the University of Pittsburgh football program to training facilities on the South Side and a new football stadium on the North Side. The 1999 schedule was the last to be played at Pitt Stadium, and it has since been leveled.

No one realized at the time of the Varsity Letter Club dinner how imminent this move was to the new stadium. The powers-that-be were already promoting the idea in Harrisburg.

Fralic, as honest and candid as ever, let his feelings be known when he spoke at the dinner, and Miller, among those in attendance, added his thoughts in an interview later in the evening. Fralic had heard the talk about Pitt considering a shift to the new stadium.

"I find as I get older," said Fralic, who would celebrate his 36th birthday on Halloween, "I come back here more often. I live in Atlanta now, but this will always be home. And when I come back, I want to watch the Pitt football team playing right here on this campus."

Miller, a hardy 96 at the time, may represent a different generation than Fralic, but he shares his passion for Pitt and Pittsburgh. An emeritus member of Pitt's Board of Trustees, Miller said, "In all probability, I could not vote for a move to the new stadium, but I don't have a vote anymore. I have enough confidence in Chancellor Mark Nordenberg and Athletic Director Steve Pederson. If they think it's profitable and right, I'd go along with their decision.

130

Pitt Stadium looked great when it was sold out.

The ghosts that still ran on the turf at Pitt Stadium included the "Dream Backfield" of the late '30s, left to right, Harold "Curly" Stebbins, John Chickerneo, Marshall "Biggie" Goldberg and Dick Cassiano.

"I believe there are different objectives in college football, and I think we should retain that rather than trying to emulate the pros. I'd like to see it remain in our stadium. But I'm all for Steve and any program he initiates. I think he's doing a whale of a job."

Miller's father, Charles Miller, served as Pitt's first athletic director from 1912 to 1925. "I grew up in the University," said Harbaugh Miller, a twinkle still evident in his blue eyes. He carried a cane to steady his walk, but he looked great. "I have problems with my balance now and then," he said.

He attended his first Pitt football game in 1910. He remembers when Pitt Stadium opened in 1925, his father's last year as head of the Pitt sports programs. It had been estimated that Miller had been in attendance at about 450 Pitt football games. He continued to live in an apartment in Oakland, not far from the Cathedral of Learning.

I saw my first Pitt football game in 1952. It was the home opener, a 26-14 victory over Iowa. Joe Schmidt was a senior All-America linebacker. I was 10 years old and had won the ticket as a prize for lining up so many new subscribers to the *Post-Gazette* on my delivery route in my hometown of Hazelwood. Pitt Stadium was only about four miles from my home, but the University and its campus in Oakland have always been another world entirely in my eyes. The 42-story Cathedral of Learning has always been a magnet, like seeing Cinderella's Castle in Walt Disney World. It's the tallest college building in the country. With its Nationality Rooms, it's a unique centerpiece on a campus that is more attractive than it gets credit for being. Beauty is in the eye of the beholder.

I feel better when I'm on the Pitt campus. I feel younger when I walk its walkways. Only the best memories come back. Most people cherish their college days, and they should, whether they went to West Virginia, Penn State, Notre Dame or Grove City. If you didn't go to school at Pitt you can't possibly appreciate the feeling.

My family knows the feeling. My older brother, Dan, had a degree in mechanical engineering from Pitt, plus an MBA.

My older daughter, Sarah O'Brien, and her husband, Matt Zirwas, were both beginning their fourth and final year at the School of Medicine at the University of Pittsburgh as the 1999 football season got underway. They have since graduated and drew residencies at Children's Hospital and Montefiore Hospital, respectively.

My wife, Kathie, got her undergraduate degree at Grove City College and got her master's degree in social work at Pitt. She cuts to the heart of the matter when she says, "You can't see the Cathedral of Learning from a stadium on the North Side."

I met and dated Kathie on the campus at Pitt, which is another reason the place means so much to me. Economic arguments can be made about why a move to a new stadium on the North Side might make sense for the Pitt football program, but this isn't about money. I believe the powers-that-be have made a business decision, not an education decision. The move off campus violates the spirit of college athletics.

Pitt Stadium's final season was marked by many events. Former Pitt All-American and pro and college Hall of Fame enshrinee Joe Schmidt of Mt. Oliver returned for reunion with old friends and Pitt boosters like Armand Dellovade of Avella.

Photos by Jim O'Brien

It's about remembering and reaffirming why there is a University of Pittsburgh in the first place. It's important to bring people to the Pitt campus, especially young fans, so that they can be introduced to the place, so that they might consider being students there someday. It's an acquired taste.

It's important for them to see Salk Hall, the Science Center, Sutherland Drive, and to learn about the Pitt history and tradition of accomplishment. It's important to answer their questions about what they see, and to be able to explain the names of the streets and buildings, to tell them the Pitt story, or about "the Pitt experience," as one Varsity Letter Club award winner phrased it.

So many alumni I know had their first sampling of Pitt as a young fan sitting in Pitt Stadium.

The new football stadium on the North Side will be a beauty, no doubt about it. Some wanted it named in honor of Arthur J. Rooney, the founder and patriarch of the Pittsburgh Steelers. His brother, Jim, played football at Pitt in the late '20s, but Art was not a Pitt alumnus. His is a Steelers' story, a Pittsburgh story, but not a Pitt story. He was always fond of the school and a fan of its athletic programs, but he was not a Pitt man. The new stadium will not be named for him because much money can be gained from selling the naming rights to a major company.

The Rooneys are not Pitt people. The schools they have been most closely associated with are, in turn, Duquesne, St. Vincent and Washington & Jefferson.

What happens if it doesn't work out to the satisfaction of the Rooneys or their peers in pro football?

I don't think the powers-that-be at the National Football League will be too crazy about the pros playing on Sunday on a real grass field after the college boys have been on it the day before, especially in bad weather, which is commonplace in western Pennsylvania.

Today's prospects, many coming from distant places, will be impressed when they come through the Fort Pitt Tunnel and are told to look to the left. "That's where we play our home games," the coach will tell the prospect. "The Steelers play there, too." Yes, no doubt, the prospect will like that.

These prospects, too often, will never come back to the campus once their eligibility is completed — notice I didn't say when they graduate — and they will never contribute money to the University. They'll be coming here to play football, not to be students at the University of Pittsburgh. The coaches and the players will have less of a bond with the school and its campus.

The primary colors at the new stadium will be black and gold, not blue and gold. It's unlikely there will be reminders on its walls about winning nine national championships. It's unlikely there will be memorials or signs paying tribute to the Pitt football players whose jerseys have been retired. Whatever is done will be a token effort at best. The Steelers are calling the shots.

134

Goldberg and Marino, Green and Ditka didn't do their thing on its football turf. Fralic, Dorsett and Schmidt didn't strut their stuff in that stadium. Steve Pederson and his predecessor, Oval Jaynes, had done much to spruce up Pitt Stadium and Pederson had put a new scoreboard and display screen to creative use, and attracted more students to Pitt Stadium as part of the 12th Man promotional program. Pederson has done much to improve things, and there was more to be done. Much money had been raised and invested in Pitt Stadium to put a shine on it. Pederson should have paid more attention, however, to Pitt's history, and the concerns of his constituents.

Some of the plans for the buildings to replace Pitt Stadium are quite exciting, and I can see how some have been moved to switch their positions on the subject because of this renovation. I say it could have been done elsewhere. I have always maintained that new dormitories are more of a must than a building to play basketball.

"I didn't come here for the facilities," said Jimbo Covert, a visitor for Pitt's spring game in April, 1999, who came to Pitt from Conway and became a Pro Bowl tackle for the Chicago Bears. "I came here for the players. I wanted to be part of the Pitt football program.

"They're building new ballparks and stadiums these days that are the way they used to be. Why are they doing that? People still love Wrigley Field. The Bears have agreed to stay at Soldiers Field and refurbish it. That's what could be done at Pitt Stadium."

Alex Van Pelt, a quarterback with the Buffalo Bills, told Covert he had visited the day before with Buddy Morris, the strength and conditioning coach at Pitt. "He showed me the new weight rooms in the stadium," said Van Pelt. "I wish we had weight rooms like that when I was here. The Bills would like to have weight rooms like that right now. I can't believe they're going to destroy that here."

Pitt Stadium, for sure, had its shortcomings. It was old, to begin with, and lacked many of the amenities of new stadiums. But super boxes, multi-million dollar weight rooms and bigger bathrooms are not as important as what the stadium signified for so many who truly care about the program and have remained through thick and thin.

Yes, there were parking problems and access problems. Improvements could have been made that would get the stadium up to snuff in areas that truly count. It required money and imagination. Such plans had already been drawn up. Why were they discarded?

"I'm surprised Pitt's doing this," said former Steelers and Notre Dame star Rocky Bleier. "The Steelers played at Pitt Stadium in my rookie year. Conversely, that was Pitt's stadium, not the Steelers' stadium. We just played our games there. We had no feeling for the place whatsoever. It wasn't ours. They would never do this at Notre Dame. They spruced up the stadium at Notre Dame. When you go there, it has so many memories. Plus, you want to be on the campus. It's so beautiful and brings back many memories as well."

135

Personally, I would have liked to see them replace the metal benches throughout the stadium with honest-to-goodness ballpark seats. They could have taken the seats at Three Rivers Stadium before it, too, was leveled and installed them at Pitt Stadium. The aisles needed to be widened, and the walkway at the top of the stadium needed to be twice as wide to permit traffic to flow better. The capacity lost through such a change could have been made up by building a new press box and VIP seating section atop the stadium at the top of Cardiac Hill. Frankly, a downsized Pitt Stadium would make sense. Better concession stands and better and bigger bathrooms needed to be built. Pederson said it would cost $40 million to do this.

It would be worth the investment in the University.

"They're going to tear down a stadium that would cost over $100 million to build today," offered Foge Fazio, the former Pitt coach who is now the linebackers coach for the Washington Redskins. "I think it would be worth the investment to improve the place. This is where Pitt ought to be playing."

There wasn't a bad seat in Pitt Stadium, except the ones at the very bottom of the bowl. It was more open and cleaner than Three Rivers Stadium. There's a different atmosphere to be found on a college campus than at a pro or city venue.

The crowd is better behaved. The tailgate parties are not drunken benders. Pitt would be a stepchild, or second-class citizens to the Steelers, in the new stadium, just as Pitt's basketball team and its fans have never felt at home at the Civic Arena. Pederson had decided not to play home basketball games there during the 1998-99 season, despite the protests of The Big East officials.

In retrospect, Pitt made a mistake when it surrendered Forbes Field and its occupants, the Pirates and the Steelers, to a new stadium on the North Side back in 1970. It would have been better to have kept the ballpark on the Pitt campus. Here we go again.

Forbes Field attracted many students from faraway places like Philadelphia and New York who thought it would be neat to attend a university where they could walk out of class and catch a major league baseball game or go to see a pro football game on Sunday. The Steelers, of course, also played their home games at Pitt Stadium in the '60s.

It was better when Pitt was the host rather than the visitor. Duquesne University even played its home basketball games at the Pitt Field House for years before the Civic Arena was built. Pitt will profit from the city having a new ballpark for the Pirates and a new stadium for the Steelers because it will enhance the appeal of the city at large to incoming students. This will help recruiting kids to Pittsburgh.

The Oakland merchants have, understandably, complained and cried about the possibility of Pitt playing its football games elsewhere. They needed to get their act together, however, and clean up the streets and sidewalks of their campus community. Too often, the streets of Oakland are strewn with garbage and it detracts from selling the school to prospective students and instructors and investors. Pitt Stadium is not a dump, but its surrounding streets are too often.

I was all for the closing of Bigelow Boulevard and the creation of more of a campus island by the Cathedral of Learning. I still believe that Panther Hollow should be used to expand the University. According to a survey, students say they want more green space on the campus. My response to that is to show them the lawn around the Cathedral of Learning, give them a walking map to get to Schenley Park, or walking papers to get to Penn State. Pitt is a city school and has strong points of its own.

Pitt Stadium was still a special place and it could have been better. It's important to know the story of the stadium and of Dr. Sutherland and Dr. Salk and Dr. Starzl and to fully appreciate the Pitt saga. So much has been accomplished in athletics and academics on these grounds.

The football program can be a great unifying force on a university campus. The North Side should be a beautiful showcase community, but for one reason or another it has never come close to realizing its potential. Oakland has much more going for it, now and into the new millenium.

Pitt will lose more than some of its most faithful alumni and fans when it moves its home football schedule to the new stadium on the North Side. "It's just a part of the college," offered Fralic when I asked him to expand on remarks he had made during the Varsity Letter Club dinner.

He and many other former players believe Pitt has made an even worse decision in joining the Steelers to use a practice and training facility on the city's South Side. They question how players are going to be able to get there if they need to take care of something between classes, like seeing a coach, checking in with the trainer, soaking an injured knee in a hot tub for a half hour, watching game film. That is easier to do when the football coaches, trainers and sports medicine facilities are housed on the campus. "Pitt Stadium was like my second home," said former quarterback John Congemi. "I was there every free moment I had."

The coaches will become professionalized, and will be operating outside the boundaries of the Pitt campus. Their association with professors and school administrators will be lessened. Football players will be hanging around the South Side, telling the coaches they'd like to be housed there as well.

Fralic has always been a forthright fellow. He fixes his blue eyes on yours. He never looks past you, or to some project beyond. He looks into your heart and soul when he says something, or voices his opinions about Pitt. He's lost about 50 pounds from his playing weight, but at 6-5, 230 pounds, he is still an imposing figure. Hopefully, Fralic will assume more of a leadership position in the sports picture at Pitt.

"As a high school kid, I was impressed when I came to Pitt to watch the football games. I don't remember the games as much as I remember the people I met here. You can't put the campus someplace else for six games a year," offered Fralic.

"I have full confidence in the people who will make the decision. I live and work in Atlanta now, but my family is still here, and so is my heart. Pitt is a special part of Pittsburgh. Pittsburgh is my home, and I gravitate toward here the older I get. I come here if the football team is 11-and-0 and I'd come here to see the people if the team were 0-and-11. I love seeing the guys at the tailgate parties. Every time I get back it's kind of a homecoming. I don't like to live in the past, but I was good at playing football. And I learned here that if I approach anything else the same way I approached football that I can be good at anything I want to be good at.

"I don't know what the week would be like if you were a football player at Pitt and you played the games on Saturday at a stadium on the North Side. I liked walking from the dorm to the stadium to practice. This was our field. These were our locker rooms. We'd run the risk of being second-class citizens in the new stadium, taking a back seat to the Steelers.

"Hopefully, the people who decide these things will do the right thing, and that there we'll always have a stadium on this campus and not someplace else. OK, I'm done preaching.

"When I was growing up, I wanted to play for Pitt. When I played at Pitt, I wanted to someday play for the Steelers. My uncle played for the Steelers. Pitt and the Steelers are a big part of this city, as are the Pirates, but I think we all ought to have our own home fields."

Dr. Edwin Assid, who came from New Castle in the mid-60s to play football and basketball at Pitt, was one of the four alumni honored as a Varsity Letterwinner of Distinction.

"You have those memories of what went on here," he said in an interview. "I remember coming here the first time as a high school student and seeing a Pitt game. What I remember the most was the Pitt band coming out of the tunnel and onto the field. First, you heard the drums and then they came fast-stepping out on the field. I'd never seen anything like it."

I had to smile because it was also one of the strongest memories I had of my first visit to Pitt Stadium, that band, those drums, the p.a. announcer introducing the Pitt Band. The band didn't seem to command much consideration when the administration made the announcement to move to the North Side. It hadn't been determined when the band would practice, or what would become of the track and field and soccer teams. Pitt has men's and women's teams in both sports.

Dr. Assid also remembers a home game against Notre Dame, and seeing the look on the face of his friend and teammate, Phil Dahar, on the sideline that day.

Former Pitt trustee Harbaugh Miller and All-American and Hall of Famer Bill Fralic had mixed emotions about passing of Pitt Stadium.

Dahar came to Pitt from Dillonvale, Ohio. He made his recruiting visit on a bleak, cold, dreary day when it began raining as he was being led around the campus. The coaches walked him around the track on the stadium to show off the home field. Dahar's dad, who had played football at Notre Dame, had died only a few weeks earlier. He had died, ironically enough, during a stay at the VA Hospital, visible above the scoreboard at the eastern end of Pitt Stadium.

Looking up and seeing the VA Hospital, Dahar decided he should come to Pitt to play football. "That way, whenever I was practicing there or playing there," said Dr. Dahar, who went to Pitt's Dental School with Assid, "my dad would be up there watching me."

Stories like that are a part of Pitt Stadium and the Pitt football tradition, and should have figured in the decision-making about where Pitt ought to play its football games. It shouldn't just be a business decision. It should be an education decision. What's best for all the students. I told that story about Dr. Dahar and his dad to Steve Pederson the same day the Pitt football team was about to board buses and leave for the Liberty Bowl just before Christmas in 1997. I pointed out the VA Hospital. I pointed out Salk Hall, named for a scientist who once conducted experiments there to develop an anti-polio vaccine. Pederson smiled, but I'm not sure he was paying attention to what I was saying.

Reunion of former Pitt performers included, left to right, Ron Delfine, Jon Botula, Ernie Borghetti and Ray Tarasi.

Pitt Varsity Letter Club

Johnny and Mary Lynn Majors join Tony Dorsett at Doubletree Hotel on eve of closing of Pitt Stadium where they enjoyed a national championship season in 1976.

Snapshot:

**Tony Dorsett, Hall of Fame football player
University of Pittsburgh, Dallas Cowboys:**

"My brother, Tyrone, was my first football hero. He was about six years ahead of me, and he was the original T.D. He was a star running back at Hopewell High School. Other than him, my sports hero was Muhammad Ali. I liked the way he backed up what he said he was going to do. My mom couldn't stand him. She said he was always running off at the mouth. I liked his style, his brashness, his looks. When I was coming out of Pitt, I met him at a Dapper Dan dinner. I've met him quite a few times. I met him on Fight Night in Dallas. When I saw him this past year, I was shaking his hand. There was a tremor in his hand. I was looking into his eyes, and you could tell by the vacant look in his eyes that he was on medication. It was sad. Now I saw him most recently at a card show in San Franciso and he was his old self. He was cutting up, joking and everything. I always make a point to get my picture taken with him. I have one on display in my home. I have boxing gloves he wore and signed for me. You couldn't help but appreciate the guy. He was a black guy who could cross over. Everybody loved him. He doesn't do his stint in the Army, but many people could relate to his case. He never went to college, but he was a smart man. He has sat down with heads of state, and he's important on a world-wise basis. I can understand his appeal. We all mimicked him, doing the rope-a-dope and the Ali Shuffle. Except for the Army thing, he never got into any trouble."

John Woodruff
He ran from Connellsville to Berlin and back

"I had a burning desire to win."

Alocal band was playing the Star-Spangled Banner in a welcome home celebration for Connellsville's own John Woodruff. A little guy named Henry Molinaro was directing the Molinaro Band, waving a baton high over his silver-gray head, beaming with pride, winking at passersby.

Legendary Olympic hero John Woodruff was leaning on a walking cane at the start of the 17th annual John Woodruff 5K Run and Walk on a Wednesday evening, July 14, 1999. The band was right behind him. It had been a sunny day, with temperatures in the 80s, and it had cooled enough so that the weather was perfect for a fun run or brisk walk through this storied Fayette County community located about 50 miles southeast of Pittsburgh.

"I think the biggest thing is that it honors John Woodruff," said Jennifer Blount of Uniontown, formerly of Connellsville, when asked to explain the popularity of this summer event that draws contestants from several states. "He put Connellsville on the map."

John Ruggieri, the track and field coach at Connellsville High School who coordinated the event, fired a starter's pistol into the air to get the race underway at 7:03 p.m. on Arch Street, just outside of Falcons Stadium where the runners and walkers would finish their tour. Several hundred contestants took off in earnest, few of them fully aware of the enormity of what Woodruff had accomplished as a runner once upon a time in Berlin and Pittsburgh.

"I want every young person to meet John Woodruff because he had a will to win," said Ruggieri. "He did it the hard way and I'm in awe of him."

Woodruff tipped his cap to the contestants, revealing wiry salt and pepper hair. He was not properly introduced, however, regardless of Ruggieri's good intentions. A word or two about Woodruff's Olympic odyssey seemed in order, just so the young people would know a little bit about the identity of this wonderful old man at the starting line. Once an athlete who ran so upright, ramrod straight, standing out from the pack at 6-4, 180 pounds, Woodruff was now slightly stooped. He had celebrated his 85th birthday nine days earlier. His Olympic spirit and his pride in being honored in his hometown, however, remained undaunted.

Woodruff wore a floppy white hat, a white jersey with red and blue stripes on the collar and sleeves and an Olympic logo over his heart, white slacks and white sneakers. He posed for photos, signed autographs and smiled for everybody who approached him. His dark weathered skin, like that of a life-long farmer, was a contrast to his

JOHN WOODRUFF
GOLD MEDAL—800 METERS
1936 BERLIN OLYMPIC GAMES

all-white costume. He was dressed to play shuffleboard on an ocean liner.

He and his wife, Rose Ella, had driven over 300 miles, nearly a seven-hour trip, from their home in East Windsor, New Jersey, 13 miles from Princeton, to attend the annual get-together. It's not an easy trip, and it's become increasingly more difficult. Woodruff had undergone several surgeries in recent years, for his back, a hernia, a prostate condition, his wrist. "They been patching me up for a long time," said a weary-sounding Woodruff. He smiled so it wouldn't come off as a complaint. He moved stiffly as the years had taken their toll.

The Molinaro Band and John Woodruff are both Connellsville icons, something that is part of the town's fabric and identity, as much as the coke it once produced in its local foundries.

The band is comprised of people of all ages, 30 or so men and women, and they were doing their best to bring a festive spirit to the annual return of one of Connellsville's most celebrated citizens.

Woodruff won a gold medal in the 1936 Olympic Games in Berlin, Germany. Those were the Olympic Games that were overseen by Adolph Hitler, the Nazi leader who was espousing Aryan supremacy propaganda. Hitler's hatred for blacks and Jews and other minority groups and his desire for world domination would intensify and ultimately set off World War II in the ensuing years. The Holocaust and all kinds of atrocities were yet ahead. The Nazi government showed off its military might at the world showcase that were the Olympic Games — the facilities were among the finest ever and the treatment of visitors couldn't have been better.

Woodruff and his teammates on the U.S. Olympic track & field team set the pace for shooting down Hitler's racist drivel. These were the Olympic Games in which Jesse Owens of Ohio State University in Columbus, Ohio won four gold medals in the sprint and long jump events. Owens gained the most fame for his achievement — he is still heralded as one of our all-time greatest athletes — but Woodruff won his share of acclaim as well. Old time track buffs still wax nostalgic about Woodruff's magnificent long stride.

"After the Olympics, I stayed close with guys like Jesse Owens, Archie Williams, Ralph Metcalfe and Mack Robinson," said Woodruff. "Mack was the brother of baseball's Jackie Robinson. We were one big family."

"Long John" Woodruff was a 21-year-old freshman at the University of Pittsburgh when he won the gold medal at Berlin. He was a tall, well-muscled, long-legged athlete who had come off a dirt farm in Connellsville to become an international track & field phenomenon. He was the core of Carl Olson's nationally respected Pitt team. He had competed in an organized track program for only three years before Berlin, but he was a natural, and the demanding Olson knew how to get the most out of him.

"I think I was a gifted athlete," said Woodruff. "And, most importantly, I had a burning desire to win.

"I was 20 years old when we boarded the SS Manhattan in early July of 1936, and I had turned 21 by the time we arrived in Hamburg, Germany. It took us about seven days to get there, and we were somewhere in the Atlantic Ocean on my birthday (his birthdate was July 5, 1915). It was quite a thrill. It was the first time I'd ever taken an ocean voyage. When I first came to Pitt, to compete as a high school student, it was the farthest I'd ever traveled from Connellsville.

"Things happened so fast. When Coach Olson asked me to try out for the Olympic team I was quite surprised by his confidence in me. I didn't even know they were having trials for the Olympic Games.

"I had no idea I'd make the Olympic team in 1936. I figured I'd go back to Connellsville for the summer; that's what I thought. Then I won the 800 in the Allegheny Mountain Association meet at Pitt Stadium, and moved on to the semi-final Olympic Trials at Harvard Stadium. I won there, too. Then I came back to Randalls Island in New York and won the finals. Each tryout I won. I was going to Berlin and I couldn't believe it."

Woodruff should have realized then that he was an exceptional performer. He beat world record holder Ben Eastman of Stanford to win at Randalls Island.

Woodruff claimed he was the lone surviving gold medal winner from the U. S. track & field team from the 1936 Olympic Games. My latest book, *Hometown Heroes*, had just gone to press; I was wiped out and I wanted to take a break. I wasn't ready to work on a new book. But I had to go to Connellsville to interview John Woodruff one more time. Who knew if he'd ever come back to Connellsville again? And Woodruff was such a good story. Time spent in his company was to be treasured forever. He had been a personal witness to history.

"Before we went over, we heard about what Hitler was doing over there," said Woodruff, "but we had no idea he'd do what he ended up doing. What did we know?

"I got to know Jesse Owens going over in the boat. I had talked to him at track meets the previous year, but we had more time to talk now. We were like one big happy family. Prior to going over, they had put us up at the Lincoln Hotel in New York. Owens was great with everyone. He was a friendly fellow, easy to be around."

Eight months after our last meeting in Connellsville, when I called Woodruff on the telephone on St. Patrick's Day — March 17, 2000 — to check on some facts from our interview, he informed me that one of his Olympic teammates, Mack Robinson, had died three days earlier. Woodruff also told me he was now the only one left from his own family. He has been the 11th of 12 children. His sister, Catherine Hill, had died six months earlier at the age of 90 to leave him as the lone survivor of the Woodruff clan of Connellsville.

Six years earlier, I spent a weekend in Connellsville when the community paid tribute to Johnny Lujack and the undefeated 1941 Cokers football team. Lujack led Notre Dame to national football championships and won the Heisman Trophy in 1947. Folks in

Connellsville liked to boast that their town produced both a Heisman Trophy winner and an Olympic gold medal winner. I was accompanied on both visits by my buddy Bill Priatko, who has been involved in athletics all his life, and loved to spend time with sports giants like Lujack and Woodruff whom he greatly admired.

"When Woodruff is with you," said Priatko, "it makes you proud to be a Pitt man."

When Woodruff walked around the oval track in July of 1999 to await the return of the runners, he was a magnet for children and their parents. In the background, just behind Woodruff where the end zone meets the oval track, there was a tall tree, a tree that ought to serve as a history lesson for everyone in the Connellsville community. History teachers at the high school ought to take their students on a field trip to view this tree each year and tell them the story of John Woodruff. I have had the pleasure of speaking to the teachers at Connellsville High School at two different assemblies during the last decade and shared my own stories of their community's rich heritage. Few communities could claim so many distinguished sports standouts.

German officials at the 1936 Olympic Games gave saplings for German black oak trees from the Black Forest as mementos to each of the gold medal-winners with the idea that they would take them back to their home countries and plant them. Thus a piece of Germany would be growing in countries throughout the world. It's been reported that many of the American athletes tossed those saplings over the ship's side into the Atlantic Ocean on the return home. Woodruff brought his sapling with him back to Connellsville. It was planted and that tree has grown tall and robust. It remains a monument to what Woodruff accomplished, and a reminder about Hitler and Nazi Germany and their role in world history. Some people refer to it as "the Hitler tree." Seeing Woodruff standing on the track with the tree behind him, with little kids circling him as they played, was a poignant moment.

"When I got back to Connellsville after the Olympic Games," recalled Woodruff, "I was informed that the tree had to be sent to the Agriculture Department in Washington, D.C. They wanted to check the dirt around it, to make sure there weren't any bugs or disease being brought into this country. When it came back it didn't look like much. It had withered and looked like it was dead. We gave it to a man named John Lewis who had a botany lab at the high school, and he nourished it and brought it back to life. It was originally planted in the grounds of the Carnegie Library in Connellsville. When they built the high school stadium it was transplanted to where it now stands at one end of the field."

That's not the only reminder of what Woodruff accomplished as an athlete. There are photos and medals and uniforms and all sorts of memorabilia that Woodruff donated to his alma mater, Connellsville High School. They are on display in glass-enclosed cases. Jim Lembo,

John Woodruff stands on oval track in foreground of famous "Hitler Tree" that stands behind end zone at Connellsville High School Stadium. Woodruff returned from 1936 Olympic Games in Berlin with a German black oak sapling and a gold medal for his efforts in winning 800-meter run.

the athletic director, who greeted us during our visit in the summer of 1999, and two of his predecessors, the late Stan McLaughlin and Michael Bell, have taken great pride in showing visitors the Woodruff collection.

It's a real point of pride at Connellsville High School. "We hope that when our kids hear about some of our former students like Lujack and Woodruff," allowed Lembo, who looked after a first-rate athletic department, "they realize that great things are possible if they have dreams and work hard to realize those dreams. You can come out of Connellsville or any community and achieve great things. Everyone is not going to win a Heisman Trophy or an Olympic gold medal, but they can do things to make their parents and the people here proud of them. Lujack and Woodruff had reputations as great kids when they were here, and everyone is capable of achieving that kind of reputation. We're proud of our tradition here at Connellsville."

It might have been the farm boy in Woodruff that prompted him to bring the German black oak sapling to his hometown. He had grown up with a respect for the land and what grew on it. He had worked the good earth. He said his family had a small farm, about three to four acres in South Connellsville. "We raised hogs and some chickens," he recalled. "I had to cut wood and bring in some coal. We had our own garden, and I had to work that. My parents didn't understand athletics. To them, sports got in the way of what we needed to be doing. There were chores to be done and that came first. When I won my first medal in track I brought it home and showed it to my mother. She looked at it and smiled. She said, 'That's nice.' And that was about it."

There wasn't much money to go around, especially during the Depression, especially for a large family like the Woodruffs.

Silas Woodruff was a hard-working man. "He was a laborer," said his youngest son, John. "He dug coal, he worked in the steel mill, and in the coke ovens in Clairton. He worked in the stone quarry. He was a powerful man, about 5-11, 240 pounds, with great girth. I heard stories about him lifting stone slabs and rocks that normally required two or three men.

"I was built more like my mother, Sarah. She was tall, about 5-9, and slim. She took in washing to make extra money. I had one sister who was younger than me. Two of my older brothers, Clarence and Roger, died during my school days. And so did several of my sisters when they were young. It wasn't uncommon in those days."

> *"I didn't get to shake hands with Hitler, but I didn't get to shake hands with our President, either."*
> —Jesse Owens

148

"Hey, Sonny, do you want to see the President?"

The Molinaro Band was a fascinating bunch that caught my eye during my visit to Connellsville in the summer of 1999. They wore T-shirts identifying themselves as members of the Molinaro Band. They were a disparate group. Their leader was a little guy with wavy silver-gray hair to be envied. He was 5-feet, 2-inches tall, standing on his toes. He appeared taller when he was directing the band. If Shirley Jones, the pride of Smithton, were on the set it would have looked like a scene out of "The Music Man."

The guy with the baton above that silver-gray head introduced himself as Henry F. Molinaro. His son was Henry L. Molinaro. He made sure I had those middle initials right. His son, a voice teacher in the music department of the local school system, was the real director of the band, but Henry F. often pinch-hit in the role with great relish. The band had been in the Molinaro family since 1913.

Michael Molinaro, the brother of Henry F. Molinaro's father, came over from Lenola, Italy and started the band. It was originally known as the Royal Italian Band. Michael had a stroke in 1932 and died in 1936, the same year that Woodruff won his Olympic gold medal. He had turned the band over to his nephew, Amedeo, who changed its name to the Molinaro Band in memory of his uncle. Amedeo directed the band until he died, at age 86, in 1998.

"We think it may be the oldest family band in America," said Henry F. Molinaro.

He said his brother, Amedeo, was about the same size as he was. So, naturally, one of his favorite marching songs was "The Little Giant." The band still played that number, as well as "Bay Meadows" and "Night Flight," and played them at the Woodruff Run.

I asked Henry F. Molinaro if he was in Connellsville in 1936 and if he remembered how the community responded to the news that one of its favorite sons, John Woodruff, had won a gold medal in the Olympic Games.

"I've lived here all my life and, yes, I was here when he returned to Connellsville. I have a story for you about that," said Molinaro, who would be 71 in a month, seizing me by the elbow — a good sign that someone is going to tell you a story. "I was eight years old in 1936. My older sister, Louise, who was like a second mother, took me one day to the Baltimore & Ohio Railroad station in Connellsville to see President Franklin Delano Roosevelt. He was running for re-election and he was making train stops in different towns throughout the country. He'd come out of the caboose to speak to people gathered at a station. It created a lot of excitement, as you might imagine.

"My sister gets me down to the train station. Now, as you can see, I've always been a little guy. Well, I was a real runt in those days. There's a big crowd at the train station. Everyone's there to see FDR. I can't see anything but other people's legs. A big man walked over to me and he said, 'Hey, Sonny, do you want to see the President?'

"I nodded that I did, and the next thing I know this big guy has me up on his shoulders. That's how I saw President Roosevelt!"

The hair stood up on the back of my neck as Molinaro neared his punch line. "And that big guy was?" I said, leading Molinaro. We could have used a drum roll.

"That big guy," responded Molinaro, slowing down for dramatic effect, "was none other than John Woodruff!"

Right then I knew I had made the right decision to travel down to Connellsville to see John Woodruff one more time. I never knew that FDR had ever come to Connellsville or that John Woodruff was there in the crowd that welcomed him.

"It's always nice to be back home in Connellsville."

John Woodruff and his wife, Rose Ella, were sitting on lawn chairs on a cement patio in the backyard of Jessie and Pete Salatino at their home at the corner of 10th Street and West Crawford in Connellsville. This was just a few hours before the race was to begin at nearby Falcons Stadium in July of 1999. The Woodruffs would be chauffeured in a pale yellow convertible to the stadium. It was truly their day in the sun.

"We graduated together from Connellsville High School in 1935," pointed out Pete Salatino, nodding in John Woodruff's direction.

"I didn't know Pete back then," said Woodruff, "but we've become good friends through the years."

Their relationship took root about 18 years earlier when Salatino, then the director of recreation in Connellsville, asked Woodruff what he thought about the idea of having a race in his honor to help raise scholarship money for local youngsters. Right out of the blocks, Woodruff's name helped the organizers land some significant corporate support for the event.

"The drive here gets more demanding each year," offered Woodruff. "I'm always looking for the Donegal exit. I'm always glad to get off the highway, and get away from those trucks. Those trucks pass you like you're standing still. I'm glad to get off the road. It's always wonderful to be back home in Connellsville. It's great to see some of my old friends."

The race route goes out to Reidmore Road in South Connellsville. "It comes within about 50 yards from where I was born," said Woodruff.

When I asked him about his own boyhood heroes, he said, "I didn't have any heroes per se. I only participated in athletics my last two years in high school. I grew up in South Connellsville and we didn't have an athletic program there. I went to our local school for

Henry F. Molinaro leads the Molinaro Band of Connellsville in celebrating return of John Woodruff to his hometown for annual July community run. Connellsville children came out to watch the activity.

Photos by Jim O'Brien

two years. I dropped out of high school for awhile, but I couldn't get a job. So I went back to school. I was lucky to get a second chance. Now I was going to the high school in the city.

"When I got to high school, I went out for the football team and stayed until a week before the first game. My mother made me quit. I was getting home too late from practice to do my chores on the farm. She told me to quit and that was it. Kids listened to what their mothers told them in those days.

"My mother went only as far as 9th grade in school, and my father went as far as 8th grade. They didn't understand athletics. They worked hard just to keep things going on the farm; it was never easy for them.

"During my short time with the football team, though, I made a good impression. The coach had the football players running wind sprints. They had a quarterback named Ralph Marilla and he was fast. Marilla was also a sprinter on the track team. The line coach of the football team, Mr. Joseph Larew, was also the track coach. He saw that when we ran that I could keep up with Marilla.

"When the indoor season started that winter, Coach Larew invited me out for the team and I went out. I remember we ran from the high school to the cemetery — Hill Grove Cemetery — and back. It was a mile up and back. We didn't have a regular track at our school; just a dirt path around the football field."

Woodruff's mother died during this period. John was just 19 at the time.

"Coach Larew was a very fine man," said Woodruff, "and he convinced me to come out and stay with track. I knew I did well at games we played, but I didn't realize what a gift I had. I did well as a junior. I ran the half-mile in 2:03. I was just under five minutes for the mile.

"I started to get better. In the WPIAL championships at Pitt Stadium my senior year, I won the mile easily. I beat the next guy in that race by 120 yards. My time was 4:23.4. It was the second fastest time in the country. A fellow named Al Zamperini who wound up at Southern Cal was the best. He was later on the same Olympic team with me. I beat him in the Olympic Trials the following year.

"In my senior year in high school, I had a 1.55.7 clocking in the half-mile, a 48.4 clocking in the quarter-mile, and I got a scholarship to the University of Pittsburgh. Larson Robinson, the head coach at the University of Pennsylvania and the U.S. Olympic coach, wanted me to go to Penn."

Woodruff was contacted by track & field coaches at several colleges, but he was leaning toward Ohio State because Jesse Owens was there. "I had met him at some meets," explained Woodruff, "and he stimulated my interest in Ohio State. But there were some people in Connellsville who convinced me to go to Pitt. They were mainly business people, and they had a Pitt alumni club. There was a dentist, Dr. 'Muzz' Campbell, and he was a dyed-in-the-wool Pitt man. He kept after me pretty good.

Olympian John Woodruff received a Pitt Bicentennial Medal in 1987 in recognition of his athletic feats as a collegiate middle-distance runner.

Bob Mathias came out to Kiski Prep to win decathlon title in 1948 and 1952 in Olympic Games.

Jesse Owens won four gold medals in 1936 Olympic Games in Berlin, Germany.

"They got me a scholarship to Pitt. If it weren't for the scholarship, I couldn't have made it. I'm the only one from my family who went to college. Things were bad. I came to Pitt with 25 cents to my name. I had to go see the coach, Carl Olson, and he let me have $5 so I could feed myself for the rest of the week. And it did, which tells you about the times."

Today, by the way, that extra meal money would be an NCAA rules violation.

"I didn't know what way to salute Hitler."

John Woodruff stared at Adolph Hitler, not sure what he should do next. Woodruff, a freshman middle-distance runner at the University of Pittsburgh, had just won the 800 meter event in a most unconventional manner in the 1936 Olympic Games, and he was standing on the top perch of the winners' platform.

Hitler, the Chancellor and Fuhrer of Nazi Germany, stood in his private box at Berlin Stadium, to acknowledge the presentation of medals, as he did throughout the Games.

Joseph Goebbels, the minister of propaganda, approached the platform. Woodruff lowered his head, and Goebbels slipped the Olympic gold medal about the young man's head.

"I was kinda confused," Woodruff told me in a lengthy interview. "They didn't school us as to how we were to respond.

"They started to play the Star-Spangled Banner, and I didn't know what way to salute Hitler. I didn't know whether to give Hitler the Nazi salute or the American salute. I went through three or four gyrations before I put my hand above my right eye, and saluted him in the American manner."

Woodruff was sure of one thing. "It was a real good feeling," he reflected on his experience as an Olympic gold medal-winner. "It was a very inspirational feeling. I did something as an athlete and for my country."

What Woodruff did was something special, all right. Until Roger Kingdom came along in 1984 and 1988, Woodruff was the only athlete in the history of the University of Pittsburgh to win an Olympic gold medal.

The 1936 Olympic Games were dominated by Adolph Hitler and Jesse Owens. Owens finished first in the 100-meter and 200-meter sprints, anchored the 400-meter U.S.A. relay team victory, and won the broad jump, now referred to as the long jump.

Owens ran the 200-meter race in 20.7 seconds, a world record, nipping Mack Robinson who ran it in 21.1 seconds. And this was on a dirt track in a light rain.

Owens was black and his success in the XIth Games was supposed to have been a jolt to Hitler's theory of Aryan supremacy. In one report of those games, it was written "the Nazi government disgracefully attempted to turn the Olympic movement into a propaganda vehicle for the glorification of their creed."

Woodruff, who is also black, says he was unaware of any political implications at the time, and believes the American athletes were just as naive, including Jesse Owens.

"You could see all those flags with the swastikas about the stadium, but they didn't mean the same thing to us then that they do now," said Woodruff. "You could see the German soldiers marching around. It was impressive.

"The treatment was superb. Everything was fine. They couldn't have treated us any better. Old-timers on our Olympic team said the facilities were the finest they had ever experienced. Everything was just right.

"A young German athlete came to our village. He spoke some English. We asked him about Hitler, and he made a statement that Hitler was doing a fine job, that he had improved the economy, and had people working again.

"We knew nothing then about his Aryan supremacy theories, that pure-blooded whites were to rule the earth. If he was advancing all this political stuff, we weren't conscious of it.

"Hitler came to the Games every day, and sat in his box with his lieutenants. We didn't pay much attention to him. I know Jesse Owens always told the story about Hitler refusing to shake his hand. He said he snubbed him. I don't know about that.

"You hear a lot of stuff about how Hitler snubbed Jesse Owens. I know that Hitler invited some athletes into his box at Berlin Stadium. Jesse Owens wasn't one of them because he was still competing in events when that took place. So was I. I saw Jesse wave from the track to Hitler in his box. He'd already won the 100 when he did that, and he was performing in the long jump. So I don't know when the opportunity came up for Hitler to snub him."

There were more than 110,000 spectators who witnessed Woodruff's winning effort in the 800-meter run that overcast and otherwise gray day of August 4, 1936.

Owens won his second gold medal that same day, with an Olympic record broad jump of 26 feet, 5 inches, but Woodruff's victory was more unexpected and certainly more unorthodox.

The race was run in bad weather conditions, the pace was slow, and Woodruff's winning time of 1:52.9 didn't threaten any existing records. It was still remarkable.

"Winning the race itself, and how I won it," said Woodruff, "is still vivid in my mind, and always will be. In the preliminaries when I ran, I jumped right out in front and stayed there. I did the same thing in the semi-final heat. Why I ran the way I did in the finals still escapes me.

"I laid back in the beginning. Phil Edwards, a Canadian who went to NYU, set the pace. He set a slow pace. I fell in behind and ran

155

second or third. I ran that way for 400 meters. Then I realized that all the field was around me, and I was boxed in. I had to get out of there."

Olympic historian R.D. Mandell wrote a report on what Woodruff did to win the race: "Seemingly disgusted, the American giant slowed his pace until he was, briefly, walking."

Recalls Woodruff:

"I actually stopped. I got spiked when I did that, but I didn't realize it until I saw the blood on my leg after the race. I moved out into the third lane, and was last in the pack. I felt I had to do something drastic. I couldn't break between the two leaders because I would've been disqualified on a foul.

"From the third lane, I got around everybody, and took the lead. They said I ran a lot more than 800 meters."

Woodruff was able to make up the lost ground because he had a running stride that hadn't been seen before in track and field competition. The average athlete took in about eight feet at a stride, while Woodruff was believed to be putting his spikes up and down nine feet apart.

Woodruff had what was described as "the longest stride of any human being in the world," and, in another report, as "heron-legged."

Jesse Abramson, the track and field writer for the *New York Herald-Tribune*, wrote that Woodruff was "the Negro wonder whose stride has to be seen to be believed." Another Abramson story described Woodruff as "an ebony vision in gold pants and blue shirt."

This tells you of the awe in which Woodruff was held, and maybe even more about the sports writing style of that era. Legendary Broadway columnist Damon Runyon referred to Woodruff as "the Black Shadow of Pittsburgh."

Whatever, Woodruff won his Olympic gold medal by beating out Mario Lanzi of Italy, who finished second, and Phil Edwards of Canada, who was third. It was the first victory by an American in the 800 meters in Olympic competition in 24 years.

The U.S.A.'s Olympic team was celebrated with a parade when it returned to New York City. Then Woodruff went home to Connellsville and rode in an even more important parade as far as he was concerned. "The people really turned out," recalled Woodruff.

According to an *Associated Press* report of that day of September 5, 1936, there were 10,000 townspeople on hand to welcome Woodruff home. It was a Labor Day event that also marked the golden jubilee of the class of 1886 at Connellsville High School.

"They presented me with a fine watch, a Lord Elgin, with an engraving on the back acknowledging my Olympic Games achievement," said Woodruff. "That fall, on the first day of practice at Pitt, we were told to put our clothes in baskets in open lockers when we changed into our sweat suits. We would be assigned lockers with keys the next day. I put my watch in the pocket of my pants. When I came back, it was gone. It was gone for good. I had it for only two months. I was told not to make a big fuss about it."

156

That watch meant a great deal to him. Woodruff's high school coach, Joseph A. Larew, presented the watch to him. His college coach, Carl Olson, was there that day, too, as were several political officials from Connellsville, including the mayor.

Woodruff was born and bred in Connellsville, and it is where he first learned, almost by accident, that he had an exceptional ability to run.

His grandparents were slaves in the Virginia tobacco fields. His parents were born free in Virginia and moved to Connellsville.

It's a town that turned out several other exceptional athletes in the mid-40s. Local heroes included Johnny Lujack, a Heisman Trophy winner at Notre Dame; Dick Pitzer, an All-American at Army; Wally Shroyer, a starting running back as a freshman at Penn State University before World War II wounds sidelined him for good, and Jimmy Joe Robinson, who became the first black ever to play football at the University of Pittsburgh.

Lujack went on to play football for the Chicago Bears. Robinson went to the seminary, and became a minister at the Bidwell United Presbyterian Church on the North Side, and team chaplain for the Pitt football team during Foge Fazio's run as head coach.

"I remember Robinson as a youngster," said Woodruff. "His home was right beside the Union Baptist Church. His father, Franklin, was a chauffeur. Jimmy Joe was raised so properly. He was like Little Lord Fauntleroy. He impressed me as a well-behaved kid. I never thought he'd be an athlete.

"Johnny Lujack's brother, Stan, would have been a great athlete if he had gone to college. He came earlier, about the class of '32 or '33. There were other good athletes, but they just finished high school and got married, and didn't have the opportunity to continue playing.

"They worked in the coal mines, or the glass factory, or the box factory, or at the B&O Railroad. I quit school when I was 16, and that's what I was going to do. I tried to get a job and make some money. They wouldn't raise my salary. So I went back to school. Looking back, that's the one time I was glad to be rejected, even if it was because I was black."

"I always had a job."
—John Woodruff

I had first interviewed Woodruff at length at the Grand Hyatt Hotel, above Grand Central Station, in New York back in 1982. I had talked to him from time to time when he attended functions at the University of Pittsburgh through the years. Pitt officials paid tribute to him on several occasions. My good friend, Herb Douglas, who was from my hometown of Hazelwood and won a bronze medal in the long jump in the 1948 Olympic Games in London, often returned to the campus from his home in Wyncote, near Philadelphia, to be with Woodruff. Douglas, who became a member of Pitt's Board of Trustees in 1999, often called Woodruff on the telephone to check on his health and latest activity. Douglas was the driving force behind a reunion dinner for former Pitt track & field athletes on June 16, 2000 at a campus hall at which Woodruff was the main honoree.

Woodruff and Marshall Goldberg, an All-American running back and a member of Pitt's "Dream Backfield" in the late '30s under Jock Sutherland, were two of the grand old men of Blue & Gold sports who returned regularly to the Oakland campus. Both had great moments at Pitt Stadium. In doing research for the reunion dinner, Douglas discovered that Sutherland was a two-time IC4A champion in the hammer throw, as well as an All-American football lineman, during his student days at Pitt. Woodruff had won WPIAL titles there as a prep star. Woodruff was dismayed by the decision by Pitt officials to level Pitt Stadium at the end of the 1999 season, whereas Goldberg was enlisted to assure athletic alumni that it was a wise decision, painful as it might be. Douglas, a retired executive with Schieffelin & Somerset Co., was one of the trustees that approved the decision.

Douglas was an admirer of Woodruff and Owens. Years earlier, Douglas talked Pitt officials into starting an annual race in Woodruff's name and donated framed photos of Woodruff that have been on display in the school's Hillman Library. He also instituted an international award and annual honors dinner at the Waldorf-Astoria in New York in memory of Jesse Owens, who had been one of his boyhood heroes and a great source of inspiration to him as a teenager.

Actually, things were looking up in 1936 when Woodruff first came on the campus at Pitt. The Depression was almost ended. Pitt, Carnegie Tech and Duquesne all had great football teams. Pitt had quite a basketball team, too, so, with Woodruff on hand. The local schools also had hockey and boxing teams that competed with local and Ohio teams. It was truly a golden era in sports at the Oakland school. "I had mixed feelings about the school," said Woodruff. "Back in those days, things weren't for the blacks. But it was a good experience for me, coming out of a small town, and never having been to the big city much." He roomed at the Centre Avenue YMCA, at Centre Avenue and Francis Street in the Hill district, just across the street from the offices of the *Pittsburgh Courier*, a nationally distributed and respected black newspaper. Two *Courier* alumni, Frank Bolden and Bill Nunn, Jr., were present at the dinner to honor Woodruff.

"That first year was rough for me, trying to get adjusted," he recalled. If God hadn't given me the ability to run I couldn't have gone to college. My first roommate flunked out and went home. I made up my mind I wasn't going back to Connellsville. I was a good average student in high school. I had to work hard at Pitt; I had to dig. And we all had to work, too, at Pitt. I cleaned up the Stadium after football games, and the Stadium Pavilion after basketball games.

"At Pitt, I reached the ultimate right from the beginning, but I enjoyed the rest of my student days, too. It was stimulating." Woodruff went on. "I got more experience and I accomplished a lot of the goals that were set for me."

He won the 440 and 880 three years in succession in the IC4A track and field championships. "That had never been done before in 58 years," said Woodruff. During the same three-year span, from 1937 through 1939, he also won the NCAA half-mile all three years. "That was quite an achievement," he said. "You can't do much better than that."

He also set records and anchored record-setting Pitt relay teams at the Penn Relays in Philadelphia and at various meets at Madison Square Garden. He won the 800 meters in the 1937 Pan American Games.

He recalled his relationship with Carl Olson, the Pitt track coach. It was a satisfying, yet stormy relationship. "Coach Olson was a very ambitious coach," he said. "He tried to get the ultimate out of you. But he had a tendency to make you run too much.

"I often ran in four events: the 220, 440, 880 and the mile," said Woodruff. "I didn't mind it so much in dual meets. But in the IC4A and NCAA, I felt you were fortunate if you could win one event. I remember in 1938 at the University of Minnesota, he wanted me to run the quarter- and half-mile events, and I had to run heats as well to qualify for the finals. He got mad at me when I protested. He was like a little dictator, a Napoleon. I just thought it was too much to ask in national competition."

Woodruff ran and won, though, and Pitt won its share of IC4A titles, and gained a national reputation as one of the top teams in the nation in those days.

In 1937, for instance, Woodruff established a world mark of 1:47.8 for the half-mile as Pitt won the IC4A title. That same campaign, he won the same event in the NCAA meet held in Berkeley, California, with a 1:50.3 clocking.

On Friday, April 30, 1938, at the 44th Penn Relays Carnival in Philadelphia, Woodruff made up a deficit to anchor Pitt's sprint medley unit (Frank Ohl, Al Ferrara and Dick Mason) to a world record 3:34.5 time, as he ran the 880 in 1:49.9. The following day, he anchored the half-mile relay team (the same foursome) to victory, and then the mile unit (Allen "Red" McKee replaced Mason on the third slot) to victory. On May 27 of the same summer, Woodruff won the 440 and 880 in the IC4A track and field meet, equaling the college mark of 47 seconds for the 440.

In his senior season of 1939, he repeated his IC4A and NCAA titles, and anchored three relay teams at the Penn Relays. The Pitt teams on which he ran, and he captained the 1939 outfit, were undefeated in dual meets.

"I graduated in four years in 1939," Woodruff was eager to point out. "Then I went to NYU for a master's degree in sociology."

While attending NYU, Woodruff worked as an elevator operator at a local department store — from 6:30 a.m. to 4:30 p.m., six days a week. He rose at 5 a.m. to start each day. They were long days, and they required a man with his determination and long stride.

Later, Woodruff served in World War II as a second lieutenant in the South Pacific, and compiled a remarkable record.

"Pitt gave me an opportunity to get a good college education," he said. "Without it, I couldn't have achieved what I did: winning the Olympics and getting a degree. It made it possible for me to make a good livelihood. Some others did better economically, but I did all right. I always had a job.

"I raised two children. My son, John Jr., became an attorney. My daughter, Mrs. Randilynn Gilliam, became a schoolteacher and married an attorney. They've both done well. I have five grandchildren and one great grandson. I always worked with disadvantaged kids, and I often served as an official at track & field meets. I liked working with young people."

Woodruff hopes his story inspires young people the way he was inspired by those who blazed trails for others.

He believed that Jackie Robinson provided the greatest inspiration to young blacks. "I knew his older brother, Mack Robinson, from our Olympic team and I later met Jackie. He told me of some of his experiences when he was coming up with the Brooklyn Dodgers. He was treated worse than a dog. But he had to take it. Branch Rickey selected him because he was the right man, as much for his great ability. He had the right temperament to break the barrier, the color line. Today's young blacks owe it all to Jackie."

They owe something to John Youie Woodruff as well.

"I haven't been forgotten," said Woodruff. "When the Olympics were held in Munich in 1972, German officials made arrangements for the 1936 Olympic champions to be there, and they paid my way there.

"We were given a tour of Berlin. We saw the Berlin Wall and we heard the Berlin Symphony Orchestra — and we went to the stadium where I'd run in 1936. I'm looking out at the empty stadium, and I had a quick flash. Suddenly, I could see all those flags, and the soldiers marching, and I could imagine all those people.

"For a second, there were over a hundred thousand people in the place again, and I was running. It was like it was yesterday."

General Colin Powell
Retired U.S. Army Commander:
"I tell young people all the time:
Disappointment and failure are part of life.
The only thing you want to do with them is
examine them, see what you did wrong — not
what somebody did to you that caused them —
and learn from that. Then bundle it all up,
wrap it up and throw it away."

Turtle Creek shares honor with Connellsville

Connellsville sports enthusiasts have often boasted that their community was the only one that could claim both a Heisman Trophy winner (Johnny Lujack at Notre Dame in 1947) and an Olympic gold medal winner (John Woodruff in 800 meters at 1936 Games), but that simply isn't so.

Move over, Connellsville, and make way for Turtle Creek.

Pat Lanigan, a funeral director in East Pittsburgh and a loyal reader of the "Pittsburgh Proud" sports book series, sent an e-mail message to correct an oversight relating to Turtle Creek.

"I wanted you to know that Turtle Creek (population 6,000) produced the same tandem of champions. In fact, both of these champions graduated in the same high school class, Turtle Creek High School, Class of 1946.

"In 1949, Leon Hart won the coveted Heisman while playing end at Notre Dame. As you probably know, he was the last lineman to win the award. He went on to have an All-Pro career with the Detroit Lions.

"In the Rome Olympics in 1960, Lt. Col. William W. McMillan, also a 1946 graduate of Turtle Creek High School, won the gold medal for pistol shooting. His other championships included 1956 and 1957 National Champion, 1958 World Champion and 1967 Pan American Games Champion. [McMillan died, at age 71, on June 9, 2000.]

"Only Mr. McMillan lived within the boundary of Turtle Creek, however. Leon Hart lived in Wilkins Township, but attended Turtle Creek schools because Wilkins Township had no high school. Years later, Paul Martha, who lived in Wilkins Township, chose to attend Shadyside Academy prior to his All-America football career at Pitt.

"I would like to mention a few other remarkable items about Turtle Creek. A 1949 graduate received the nation's highest honor, the Congressional Medal of Honor. Michael John Estocin was shot down in Vietnam while piloting a fighter jet and was posthumously awarded the Medal for bravery and service beyond the call of duty.

"The Vogues, a hit recording group from the 1960s and early 1970s, was comprised of four Turtle Creek High School grads. They had a No. 1 hit, two No. 2s, and four other Top Ten hits.

"And one of the great historic events in the nation in this past century took place in Turtle Creek. In 1920, atop the K Building at the Westinghouse East Pittsburgh Plant, KDKA broadcast the returns from the Presidential election. It was the first commercial radio broadcast in the country.

"So you can see that, indeed, Turtle Creek is a special place. Probably no other community in the country can boast of graduating from its community high school a Heisman Trophy winner, an Olympic gold medalist, a Congressional Medal of Honor awardee, and a recording group with a No. 1 hit."

A good soldier
World War II medic completes his mission

*"I was able to do something
I've wanted to do."*
—Gregory Kirchner

A 54-year mission has come to an end. An Army medic who served in World II has finally found the wife of a soldier he tended to in his dying moments in the midst of a battle in Germany.

He has wanted to tell her all this time that her husband's last thoughts were about her.

Thanks to Tom Brokaw and his staff at NBC-TV, Gregory Kirchner, an 85-year-old retired postal worker from Bethel Park, was able to do just that.

Kirchner was among those who were emotionally moved in 1999 by Brokaw's best-selling book, "The Greatest Generation," that detailed the stories of the men and women who came out of the Depression and World War II to build the world we have today.

After the war, Kirchner worked for the postal service for 36 years and raised ten children, nine of whom are college graduates.

Kirchner was among the thousands who wrote letters to Brokaw about his book, telling their own stories. These letters and reflections are the stuff of a second book by Brokaw, called "The Greatest Generation Speaks." Kirchner's story is included in this sequel.

In his letter, Kirchner complimented Brokaw on his book, and the immense research that went into it, and asked for help in finding the widow of his wartime friend Glenn Jones.

During the Battle of the Bulge in 1945, Kirchner was one of three medics serving with Company I, 417th Regiment, 76th Infantry Division. One of the medics was killed during the action, one was wounded and Kirchner came away unharmed, but haunted by the words of a dying friend.

"For a while, I was the only medic in the field that night," recalled Kirchner.

Since I spoke to Kirchner, I caught the first 15 minutes of the movie "Saving Private Ryan" once again. It was on HBO. The first 15 minutes of Stephen Spielberg's movie that begins with the landing at Normandy on D-Day is difficult to watch. It is 15 minutes of absolute horror.

To think that Kirchner came through such a battle episode, or anything approximating it, helps one to appreciate the contribution Kirchner and his fellow soldiers and nurses made in our lives.

"We set out on a dark night to surround a German pillbox or gunnery postion," recalled Kirchner. "The rain was falling. We had

162

gone through a minefield and five of our fellows lost a leg or part of it. I was tending to one of them. The whole front of his foot was gone.

"When I tried to raise him up, I placed my hand on another mine. It was what they called a 'Bouncing Betty.' Just a slight contact and the mine would pop up about six feet and explode. I paused. I didn't dare move. I was lucky to survive that.

"We had seven men suffer injuries in 15 minutes. One of them was Glenn Jones. We'd become friends. He had shared letters and news from home. All I knew was that Glenn was from the Southern States. Three days before he was hit, he had received a letter from his wife stating that she was about to enter the hospital to have their first child.

"As I treated him, he said, 'My God, what will my wife say?' There he was, his leg blown off at the hip, and he was thinking of her, not himself. Later, he said, 'I hope she will be okay.' He died in an ambulance on his way to a field hospital."

Kirchner made several attempts through the years to try to locate his friend's wife, but was always frustrated by the red tape. Brokaw and the NBC people had better luck. They had better connections, of course. With the help of the Veterans Administration, they found Sgt. Jones' wife, Virginia, living in a rural part of western North Carolina.

Kirchner and Virginia had a long conversation. He had promised in advance not to tell her any of the gory details of her husband's death. She was glad to hear from him. "It was almost like getting a message from Glenn," she said.

"My wife Mary and I watched the 'Today' show recently because we heard Tom Brokaw would be on with Katie Couric," said Kirchner. "He mentioned my name and our story when he was on. I'm grateful to him. Thanks to Brokaw's book I was able to do something I'd wanted to do for a long, long time."

Gregory Kirchner reads about the end of World War II in 1945 while in Erlangen, Germany.

Pete Maravich
A court magician

"I think basketball's the most exciting game in the world. It's entertainment, or it should be, for both the players and the fans. It's something you just have to feel. The people are so close to you. You can see the faces and they can see yours, not like some football game where you're 50 miles up in the boondocks trying to make out some guy's number. It's all right there in basketball. I mean they see you sweat!"

—Press Maravich

"Basketball is not a profession. It's a rat race. If you're going to stay in it, you have to be a rat!"

—Pete Maravich

A rat. That's it. Pete Maravich reminded me of a rat, a scared rat, the first time I ever personally saw him play basketball. It was the look in his eyes, a worried, wild, almost frantic look, deep in those dark sockets. It was the same look I had seen years before in the eyes of a cornered rat, a rat I'd come upon soon after it had attacked and killed one of three pet ducks in our backyard in Pittsburgh. It wasn't called the City of Champions back then. It was just up the river from Aliquippa, Pa., where Pete Maravich was born, and Aliquippa was just across the river from Ambridge, where his dad, Press Maravich, was coaching at the local high school at the time.

Pete Maravich was born June 22, 1947 at Aliquippa Hospital, where another Hall of Fame athlete, Tony Dorsett, would be born seven years later.

Pete "Press" Maravich was one of Pittsburgh's sports pioneers. He had grown up in Clairton and Aliquippa, and made a name for himself as a hotshot basketball player. He was a dark-eyed young man of Serbian heritage, and he had a passion for playing basketball. He wore a crewcut into his senior years. He was getting paid to moonlight in semi-pro games even while he was a student athlete at Davis & Elkins College. He later played for the Pittsburgh Ironmen in the Basketball Association of America — the BBA — which preceded the National Basketball Association, or NBA. Paul Birch was a player-coach for the Ironmen. That 1946-47 season is now considered the NBA's first official season.

Because we shared similar roots, and because I met Press Maravich on a few occasions when he was coaching at North Carolina State University and Clemson University, while his son was playing ball as a schoolboy in Raleigh and then Clemson, the Maraviches always held a special fascination for me. I kept an eye on them when they moved on to Louisiana State University. They gained a lot of attention in Baton Rouge as a father-son coach-and-player parlay.

Press Maravich, above, and his son, "Pistol Pete," were quite a parlay during their days at Louisiana State University in late '60s.

Knowing his dad gave me a distinct advantage with Pete because he was wary of most sportswriters. He often referred to sportswriters as creeps. "If you're not totally on Pete's side," said a friend, "you're an enemy for life."

Pete could be a lot of fun, and he could talk a blue streak, just like his dad, but he always seemed tormented. The pressure on him to perform was unrelenting. He never seemed to satisfy himself or anyone else. Rick Barry, another great basketball player, was like that. Pete's father, in a sense, had created a monster. It was so demanding to live up to the advance billing. It was difficult to be Pete Maravich. He often felt put upon, unappreciated by teammates, coaches, administrators and fans.

"Basketball used to be so much fun," he complained late in his NBA career. "Now I don't sleep for a week at a time. There's a reason I never smile out there anymore. This is the coldest, flesh-peddlingest business around."

I treasure some of the images that stay with me of Press and Pete Maravich, in Pittsburgh, in Baton Rouge, the Catskill Mountains, in New Orleans and Dallas.

The first time I saw Pete play was in the campus field house at Louisiana State University. We were watching him from a press table directly behind one of the baskets as Pete — "Pistol Pete" they called him — played against Auburn University in a Southeast Conference contest. His dad was hollering out instructions to Pete and — at times — the other players in LSU's purple and gold uniforms.

It's a scene that sticks in the mind, the way a spinning basketball stuck on Pete's fingertips. It took place on January 10, 1970 and was the first college basketball game I saw in the '70s. I sat between Dave Anderson of the *New York Times* and Edgar Allen of the *Nashville Banner*. We'd driven up from New Orleans, where the Kansas City Chiefs and Minnesota Vikings were to meet in Super Bowl IV at Tulane Stadium the following day. George Solomon, then a pro football beat writer at the *Fort Lauderdale News*, was with us. Solomon has been the sports editor of *The Washington Post* for nearly 30 years. At the time, I was on the Miami Dolphins beat for *The Miami News,* traveling to road games with Solomon, among others.

This was during Pete's senior season and he was shooting for this third straight national collegiate scoring title. Gunning for it, to be more accurate. He would end up averaging 44.5 points per game that season, the most anyone has ever averaged on that level. For three seasons, he averaged a record 44.2 points, and nobody — not Oscar Robertson, or Elgin Baylor, or Jerry West, or Julius Erving, or Wilt Chamberlain, or Bob Cousy, or even LSU's own Bob Pettit — ever did better in college basketball.

Think about it, though. Every time Pete Maravich moved off the bench to begin a game he had to score about 45 points just to stay even. And there were no three-point field goals then, though Pete could pump in a lot of long jumpers with the best of them. Naturally, there was quite a bit of pressure on "Pistol Pete," and he put even more on himself because he had to find time for his self-proclaimed "Show Time" antics as well. It was like playing "Beat The Clock" every night out. A game wasn't complete unless "Pistol Pete" had put the ball between his legs a few times, flung a ball behind his back to a teammate who just might be looking for such a pass, spun the ball on his fingertip during a timeout, or did a double-pump jumper to pull the fans right out of their seats. "When I hear that crowd roar," he once said, "I swear I go wild, crazy."

Those eyes — like those of a frightened rat ready to pounce on an intruder — his dark hair flopping over his face, that skinny body with all the sharp edges, those old gray sweat socks as he raced, relentlessly, from one end of the court to the other, in search of a shot, his "fix" so to speak, an opening, the ball. The memory remains vivid. He needed the ball. He owned the ball. As a youngster, he'd gone to the movies at the local theater, and always sat in a seat on the aisle, so he could bounce a basketball in the aisle while he was watching the movie. Can you picture that scene? His dad, Press, gave him his first ball, showed him what to do with it, and pushed Pete to practice and practice. He became a gym rat.

To break the boredom, Pete improvised. And he improvised like no other youngster before him had ever improvised with a basketball. John Wooden, the legendary UCLA coach, once said Pete Maravich could do more with a basketball than anyone there ever was. Adolph Rupp, an all-time coaching great at the University of Kentucky, said of Maravich: "This boy is as near the complete basketball player as you'll ever see anywhere."

Midway through young Maravich's days at LSU, his father conceded, "I think he's starting to think basketball instead of playing like an animal, with instinct."

As a junior, Pete tried to put it all in perspective when he said, "If I took it seriously, I'd be in an insane asylum right now."

He certainly seemed to be taking it seriously, too seriously, the night we saw him against Auburn. He looked like he'd just escaped from an insane asylum. You had to feel sorry for him.

You also had to feel sorry for Henry Harris, a handsome young guard, a sophomore in his first varsity season for the Auburn team. Harris had broken the color line in SEC basketball; he was the first black performer on the circuit. He was in the visitors' dark uniforms, burnt orange and navy blue, and he was an object of ridicule for a few of the fans, just enough to be heard and turn the scene, at time, into an ugly one. Several people in the stands kept shouting at Harris, calling him "Leroy," a derisive racial remark.

When the game was over, two state troopers came to mid-court and stood there while the referees donned their jackets, and then escorted them to the locker room. It had not been a controversial contest. It appeared that this was standard procedure. SEC basketball was serious stuff.

167

Henry Harris, after his days at Auburn, would commit suicide as a young man. The pressure had taken its toll.

Auburn beat LSU, 79-70, that night in Baton Rouge. John Mengelt, a tough guard who would go on to the NBA the next year, led Auburn with 23 points, playing alongside Harris, who had eight points. Maravich matched his average, scoring 44 points. But he took 46 shots, hitting 18, and was 8 for 11 at the foul line. He had two assists. LSU had only six assists, as Pete pounded the ball the length of the floor before firing most of his shots. But he never ran out of gas. We did, however, on the way back to New Orleans. We spent some uneasy hours on the side of a highway, keeping one eye on the steaming bayous nearby, and the other for a passing motorist, a Good Samaritan who might stop and help. Our prayers were answered, someone stopped to assist us, and we didn't miss the next day's kickoff.

"We're basketball coaches."
—Press Maravich

During my student days at the University of Pittsburgh, my senior year of 1963-64, Press Maravich came to Pittsburgh on a scouting trip. Pitt ripped Dartmouth, 107-63, that night at the Pitt Field House. Alvin "Doggie" Julian, the Dartmouth coach, joined Pitt coach Bob Timmons and Maravich for a drink after the game. They got together in the back room of Frankie Gustine's Restaurant in Oakland, right on the Pitt campus. Opposing coaches used to get together at Gustine's after games in Oakland. Dudey Moore, the former coach at Duquesne, always did it when he brought his LaSalle team to town. Red Manning, his successor, could be coaxed into coming on occasion. Coaches were more of a fraternity in those days.

Sports writers, even sports writers on the student newspapers, were permitted to join the coaches for the post-game jam session. Maravich and Julian started moving salt and peppershakers and ash-trays around a tabletop. Maravich and Julian were demonstrating plays and defensive schemes. A Heinz catsup bottle might be one team's center. A few years later, I recall seeing some military officers doing something similar while simulating war games on a tabletop at a cafeteria at Fort Leavenworth in Kansas City, Kansas.

When Gustine's Restaurant closed about 2 a.m., Julian and Maravich were still going at it. Maravich was boasting about his new "special x-ray defense." They took their game to the sidewalk in front of Gustine's. Maravich and Julian were using garbage cans as players now, and they were running around and over the cans. The clanging noise caught the attention of police in a patrol car cruising by on Forbes Avenue.

168

When the police asked what was going on, Maravich hollered back, "We're basketball coaches!"

"Oh," said the police officer. "That explains everything. Keep it down a little, OK?" And he kept going. No arrests were necessary.

"How long did it take Pete to learn all that?"
—Kid at Clair Bee basketball camp

A few weeks after that Super Bowl I covered in New Orleans, I left Miami, where I had been working, and headed for New York, where I would spend nearly all of the '70s. It was in April when I made the trip north. I was driving through northern Florida when I learned on the radio that the Atlanta Hawks had made Pete Maravich their No. 1 draft choice. Later, I drove through the Carolinas. The Carolina Cougars were anxious for Maravich to play for them in the ABA. Both teams went into a bidding war. Pete picked the Hawks and the established NBA.

To me, Pete Maravich symbolized basketball in the '70s as much as anybody. He had a well-publicized and glorious college career. He was a controversial figure in pro ball. He was too rich and too white to suit some of his teammates. He ended up playing for four different teams in the NBA, at Atlanta, New Orleans, Salt Lake City and Boston.

In the summer of 1970, I traveled to Kutsher's Country Club in New York's Catskill Mountains to see Clair Bee, one of the greatest basketball coaches of all time. Bee was running a basketball camp there for youngsters.

Kutsher's was also the site for the annual Maurice Stokes Summer Game. Some of the top pros, like Wilt Chamberlain, played in an exhibition game to raise funds for the rehabilitation program for Stokes, a former NBA All-Star from Pittsburgh who had been struck down by a crippling brain disease.

Bee had written a series of books about Chip Hilton, a mythical young athlete he had modeled after Bobby Davies, a basketball Hall of Famer. Meeting Bee was a special thrill.

Pete Maravich and his dad and his mother and his kid sister, Diana Maria, were at the camp at Milt Kutsher's mountain retreat. Pete and former Globetrotter Marques Haynes put on some ballhandling exhibitions. A kid at the camp asked Press Maravich, "How long did it take Pete to learn all that?"

Press replied, "All his life."

"Oh," said the youngster, turning away. "I don't have that much time."

I remember seeing Maravich's mother scolding her husband and her son in a parking lot at Kutsher's because they had left her alone the day before.

Maravich's mother had her own demons. She committed suicide in 1974. She always felt like she was on the outside looking in on their lives.

"For the longest time, Pete just couldn't get over that," said Press Maravich. "It hurt him deeply. Deeply. You see Pete is a tremendously loyal person, and those close to him have all his love, and he is a deeply emotional person, too. We are Serbian and we have very violent emotions which are hard, very hard to contain."

"He wasn't a hero anymore."
—Ronnie Maravich

When I was checking out the materials in my Pete Maravich file, I found an official scorer's sheet I didn't know I had of the game in which Maravich scored 68 points, the most ever by a guard in the history of the NBA. That occurred on the night of February 23, 1977 at the Superdome in New Orleans. I should frame that boxscore.

Maravich took a shot a minute that night, hitting 26 of 43 field goal attempts in 43 minutes of action. He hit 16 of 19 field goals. He had six assists and six rebounds, and three steals. Maravich might have scored more if he hadn't fouled out on an offensive charge call with 1:18 to play. The Jazz beat the Knicks, 124-107.

Only his coach, Elgin Baylor, who had scored 71 points against the Knicks in 1960, and Wilt Chamberlain, who had scored 68 points or more seven times, had surpassed him for a single night's output.

Maravich was unreal. I had sat in on history. It had been quite a day. Everything seemed to go right, for Maravich and me.

The Knicks were staying at the Hyatt Hotel that was connected to the Superdome. During the day of the game, I was holed up in my room. I was 34 years old. I was watching one of my all-time favorite movies on the TV. It was "One Flew Over The Cuckoo's Nest," starring Jack Nicholson. I had ordered a shrimp cocktail, a club sandwich and a Diet Coke, and was enjoying my lunch as I watched the movie. It suddenly dawned on me that life was pretty good, that being a sports writer for *The New York Post*, and traveling with teams like the New York Knicks was a good way to make a living. I felt fortunate.

When the movie was over, I went down the hall to the suite where Red Holzman, the Knicks' coach, was staying. I knocked on his door. Frankie Blauschild, the Knicks' lead public relations man, opened the door and ushered me in. Holzman was having a mid-afternoon drink. I told him what I was thinking, about my good fortune in being in New Orleans. Holzman smiled. "Jim," he said, "this would be a great life if it weren't for the damn games!"

Maravich had scored 40 or more points six times — all on the Superdome court — that season. In *The New York Post* that day, I had written, "and he might just do it again tonight against the Knicks."

Photos from Street & Smith's Basketball

Pete Maravich

Pete Maravich, in his Jazz days, shoots over Denver's Dan Issel, and in his Celtics' days, sits next to Larry Bird on sideline.

I didn't know that Maravich would score even more points that night. Before the game, I spoke to Press Maravich, who was at courtside with his daughter, Diana Maria. He introduced me to Pete's two attorneys, who were in from Pittsburgh. Pete was in the final year of a three-year, $1.2 million contract, big for those days, and his attorneys were in town to negotiate a new contract.

His attorneys, Arthur Herskovitz and Lester Zittrain, were both originally from Aliquippa. Zittrain was, by this time, working out of an office in downtown Pittsburgh. Talk about hometown attorneys. They were friendly fellows, easy to talk to, and they had Pete's best interests at heart. Press insisted that his son use them to represent him. It didn't matter that Pete was only six years old when he left Aliquippa when his father got his first college coaching assignment.

Pete certainly put them in the best possible negotiating position by the way he played that night. He ended up signing a five-year contract at $700,000 per year — even more than Kareem Abdul-Jabbar was making at the time. "That game couldn't have come at a better time," Zittrain recalled when I visited him in his office in Pittsburgh in 1980.

Pete put on quite a show. Before a crowd of 11,033 in the cavernous Superdome, Maravich scored 68 points, or most of them anyhow, against Walt "Clyde" Frazier, who had been named to the NBA's All-Defensive team seven years in a row. He was having a great season. So was Maravich, who would average 31.1 points a game that season.

Butch Beard, Dean Meminger and Ticky Burden would have to share the blame with Frazier for surrendering some of those 68 points.

After Maravich racked up the eighth-highest scoring performance in NBA history, "Hot Rod" Hundley, the Jazz broadcaster, brought him to the microphone and announced him to the crowd, "Here comes Pete Maravich, who could be the next Governer of Louisiana!"

Hundley, who had played basketball with great style as a schoolboy at Charleston and with with West Virginia University, and later with the NBA Lakers, and Maravich were quite a parlay. They thought basketball should be fun.

The New Orleans Times-Picayune newspaper the next day had a display of pistols across the top of its front page and a banner headline that read, "The Pistol Was Hot."

Pete admitted he was eager to see the reports on his game, and didn't sleep well after his great game. He said he felt like a movie star or actor waiting for the reviews.

"I tossed and turned a lot trying to fall asleep after I got home," said Maravich. "I was all keyed up. I get that way after some big, emotional events in my life.

"I'm kind of glad our victory was telecast back to New York. That's the big fishbowl. That's where everything starts. I also was happy when I heard that the game was seen on cable TV in Aliquippa, Pa., my hometown. We have a lot of family back there and there are a lot of Serbs like me, and don't you think they had a drink or two watching me?

"I took a kidding from the bench when I started to get close to Elgin's 71 points," Maravich continued. "Someone yelled at me, 'Elgin is going to take you out because he's afraid you're going to break his record.'"

After the game, Baylor laughed at the coincidence that Maravich and he had scored their high point games against the Knicks.

"The Knicks are good for history," said Baylor. "Chamberlain also scored his 100 against them and Jerry West had 63 against the Knicks, which was the record for a guard until Pete did this."

Asked to rate Maravich, Baylor said, "I don't rate players. But I'll say this. Oscar Robertson was the best guard I ever played against; Jerry West the best I ever played with and Pete's the best I've ever seen."

Chamberlain, Baylor and West turned in their record performances during the 1960-61 and 1961-62 seasons when the NBA was a struggling league with eight teams and the Knicks were a struggling franchise in last place.

The Pistol would later recount to his friend, John Lotz, a former University of Florida coach, that at one point during the game Frazier had turned to teammate Earl Monroe and suggested they switch defensive assignments. "Uh uh," said Monroe. "You're the defensive expert."

"A thing like this catches you a little by surprise," said Maravich, who scored 69 points and 66 points in games at LSU. "I didn't know I was close to a record until one of my teammates told me during a time-out I needed only a few more. I could have scored more. I missed a lot of easy shots early in the game."

He had scored enough, as far as Frazier was concerned. A few nights later, after a Knicks' game at the Garden, I was walking along 33rd Street when I spotted some young fans hollering at Frazier as he was coming out of an underground parking lot.

There wasn't a cooler or classier athlete than "Clyde" Frazier in those days. He dressed the part and then some. This night he was wearing a black, wide-brimmed hat that went well with his long black sideburns. He flashed a big smile to the fans as he appeared at the wheel of a two-tone beige-brown Rolls Royce. The kids wanted autographs, but Frazier kept moving forward slowly in his car. As he turned to enter the street, the kids turned a little hostile and started hollering at him. "Sixty-eight!" they screamed at him. "Sixty-eight!"

The fans weren't going to let Frazier forget that night in New Orleans, not too soon anyhow.

I had another souvenir from that visit to New Orleans. Pete's older half-brother, Ronnie, was bartending at a place in the French Quarter called Ye Old Absinthe House. I had a souvenir glass that

Ronnie had given me during a visit, and I had it for over 20 years. Now I can't find it. Ronnie worked at other spots later on, such as Moran's Riverside Restaurant, and, in time, gained a reputation as "the mayor of the French Quarter."

Ronnie worried about Pete. "There is a certain paranoia," related Ronnie. "Peter just doesn't trust people. It started in Atlanta where they froze him out and he was too young to understand. It was a business, nothing personal. Except — hah! — black versus white. That's all. LSU was Tigertown and lots of laughs. Then all of a sudden there was no Tigertown. He wasn't a hero anymore."

"Do you remember the date?"
—Les Zittrain

In June of 1980, I visited Les Zittrain in his office in the Grant Building. He had represented some of the Steelers, like Terry Bradshaw, Joe Greene and Rocky Bleier, which prompted my visit, but his first and most famous sports client remained "Pistol Pete" Maravich.

He greeted me by saying, "Hey, do you remember where we last saw each other?"

"Sure," I said, "that night in New Orleans."

"I'll never forget it," said Zittrain. "Do you remember the date?"

"Wait a minute — not really," I replied.

"C'mon," said Zittrain, "you guys are supposed to be trivia experts."

"I'm sorry," I said, "but I don't really remember."

"It was February 25th, 1977," said Zittrain. "It's a night I'll never forget."

The last image I have of Pete Maravich was bumping into him as I was getting on an elevator at the NBA All-Star Game hotel headquarters in Dallas in 1986. I had just had lunch with George Karl, a former pro player and coach from Pittsburgh's Penn Hills. As Karl and I were saying goodbye, we both spotted Maravich.

Pete was pleasant with both of us. "I like guys from Western Pennsylvania," said Maravich with a twisted smile. "You can't be all bad."

He was suffering from Bell's palsy, however, and his jaw was sagging. He looked thin; he didn't look good.

The following year, 1987, Pete was inducted into the Basketball Hall of Fame. That same year his dad died. Following his father's wishes, Pete placed a basketball in his dad's coffin.

Pete died on January 5, 1988, collapsing while playing in a pickup basketball game. He suffered a heart attack and died due to an undiagnosed heart defect. He was 44 years old.

He was one of the few players missing when the NBA announced its 50 greatest players on its 50th anniversary at the league's all-star game in Cleveland in 1997. It was a thrill just being in the same building as all those great ballplayers. It would have been fitting to see him honored at halftime with the likes of Michael Jordan, Bill Russell, Oscar Robertson, Wilt Chamberlain, Bob Pettit, Magic Johnson, Larry Bird and George Mikan. He belonged in that lineup.

Pete Maravich, in his early NBA years with Atlanta Hawks, drives by another future Hall of Fame guard Lenny Wilkens.

Mace Brown
He rubbed shoulders with Ruth and Williams

"Impossible to find a nicer guy."
—Ted Williams

A rookie pitcher in only his fifth day with the Pittsburgh Pirates in the summer of 1935, Mace Brown was at Forbes Field when Babe Ruth hit three home runs. Ruth rounded the bases as only he could after he hit his third home run of the game, this one coming in the seventh inning. Ruth tipped his cap to the crowd as he crossed home plate, and kept running straight ahead.

"He ran directly into our dugout," recalled Mace Brown, "and sat right beside me on the end of the bench! He sat there for four or five minutes, right next to me! The only thing I remember him saying was, 'Boy, that last one felt good.' I'll never forget that."

Ruth retreated from there to the Pirates' clubhouse and then the visitors' clubhouse, removing himself from the lineup, done for the day.

This special day in Pittsburgh baseball history was Saturday, May 25, 1935, and Brown has been asked to recount it on a regular basis ever since. Brown had celebrated his 26th birthday only four days before Ruth's historic day.

Ruth was 40 years old, in poor health, and worn out. He was playing for the Boston Braves of the National League after starring the previous 15 seasons with the New York Yankees of the American League. He was batting only .181 after 28 games. He would retire from the game eight days later. His three home runs at Forbes Field, however, created a real buzz in Pittsburgh. Those who were there boast about it with the same fervor as those who were at the same ballpark when Bill Mazeroski hit the home run to win the 1960 World Series.

They were the 712th, 713th and 714th home runs of Ruth's storied career, and that would be the record Henry Aaron of the Atlanta Braves would chase and eclipse in the mid-'70s.

Ruth's third home run cleared the right field stands at Forbes Field. He was the first ever to do so in a game since the stands were erected in 1926. Some had done it in practice. Ruth hit his first home run that afternoon into the lower deck in right field. It came in the first inning off pitcher Red Lucas.

Ruth hit his second home run into the upper deck in right field in his next turn at bat in the third inning. This time Guy Bush was pitching for the Pirates. Ruth hit a run-scoring single in the fifth inning. Just to show there was still some life left in those old legs, he raced from first to third on an ensuing single and slid safely into the bag. Then he crushed another home run off Bush in the seventh. So

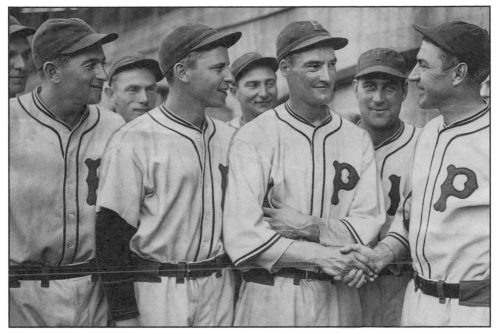

Pirates manager Pie Traynor, at far right, congratulates Gus Suhr on September 5, 1935 when Suhr tied the National League's "Iron Man" record by playing in his 618th consecutive game. Pirates, from left to right, are Mace Brown, Bud Hafey, Floyd Young, Woody Jensen, Paul Waner, Suhr, Ralph Birkofer and Traynor.

Four Pirates pitchers warm up at spring training in mid-March of 1937. Left to right, they are Red Lucas, Waite Hoyt, Ed Brandt and Darrell "Cy" Blanton. They were all on same staff as Mace Brown.

Photos from Pittsburgh Pirates

each of his three home runs went a little higher and a little farther. Ruth drove in six runs, yet the Braves lost to the Pirates, 11-7.

Bush, the pride of Aberdeen, Mississippi, indeed "The Mississippi Mudcat," was in the twilight of a terrific 17-year career. He had won 20 games with the Cubs two years before, and he posted a career record of 176-136. Red Lucas was a good pitcher, too, with a 15-year record of 157-135, so Ruth ripped into some top-notch hurlers in his four-hit assault.

Sports writer Volney Walsh's report in *The Pittsburgh Press* the next day began like this:

"George Herman Ruth — the Great Man of Baseball — lighted the twilight of his career with a fantastic display of home run hitting at Forbes Field yesterday — a gaudy exhibition that was dimmed not one whit because his Boston mates could not prevent the Pirates from winning, 11 to 7.

"The Bambino pyramided three home runs, equaling his previous record set back in the days when he was a young giant and not a man of 40. When he piled on the third and final home run it was the longest drive ever seen in the Oakland flats — a prodigious wallop that carried clear over the right field stands and lit somewhere down in the hollow."

Another great athlete of that era, Jesse Owens of Ohio State University, was pictured on the same front page of the Sunday sports section of *The Pittsburgh Press*. Owens, billed as the "World's Fastest Human," broke three world records — in the 220-yard dash, the 220-yard low hurdles and the running broad jump — and tied another in the 100-yard dash in the Big Ten Track & Field Championships. He was referred to in the photo caption as "Jesse Owens, above, Ohio State Negro athlete."

So it was quite a Saturday for Ruth and Owens, two of the all-time great athletes in the world of fun and games.

As the 2000 Major League Baseball season began, there were only three Pirates still living who were witnesses to Ruth's final home run outburst. That trio was Mace Brown, first baseman Gus Suhr and outfielder Woody Jensen. All were 90 years of age or older.

There was no TV in 1935. Ruth's feat was not seen by sports fans across the country the way it would be these days, again and again. There were just over 11,000 fans at Forbes Field that afternoon. In those days, sports writers did not run to the clubhouse to interview ballplayers to record their thoughts about what they had done. There were no quotations from Ruth in the Sunday newspaper, nothing about how he felt when he hit those three home runs. Mace Brown's tidbit was not in the newspapers. He was never mentioned. Sports writers wrote what they saw from the press box. There was no radio broadcast of that ballgame, either. It wasn't until 1937 that Rosey Rowswell began the first full-season broadcasting of Pirates baseball games, details of the away games being transmitted to a Pittsburgh-based radio studio by Western Union.

BABE RUTH
In Boston Braves days

MACE BROWN
All-Star pitcher for Pirates

Dapper Honus Wagner is flanked by two other Hall of Fame baseball luminaries, Joe Cronin, left, manager of the Washington Senators, and Bill Terry, manager of the New York Giants, just before the fourth game of the 1933 World Series.

Photos from Street & Smith's Baseball

Guy Bush became one of Mace Brown's biggest boosters. "Mace is as likely to succeed as any youngster I've seen," said Bush during the 1935 season. "He someday ought to round into one of the best pitchers in the National League."

"I liked him a lot, too," Brown said of Bush. "He helped me a whole lot."

"It was the greatest thrill of my life."
—Gabby Hartnett

Mace Brown, a 6-1, 195-pound right-handed pitcher would become quite a ballplayer for the Pirates, even representing the team, along with Lloyd Waner and Arky Vaughan, in the 1938 All-Star Game. Brown posted a 15-8 record that year, his career best.

Brown is better known in Pirates history, unfortunately, for giving up a home run that same season that may have cost the Pirates the National League pennant.

The Pirates were leading the pack by seven games on September 1. With six games left on the schedule, the Pirates led the Chicago Cubs by a two-game margin. By the time the Bucs got to Chicago for a three-game series, on September 27, their lead had been trimmed to 1 1/2 games. They lost the opener, 2-1, to reduce their advantage to a 1/2 game.

The Pirates were leading by 5-3 in the 8th inning in the second game of that stretch series, but the Cubs came back to tie the game in their half of the inning. It was getting dark in Chicago and the umpires were going to call the game if it was still tied at the end of nine innings.

Mace Brown was pitching in relief for the Pirates. He got the first two Cubs batters out in the ninth inning, and threw two curve balls for strikes past Gabby Hartnett, the player-manager for the Cubs. He threw a third curve ball, when most second-guessers thought he should have thrown a fast ball, and Hartnett hit it out of the ballpark for a 6-5 victory for the home club. Because it was so dark, it was referred to as a "home run in the glomin."

"It was the greatest thrill of my life," said Hartnett, a future member of the Baseball Hall of Fame. "I figured Brown for a curve on that oh-and-two pitch, and I got set. I sort of felt it was a home run when I hit it."

The Pirates never recovered and the Cubs won the National League pennant. Pirates owner Bill Benswanger, believing the Pirates would be in the World Series, had already made some changes at Forbes Field. He had built an enlarged press box and was putting in temporary bleachers in center field to better accommodate the crowds a World Series would draw.

180

The new press box Benswanger built was never used for its intended purpose, but remained a monument to the disappointment of the 1938 season. Until the day Forbes Field was razed in 1972, the would-be press box was known as "Mace Brown's Folly."

Brown pitched for the Pirates for six full seasons (1935-1940), was traded at the outset of the 1941 season to the Brooklyn Dodgers, and a year later was sent to the Boston Red Sox for a three-season stay in the American League. He was with the Red Sox when they competed in the World Series in 1946. His 10-year pitching record was 57-31 with 48 saves. He stayed with the Red Sox as a pitching coach and then as a scout for over 50 years before retiring from baseball in 1992. Baseball became a lifetime involvement.

"I went with them in 1942. I was in the Navy in 1944 and 1945, and back with them in 1946. I worked for them ever since until I was 80."

It was during his long stay with the Red Sox that he befriended Ted Williams, one of baseball's greatest players. Brown has great memories of those days.

Don Schwall, a stockbroker for Paine Webber in Pittsburgh and the director of Bob Prince Charities, pitched for the Red Sox and Pirates. He was with the Red Sox in 1961 and 1962 before he was traded along with Jim Pagliaroni to the Pirates in exchange for Dick Stuart and Jack Lamabe. "He was a fine pitcher," said Brown, when I told him over the telephone that I had seen Schwall at a sports banquet in Pittsburgh.

"Mace Brown was our pitching coach for the Red Sox, and he was a great guy," said Schwall, a 6-6 right-handed pitcher with a 49-48 lifetime record for seven years in the big leagues. "I remember I stayed out too late one night at spring training, and Mace put me through a punishing workout the next day. That's what it was — a punishment. He kept hitting grounders to my left and to my right; he had me running back and forth off that mound for a long while. I was dying when he was done. He said he was sorry, but he had to do it to teach me a lesson. Danny Murtaugh used to do the same sort of thing with the Pirates."

I asked Mace Brown if he knew Socko McCarey. When I was a student at Pitt, I used to see Socko McCarey on occasion at his friend Frankie Gustine's Restaurant. McCarey wore a hat all the time, and he looked a little bit like Jimmy Durante. McCarey was always complaining about hearing a ringing in his ear. His buddies at the bar in Gustine's were always giving it to him pretty good. "Answer the phone, Socko," they'd holler at him. "The phone's ringing!" McCarey was a real character, one of many to be found in Gustine's. McCarey was a scout for the Red Sox. "Joe Cronin liked him, that's why he was with the Red Sox all those years," said Brown. "Socko was the clubhouse boy at Forbes Field when Cronin played for the Pirates, and Joe never forgot him. He used to stay late and pitch to Cronin for extra batting practice. I don't think he could have been much of a pitcher.

That's where I first met Socko. Socko was something. Socko would come down to Florida for spring training and during the winter instructional league, and he'd look after the equipment. I knew Frankie Gustine, too. I knew him when he first came up to the Pirates (in 1939). He was a fine fellow."

"I was always a baseball fan."
—Sue Brown

I visited Mace Brown at his three-bedroom ranch-style home in Greensboro, North Carolina twice in three days, on October 23 and October 25, 1998, and talked to him over the telephone a few times after that. I visited him again in late April of 2000. He was 89 and moving around with a cane at the time of our initial interview. He sat in a comfortable chair in a wood-paneled den where framed baseball photos filled the walls. Most of the photos were from his days with the Boston Red Sox rather than the Pittsburgh Pirates.

Behind his head, I recognized the photos of Bobby Doerr, Ted Williams, Joe Cronin, Tony Conigliaro, Carl Yastrzemski, Jim Lonborg and Rico Petrocelli. I saw pictures there, and in the living room, of Mace Brown. They were tinted the way they used to color photos. He looked so young in those photos. He was in his mid-20s in most of those photos.

On the Williams photo is this inscription: "To Mace, Impossible to find a nicer guy."

Brown was born May 21, 1909.

Brown's wife, Sue, was sitting there in the family room. She had a portable oxygen tank with her, with tubes attached to her nostrils to ease her breathing. She had been a cigarette smoker for years, she confessed with a resigned sigh, and she was suffering from emphysema. The lungs are damaged and it's difficult to draw the next breath without an oxygen tank or medication.

Mace said he once smoked, but had quit 25 years earlier. Sue was a pleasant, good-humored woman, so sweet, doing her best to be a good host despite her health problems.

Mace was understandably concerned about Sue's situation. The love between the two was so evident. It was uplifting to witness, yet you couldn't help wonder what one would do without the other. The downside of a good marriage is that you are often lost without your mate.

"With my cane and her breathing apparatus, we don't move around too easily," said Mace, lightening the mood of the moment.

Seeing Sue and her difficulty with breathing brought an image to mind of my visit seven years earlier with former Pirates pitcher Harvey Haddix at his home in Springfield, Ohio. Haddix had some

Mace Brown shows off his Wall of Fame at family room in his Greensboro, North Carolina home. Pictured at right are former Boston Red Sox stars Bobby Doerr and Ted Williams, and Mace in his days as Red Sox coach with wife, Sue.

Mace and Sue Brown in 1998.

Photos by Jim O'Brien

Old Mace shows off Young Mace.

sort of breathing-assistance equipment in every room of his home. He, too, had emphysema. He'd lose his breath just walking up or down stairs. I felt guilty after I asked him to take me downstairs to his game room where his mementos were on display. His emphysema taxed him greatly. He would die from it a year later. My father had died from emphysema and pneumonia at age 63. When I spoke to Mace Brown a year after my visits to his home, he said he was fine, but that Sue was not doing so well.

We sat there in the fall of 1998, however, and reflected on Mace Brown's ball-playing career. Mace and Sue were so accommodating. My wife, Kathie, came with me, but left after saying hello to the Browns to check out a nearby shopping mall. Mace and Sue had been down some interesting roads together, and met a lot of famous and not-so-famous people. They were both dealing with health challenges. They were about ten years older than Kathie's parents, so the scene was a familiar one. They were a team.

I would learn upon returning home to Pittsburgh that my father-in-law, Harvey Churchman, was called "Mace" as a young sandlot baseball pitcher in McKeesport.

Kathie and I were visiting her brother, Harvey, and his wife, Diane, at their home in Raleigh on a rest and recreation getaway. I stopped en route to visit with the Browns. I enjoyed my visit so much that I returned two days later. In between, I visited with Sean Miller and Larry Harris, two former Pitt basketball players who were working as assistant coaches on the staff of Herb Sendek at North Carolina State University. Sendek hailed from Penn Hills, a suburb just east of Pittsburgh. I enjoy spending time with such people.

The Browns were both so engaging, easy to be with. There was also the thought that there might not be many opportunities to talk to Mace and Sue Brown on some subsequent trip to North Carolina.

The Browns' daughter, Carolyn, who also lived in Greensboro, came by to check on them, as she often did. When she left, Carolyn called out, 'I love you, Daddy,' and he hollered back to her, 'I love you, too.'"

I asked her dad to go back to the beginning, to get his story started.

"I grew up in North English, Iowa, about 50 miles south of Cedar Rapids," began Brown. "There were 780 people in our town. It's grown since then. There are probably about 1,000 there now. I played catcher on our town team. We didn't have a high school baseball team. The athletic department didn't have enough money.

"I went to the University of Iowa. I was a catcher my sophomore year. In my junior year I started pitching. Our coach was Otto Vogel. He played two years for the Chicago Cubs. I hooked up with the St. Louis Cardinals organization after my junior year, but they cut me during spring training in my second year with the club. I caught on with Durham in the Piedmont League, and I moved from St. Joseph, Missouri to Greensboro, North Carolina. The Cardinals had a farm

184

team in St. Joseph's. Dizzy Dean and Bill Lee were there at the same time I was."

I mentioned to Brown that I had been to St. Joseph's, during my days in the U.S. Army, and recalled seeing a statue in the center of town commemorating the Pony Express, which began in St. Joseph's. "It's also famous as the place where Jesse James was shot," said Brown.

It was when he came to Greensboro that Mace met Sue, who was then Sue Talley.

"He had seen me, and he asked a friend of mine to get a date with me," Sue recalled. "It was a bit of a blind date. I let my friend talk me into it. I knew I wouldn't like him. I just didn't think I would. I wasn't interested in the least in marrying a ballplayer. I was 19 at the time.

"I went to the ballpark a lot. I was always a baseball fan. It wasn't long after we met that we got married. My dad was dead, but my mother wasn't too thrilled about the idea. After all, I was only 19. But it's worked out fine. We've been married for 68 years."

"I saw her at the ballpark. Later, I saw her at a miniature golf course nearby," said Mace.

"I think he came so he could meet me," said Sue.

Mace Brown smiled at his wife's remarks. "We did fall in love," he said. "It was right during the Depression. It was 1930. Those were tough times. When I signed with the Cardinals I was given a $750 bonus. My first year I made $400 a month. My second year I was cut to $250 a month. I was with two different professional teams in 1931. I was with the Greensboro Patriots and then the Durham Bulls in 1931. They were in the Cardinals' organization.

"When I got to the Durham Bulls they ran out of money and couldn't pay us. Worse yet, I pulled a ligament in my elbow. We went from last place to first place and won the pennant. After the ball club went broke, they just gave us enough to pay for the necessities. I wasn't able to pitch, but I was permitted to remain with the club. We all ate in a rooming house; it was good food. They gave me enough money to get back to Iowa at the end of the season.

"I was able to get a job at a service station there. The fellow who owned the service station had a stroke, and he asked me to run the station. I was in love and wanted to get back to Greensboro somehow. I was dead broke, but I was happy when I was with Sue. You can't imagine what it was like during the Depression, but at the same time we were never hungry.

"I finally got my money back from the Durham Bulls. They had to clear up their debts if they were going to operate the next season. I got $400. We were rich. I caught on with Des Moines in the Western League. I signed a minor league contract in Des Moines in 1932.

"The owner of that ball club bought a team in Kansas City and that's where I went in 1933. We had a terrible team. We lost 100 games and finished in last place. I won four and lost 16. I was wild as can be. A fellow named Lee Kaiser was the owner of the team. He told me the manager wanted to release me. He said he didn't want to do that.

"A fellow named Art Griggs owned a ballclub in Tulsa, and I had talked to him the year before. I told Kaiser I wanted to go to Tulsa. So I got to Tulsa. I pitched my first game on May 30. I won 19 games that summer and struck out 167. Then I got a call from Pittsburgh. They bought me during the winter.

"I never forgot. I saw the news that Pittsburgh got me in *The Sporting News*. We were tickled about that. Art Griggs thought I belonged in the big leagues. He said to me, 'What the hell are you doing down here?' I said, 'Cause I'm wild. They sent me here.' Griggs was a former manager and he knew something about talent. He got Arky Vaughan.

"I liked Arky Vaughan. I was a good friend of him and his wife. It was a shame the way he drowned. He was fishing in a lake in (Eagleville) California, a crater lake. It was chilly weather and he was wearing a lot of clothes. His boat tipped over. He wasn't far from shore. But he couldn't get to shore. He was so young (40) and it was a real blow to everybody who knew him.

"I remember him real good. We lived in the same apartments in Pittsburgh for three years. Arky and his wife, Margaret, were good company. When he got into the Baseball Hall of Fame (1985), we went up to Cooperstown for that.

"We had a son in Pittsburgh. His name was Ronald Allen Brown and he was born in Canonsburg Hospital. The doctor who delivered him was Dr. James Wilson, who was a personal friend of ours.

"We were living in Oakland, in the Coronado Apartments, on Centre Avenue near Bellefield Avenue, and you could walk to the ballpark. I liked Forbes Field. It was a good ballpark to pitch in. Billy Conn, the boxer, was big in Pittsburgh in those days. He fought at Forbes Field. I saw him fight there one night. I saw him fight in New York. Arky Vaughan and Paul Waner went to the fight; we were guests of some politician. We watched Carnegie Tech. They had a good football team in those days. We watched them work out a few times. I liked it. I remember Mel Cratsley played sports at Tech in those days. The coach, Bill Kern, invited me to be on the bench when they played down here in North Carolina. We never went downtown too often, but we liked the city. We went to Pitt games, too. That's when they had Marshall Goldberg and 'The Dream Backfield.' Jock Sutherland was the coach and they had one of the best teams in the country. They invited us to come see them play when they came down here to play Duke at the end of the season (in 1937 and 1938)."

"I enjoyed Pittsburgh and I enjoyed Oakland," said Sue. "We women, the girls on the ballclub, we joined the YWHA. We had a good time going to the Y. We'd go there twice a week. We'd work out and get in shape. We'd go to the First Baptist Church. The minister there was a good man. We watched them build the Mellon Institute. We

Sue and Mace Brown with son, Al, in Greensboro home.

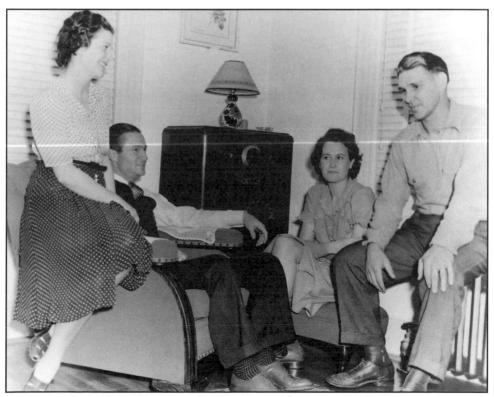

Frances and Lloyd Waner visit with Sue and Mace Brown at their apartment in Pittsburgh in late '30s.

were within short walking distance of the Cathedral of Learning, Webster Hall and St. Paul's Cathedral. It was an interesting neighborhood.

"I'll never forget the first day I went to Pittsburgh," Sue continued. "We went to Webster Hall. There was a long lobby and all the boys were sitting out there. I had never seen any of them in my life. I got to know all of them. All of my life I'd been a baseball fan. I used to go with Mace when he'd go somewhere to do a talk.

"My father loved baseball. My older brother, he was a baseball nut. I was a girl in between a bunch of boys. It was a natural thing for me to like baseball."

Mace smiled at Sue, picturing some of the same scenes she spoke about. Always the relief pitcher, he took the ball from there, and exhibited the kind of recall that most pitchers possess. They can give you pitch-by-pitch accounts of games that were played 50 years earlier.

"Baseball has been good to us," said Mace. "Growing up in Iowa, our favorite baseball team was the Chicago Cubs. We'd get the Chicago newspapers now and then. I'd follow them that way. Gabby Hartnett was one of my favorites. Hartnett played for 20 years. He started out with the Cubs in the early '20s. He managed them from 1938 to 1940.

"I still remember that game against the Cubs in 1938, the one everybody likes to remind me about. I remember it all. Pie Traynor was our manager, and he put me in to pitch in the seventh inning. Bob Klinger, a rookie pitcher, started for us that day. He pitched real well.

"At the start of the seventh inning, we were ahead 5-3. Klinger walked a batter and Traynor took him out. He brought in Bill Swift. We were both warming up at the same time. He was a right-hander and it was the first time he pitched ahead of me. He went in. They tried to bunt the guy to second. Swift got two strikes on him, so he hit away and hit a single to right field. The next guy tried to bunt, too, and he ended up hitting a single. Before you knew it, they tied us 5-5.

"Someone hit a line drive to right field and Paul Waner threw the guy out at home. That was one out and there were runners at first and third. That's when Traynor put me in. Frank Demaree was the first batter for the Cubs. He hit the first pitch into a double play. He hit it right to Arky Vaughan. I got out of the inning. I got them out in the eighth inning, too.

"They had a meeting at home plate of the umpires and managers to decide whether to continue the game or not. It was getting dark, real dark. We didn't score in the top of the ninth even though some of our best batters came up. I got the first two guys out in the bottom of the ninth, and I had two strikes on Hartnett. Two strikes and no balls. I threw him two curve balls and he looked bad. If I could have gotten the next pitch where I wanted to, I'd have struck him out. When you can't put it where you want to you get in trouble. Hartnett hit it out of the park.

"We were one and a half games ahead of the Cubs when we came in to Chicago. We lost the opener, 2 to 1. Dizzy Dean pitched for them and he didn't have nothing. I don't know how he held our ballclub to one run. Then I give up the home run to Hartnett and we lose, 6 to 5. The next day they beat us bad. They won all three games. We couldn't stop the bleeding. We went to Cincinnati to close the season and they went to St. Louis. We had a five-game lead on Labor Day. We won 14 of our last 22. The Cubs won 21 of 22 or 21 of 23. They had changed managers during the season. Harnett replaced Charlie Grimm. He was a good catcher and he was a good manager that year, too.

"After we lost those three games in Chicago, I can remember walking with Woody Jensen down to the train station from Wrigley Field. We tried to walk off our disappointment. The train left at midnight. Woody liked to walk. One time we walked from our hotel to the Polo Grounds in New York. We walked through Harlem all the way, and never thought a thing about it. That was the day after Joe Louis had fought Max Schmeling at Yankee Stadium. Now Woody and I and Gus Suhr are the only ones left from my first year with the Pirates. The Pirates had us back to Pittsburgh a few years ago for a reunion.

"I really liked it. I liked baseball. It's what I always wanted to do. In eighth grade, our teacher had us write a theme on our ambition. I wrote that I wanted to be a ballplayer and she thought I was crazy. But it's all I ever wanted to do.

"I still feel a part of the game. I still get baseballs sent to me with requests to sign them."

Every time Brown is asked about what it was like that day at Forbes Field when Ruth hit the three home runs, he provides a few more details. He also revealed something that is disturbing to anyone interested in preserving history.

"Sue brought a movie camera to the ballpark that day," said Mace. "She shot some footage. It was a cheap movie camera. The film came out real light. Eventually it was no good. We didn't take care of it. We don't have it any more."

The only pictures that remain are the ones Brown can provide from memory. "I was sitting on the bench at the end of the dugout," he recalled. "When Ruth hit the first home run it went out real high and it dropped just under the 315 sign in right field. His next home run was in the upper deck, about 375 feet out. The third one cleared the whole stadium. He really hit it.

"He ran around the bases and ran into our dugout instead of the dugout along the third base line. There was some space between me and the end of the bench. He just flopped down there. He said, 'Boy, that last one felt good.' It was the seventh inning and he quit for the day."

Brown was glad just to be there that day. He felt that way about his whole baseball career. He was once quoted by Chilly Doyle, the sports columnist for The Pittsburgh *Sun-Telegraph*, as saying, "I'm a lucky guy to be out there on the ball field. If I were back home on the farm in Iowa I'd be out there in the hot sun trying to hoe some corn. If I couldn't throw a curve ball, that's where I'd be."

Doyle dubbed Brown "The Iowa Farmer," and wrote about "the big Iowan who married a Southern belle." Doyle also declared that Brown was one of the best relief pitchers in the history of baseball.

"Every time you leave the bullpen and take that long trek," Brown related to Doyle, "you experience a thrill. The bases are loaded and you're coming in to face someone like Joe Medwick. It's almost like climbing through the ropes to start a fight with Joe Louis."

Brown's father boasted that he had been a catcher and that he caught without a glove. Mace's older brother, Rex, was a semi-pro baseball player. "He was a pretty good hitter," said Brown, "but he couldn't run a lick." Mace had another brother, Vaughn, who died from flu while serving in the U.S. Army in France during World War I. "He died one day before Armistice Day," said Brown. "He was ten years older than me. I was eight years old at the time he died. Our birthdays were on the same date.

"I was in school when my family got word that he had died. We were going to have a parade at school to mark the end of the War. They got me out of class and told me they had gotten word that he had died."

He remembered another time when he learned about a more positive event in his life. "I was pitching against the Braves in Boston and we won, 10-4," said Brown. "Right after the game they handed me a telegram telling me Sue had given birth to a seven pound boy. That was our son, Al. I felt like a million dollars."

Al was 63 at the time of our visit to Greensboro, and his sister, Carolyn, was 57. Al was living in Bellhaven, near the North Carolina coastline.

"The doctor who delivered my son also delivered Perry Como, the famous singer, at that same hospital in Canonsburg. I used to hang out with the doctor. He came down to see me a few times in Greensboro. I saw him take out Perry Como's tonsils when Como was an adult. I had to leave; I got light-headed."

Brown remembered that Les Biederman, the baseball writer for *The Pittsburgh Press*, called him "Fireman," and Sue recalled that the two of them went to a fire station in Pittsburgh one day so Mace could be photographed sitting in a fire truck.

Sue said she still had a book of poems by Rosey Rowswell, which he had given her. She brought out some scrapbooks that had clippings about her husband and the Pirates pasted in them. It was a trip down memory lane for them.

"I was making $500 a month my first year with the Pirates," said Mace. "I remember I bought a 1937 Plymouth early on, from a dealership out in East Liberty. Some one gave me a great deal on it. It was the worst car I ever had. It had no power, no pull."

"It was a lemon," said Sue.

Brown brought up two of the Pirates' most famous ballplayers, Pie Traynor and Honus Wagner, and what he remembered best about them.

"Pie Traynor was our manager and he was an easy fellow to play for. If you couldn't play for Pie, you couldn't play for anybody. I didn't have a thing in the world against Pie. He was easy-going. He never got on you or raised any cane with you.

"Honus Wagner was an honorary coach. He suited up for every game. He'd sit on the bench for awhile at every home game, and go home before the game was over. He'd go back and forth to his home in Carnegie on a train that stopped there."

"We visited with him out there," recalled Sue.

"I liked Honus," said Mace. "He'd walk out of the dressing room and down under the stands to get to our dugout and everyone watched him. Red Lucas was always teasing Honus Wagner. They were always having fun at each other's expense.

"Honus would be there with his ear up against the wall. We'd see him and someone would say, 'Don't ask him what he's doing. He wants you to.' Then Red Lucas would say, 'What in the world are you doing there?' And Honus replied, 'I'm counting the cars going through the Liberty Tunnels.' Silly stuff like that.

"In New York, we followed Honus Wagner around one day. He stopped in every tavern and had a beer. He was a fine fellow, easy to be around. He liked still being a part of the team. It was great traveling in those days. We went to San Bernardino in California and we went by train. It took us four days and four nights to get there.

"We stopped in Hutchinson, Kansas on the way out. We had a ballclub there. They took us down into a salt mine there. Everyone in town wanted to see Honus Wagner. He was a big hit. We played exhibition games at different stops on the way back from San Bernardino. We played in Needles, California. We played in Albuquerque, New Mexico, and we played in Phoenix and in Tyler, Texas. We played in San Antonio, Austin and Amarillo. We played in New Orleans. We rode in Pullman cars. We traveled once with the Chicago White Sox and played exhibitions, and we traveled once with the Athletics.

"The guys used to play cards on the train, but I never did. I didn't want to gamble. I never gambled much.

"Paul and Lloyd Waner were two of the great ones I played with. Lloyd could fly to first base. He had some hands and he had a good strong arm. He wasn't the hitter Paul was, but he could run, and he got a lot of singles that way. I think he had 199 singles one year. Paul was the best hitter I ever saw until I played with Ted Williams. He was one of the few hitters who could tell you where he was going to hit it. He'd foul off balls until he got a pitch. There were several years (three, in fact) when they both had 200 or more hits. Pound for pound, the Waners were as good as anybody.

Honus Wagner Still an MVP

A near-mint condition baseball card of Pirates Hall of Fame shortstop Honus Wagner that was issued in 1909 was sold for a record $1,265,000 in mid-July, 2000 over the Internet auction house eBay. The card's price was driven by its rarity, as only about 50 are known to exist.

"Waite Hoyt, who's in the Hall of Fame, was on our pitching staff when I was in Pittsburgh. He and Cy Blanton (in 1935) were the best on our team. Blanton was among the leaders in several categories that year (shutouts with four, 2.58 ERA, 18-13 record). He had a great year when I was a rookie. The best pitcher I saw then was Carl Hubbell (253-154 record in 16 years). He was like Greg Maddux of the Braves. He wasn't overpowering, but he was so smart. Maddux doesn't pitch that hard, but he puts it wherever he wants to. I've seen the best up close over a long period of time.

"One of my big thrills was pitching in the All-Star Game in 1938. I pitched the last three innings. We won, 4-1. They got a run off me in the ninth inning. Joe Cronin and Joe DiMaggio got hits off me to produce the run.

"I worked after Johnny Vander Meer and Bill Lee had pitched the first six innings. I fanned Rudy York with the bases loaded on a 3-2 count to end the first inning I pitched. The three runners on base were Joe Cronin, Lou Gehrig and Jimmy Foxx. They all ended up in the Hall of Fame. I struck out Bob Johnson of the Athletics to end the game. All things considered, I would have rather struck out Gabby Hartnett that day in Chicago.

"I scouted and coached with the Red Sox. They took me to spring training every year until I was 80. I signed Jim Rice. He was a pretty good one. I signed Jim Brewer, Willard Nixon and Don Buddin.

"The best thing about the Boston Red Sox had to be Ted Williams. To me, he's the best hitter I ever saw. He's the best who ever lived.

"He went into the military service toward the end of 1942. He was a pilot. He missed nearly five years from his baseball career when he was at his peak. He was in the service during World War II and then recalled for the Korean Conflict. He got shot down in Korea, and survived that. There was no stopping Ted Williams."

"It's all I ever wanted to do."
—Mace Brown

On my second visit to the Brown home in Greensboro two days later, I asked Mace to tell me more about Ted Williams, and I asked Sue to tell me more about Mace Brown.

"I thought he was a nice fellow when I first met him," Sue said of her husband. "He was nice and pleasant. He was a gentleman. He stayed that way.

"When I first met him, it was the first time he'd been away from home. My family was concerned about our relationship because of my age (19) and that we didn't know each other that well. But it was great to be married to him, and to move to Pittsburgh when we did."

"I liked it very much, being with Pittsburgh," said Mace. "I especially liked that ballpark. Forbes Field was a great ballpark to pitch in. I liked the Pirates, too. We had a good ballclub. They had the Waner boys and Arky Vaughan. We were contenders nearly every year. We were fourth or better."

"It was all very satisfying, and he was proud to be a Pirate," said Sue. "We got along well with everyone."

"Forbes Field had a big playing area. Even I found an opening for a hit. Right field was the only place that was short. The fence was probably 15 or 20 feet high. It jutted out real quick. I was a lousy hitter, but I got a double off Johnny Vander Meer there in a July 4th game. There was an overflow crowd. They had fans against the wall in left field and center field. They roped off the crowd out there. There was a sign in left field indicating it was 406 feet. I happened to get hold of one and hit that sign out there. The two Waner boys both got singles behind me and I scored. We won, 4-3, that day."

When I complimented Mace on his memory, Sue interjected, "He cares so much about baseball. He reads so much about baseball and he likes to talk about baseball. I don't always pay him any mind. We always enjoyed being around people who played ball. We enjoyed our days in Pittsburgh, we enjoyed our days in Boston, and we enjoyed our days with the ballclubs in spring training in Florida. We made a lot of friends there. I went with Mace when he went down there for winter instructional league sessions, too."

Then Mace Brown wanted to talk about Ted Williams. "We became good friends of Ted and his second wife, Lee," recalled Mace. "I always got a kick out of him. He really worked at being a great hitter. He had such great hand-eye coordination, and he saw the ball better than most people, I think. I was there in 1941, the year Williams won the batting title with a .406 average.

"I remember one game I'm pitching against Detroit and they scored a run off me in the ninth inning. I came in after we got out of the inning and I'm sitting at the end of the bench. Williams said, 'What the hell are you doing out there?' Then he smiled and assured me that everything would come out OK. '(Johnny) Pesky is going to get a hit,' Williams told me, 'and then I'm going to hit one outta here. If Pesky doesn't get a hit I am going to hit one outta here anyhow.' He liked to say things like that. Sure enough, Pesky got a hit, and Williams hit one outta the park.

"He could do whatever he wanted to do. He could tell you where he was going to hit the ball. In 1942, we were playing the White Sox in Chicago. There were two weeks to go in the season, and it wasn't an important game. Ted was going up to the plate, and he told us, 'Watch me give them my Mel Ott stance.'

"He raised his front leg as the pitch came toward him. He hit a pop fly. I scolded him when he came into the dugout.

"I told him my mother and sister had come in from Iowa to see us play. My dad had already passed on. I told him I wanted my family to see the real Ted Williams I had told them about. I told him my mother would be disappointed. Johnny Rigney was pitching for the White Sox, I recall. The next time up, Ted hit one into the upper deck in right field. When he came into the dugout, he told me, 'Tell your mother that one was for her.'

"I'll tell you another Ted Williams story, one I was sometimes hesitant to tell. We're playing in New York that same year — 1942 — at the end of the season. The Yankees beat us by ten games for the American League pennant that year. We couldn't pass them. It was too late. There was only a week to go. But there were over 30,000 there to see Williams and Joe DiMaggio. Williams won the batting title (.356) that year. The New York crowd really got on Williams. The crowd was booing him before the game. People were hollering stuff like, 'Why aren't you in the (military) service?' I was out in left field shagging fly balls before the game. Williams came out there. 'I'm going to give them an exhibition they'll never forget,' Williams told me. 'I'm going to strike out every time up.' I snapped at him, 'You can't do that.' And he said, 'Watch me.' He took three strikes the first time he came to bat. I told the guys in the bullpen that he said he was going to do that. Ted did the same thing the next time up. He didn't swing at a single pitch. Marvin Breuer was pitching for the Yankees. He wasn't a regular on their staff, but they were setting up their pitching for the World Series. Breuer had a no-hitter going for seven innings. Johnny Pesky or Dom DiMaggio got the only hit. Ted came up in the seventh inning and took three strikes again. We were behind, 1-0, in the ninth inning. Our best pitcher, Tex Hughson, was pitching for us. He was a good one. He'd won 20 games already (he finished with a 22-6 record that season). Williams comes up to bat again. Joe Cronin was coaching third base for us. He came in and he was seething. He stepped in front of Williams by the dugout, and he really let him have it. Ted was the second batter up in the ninth inning. You could see him gripping that bat, turning his wrists like he did. Like he was going to grind it down to sawdust.

"The first pitch from Breuer was a ball. On the next pitch, Williams hit a home run. He hit it into the upper deck in right field. We won the game on that one. I never did tell that story to anyone. I was always afraid Ted wouldn't like it.

"I was sitting on the bench in Philadelphia early in the 1942 season. I was sitting next to Joe Cronin, the manager. Ted came to bat in the sixth or seventh inning. We had a couple of men on bases. The count went to 3-and-0 on Ted. He hit the next pitch out of the ballpark. Cronin nudged me and said, 'They don't do that in the National League, do they?' He meant swinging at a 3-and-0 pitch. I said, 'No, sir. They would've taken that last pitch.'

"He was something. We became real good friends with Ted. After he retired, he would come to spring training and work with the kids. He'd spend a month with us. He usually stayed in our home. He did that for seven or eight years."

194

Jim O'Brien

Mace Brown's daughter, Carolyn, looks after him these days at their home in Greensboro, North Carolina.

"Ted loved working with young people," said Sue.

I asked Mace Brown about Joe DiMaggio, and how he had fared against him. "I faced him four or five times and he didn't have any hits against me," said Mace.

"Didn't you pitch against him the first day in Boston?" said Sue. "It was the first time Mace relieved for the Red Sox, and he did it against the Yankees. He managed to get DiMaggio out and we won the game. We had a big newspaper cartoon showing Mace pitching in the 9th inning against different great hitters, including DiMaggio. But Mace gave it to his great-grandson. He has a baseball room, too, and that's where it is."

What did they think of baseball today?

"I can't believe the pitching is as good as it was in our day," said Mace. "Too many guys are hitting 40 home runs. There are too many clubs. It thins out the talent. I don't like the way they pull a starting pitcher so fast today, and they way they run pitchers through a game. I don't see it. I'm old fashioned. I can't see taking out the starting pitcher to get the closer in there all the time."

"If I were a pitcher I wouldn't like it," said Sue.

I asked Mace Brown to sum up his life, as a ballplayer and as a family man.

"If I had my life to live over, I do the same thing," he said. "Only I'd be a better pitcher. I could have been a better pitcher. I enjoyed my life. I enjoyed my family. I couldn't want any better. I'm blessed. Fine wife and two fine kids. They all liked what I was doing and we got along good. My wife never one time ever complained about me going on road trips or scouting and doing my job. Never griped about it. She knew I was doing what I wanted to do, and she knew we all benefited by what I was doing."

"You're never ready for it."
—Mace Brown

I called Mace Brown on April 18, 2000 to check with him about some details in his stories. During our conversation, he said, "My wife, Sue, died this year. She was 89. She died on January 26. She was sick for a long time with that emphysema. I knew she was having a tough time, but her death was hard to deal with. You're never ready for it. We were married for 69 years. I was lucky to have her for 69 years. I'm 90 now. I'll be 91 in May. We'd have been married 70 years this June. My daughter, Carolyn, is living with me now, looking out for me. She's divorced and she has twin daughters, who are 35 now. They're on their own. I wouldn't be able to stay here if I didn't have Carolyn taking care of me. I'd have to go to a nursing home. I'm lucky to have her."

I spoke to Carolyn later, when I called back and Mace was taking a shower. "My mother suffered a broken hip, and I moved in here last August to help them," said Carolyn. "They couldn't operate on her because she was too weak. I quit my job to come here. I had been working at 911, taking calls. My father has been in deteriorating health, too. I thought my responsibility was to them. That was the least I could do for my mom and dad. They've always been so good to me. He misses her a lot, and he's had some tough times. He's scared us a few times. His mind's still as sharp as ever. His health isn't that good, though. I think he wants to go, too."

I felt badly for Mace Brown when I got off the telephone. My wife, Kathie, called me from work within minutes of my conversation with Mace Brown. "That's a shame," she said when I told her Mace Brown's wife had died. "She seemed so nice. You could tell how devoted they were to one another. We'll have to send him a card."

I was traveling through North Carolina in late April, 2000, and decided to visit Mace once more. I stopped by his home on Saturday morning, April 29. Carolyn came to the door to greet me this time. Mace remained in his favorite chair in the family room, and called out to me when I came into the kitchen. He had a walker in front of him. He said it was difficult for him to get around anymore. When I said goodbye to him this time, I gave him a hug.

I noticed a new photo in the room, a studio portrait of his late wife. Carolyn said she had put a hospital bed by the window in that same room for her mother in her last months. "It was so they could be together during the day," said Carolyn. "They liked it that way."

Mace and Sue Brown check out game program from 1946 World Series when Brown was with the Red Sox.

Swin Cash
Mother's Day in McKeesport

"I want to realize all my dreams."

Swin Cash seemed as sweet as the raspberry iced tea she was drinking. There was an absolute gayety about her, a light-hearted spirit to her speech, often a laugh. She had an attractive appearance, to begin with, and this even made her more appealing. She set one completely at ease the way she shared her personal thoughts and goals and talked about her upbringing, right from the outset. She could be a model in every sense of the word.

The light was on in her dark eyes. This was a young woman who was clearly happy to be home with family and friends, yet confident that there were more worlds for her to conquer at the University of Connecticut where she was a starting sophomore forward for an NCAA championship basketball team.

Swin Cash had come home from Storrs, Connecticut for a week's visit. She was in McKeesport, Pennsylvania on Mother's Day, to be with Cynthia Cash, the mother she credits for showing her the way, making personal sacrifices and always supporting her efforts and dreams. This was the day after Mother's Day, May 15, 2000, and Swin was sipping raspberry iced tea at lunch at the Eat'n Park Restaurant on Lyle Boulevard.

This is a busy stretch alongside the railroad tracks and the mills that once made McKeesport huff and puff. It had been a smoky and sizzling Class C-sized city, a gritty industrial mecca along the Monongahela River. Those mills became haunted shells just before Swin Cash was born there 20 years earlier, and the city is still trying to mount a comeback. Old men sitting on benches nearby still believe those mills will re-open and flourish again some day. Here's a reality check, fellas, those days are long gone.

Across the river in Duquesne, and down the river in Munhall and Homestead and Glenwood and Hazelwood, the mills, once parts of the U.S. Steel, LTV and Jones & Laughlin Steel empires, are gone. New centers of commerce are emerging along the Mon shorelines. They don't make steel in Pittsburgh anymore.

It was a bright, sunny day this Monday in McKeesport, a bit deceptive because temperatures had dipped to 38 degrees overnight and were now about 60 degrees. The wind was gusting and it was on the cool side. Even so, Swin Cash came to the restaurant in a short-sleeved lilac jersey, some simple gold chains and bracelets, and black slacks. Swin Cash was as cool as this May day.

She was a willowy 6-1, 164 pounds ("Do I have to tell you that?"), seemingly too thin to get her way on a basketball court, but that was deceptive, too. Make no mistake about it, Swin Cash has got game.

Bob Stowell/University of Connecticut Sports Information

Photos by Jim O'Brien

Swin Cash came home to McKeesport for Mother's Day of 2000 and checked out some local landmarks. She posed in front of statue memorializing President John F. Kennedy, who spoke on the same spot in a park on Lyle Boulevard when he was campaigning for office.

I could still see Swin Cash in her white basketball uniform with orange and blue trim and lettering. She wore uniform No. 32, the number Franco Harris, O.J. Simpson and Jim Brown made popular for star running backs in football.

Even as she sat across the table from me, I could see Swin Cash sliding across the floor, flopping at mid-court to join her teammates as they hugged and squeezed each other, and carried on like young women would be expected to carry on after winning the NCAA women's basketball championship five weeks earlier. I remember how I felt good for her, even though we had never met, because she was from McKeesport, a local girl making good.

My wife, Kathie, comes from McKeesport. Kathie spent the first few years of her life in a modest home on Jenny Lind Street, just around the corner from Soles Street, where Swin's family makes their home these days. Swin had grown up in Harrison Village, a stark public housing project in the city. Kathie had grown up in White Oak, a comfortable suburban stretch on the outskirts of McKeesport.

They came from different environments, but they were both Tigers.

Soles Street was seven-and-a-half to eight hours away from Storrs. The brick buildings of Harrison Village were hardly as idyllic as the South Campus dorms where Swin resides at Connecticut. It's a different world. The true beauty of Swin Cash seems to be her ability to switch back and forth, and not make judgments about either. She adapts well. She is comfortable in the company of old friends and new friends.

There simply is no snob in Swin Cash. She had gone to Europe twice over a three-year period. She had seen the Pope in Rome and been to Paris. She preferred Pittsburgh and her parents and pals.

"I'm looking forward to spending this summer at home," she said. "It seems like the right time to do this. I feel like I need to be home."

Cash had contributed nine points and strong defensive play to the Huskies' 71-52 victory over Tennessee in the *ESPN*-televised championship contest from Philadelphia's First Union Center. Her coach, Geno Auriemma, who grew up in Philadelphia, was on top of the world. His team had won its second national championship in six years.

It was the best Swin Cash had felt on a basketball floor since her All-State days at McKeesport High School when she led the Tigers to a Quad A WPIAL championship in 1998.

When Swin was a freshman at McKeesport High School in 1994, the school's football team, led by All-American Brandon Short, won the Quad A WPIAL and PIAA championships. Short also grew up in Harrison Village. They were friends and played some basketball together. They both dreamed of being All-American players and pros. Short had graduated after an All-America career at Penn State and had been drafted by the New York Football Giants.

200

I had walked through Harrison Village and some of the nearby streets with Brandon Short five years earlier. I knew the territory and remembered houses where he had introduced me to friends and teammates. Short and Cash came from the same stock, and they were able to tip-toe through the minefields of their youth to become sterling citizens and leaders.

Street gangs, drugs and out-of-marriage pregnancies were prevalent, and only the strong were able to resist getting waylaid by these obstacles.

What Brandon Short and his teammates had accomplished in football at McKeesport High, and what Swin Cash and her teammates had accomplished in basketball brought great pride to the community, and gave the local folks something to cheer about. There were still signs posted about town calling attention to those two feats. They remained a point of civic pride, something to boast about. Hey, Penn Hills, Monroeville and Trafford, take that.

Cash scored 2,678 points and grabbed 1,782 rebounds in her sterling career at McKeesport High School. She was the *Post-Gazette* Player of the Year as a senior for the second year in a row, a first-team *Parade* and *USA Today* All-American. She was MVP in the Nike/WBCA All-Star Game, which featured the top players in the country. She also played for the U.S. team in the Junior World Championships in Louisiana after graduation.

She averaged 29.8 points, 17 rebounds, 5.7 blocks, 4 steals and 3.1 assists a game. Against North Allegheny High School in the championship game, Swin was sensational with 40 points, 21 rebounds and 10 blocked shots.

"It's hard to put a value on her presence here at school," said McKeesport principal Joe Catalina.

Cash was a solid student, president of student council and a finalist for homecoming queen. She carried herself with style.

"All I want to do is live life to the fullest," she said. "I want to realize all the dreams I have — going to the pros, coming back to McKeesport someday and setting up a Swin Cash Foundation. I know those things are possible."

The best was surely yet to come for Swin Cash. She had a name and a game that promised even more fame. Barbara Cloud, a weekly contributing columnist for the *Pittsburgh Post-Gazette* and a former fashion writer, had suggested Swin Cash had the lean clean looks to be a fashion model.

Her full name is Swintayla, but that's more than a mouthful. Swin Cash is a great name for a great athlete. It's short and sweet and different. There hasn't been a Swin in basketball. The closest would be Swen Nater of UCLA and the San Antonio Spurs. Swin is one of those names that can stand alone. Cash works well for headline writers.

"The older guys paved the way for us."

When Swin was a freshman at the University of Connecticut, the men's basketball team, led by Richard Hamilton and Khalid Al-Amin, won the NCAA title.

"We were really close to the guys' team at McKeesport and Connecticut," recalled Cash. "When I was a freshman at Connecticut our class was regarded as one of the best to come along in a long time. We just thought we'd win four national championships. But it's not that easy. We saw how hard it was for the guys to do what they did, and what it took to win a national championship. I think it helped us the second time around. It was that way at McKeesport High School, too. The older guys showed us the way; they paved the way for us."

As a freshman at UConn, Swin suffered a stress fracture of the right shin that caused her to miss 12 games. Even so, she averaged 9.5 points and 5 rebounds a game. As a sophomore, she boosted that a bit to 10 points and 5.5 rebounds. "My friends tell me I should shoot more, but I know what my role is," she said.

"My coach explained that to me right off the bat. He told me straight out that I would have to be patient. He said it's going to be a process, one year at a time. They keep building on your game. You have to wait your turn. It's a process and a business."

With increased playing time, it wouldn't surprise anyone if Cash averaged 12 or 13 points and eight rebounds a game as a junior. And UConn figures to be a favorite for national honors again in her junior and senior seasons.

"I'm coming home for two months this summer and I plan to work on my game," she said. "I'm going to get stronger and better. I'm stronger for my size than you might think."

I'd seen her play and I suggested there must be two Swin Cash personalities, the sweet one sitting across the luncheon table, and the Tiger who grabs rebounds with a special vehemence and swats shots back by opposing players. I asked her if she had a tiger in her. Swin smiled at my comment.

"I think so," she said. "When you get into the atmosphere that we play in it helps if you can play with some aggression. I think I have that and it separates me from many of the other girls. That's something I bring to the team. The coach tells me that. He wants me to be really aggressive. I can guard someone on the outside and go inside with them if necessary.

"The coach wants me to work on 3s and my ballhandling. You have to start to develop in all those areas. You have to keep getting better. You have to work at it. I'm doing what I dreamed about doing as a kid. Who didn't practice shooting the shot that won the national championship?"

That's no pipe dream at Connecticut. The Huskies play their home games at the Harry A. Gampel Pavilion (10,027 capacity) and the Hartford Civic Center (16,294) and the men's and women's teams regularly play to sellouts. The men's team stumbled in 1999-2000 after being rated as a possible NCAA repeat champion. The women's team posted a 36-1 record, losing only to highly-rated Tennessee by one point on February 2 on the Huskies' home court. They had won at Tennessee, 74-67, earlier in the campaign.

Connecticut has become one of the bastions of college basketball. Jim Calhoun consistently puts a national contender on the floor, and has had the winningest program in The Big East in the 90s. Gene Auriemma has done the same for women's basketball. His teams qualified for the NCAA tournament 11 straight seasons. So the whole campus and the whole state rally around the school's basketball teams. The home court advantage is a real one.

"It's an eye-opener the first time you play in our place," said Cash. "I've gotten used to it now. It's really exciting. There's always so much noise. Everybody's always yelling. They go crazy. It really helps us. It gives us an edge."

"My mom and I have always been so close."

Swin Cash recounted her Mother's Day strategy with her mother, Cynthia Cash. It sounded like she was teasing her mother, trying her patience. "My mom was there, and my best friend was in from college," recalled the young Cash, referring to Danielle Johnson, a former AAU teammate who went from Woodland Hills High School to American University. "Everyone was telling her 'Happy Mother's Day,' but I was holding back. My boyfriend, Courtney Wallace, called, and he wished her a 'Happy Mother's Day.' She kept looking at me, like she was trying to figure out why I hadn't said anything to her.

"We went upstairs together. I had made her a special CD. I had a message on it just for her. I gave her a card with some hand-written words just for her. I gave her a plaque we received for being in the NCAA Final Four. There were only a few made. It had all of the signatures of the team members on it. I played the CD for her. She just loved it. When she was reading the card, I started talking and telling her how I felt about her. I had written out ten reasons why I thought she was the best mom. One of the things I wrote was a thank you for fixing me all the peanut butter and jelly sandwiches. And thanks for helping me through tough times. Stuff like that. And she started reminiscing. 'Do you remember the time you fell down the steps when you were ten?' And, 'Do you remember when you were five and—?' I said, 'C'mon, Mom.' And I told her that with all the yelling, scolding and screaming that she turned out pretty well. I reversed our roles. I told her she had to work on her 'crunches' because she wants to have tighter abs. We were just telling each other stories, laughing, crying a little, you name it. It was great. My mom and I have always been so close."

Cynthia Cash was 37 years old at the time of my meeting with her daughter. She was 17 and ready to start her senior year at McKeesport High School when she gave birth to Swin on September 22, 1979. Cythia came back to school afterward and was one of the star players on the girls' basketball team. She raised Swin alone until she married Kevin Menifee and they have raised three more children together.

"She sacrificed a lot to give birth to me," said Swin, "and I don't forget that. If she didn't have me, maybe she could have gone on to college. I asked her, 'Mom, are you sad you had me when you did?' And she said, 'I wouldn't trade you for anything.' So I wouldn't do anything to hurt my mother."

Cynthia Cash works in a mechanical maintenance job for the McKeesport public housing authority. The three other children include, Steve, 22, a senior basketball player at Indiana University of Pennsylvania, Kevin, 15, and Angelique, 6.

Swin's boyfriend, Courtney Wallace, was a 6-4 junior point guard at Duquesne University. He was from the Hill District and played previously at Perry Traditional Academy, the same background as his coach Darelle Porter. "The first time I saw him he was playing against my brother Steve," said Swin. "At first, I couldn't stand him. He scored so many points against my brother."

She said she and her friend, Tionda Jennings, who plays for the women's basketball team at Duquesne, would be going down to the playground at Kinnard Park in the Hill District to play with the guys in the summer.

"Some of my friends don't like me playing with the guys," she said. "They get on my nerves sometimes. I think it's important to play against guys because they are stronger, not necessarily better basketball players. If I can do it on a guy I know I can do it on a girl."

She said that her assistant coach at UConn, Chris Dailey, keeps a close eye on her and her teammates when they are off the court. "She makes sure we eat the right way, dress properly, how we sit, and so forth," said Swin. "We're always going to fancy, expensive restaurants. They give you steaks that are so expensive but they bring your plate and those steaks are as small as peas. I'm used to bigger portions. My family cooks big. I've gotten the team to eat soul food a few times. I love my mom's home cooking better than anything.

"When I was about seven years old, my mother was a crazy basketball fan. She was a big fan of Dominique Wilkins and Michael Jordan. So I learned a lot about basketball from her early on. My family is big. There are a lot of boys and they'd be out playing ball. That's how it all started. I'd be out in the playground at Harrison Village. The playground was right across the way from the building where we lived. I could see the curtain cracked in our window. I knew she'd be looking at me.

Swin Cash signals that the University of Connecticut women's basketball team defeated Tennessee for the national championship.

"My mother coached some basketball. I could play my best game and mom would tell me what I did wrong. She wanted me to hustle, dive for loose balls and get every rebound. The guys would give me a tough time on the basketball court. They all wanted a piece of me. They wanted to make me stronger.

"We were out there every day. People in our community knew we were going to do something special. We ran around Moran Field together. We supported each other.

"I had 11 aunts and uncles. My mother was one of 12 children. When my grandfather passed away in 1993 or 1994, I remember there were 75 grandchildren and 12 great grandchildren. I remember saying to my mother, 'Mom, do we really have so many people in our family?' I think there are even more now.

"I have so much support. I always know they're there. One of my teammates at Connecticut, Tamika Williams, came to my house with me. She said, 'Not only do you have so much family, but they all look alike.'

"It's more a family thing. I need to be there. Even if I move — I've talked to Courtney about this — I'd always want to have a home somewhere here. I have so many ties. This is where my roots are. My gym teacher, Miss Apple, in high school was my mom's high school basketball coach. She said, 'I remember holding you when you were in diapers.' Everyone knows all about me here.

"It's tough to be away so much. When I was a freshman, I came down with mononucleosis. I just knew if I came home I'd get better. And it worked."

There was some talk at the time that Swin was homesick that she might not return to school. But she did and she's glad she did. "Truthfully, I was homesick the minute I got to school," said Swin. "I called home a lot to talk to my mom, my aunts, my cousins. It just took some getting used to.

"I consider myself a city girl," she continued. "I'm used to having different people around me. Storrs is so remote. There's not a McDonald's for miles. It's so isolated. There's nothing there. I'm used to going down the street and having everything there for me."

I mentioned to Swin that there used to be a McDonald's about a half-mile east on Lyle Boulevard, in the heart of the downtown McKeesport community, but that it went out of business several years before. A McDonald's doesn't go out of business too often. That tells you something about McKeesport, too. You can't trap Swin Cash, though. She's too quick. She is never going to say anything that sounds like a snipe at her hometown. She doesn't see it the way somebody who lives in the suburbs might see it.

The kids in my hometown of Hazelwood now call if Plywood because so many of the storefronts on the main street, Second Avenue, are all boarded up. Hazelwood has a lot in common with McKeesport.

"These are my friends," Swin said of the folks she knows in McKeesport. "I have a photo album at home and it's filled with photos of me and my friends from high school. You have different kinds of friends when you go away to college. I haven't left any of my old friends for new friends. I've just added to my list of friends. Now I have an even bigger support group.

"When I was younger, I lived two buildings apart from Brandon Short. We grew up together. We had our own little group. They were good for me. They were making a path for myself. When they won the WPIAL and the PIAA it was so great for everyone. Everyone shared in the glory.

"There was a lot of opportunity to get in trouble in my early years. My mother took a novel approach. My mom always used to say that she couldn't tell me what to do. She let me fall a few times before she showed me the right path to walk. She let me make mistakes. All she could do was guide me and lead the way. She showed me the right path to take."

"Swin refuses to come in second."
— Gerald Grayson

While Swin Cash is best known as a basketball player, it was her achievements in track & field in her senior year that really revealed her athletic and competitive spirit at its best.

She had never run track before the spring of 1998, but she quickly established herself as someone to be feared. She made it to the 100-meter hurdles final of the WPIAL Class AAA championships in May of that year. Midway through the race, Cash was in the lead.

As Cash came over the sixth hurdle she hit it squarely with her right knee and nearly fell down. The hurdle fell to the ground, but Cash kept her balance somehow, stumbling and touching the ground with her long fingers. Somehow she righted herself and continued to run. She made up the ground she lost in the last 30 meters and won the race.

Her time was 15.1 seconds. As an observer put it at the time, Swin Cash's life is about overcoming hurdles — from growing up poor in the projects — to becoming a national-class athlete.

One of her biggest boosters watched from the stands that day. Gerald "Puddin" Grayson was her coach on the basketball team at McKeesport High School. He had been a football star there and before that with Bill Lickert's McKeesport Little Tigers and remained a local legend.

"Anybody else would've lost that hurdles race," Grayson said. "But what people don't know about Swin is that she refuses to come in second. If she played marbles, if she played tiddly winks, she would finish first because that's her nature and she just has a will not to lose.

"The important thing to remember about Swin is that she's a better person than basketball player."

That sounds like something Coach Grayson might say, as Swin sees it.

"He was more of an influence as a black male, someone who accomplished a lot," said Swin. "He talked to me a lot about life in general. He kept after me to stay humble. He tried to keep me level-headed. His constant speech was not about scoring 30 points a game; it was about what I needed to do to be a success in life.

"I remember in my first game when I went out for the high school team. I was going up against some seniors. One of the girls went to shoot the ball, and I blocked it really hard. That's when I knew I could play with the big girls. I knew I was going to go to school. I knew I was going to get a scholarship. I dreamed about playing for a championship team.

"I always had faith in myself. I wanted to be a pro basketball player someday before there was even a professional league for women. I watch the WNBA games and I want to be part of that someday. I've got to wait my turn, work on my game, get better and stronger."

Swin had another booster in Freddie Lewis, the only athlete to come out of McKeesport who played pro basketball, 11 years altogether, the first and last in the NBA and the other nine, mostly with the Indiana Pacers, in the ABA. He was in the ABA when it started in 1967 and when it was absorbed into the NBA in 1976. He played in four ABA all-star games and was a solid performer and one of the nicest guys in the league. He had been a classmate of my wife, Kathie, in high school and that helped us develop a long-time relationship.

Lewis came back to Pittsburgh from Washington D.C. in the spring of 2000 in an attempt to help bring a pro basketball team to Pittsburgh as a member of ABA 2000. It seemed like a long shot at best, but Lewis was always a great long shooter.

"I worked with Swin when she was in seventh grade," recalled Lewis. "I worked in some summer camps in McKeesport and Swin was always there. She knew back then that she wanted to be a college and pro basketball player someday. She was always working on her game. She was a good kid, someone you enjoyed working with."

Swin was lucky to have someone like Lewis, a good friend of her mother, to help show her the way. He was a far better role model, for example, than Allan Iverson, whom the NBA portrays in TV public service announcements as a good influence on street kids trying to find their way.

Her UConn coach, Geno Auriemma, has picked up the baton. "When she first came here I was surprised by her court knowledge and her defensive play," said Auriemma. "She's the quickest player on the team. She makes our press very tough. She has the talent to be a terrific player."

Cash made her mark immediately at UConn. She won several Rookie of the Week awards in The Big East. Her freshman class included a group of great high school players. They included Tamika Williams, Asjha Jones, Swin Cash, Sue Bird and Keirsten Walters. They were likened to the Fab Five of the Michigan men's team a few years earlier. They preferred being called the TASSK Force (using the first initial in their first names in the same order they appear above). Much was expected of this team. They were to get UConn back to the NCAA Final Four for the first time since 1996.

It made Swin feel she had made the right choice. Pitt came after her early and hard to stay at home. It began with Kirk Bruce and then with his successor, Traci Waites. If Waites would have gotten Cash it could've turned things around immediately. "I liked the people at Pitt, but it wasn't one of my top choices," said Swin.

"My top three choices were Penn State — a lot of people wanted me to play there — and Tennessee and Connecticut. Those two had the two best programs in the country. I wanted to go with the best. I couldn't have gone wrong either way." She chose UConn because she believed it offered her more opportunities for "what I really wanted to accomplish for myself."

One reason she picked UConn was so her family could see her play a lot at Georgetown (Washington, D.C.), Pitt and West Virginia.

She majors in communications with a sports marketing minor. She says it's all she expected it to be. "It's an adventure," she said. "It is everything I expected and more. Big crowds, pressure practices, pressure games, pressure to compete. It is right where I want to be to get to the next level."

UConn faced Penn State (30-4 at the time) in the national semi-final and came out on top. Tennessee beat Rutgers in the other semi-final to advance to the showdown with UConn. It was the fourth time in nine years UConn had made it to the Final Four.

"Our freshman year we came in and there was so much pressure, national championship talk every day," recalled Cash. "This year, there wasn't national championship talk every day. It was one long road with lots of little steps along the road."

Cash contributes a sense of peace to the UConn club. "I have a ritual," she said. "In the huddle before every game, I just tell my teammates 'take care of business.' That's what we have to do.

"I used to take extra shots in warm-up or change something before a big game, especially last year as a freshman. Then I kept telling myself business as usual, keeping the same mindset no matter who we were playing — Syracuse or Tennessee. I started telling my teammates that, too.

"Starting is an honor for me. My coach has shown he believes in me. And I've proven that I can handle it. Starting is something you have to earn every day in practice. It is motivation for me. Just because I started one game doesn't mean I am going to start again. I have to earn it. I have to prove myself every day.

"The competition can only make you better. When you sign a letter-of-intent to attend the University of Connecticut you know the competition is going to be great. You wouldn't have signed if you didn't want to compete.

"Coach Geno is great. He gets on you and really grills you in practice. He will ride you hard in practice to get the best out of you. Off the court, he listens to you. He has a different relationship with every player. He doesn't pick favorites and you know you can always talk to him or any of the coaches.

"I love traveling. Coach Auriemma always takes us here or here in different places. It's really nice because you never know when you'll have that opportunity again. When we were in Washington, we visited the capital, and stuff you don't know about you can learn first hand."

During the summer of 2000 she planned to work with kids in the public housing recreation center in McKeesport. "This won't be about basketball," said Swin. "I'll be talking to these kids about other things. I'll be talking to them about their social life. I want to show them the way like others have done for me. I want to help my community. Now it's my turn."

Jim O'Brien

Swin Cash feels comfortable when she's home with family and friends.

Jim O'Brien

Mark Recchi, Philadelphia Flyers:
"My hero was Bryan Trottier. I was playing in the Western Hockey League in Kamloops, British Columbia when the New York Islanders were winning all those Stanley Cups in the early '80s. I enjoyed the way he played. I enjoyed watching him. Then I got to play with him in Pittsburgh (1990-1992). I sat next to him in the locker room. It was a great thrill. I loved talking to him and learned a lot from him. It's one of the reasons I was often getting onto the ice late at practice. We had so many great guys on the team then, beginning with Mario Lemieux. I was a part of the first Stanley Cup champion team (1991). I've helped knock them out of the playoffs twice in recent years."

Jaromir Jagr
The Czech who came to play

"We have the best player in the world."
—Mario Lemieux

Penguins' fans were rooting for a hat trick in Toronto. Team captain Jaromir Jagr had a shot at coming home with three of the most prestigious honors at the National Hockey League's annual awards ceremony at Air Canada Centre.

Jagr went to Toronto assured that he wouldn't return empty-handed. He had already staked a claim to the Art Ross Trophy as the league's leading scorer. No one could deny him that. All he had to do was pick up the hardware. He achieved that with 42 goals and 54 assists for 96 points, even though he missed 19 games because of injuries. He and Mario Lemieux are the only players in league history to finish first in scoring while missing more than ten games. It was Jagr's fourth Ross Trophy, his third in a row.

This was Thursday, June 16, 2000. Jagr had come to Canada from the Czech Republic to pick up some more trophies for his sterling silver collection.

During the day, Jagr learned that he had won the Lester B. Pearson Award, given to "the league's outstanding player" in a poll of NHL players. He had won the same award a year earlier.

That seemed to bode well for Jagr's chances of taking home the Hart Trophy for the second consecutive season. The Hart Trophy is the older and more celebrated MVP award, voted on by the media. It dates back to 1924 and goes to the player adjudged to be "the most valuable to his team." Usually, both awards go to the same player.

Then, too, the Penguins were faring well that same day as far as honors were concerned. Former Penguin Joe Mullen received a telephone call at his home in Upper St. Clair around 11 a.m. from an NHL official in Toronto telling him that he had been voted into the Hockey Hall of Fame in his first year of eligibility.

Mullen had been a high-scoring contributor to Stanley Cup championships in Calgary and twice in Pittsburgh during a 16-year NHL career, six of them with the Penguins. He worked in community relations for the team, and helped to coordinate alumni activities, during much of the three years since he retired as a player. He was to be added to the coaching staff for the 2000-2001 season.

Hailing from Hell's Kitchen in New York City and the son of a facilities maintenance man at Madison Square Garden, Mullen was the first American-born player to record 500 goals and 1,000 points in an NHL career. His final numbers were 502 and 1,063, respectively. He was always popular with the players and the press.

Jagr photos by Matt Polk/Pittsburgh Penguins

So good news was coming out of Canada during the day. I was listening to the reports on ESPN Sports Radio (WEAE) throughout the day. The suspense surrounded the announcement yet to come at the awards ceremony dinner regarding the winner of the Hart Trophy. I wanted Jagr to capture all three awards, another hat trick in his fabulous career.

As it turned out, however, Jagr didn't get his hat trick. He lost out for the Hart Trophy by one point to St. Louis Blues defenseman Chris Pronger. The winner had 396 points to Jagr's 395. Florida Panthers right winger Pavel Bure, who was the league's leading goal-scorer with 58, finished third with 346 points. Pronger had a 25-18 edge in first place votes. Bure had 11 first place votes.

What cost Jagr the Hart Trophy was that four hockey writers gave Jagr fifth-place votes and, as it developed, a Pittsburgh writer picked Pronger over Jagr in his ballot. Each writer was to list five players on their ballot in the order of their value to their team. Four of them thought there were four players in the league who were more valuable to their team than Jagr. That's difficult to comprehend. If one of them had listed him one notch higher — fourth rather than fifth — Jagr would have won the Hart Trophy.

The *Pittsburgh Post-Gazette* carried a banner column at the top of its Sunday edition in which Dave Molinari, who had covered the Penguins for 17 years, disclosed that he had Pronger in first place and Jagr in second place on his ballot. Molinari offered a well-thought-out explanation to defend his choice. He mentioned that his vote cost Jagr a contract bonus of $100,000. Molinari believed that Jagr was the outstanding player in the NHL, but that Pronger was more valuable to his team during the 1999-2000 season. The disclosure would more than likely end up costing Molinari something, too. Team officials, players and fans didn't figure to be too forgiving no matter Molinari's reasoning. They tend to view these things while wearing blinders.

Pronger, in a diplomatic gesture, suggested the difference might have been that Jagr missed 19 regular season games, nearly a fourth of the schedule. That's a valid point, and Molinari mentioned that as well.

Players always say it means more to them when they are honored by their peers than by the press. Jagr was no different in that respect. The year before, when he won both the Ross Trophy and the Pearson Award, Jagr had said that the latter was the most coveted. "It's a trophy voted on by the players you play against, the players you face every night," offered Jagr.

Be assured, however, that most media take their voting much more seriously than the players or coaches in any sport. They do their homework before filling out such ballots.

As for the Ross Trophy, Jagr passed the praise generously to his fellow workers in the Penguins organization.

"To win this trophy," he said, "you've got to be lucky and have a lot of help. This year, I wasn't really lucky. I had a lot of injuries. But

I did get a lot of help from the coaching staff and, of course, the players."

The brass of the Penguins offered much praise for their captain. Before the announcement, Lemieux made it known how he felt about his team's leader. "We have the best player in the world," Lemieux proclaimed. "He had a great year, and I'm looking forward to a lot of great things from our captain in the next few years, too."

Craig Patrick, the Penguins' general manager, was just as much a Jagr booster for the Hart Trophy. "Just look at what he's done for us," said Patrick prior to the awards ceremony. "The way he competed for us, the way he came up big for us all season. Anytime we needed a big goal or a big play, he was the guy. And he really seemed to take to the challenge. He's grown into a great leader as well as a great player."

"I'd like to do what Mario did."
—Jaromir Jagr

Time flies when you're having fun. It seems like only yesterday when Jaromir Jagr joined the Pittsburgh Penguins, and teamed with Mario Lemieux & Co. to win two consecutive Stanley Cup championships.

That was in 1991 and 1992, and that's almost ancient history. Jagr was just 19 and 20 years old, respectively, during those giddy times. He came from Kladno, a small town just northwest of Prague in the Czech Republic, and became an instant sensation at the Civic Arena. He won over fans with his handsome smiling face, his hard-working ways and, most of all, his ice-skating and stick handling ability that was right up there with Lemieux and Paul Coffey in a star-studded lineup.

He was surround by some terrific players, such as Mark Recchi, Kevin Stevens, Joe Mullen, Larry Murphy, Rick Tocchet, Bryan Trottier, Ulf Samuelsson, Tom Barrasso and Ken Wregget.

Jagr was known for his speed, on and off the ice, his passion, strength and shooting accuracy. The Kid from Kladno captured the hearts of hockey fans everywhere. He was the pink-cheeked darling of the Civic Arena, now known as Mellon Arena. His shoulder- length dark brown locks appealed to many of the fans, especially the young ladies.

Someone figured out that if you jumbled the name Jaromir you could come up with Mario, Jr. Stan Savran made sure we knew about it. That said it all. He was the obvious successor to Lemieux as the leading scorer on the Penguins.

Jagr struggled at the start, with the English language and his role on a team stocked by general manager Craig Patrick with many well-established veterans. Most of the other Penguins seemed so serious at times, and Jagr — or "Jags" as he was called — just wanted to have fun.

It was a great time for sports fans and citizens of Pittsburgh. They were having fun, too. Once again, Pittsburgh was the "City of Champions." Mike Lange, "the voice of the Penguins," was delighting them with his descriptive phrasings ("scratch my back with a hacksaw" and "buy one for my dog, too") in radio and TV broadcasts of the games. Elvis and The Fat Lady were leaving the building together. Pittsburghers hadn't felt so good since the '70s when the Steelers won four Super Bowls, the Pirates won two World Series and the University of Pittsburgh won a national football championship, among the many achievements accomplished by local teams.

I can recall seeing "Jags" — pronounced "Yags" — in the Penguins' locker room after games and practice sessions. He was constantly cutting up, flexing his muscles in the mirror, talking aloud to no one in particular about his handsome appearance, nudging the white towel wrapped around his middle to make himself look like more of a hunk as he studied his bare-chest form. He moved to the music blaring from stereo speakers. He made fun of himself and everyone around him. It was no wonder young women loved this newcomer so much. They would have gone crazy if they could have seen him standing in front of a locker room mirror, flexing his muscles and fooling with the edges of his wrap-around towel. He would have been a big hit with his "tease" routine at a bachelorette party. I remember seeing him riding around on the back of a convertible automobile at a Stanley Cup celebration held at Three Rivers Stadium. He waved to the crowd and he couldn't have looked happier.

Some of the women fans waved back and blew kisses at him.

There were stories making the rounds about Jagr's love for fast cars and fast women. He was stopped for speeding on more than one occasion, but he managed to get out of most jams. No one was going to put Jaromir Jagr in front of a judge, or worse yet, in jail. He had the cherubic face of an angel.

"Every young girl in Pittsburgh wants to marry him," said teammate Rick Tocchet. "Of course, every cop in the city knows him, too."

Those who knew their Penguins history hoped Jagr would be luckier than Michel Briere, a 20-year-old center with great promise who died from injuries suffered in a high-speed auto crash back in 1970. That was a dark day in the team's history. One of the team's executives, Baz Bastien, also died from injuries suffered in a solo auto accident in Pittsburgh's South Hills. Time passes. Since the Toronto Maple Leafs left Maple Leaf Gardens two years earlier, the Civic Arena, which opened in 1961, became the oldest building in the National Hockey League. The NHL landscape was changing. There was an NHL team in Charlotte and Nashville and one was coming in Columbus. Jagr wasn't a kid anymore.

Jagr was born February 15, 1972, the same year the Steelers qualified for the National Football League playoffs for the first time in

the team's 39-year history. Two weeks before Jagr's birth, Red Kelly surrendered the position of general manager of the Penguins back to Jack Riley, but Kelly would continue to coach the team. The Penguins, in their fifth year of operation, would finish fourth in the West Division and were swept in four games in the first round of the NHL playoffs. The Penguins had no captain that year. They had new owners —Tad Potter of Pittsburgh headed the group — but in a few years they would be in bankruptcy court. The team's offices would have its doors padlocked by IRS agents. Lemieux is the first Pittsburgher since Potter, by the way, to be the team's principal owner.

That helps put Jagr's birth in its proper historical perspective.

Like Lemieux, he would prove to be something of a savior for the franchise. Both were pictured on the cover of the Penguins 1999-2000 press guide. Lemieux had put together yet another new group of owners to rescue the financially strapped franchise from being folded by the NHL. Jagr was going to be a captain who was expected to play up to the same standards set by Lemieux. That meant leading the team back to winning the Stanley Cup.

The torch had been passed.

As the 2000-2001 season approached, Lemieux, who would be 35 in October, had been retired as a player for the previous three seasons. Jagr was now 28 years old and had played ten seasons for the Penguins.

"It's been a long time since I won the Stanley Cup," Jagr said during the playoffs that culminated the 1999-2000 season. He was talking as he stood by his locker at Iceoplex at Southpointe, the Penguins' practice facility. The Penguins teased their fans, by upsetting the favored Philadelphia Flyers in the first two games of their best-of-seven series, then folded in four straight. If the Penguins had gotten past the Flyers, their fans would have been riding high. Anything would then seem possible.

Patrick had made trades for six players just before the NHL's trading deadline, so a third of the skaters were new to the team at season's end. They finished strong and, led by a rejuvenated Jagr, looked capable of going all the way. It wasn't to be, however, and Jagr could foresee the disappointment of Pittsburgh fans. He was still not a hundred percent healthy in the playoffs.

"I know people are going to judge me by how many times I've won the Stanley Cup and if I can get the team there," he said. "Right now, I'm the captain and I'd like to do what Mario did. He brought the Stanley Cup to Pittsburgh."

Jagr has been successful in succeeding Lemieux as the league's scoring leader, but a third Stanley Cup has eluded him. The Penguins, thanks to Lemieux and Jagr had won 10 of the previous 13 scoring titles, with Wayne Gretzky gaining the honors the other three times.

With Lemieux and Gretzky gone, Jagr had clearly established himself as the best player in the league. It would be hard to comprehend what the Penguins' appeal in Pittsburgh would be like without

Lemieux and Jagr in the lineup. Having such great players skating for the home club over such a long span has spoiled Penguins' fans.

Still, Jagr was hardly satisfied. Personal accomplishments are fine, but team accomplishments are more important. Asked how he felt about winning the scoring title again, Jagr said, "I would lie if I said it wasn't important. Yes, it was important. I consider myself a scorer. That's how I judge myself compared to other players. Winning the scoring title is a big thing for me. But it's not the most important thing. Winning the Stanley Cup is the most important thing. It's been too long."

Jagr's name appears twice on the Stanley Cup, but he knows that the great ones appear more often. That's Jagr's goal in the new millennium. "People say I should be able to do it," he said.

He was paid $10.5 million to play for the Penguins in 1999-2000. He played only 63 games, missing most games because of leg injuries. Playing in 81 games the previous season, he had 44 goals and 83 assists for 127 points.

"It was a pretty tough year for me," Jagr said of the 1999-2000 campaign. "I had a lot of injuries, and I didn't play many games. Every time I came back, I didn't have a chance to practice properly, and something else would happen."

Even so, there were some playoff games in which Jagr was downright spectacular. Herb Brooks, who replaced Kevin Constantine as coach during the season, stepped down at the completion of the playoffs. Brooks is a big fan of Jagr. "He can lead the team to higher levels and to the Stanley Cup," observed Brooks. "There's no question in my mind. That's how good he is."

Jagr was now mentioned with the likes of Lemieux, Gretzky, Bobby Hull, Gordie Howe and Bobby Orr as one of the greatest players in NHL history. Jagr knew he was good, real good, but he had difficulty feeling that he belonged in that kind of esteemed company.

Jagr was back home in the Czech Republic in late May, 2000 when one of hockey's all-time great players, Maurice "The Rocket" Richard, died at age 78 after a long battle with abdominal cancer and Parkinson's disease. Richard's death caused mourning throughout Canada and, most of all, in Montreal where he once led the Canadiens to a string of Stanley Cup championships. His body lay in state at the Notre Dame Basilica and thousands came to pay their respects. It got front-page attention in the Pittsburgh papers as well.

Jagr is still too young to appreciate what Rocket Richard was all about. I remember how impressed I was with meeting and shaking hands with Richard and Jean Beliveau once in the media dining room at the Montreal Forum. Beliveau was a senior vice president of the club at the time.

Jagr did see Richard, looking poorly from his health challenges, at the league's All-Star Game in Toronto at mid-season. The NHL was hosting its 50th All-Star Game at the Air Canada Centre. Jagr scored a goal in that game and attracted a lot of attention. Maurice Richard was one of the dozen or so players present who had played in the 1947 All-Star Game. His kid brother, Henri "The Pocket Rocket" Richard, was among the many former outstanding players who were showcased at the weekend extravaganza February 5-6, 2000. So Richard's death should have hit home with Jagr. As he gets closer to being 30, he has matured, and he has learned to appreciate what the NHL is all about.

In short, he has learned that hockey did not start with Lemieux or Jagr. (By late June, the Canadiens would be put up for sale by the Molson Brewery Co.)

The Canadiens were a dynasty in the 1950s. Among the mourners were some of Richard's former teammates such as Jean Beliveau, Dickie Moore and Elmer Lach. The Penguins didn't come close to the success of those Canadiens. Lemieux, who grew up in Montreal not far from the ice rink where the Canadiens competed, was more familiar with Richard and the tradition of the Montreal Canadiens.

Jagr received more votes than any other player in a public voting for the NHL All-Star Game. He was the first, in fact, to receive more than a million votes. He could be forgiven if he thought he had arrived. He knew, though, that it was not enough.

"To be on top for a little time is not good enough," said Jagr during the playoffs. "You want to be there for a long, long time."

Eddie Johnston, the assistant general manager of the Penguins, also grew up near the Montreal Forum. He was playing goalie in the NHL at age 42. He was the last goalie to play every game in a season. He played in the days before goalies wore masks. In short, he's been around the league a few times as a player, coach, scout and executive.

He played in the Mellon Mario Lemieux Celebrity Invitational at Nevillewood in early June of 2000. I asked Johnston about Jagr. "He's the best in the game, by far," Johnston said. "He's so strong, so powerful, and he comes out of the corner with the puck, and flies past people in traffic like no other since Lemieux and Gretzky. He was fortunate to come along behind Mario. He learned a lot from him about how to play the game. He also learned how to be a good captain. I don't like comparing him to Mario or anyone else for that matter. Jaromir Jagr can stand on his own."

There's a game that sticks out, as many do, that gives you an idea of what Jagr is all about. Jagr stole the spotlight away from Gretzky on a special night the New York Rangers were holding at Madison Square Garden to say goodbye to one of the greatest players in league history during his final season. Jagr scored a goal in overtime in a 2-1 victory for the visiting Penguins. He scored on a one-on-one breakaway against Rangers' goalie Mike Richter. Jagr had his stick ahead and behind the puck — forehand, backhand, forehand — and drilled a shot between Richter's pads. Jagr apologized to Gretzky afterward, "I didn't mean to do that." Gretzky grinned when Jagr said that. "That's what I used to say," gushed Gretzky.

Always knowing the right thing to say, Gretzky told reporters, "Maybe it was only fitting that the best young player in the game scored the goal in overtime. Everyone always talks about passing torches and all that kind of stuff. Well, he caught it. That's what I told him after the game."

When that remark was relayed to Jagr, he was just as smooth in his response. "I appreciate it," said Jagr. "Especially from a guy like him, the best player ever."

"I feel I'll be better than everybody else."

Jaromir Jagr lives in a stately two-story brick home on a quiet cul-de-sac in Upper St. Clair, about three miles from my home in the South Hills of Pittsburgh. His home is at the southern tip of the community, amid newer and bigger homes, near the border that separates Allegheny County from Washington County. People have pointed out his home to me when I've traveled on Route 19. His home is about seven miles from the Iceoplex at Southpointe, the Penguins' practice facility in Canonsburg, so it's a quick commute for him to work.

Mario Lemieux used to have a mansion-like home in Mt. Lebanon, when the Penguins practiced at the public rink in that neighboring suburban community. In more recent years, Lemieux has lived in an older equally large home in Sewickley. He lives there with his wife, Nathalie, and their four children.

Jagr was still single. His mother often stays at his home and looks after him. Previously, they lived with a Czech family in West Homestead, once a bustling mill town.

Even though he makes millions, Jagr has a millworker's mentality when it comes time to go to work. No one works harder at practice. Often, he is the last to leave the ice. He feels it's important for him to build his strength and stamina. The effort will pay off dividends when he's playing in NHL games, especially late in NHL games, especially in overtime periods. He seems to excel in marathon contests.

"I know I have some kind of talent," said Jagr, "and I know what I've got. And I know that if I work very hard —more than anybody else — I feel I'll be better than everybody else."

His new boss believes Jagr is now the NHL's finest player. "He's awesome," allowed Lemieux. "Right from the start, you knew he was going to be a special player."

Jagr has always been deferential to Lemieux. After all, Lemieux won six league scoring championships, three MVP awards, two Conn Smythe Trophies as MVP of the playoffs (1991 and 1992) and the Calder Trophy as rookie of the year in 1984-85.

Talking about Lemieux, Jagr said, "I know that no matter what I would do, if he would do the same thing, I would never be better than him. There was a big distance between us. It would be tough to match him.

"When he wanted to win something, I didn't have a chance. He was the one guy I could never beat. When you look at the last five years, I won the scoring championships because Lemieux didn't play. When he played, I always finished second or something. Nobody had a chance when he played."

Jagr, like Lemieux, has some scoring sequences that are highlight reels. He says they are all improvised. "I don't think at all," said Jagr. "Natural things come to me, how I'm going to play. I cannot explain it. But I don't think I'm going to do this and that and that. Hockey's so quick you cannot think about something before you do it. It's impossible. "

"He's a very emotional kid."
—Mike Lange

His parents started taking him to public skating sessions when he was two years old. At 5, he played on his first hockey team.

"I wasn't good at all," recalls Jagr. "I always played with people two years older. My dad knew the coach and that's what he thought would be best for me."

That's also when Jagr began doing knee-bends and push-ups at his father's behest. When he was 6, Jagr was able to do 600 knee-bends. When he was 8, he claims he was up to 2,000 knee-bends and 100 push-ups every day. That's why his legs are so strong. Today, Jagr is one of the hardest and most impressive workers in the weight room.

In his youth, his bedroom walls were lined with posters of his favorite Czech hockey players. "We never really heard about the NHL," he said.

When Jaromir was six, he practiced hockey with three different age groups, getting three times as much ice time as his peers. "That was my father's idea," said Jaromir. "When I played against other six-year-olds, I was great. When I played against 10-year-olds, I was average. My father wanted me to play where I was average."

His father played street hockey with his son after school. They played in a dirt yard between the family's house and barn, often scattering a dozen chickens that the family kept in the yard.

His dad used an axle off one of his old tractors to craft a homemade set of barbells for Jaromir.

When Jagr was eight years old, he started hearing about Gretzky scoring goals and racking up assists at an unprecedented pace. That's when he was hungry to learn more about what was going on in the NHL.

At age 13, Jagr saw Gretzky and Lemieux play in Prague in the World Championships in 1985.

"Those were the only names I knew," recalled Jagr. "But I knew about life in America, and I knew about the NHL. My first goal was to play for the local team in my city. My second goal was to play for the national team of Czechoslovakia, because that is my country. But my third goal was to play in the NHL, because that is the best hockey in the world."

As a 12-year-old, Jagr had a paramount goal to come to America and to play in the NHL. He carried a picture of then-U.S. President Ronald Reagan in his schoolbooks to remind him of his mission.

This was not a smart thing to do in a Communist country. He was scolded by a teacher for carrying the picture, and he was told to get rid of it. He did, but later reclaimed the photo. There was no stopping the jingoistic Jagr.

In late 1992, when Reagan's aides heard about the story after the Penguins won a second straight Stanley Cup, they set up a telephone call between the former chief executive and the emerging NHL star.

"He told me 'thank you' for the nice talk about the U.S.A. and about him," recalled Jagr. "It was my best day. I never talked to a guy like him. Ever."

Jagr has expressed an interest in learning more about Czech history, spurred perhaps by what he has learned about his own family's proud heritage. Jagr's grandmother, Jarmila, told the boy about the first Jaromir Jagr, his grandfather and her husband.

That Jaromir had his own farm that the Communists took over in 1948. They took all his land, and took most of his livestock. They left him with the house, barn and yard where the family still resides today.

His grandfather was thrown into jail for refusing to cooperate with the Communists. He was imprisoned for two years.

Jaromir Jagr, the Penguins' player, never knew his grandfather. His grandfather died in 1968, four years before the younger Jaromir was born.

"In school, we were always taught the Soviet doctrine," said the Penguins' Jaromir Jagr. "We were taught the U.S.A. was bad and wanted war. Russia was a friend and was preventing the U.S. from bombing us. Even my father didn't tell me the truth, because he was afraid I'd say something in school that would get us into trouble. But my grandmother told me the truth."

Jagr was the Penguins No. 1 draft choice in the 1990 entry draft. Patrick took a risk in drafting Jagr. There was no assurance at the time that he would be able to come to America. Czechoslovakia was in political turmoil at the time, and a revolution against a Soviet-controlled government had broken out.

His homeland's revolution allowed him to be one of the first Czech athletes who didn't have to defect to perform in the United States. Out of respect, he chose uniform number 68 to commemorate the year when Soviet troops stormed the country he still calls home. He became the youngest player on a team primed for its first taste of glory. He was known to have "big hair and hot air" and the older players got a kick out of him.

Even after Jagr was in Pittsburgh a few years, he was still feeling his way in the dark. "He's a very emotional kid," Penguins' broadcaster Mike Lange said at the time. "I don't think people realize how emotional he is, day-to-day. We all lose sight of the fact that he's 21. His mom is here with him now, and she's emotional, too. She'll read things in the newspaper about him and she'll start crying, and we don't know why."

Jagr did his best to explain his dilemma.

"The hardest part for me is, you know, I can watch TV and I can talk to people, but I never find out who is a good person, who is a bad person," he said. "Maybe I will never find out, because I wasn't born here. Maybe I will never speak so good English that I will ever find out. That's the biggest problem, you know. Should you be friends with somebody or should you not? It's hard, you know, it's very hard."

It was evident by those remarks that Jagr, just like most American youngsters, had learned to pepper his conversation with the "you know" phrase.

"I was born to have fun all the time."
—Jaromir Jagr

Asked why he cut his hair short for the 1999-2000 season, he said, "I just decided it was time." Some saw it as a sign that Jagr was growing up, becoming a man, becoming someone, like Lemieux, who could lead his team to greatness.

Reflecting on his early days with the Penguins, Jagr said, "I was lucky to play with a team with so many great players. I think that's the best thing that happened to me. Everything I know I learned from them.

"You think you know everything when you are 18, but you know nothing," Jagr says now. "In some ways, it helped me. I was cocky. I always did my thing. I didn't think about if it can hurt me. I just did it my way all the time.

"Now I'm still doing it my way, but when I look back and think about what I did when I was younger, I say, 'What was I thinking?' I was the kind of player who, one-on-one, tried to beat everybody by myself. Now I use the players around me more often.

"When I first came here I played ten minutes a game. Now I play 30. That's a big difference. You have to know how to save energy when you're on the ice.

"To have fun during a game, to have real fun, you've got to be in good shape. Because if you're better than the other team, if you're in better shape and can skate better, you can make it fun. Winning is fun.

"If you're better than the other team you can make it fun on the ice. You can laugh. If you're losing, you cannot have fun. Everybody's laughing at you."

He's putting in more playing time and he's getting paid a little better per hour, too. In 1998, Jagr signed a six-year deal worth about $48 million.

"I just love the game. People don't understand why you can like it so much, but you have so much fun. I play for more than the money. What are you gonna do with it? Five million, 40 million, 50 million, it's the same thing. You're still gonna die."

Jagr knows that the future of the Penguins was in jeopardy in the summer of 1999, and credits Mario Lemieux for saving the franchise. Asked about his relationship with Lemieux, who became his boss, he said, "It's the same. He's a very nice guy, a funny guy, who loves to have fun. But very private."

Jagr also won a 1998 Olympic gold medal with the Czech Republic and so many individual awards in recent years.

When he won the Lester N. Pearson Award as the MVP as voted by his fellow players, Jagr designated an orphanage in the Czech Republic as recipient of the $10,000 that went with the award.

It should be pointed out that he does participate in several Pittsburgh-based fund-raising projects. He has participated in the Pittsburgh Penguins Cystic Fibrosis Dinner, the Penguins' Make-A-Wish Party, and has made team-sponsored visits to Children's Hospital.

"I wish I could play till I'm 40," he said, "but the guys are getting so big, so strong. It'll be tough. It's very tough."

Like Lemieux, he also complained about growing trends around the NHL that were taking some of the fun and finesse out of the game. He was talking about the clutching and grabbing of goal-scorers, and using conservative strategies to stop or limit talented players like Jagr.

"I don't think it's the defense," he explained. "It's the system the players play. It's getting close to football. Pretty soon everyone is going to have microphones in their helmets, and coaches are going to tell you, 'Skate this way' and 'Skate that way.' Everything is so organized.

"When I came here, my first two years, everybody played man on man. If you were good enough to beat the guy, you had a free way to go to the net. Now, everybody plays positions, like a unit. If somebody loses the man, somebody else steps in, just like basketball. They double-team you."

Jagr has gotten himself in a jam from time to time with something he said, or something someone figured he'd said. Sometimes something is lost in the translation, Jagr's translation usually. He suggests that everyone should be cautious of being critical of what he says, or is supposed to have said.

225

"Whatever I say, 90 per cent of the time, I'm just joking. I don't stay serious. I like to have fun all the time, make fun all the time about everybody. People want to be serious all the time. I was born to have fun all the time."

JAROMIR JAGR

Jim O'Brien

Mark Malone, former Steelers quarterback
ESPN TV and Radio sportscaster:
"Willie Mays was my main guy. I played a lot of baseball long before I got into football. I pitched and played centerfield and he embodied everything a centerfielder was supposed to be. I had a Willie Mays autographed mitt and a Willie Mays autographed bat. I think I asked for No. 24 and I'm not sure you could do that then. I watched Willie on TV, but I never had a chance to see him play in person. Two years ago, I was at Bally's in Atlantic City and I had an opportunity to meet him. He works for Bally's. Someone took a photo of me speaking to him. I had him sign it. It's the only thing I possess that has an autograph."

Wilt Chamberlain
A giant in every way

"Nobody loves Goliath."
—Jerry West

I couldn't believe that Wilt Chamberlain had died. He was a giant, seemingly indestructible, the most physically impressive person I have ever met. So I was stunned when I heard he had been found dead in his home in suburban Los Angeles. He died at age 63 of congestive heart failure on Tuesday, October 12, 1999.

I agree with those who say that while Michael Jordan was the best basketball player there ever was, Wilt Chamberlain was the most dominant.

Chamberlain was a compelling figure, for sure. He was one of the first sports personalities who demanded our attention. Chamberlain was a constant enigma, which was part of his charm.

He stood above every crowd and he was a cool customer. He always looked good, and dressed the part of a successful performer.

He didn't win as many NBA titles as Bill Russell and the Boston Celtics, but his supporting cast was seldom as good. As great as Russell was, he was not as good as Chamberlain. No one was. No. 13 was special.

A native of Philadelphia and the best basketball player ever to emerge from Pennsylvania, Chamberlain was a controversial and fascinating figure in the world of sports. Love him or hate him, Chamberlain left his mark, and set one of his NBA records in Pittsburgh, of all places. He retired as the leading scorer and rebounder in NBA history. He held the pro scoring record of 31,419 points, the highest lifetime average of 30.1 points, the most minutes played and the most rebounds. Some of those have since been surpassed. He never fouled out of a game.

He won seven scoring titles, 11 rebounding titles and there was that 100-point game in Hershey, Pennsylvania.

Three of his most outstanding efforts came in three unlikely outposts, namely Hershey, Bethlehem and Pittsburgh. Even though the 76ers had the best player and one of the best teams in league history, they had to farm out some of their home games to meet the payroll. That tells you something about the economics of the NBA in those barnstorming days. Those are the sort of thoughts that raced through my mind as I motored along Route 30 after learning of his death.

I was leaving Latrobe en route home from an appearance at a business fair at the Latrobe Area High School gymnasium sponsored by the Latrobe Chamber of Commerce when I heard on the radio that Chamberlain had died. It hurt to hear that news. I heard it on WCNS Radio, the Latrobe station. Its owner and general manager, John Longo, had invited me to Latrobe that night.

Chamberlain shows sign after scoring 100 points at Hershey.

Wilt wears Lakers colors.

Photos from Street & Smith's Basketball

Chamberlain is doused with champagne by teammates after leading 76ers past Boston Celtics, 140-116, to win NBA championship series four games to one in 1967.

I had seen a portrait of Arnold Palmer on display in the lobby at Latrobe High School. I wasn't aware of that portrait's presence at his alma mater when I wrote a chapter about Palmer in my most recent book, *Hometown Heroes*, and I was wishing I had known about it when I wrote that piece. If Palmer was the most popular sports performer to ever come out of Pennsylvania, then certainly Chamberlain was one of its most intriguing.

I was driving down Route 30 West, moving past the Arnold Palmer Cadillac agency, then the Arnold Palmer Airport — there was a road nearby named in Palmer's honor as well — and then the entrance to St. Vincent College. Mixed memories were swirling through my mind. It's easier to picture the past when you are driving in the dark of the night.

I had thoughts of covering the Super Bowl champion Steelers in the late '70s for *The Pittsburgh Press*, and times I had spent at their summer training camp at St. Vincent's. Those thoughts were fighting for attention with memories of times spent interviewing and watching Wilt Chamberlain when I covered the New York Knicks in the NBA title series with Wilt's LA Lakers at the outset of the '70s.

It struck me that I was bothered more by the news that Chamberlain had died than I was when my mother woke me up on New Year's Day in 1973 to tell me the Pirates' Roberto Clemente had died the night before in an airplane crash in his native Puerto Rico. More mixed memories.

It struck me that my father was also 63 when he died. I thought my dad was old when he died. Now I was 57. I no longer thought my dad was so old when he died.

Wilt was always one of my favorites.

Wilton Norman Chamberlain had been a well-known scholastic star at Overbrook High School in Philadelphia. They ruled the Philly prep circuit. I recalled how Ed McCluskey's Farrell High School team had upset Overbrook in a holiday tournament in Farrell.

Chamberlain had led Overbrook High to three public league championships and two all-city titles in Philadelphia. He set off a recruiting war among 200 colleges. He went to Kansas where he played two varsity seasons. Freshmen weren't eligible for varsity competition in those days. In his first varsity game at Kansas, he scored 52 points against Northwestern, a total he never topped the remainder of his college career. As a junior, he led Kansas to the NCAA championship game with North Carolina, but his team came up short against Frank McGuire's Tar Heels.

He was frustrated by the double-teaming he constantly confronted. He said later, "I was guarded so closely that I thought I was going to spend the rest of my life looking out at the world through wiggling fingers, forearms and elbows."

Chamberlain had grown up in a family of nine children. His father was a handyman and his mother a domestic. He was 22 inches long at birth. At 15, he grew four inches in three months and he was

Wilt, at right, in U. of Kansas days

230

6-11 when he entered high school. He grew to be 7-foot-2, 275 pounds. He was one of the first giants to be athletically coordinated. He could do anything he liked, and he liked to tell you about his athletic prowess as well as his sexual prowess. He loved the women, but he never married.

He was a track & field star at the University of Kansas as well as the best college basketball player in the land. He was the Big Eight high jump champion three years in a row, he put the shot 56 feet, ran the 100-yard dash in 10.9 seconds, and triple jumped more than 50 feet. A bright man, he once said if he had been 6-foot-2 or smaller, he'd have been a Philadelphia lawyer. His size was both an asset and a burden. Everybody expected more of him than he could deliver, and his feats were often dismissed because he was bigger than everybody else. Some of his critics didn't think Wilt was a winner. Explaining Chamberlain's difficulties at pleasing people, Jerry West once said, "Nobody loves Goliath." It was a constant refrain.

I remembered that when the great sportswriter Jimmy Cannon was dying in a hospital in New York City in the mid-70s, I overheard Cannon telling a nurse about Wilt Chamberlain and he recalled that line about how "nobody loves Goliath."

I liked Chamberlain, however, and recall many satisfying and rewarding interviews with him. In the early '70s, for some inexplicable reason, there were several controversial sports figures with strong Pennsylvania links. They included Chamberlain, Joe Namath, Bill Hartack, Rich Allen and Muhammad Ali.

Namath, the New York Jets quarterback, hailed from Beaver Falls and we knew some of the same people. Hartack, a tough-talking first-class jockey, came from Johnstown. Allen, a power hitter in baseball, was from Wampum. When Chuck Tanner of New Castle was managing the Chicago White Sox, he helped me with Allen, who wasn't talking to most newsmen at the time. Ali, who came out of Louisville, often trained in the Poconos and once made attempts to buy a home in the Mt. Lebanon section of Pittsburgh, before he realized that he would not be welcome by his prospective neighbors. Chris and Angelo Dundee, two key boxing figures in the formative years of Ali (aka Cassius Clay) when he trained in Miami, were from Philadelphia. They were friends of Steelers owners Art Rooney and Barney McGinley in Pitttsburgh. So my Pittsburgh background was a big plus in being able to interview these often recalcitrant and moody men.

Chamberlain had a bad stutter in his early school days, but overcame the handicap to become a glib, smooth-talking individual as an adult. He had a great voice, rich and warm, and he could tell stories with the best of them.

Chamberlain never kept his thoughts to himself. Some were turned off by a black man with so much to say, especially during the racially charged '60s and early '70s.

He talked about becoming an Olympic decathlon performer, and often said he was willing to fight Ali if the price was right. He talked about becoming a pass-catcher in the NFL. He boasted about his ability as a volleyball player and frequented the California beaches to play against the best in that game. After retiring from basketball, he starred in the short-lived International Volleyball Association. He loved to discuss geography and politics, anything for an argument. He had an opinion about everything. He called friends at three in the morning to offer his thoughts on sundry subjects.

"He was genuine," said Gail Goodrich, a great guard and one of his teammates on those outstanding Lakers teams of the early '70s. "He was just a nice guy who liked people.

"He liked to hold court and he loved attention and he loved controversy. As a result, I think the media fed of that and you didn't really get a feel for who he really was."

Chamberlain could be difficult and he could be so much fun, so entertaining. He had a hearty laugh and a great smile. Everything about him was larger than life.

"He was loving and caring," said Billy Cunningham.

"The Knicks didn't want him to get a hundred."
—Paul Arizin

I remember visiting the Hershey Arena in the early 70s when I was in Hershey for a weekend getaway with my family. I saw the plaque that commemorated Chamberlain's record 100-point night there on March 2, 1962 against the New York Knicks.

A notoriously poor foul shooter — ala Shaquille O'Neal — Chamberlain also set another record that night when he hit 28 foul shots, missing only four from the foul line.

Paul Arizin was in the Warriors lineup that night at Hershey. Arizin had been an All-American at Villanova and one of the NBA's early scoring leaders. I saw him play for the Quantico Marines at the Pitt Field House during the 1952-53 season when he was in the military service. Dick Groat played at the Field House that same year with the Ft. Belvoir basketball team.

"As the game wore on," Arizin said of that night in Hershey, "no one realized he had scored so many points. We had a 15-point lead over the Knicks for most of the game. We were in command so I sat out the fourth quarter.

"We didn't realize how many points he had until late in the game when the public address announcer began to say how many points he had. He was already in the high 80s. Then it became a game in reverse. The Knicks didn't want him to get 100.

"They were trying to freeze the ball. Or, if we got the ball, they would foul our guards before we could get the ball to Wilt. But he did it, and the Knicks didn't give him one easy basket that night."

For the record, Chamberlain also had the highest-scoring game for a rookie, scoring 58 against the Detroit Pistons on January 25, 1960 in Bethlehem, Pennsylvania, of all places.

Chamberlain claims so many records. He had 118 games in which he scored over 50 points. During the 1961-62 season, he had 45 games in which he scored more than 50 points. He scored 50 or more points in seven games that same campaign.

He joined the Philadelphia Warriors of the NBA in 1959. He was Rookie of the Year and Most Valuable Player, setting league records for most points with 2,707, most rebounds with 1,941, and most points per game with 37.6.

He broke his own records each of the next seasons, peaking at an incredible 4,029 points, an average of 50.4 a game, in the 1961-62 season.

He went with the Warriors when they moved to San Francisco for the 1962-63 season, and then joined a new Philadelphia team, the 76ers, in 1964. Chamberlain's teams had lost five times to the Celtics in five playoff meetings, but they finally beat the Celtics and won the NBA championship in 1967.

The following season, Chamberlain changed his game entirely, and concentrated on passing to the open man when he was double-teamed. He led the league in assists, the only center ever to accomplish that. Chamberlain liked to take on challenges like that, to amuse himself and show everyone how versatile he was. He was the league's MVP for the third year in a row.

He was traded to the Los Angeles Lakers in 1968. In 1972 he played on his second NBA title team, as the Lakers won 12 of 15 playoff games, beating the Knicks 4 games to 1 in the final series. Chamberlain retired after one more season with the Lakers.

Practicing Wilt's finger-tip roll shot

As a teenager, I kept a close watch on Wilt Chamberlain. I read every story about him in *Sport* magazine, the daily newspapers and looked forward to when he would appear on the Sunday NBA telecast on ABC-TV, with Chris Schenkel and Pittsburgh's own Jack Twyman calling the shots.

As great as Chamberlain was, you didn't get to see much of him on TV in the late '50s and early '60s. There were no round-the-clock sports shows on TV or radio back then. There was no ESPN, no sports talk shows. So every game on TV, no matter the sport, was special.

In Pittsburgh, we got to see the Steelers and the Baltimore Colts on TV, which meant I had a chance to see another boyhood hero,

Pittsburgh-born Johnny Unitas in action on the black and silver screen.

Chamberlain was the biggest of sports stars. When I would be fooling around with a basketball at the hoop in front of my house, I would mimic my favorite pros and attempt to shoot shots the way they did. Wilt had this finger tip-roll shot in which he would extend his right arm and let the ball roll off his fingertips down into the hoop. It helped to do that shot effectively if your hand was extended higher than the hoop.

I'm not sure why I was so enamored with Wilt Chamberlain. Maybe it was because I was the smallest kid my age in my neighborhood and in my class at school. I was a little boy who loved a giant.

He left Kansas after his junior year and signed to play with the Harlem Globetrotters. After a year with the Globetrotters, he took the NBA by storm, winning both the Most Valuable Player and the Rookie of the Year awards with the Philadelphia Warriors in 1960. That was my senior year at Taylor Allderdice High School, and I cared more about Chamberlain than most of my subjects in school.

Chamberlain could do whatever he wanted to do on the court — and off it as well — and he could lead the league in assists or average 50 points and nearly 30 rebounds a game, depending on his personal goals for that particular season.

George Kiseda, a Pittsburgh-born sports writer of real merit, covered the 76ers for *The Philadelphia Daily News* and wrote some great stuff about Wilt. Kiseda shared my enthusiasm for Chamberlain. Beano Cook, the Pitt sports information director, used to share Kiseda clippings about Chamberlain with me during my student days at Pitt.

When I went to New York in 1970, I was immediately assigned by *The New York Post* to cover the New York Knicks in the NBA playoffs. I was part of a four-man team of reporters who covered the Knicks in the Eastern finals against the Baltimore Bullets and then the NBA finals against the Los Angeles Lakers.

The Lakers included Chamberlain, Jerry West and Elgin Baylor, three of the best who ever played the game. Yet the Knicks prevailed, winning the first NBA title in the team's history. I remember Bill Bradley, one of the Knicks standouts who was running for President of the U.S.A. at the time of Chamberlain's death, telling me that his mother had uncovered an album Bradley kept as a child that was devoted exclusively to newspaper and magazine clippings of Chamberlain.

**Willis Reed and Walt Frazier
of Knicks collapse on Wilt
Chamberlain, at right, in the 1970
NBA playoff championship.**

Street & Smith's Basketball

A giant comes calling at Kutsher's

A special time comes to mind. It occurred a year or so later at Kutsher's Country Club in the Catskill Mountains north of New York City. NBA players gathered there each summer to play a benefit basketball game to raise funds for Maurice Stokes. He had been a great player at Westinghouse High School in Pittsburgh, and at St. Francis of Loretto and in the NBA. He was stricken with a crippling brain disease. He died in 1970 at age 36, but the game continued in his honor to help needy ex-NBA players.

Chamberlain always came to the Stokes game at Kutsher's. A friend of mine, Jim Bukata, knew how I had idolized Chamberlain as a kid and urged him to go to my room at Kutsher's. Bukata had come out of Munhall to become the sports publicist for the American Basketball Association. I was in my room when there was a knock at the door. Imagine my amazement when I opened the door and Wilt Chamberlain was standing there. He ducked under the doorway and filled the room. I still have photos of him I took during his surprise visit.

That night, Chamberlain came to the hotel bar and entertained everyone with his stories. He had a rich baritone voice, an easy smile and hardy laugh. He wore a white blouse, with a turned-up collar and puffed-out sleeves, looking like a swashbuckling Errol Flynn in one of those pirate movies.

Chamberlain was always a flamboyant dresser.

"They called him Big Musty."
—Bill Melchionni

Chamberlain liked to be called "The Big Dipper." He hated being called "Wilt the Stilt." He had another nickname, not well publicized, that I had learned about when I was covering the New York Nets of the American Basketball Association in the early '70s.

Bill Melchionni was the point guard for the Nets, whose star was Julius Erving, better known as Dr. J.

Melchionni, a bright young man who read books on the airplane on every road trip, was a rookie reserve out of Villanova on the Philadelphia 76ers' 1976-77 team that has often been called the best basketball team in NBA history. Alex Hannum was the coach of that team. Chamberlain was the star. Hal Greer, Chet Walker, Larry Costello and Billy Cunningham were on that club. So were Wally Jones, Matt Guokas, Luke Jackson and Dave Gambee. Jack Ramsay was the general manager.

Melchionni said the Sixers called Chamberlain "Big Musty," but only behind his large back. None of them would have dared say it to Chamberlain's face.

"Wilt had some unusual personal habits," Melchionni recalled, chuckling at the memories. "He used to eat sandwiches and pies in the locker room and even at halftime. Wilt had enormous appetites, in every respect. He'd stick sandwiches he'd get on the airplane in his travel bag. Sometimes he'd forget about them.

"Our trainer, Al Domenico, who loved Wilt, would open that bag from time to time when Wilt was in the showers, or doing something somewhere else. Al would clean out that bag. Sometimes he had to scrape stuff out of the bottom of that bag. There'd be dirty socks or jocks, sweaty T-shirts and jerseys, you name it, in that bag. It would stink something awful. Sometimes Wilt would skip showers after a game. So the guys started referring to him as Big Musty."

The 76ers had the best record (68-13) in the NBA by far that season. Chamberlain led the league in rebounding with 24.2 a game, better than Bill Russell's rebounding average of 21 a game. Chamberlain led the league in field goal percentage (.683), was third in scoring (24.1 ppg) and assists (7.8 apg).

They beat the San Francisco Warriors in six games to win the NBA playoff title.

That team, by the way, played six of its home games at the Civic Arena in Pittsburgh. That tells you a lot about the state of the NBA in those days. Jason Shapiro, the owner of National Record Mart, was the man who brought those 76ers to Pittsburgh. He made a deal with 76ers owner Irv Kosloff that is hard to believe, especially in light of today's sports economics.

Shapiro was able to get a six-game regular season package by paying $50,000 in advance to Kosloff. One of Shapiro's friends, Gabe Rubin, who owned the Nixon Theatre, was an investor in this entrepreneurial effort. A year later, Rubin and Shapiro, in that order, would bankroll the Pittsburgh Pipers in the newly formed American Basketball Association.

Connie Hawkins, who had challenged Chamberlain in summer basketball outings in Harlem and Philadlephia, was the star player for the Pipers, who would win the first ABA championship.

In one of those half-dozen games the Sixers played in Pittsburgh, Chamberlain took 18 shots and made all of them, mostly dunk shots, against the Baltimore Bullets on February 24, 1967. That's still an NBA record. During that same stretch, Chamberlain canned 35 straight field goals. He had other games in which he hit 16, 15 and 14 shots without a miss. He had three games in which he attempted 60 shots or more.

In his second pro season, he had a record 55 rebounds in a game against Russell and the Boston Celtics on November 24, 1960.

Some other memories of Chamberlain come to mind. When Joe Mullaney was coaching the Lakers during the 1970 season he started a practice of having his team loosen up with an afternoon shoot-around at the arena where they would be playing that night. Wilt skipped those sessions.

"I'm only going out there once a day," Chamberlain informed Mullaney, who had gained fame as a coach at Providence College. "You can either have me for the shoot-around or for the game. But you can't have me for both. You make the choice."

After retiring following the 1972-1973 season, Chamberlain had a brief stint as a coach with the ABA's San Diego Conquistadors. He seldom came to practice, leaving those duties to one of his assistants, Stan Albeck. Wilt would even disappear for a few days now and then. Wilt was always his own man. Who else wore sandles on the sidelines?

That's why we will all miss The Big Dipper.

Wilt Chamberlain coached the ABA's San Diego Conquistadors.

Wilt's 100-point basketball nets $551,844

Kerry Ryman was a 14-year old basketball fan who was at the Hershey Arena the night Wilt Chamberlain claimed the NBA's all-time single game scoring record with a 100-point performance against the New York Knicks.

There were only 4,124 fans in attendance that night — March 2, 1962 — though the number has grown considerably since then as it always does with magic moments in sports history. Ryman was among those who swarmed onto the court when Chamberlain scored his 100th point, and interrupted the contest.

Ryman shook Chamberlain's hand, took the ball from him, and ran home with it. He had to vault a fence outside the Arena with a security guard in pursuit. The guard, Gabe Basti, recognized Ryman and knew where he lived, but Chamberlain declined his offer to go to Ryman's home to retrieve the ball.

"Let the kid have it," said Chamberlain, according to Basti.

The NBA game was never completed. The Warriors won, 169-147.

Ryman later moved to an apartment in Annville, Pennsylvania, about seven miles northeast of Hershey. At age 52 in April of 2000, he still had the ball, keeping it in a plastic bag in recent years. He and his friends used to play with it in local playgrounds when he first got it. He was working as a crane operator, making about $30,000 a year.

"It has been a burden in some ways," Ryan told the *Associated Press*. "With Wilt's death, and every anniversary of the game, people call wanting pictures and interviews. I'm tired of it. I want to put it to rest. Plus, I was never particularly proud of the way I got it in the first place."

So he agreed to allow it to be sold through a Manhattan auction agency. It sold for $551,844 on April 28, 2000. Ryman was to receive just under $500,000 as his share.

"I don't feel the need to radically change my life," said Ryman after receiving the good news. "I am content with my job and my life."

Gus Suhr
Still an "Iron Man" at 94

"Babe Ruth had quite a day, but we still beat 'em."

G us Suhr was something to see. He was 94 years old and a living link to the distant past of the Pirates. He personally knew people who can only be found today in history books and record books. That's why it was so special to see him, speak to him, take pictures of him, get him to sign a photograph and simply to spend time with him during PirateFest 2000.

What wonderful things this man had seen and experienced in the past century. He was at Forbes Field, for instance, the day Babe Ruth hit three home runs, and remembers when Honus Wagner would continue to work out with the team and sit on the bench after he had retired as a ballplayer. Talking to Gus Suhr, and hearing some of the names he casually tossed out was like spending an afternoon flipping through the pages of *The Baseball Encyclopedia*.

He was unsteady at times, but he carried himself with great dignity. His signature was shaky, but his smile was constant and genuine. He lit up and warmed every room he graced.

When I mentioned Gus Suhr to a neighbor of mine, Jack Curley, age 70, Curley smiled and said he remembered him playing for the Pirates during Curley's boyhood days atop Mt. Washington. "They never had a drainage problem at Forbes Field," cracked Curley, "because they had a Suhr at first base."

It was a refrain I'd never heard before. So now you know how to pronounce the name of this distinguished old Pirate. "It's nice to be here," Suhr kept saying. "I can't believe how many people are here. They're all so nice."

Suhr played 1,339 games at first base during his ten years (1930-1939) with the Pirates, nearly 300 more games at first base than anyone else in team history. You could look it up, as Casey Stengel liked to say. Suhr was a bit of an "iron man," the Pirates answer at the position to Yankees' great Lou Gehrig. Suhr still holds the Pirates' record for consecutive games played with 822, from 1931 through the 1937 season. He wore No. 24. "That's the same number Willie Mays wore when I used to see him play for the Giants in our town," said Suhr, who was from San Francisco.

Suhr is the third oldest living Pirate, according to Sally O'Leary, who looks after the Pirates' alumni newsletter, Black & Gold. Her records listed former Pirates' coach Clyde Sukeforth and left-handed pitcher Ralph Erickson as 98 years old at the time, Sukeforth first by a few months. Erickson pitched exactly 15 innings over two seasons (1929-30) for the Pirates, so Suhr was certainly the oldest living Pirate who had a significant career with the ball club.

BABE RUTH

PIE TRAYNOR

ARKY VAUGHAN

HONUS WAGNER

Suhr was not able to expand on his stories. He did his best to answer all my questions. He glanced at his son from time to time, inviting some assistance. His son tried to fill in the memory gaps. Somehow it didn't matter. Just being in his company was a big thrill. What ballparks he had seen, what pitchers he had faced, what fun he had, how many trains and buses he had boarded and rode to magical places, what those washed-out old eyes had seen.

"He's shy," said his son. "But he's loving this. He said he had his day in the sun. That day is past. He's an old man now and this could be his last go-round. Everybody's so friendly. So he's enjoying this. When he first got the call to come here, he said, 'Do I have to come?' It's like he just didn't want to go any place. Here he is now, having the time of his life. Back home, he gets a letter a day, it seems, asking him to sign a card or answer a question, some kind of request. He remembers the Ruth game very well. He's in pretty good health. His legs give him some problems now and then, but so do mine.

"My sister, Barbara, died on October 18 this past year. She was 69. That was a sad time for all of us. But he seems to be getting over that. Barbara kept scrapbooks about Dad.

"After he left the big leagues — he finished up with the Phillies in 1940 — World War II broke out. After he returned from a stint in the military service, Suhr played three more years (1943-1945) in his hometown with the San Francisco Seals of the Pacific Coast League. Then he owned a liquor store in Millbrae, California.

"He lived in the same house for 66 years. His wife, my mother, Helen, died in 1944 when I was 12 years old. He remarried. His second wife, Lillith, died in 1980, twenty years ago. We talked him into moving into a retirement community in Scottsdale a few months ago.

"His father owned a livery stable in San Francisco before the turn of the century. He had three brothers, Fred, Herb and Bill. He was the baby of the family. They all grew up in San Francisco and they all wanted to be ballplayers. They were earlier than the DiMaggio Brothers, but my dad knew them. My dad said Joe was an introverted, laconic kind of guy. But he was always friendly with Dad. He was about ten years behind Dad.

"I wanted to be a ballplayer, too. I played three years of ball at Santa Clara University. I was signed by the Yankees — the Pirates wouldn't have me — but I wasn't good enough to be a big leaguer."

"I don't know if Dad's up yet."

I awoke at 5:20 a.m., ten minutes before the alarm was to sound on my bedside clock, on Sunday, the final day of PirateFest 2000. I was scheduled to meet Gus Suhr at 9:30 a.m. for breakfast at the Doubletree Hotel in downtown Pittsburgh. I had to get an early start to squeeze that into an already demanding schedule.

The Sunday program at PirateFest 2000 would begin at 10 a.m. and last until 5 p.m. I was signing copies of the books in my "Pittsburgh Proud" sports series. I knew the fans wouldn't be showing up in any great numbers before 11 a.m. so I could have a good hour with Suhr before going back across the Roberto Clemente Bridge to the North Side.

I walked my daughter's dog, Bailey, before departing home for the Carnegie Science Center. I wanted to get there early to set up my table, so it would be ready when I returned after my breakfast meeting with Suhr and his son, Gus Suhr Jr. and his daughter-in-law, Ann.

Gus Jr. and Ann told me they were going to the 8 a.m. mass at St. Mary of Mercy Catholic Church at the Point, at the other end of the downtown area. They thought they'd be back a little after 9 a.m. They entered the lobby at 9:10 a.m. "I don't know if Dad's up yet or not," he said as they passed me, "but we'll meet you upstairs at 9:30."

I waited in the lobby for awhile. I saw the concierge chase a drifter out of the lobby. "I have to go now, huh?" the homeless man asked as he backed toward the door. "Thank you, friend. Bless you."

A group gathered nearby and I heard a man and woman speaking French. He was flipping through a French language newspaper. I learned that these people were from Paris. They were associated with Pittsburgh-based companies such as PPG, Bayer, Wyeth and USAirways. Their guide was Ines Schaffer, a native of Uruguay whose husband, Juan, was a professor at Carnegie Mellon University. They would soon board a bus and tour the town, going through Mt. Washington, the South Side, Oakland, Squirrel Hill, Bloomfield, Lawrenceville and The Strip.

An emergency medical service van pulled up in front of the hotel with red and blue lights flashing and whirling. My first thought was that something might have happened to Gus Suhr. After all, the man was 94. I was relieved to spot Gus Suhr standing along a brass rail a floor above me in the dramatic atrium entryway. I waved to him and he smiled and waved back.

He was standing outside the Harvest, where we would have breakfast. It was on the second floor, where the meeting rooms and ballrooms were located. They were named after counties in the western half of Pennsylvania: Westmoreland, Cambria, Allegheny, Butler, Armstrong, Somerset, Bedford and Fayette, to name a few.

Gus said his son would be down soon. It was a gray February day in Pittsburgh. Snow had fallen on 17 of the 20 previous days, and temperatures had been above freezing only twice since January 16 so the snow hadn't melted. The streets were clear but snow covered most of the landscape. Ann Suhr slipped and fell while touring Point State Park the day before and struck her elbow. It still pained her.

The PirateFest was a welcome respite from the winter gloom. It was important to look ahead to spring training and one last summer of baseball at Three Rivers Stadium before the team shifted to a spanking new, state-of-the art ball field PNC Park, that would be better for baseball, cozy and comfortable like Forbes Field.

251

Hope always springs eternal for the city's baseball team at this time of year, even though it was unlikely the Pirates would put a real contender on the field. Their payroll paled by comparison to the legitimate contenders. Then, too, things would get tougher within the week when the Cincinnati Reds would acquire and sign Ken Griffey, Jr., the gifted son of a major leaguer of the same name who grew up in Donora, Pa. Young Griffey was regarded as the best all-around player in the game today. He was coming over from the Seattle Mariners and the American League to play in the National League's Central Division. Griffey would be joining Mark McGwire of the St. Louis Cardinals and Sammy Sosa of the Chicago Cubs and Jeff Bagwell of the Houston Astros to give the division the best home run hitters in all of baseball. This could give Pirates pitchers some nightmares.

Then, too, things were not going well for the Steelers who had finished with a 6-10 record, their second straight losing season and there was turmoil in the ranks. It seemed like a good time to get out of town, yet Tom Donahoe turned down a front-office job with the Miami Dolphins to remain close to his family in the Pittsburgh suburb of Mt. Lebanon. Donahoe had lost out in a power struggle with Steelers coach Bill Cowher and was fired January 14 as director of the team's football operations by owner Dan Rooney.

Donahoe was shocked by the move. He had turned down a generous offer the year before from the Seattle Seahawks to stay with the Steelers. Now he was on the outside looking in. So he would stay home and let Rooney pay him for a sabbatical from pro football. Temperatures were in the 20s in Pittsburgh and in the 60s in South Florida, but Donahoe didn't take the bait. Being a "Pittsburgh guy," in the parlance of the late Art Rooney, may have put Donahoe deep in quicksand instead of snow. He couldn't leave his hometown.

While Suhr was a reminder of the Pirates past, those who attended the Piratefest also had an opportunity to take a peek at the progress of PNC Park, the future home of the Pirates, as well as the stadium being built for the Steelers and Pitt Panthers. In dramatic fashion, fans who were at the Carnegie Science Center on Sunday afternoon had a chance to see barges bringing pre-fabricated steel for the new baseball park. They could look out the windows in the direction of the Point and see the barges coming down the Monongahela River and making the turn to the Allegheny River. It wasn't planned that way, but it was a dramatic manner in which to wrap up the weekend schedule.

The barges began the trip earlier that day at Wilhelm and Kruse Inc., a fabricating plant in Brownsville, Fayette County. A large Pirates banner was draped across the steel beams, with a Pirates flag flying from the rear of one barge.

PAUL "BIG POISON" WANER and LLOYD "LITTLE POISON" WANER

Honus Wagner loved to tell stories and he had an attentive audience here, with Pirates' manager Frankie Frisch, left, and his staff in Bucs' clubhouse at spring training at San Bernardino, California camp on February 25, 1941.

"That was wonderful being with the guys I was with."

Gus Suhr said he remembered the first time he came to Pittsburgh, back in 1930. "I thought it was great," he said, "but you couldn't see too good. There was a lot of coal dust in the air, from the smoke coming out of the steel mills."

He offered thoughts on several subjects, not in any particular order.

"Honus Wagner was a wonderful fellow, a real good guy on the bench. I think he had a sporting goods store in Pittsburgh at the time. He was awful easy to get along with. No one said anything bad about anyone. Geez, that was wonderful being with the guys I was with. The Waners were great ballplayers, in every way. I think Paul was just as great a ballplayer as Babe Ruth. Paul was the best hitter in the National League. He and Lloyd were magicians the way they hit the ball wherever they wanted to hit it. Vaughan was a good hitter and a good shortstop. Cy Blanton was my roommate. You can put him down, too, as one of the best guys I played with.

"Forbes Field was a darn good ballpark. There were no cheap home runs in that place. A left-hander never hit them over the left-field fence. It was 457 to center field. You had to earn home runs there, but it was a good hitters' park because there was a lot of space in the outfield.

"I was 24 at the time and I'd never been that far east. I came here by train from my hometown of San Francisco. It was quite a long trip. I liked being a big league ballplayer. It was very good. As far as having girls and all that stuff, I don't know. We'd play cards in the clubhouse or on the train for two bits a pot. We played all day games back then, so we went out at night a lot and had a good time. The players were closer in those days.

"I remember batting against Dizzy Dean and Carl Hubbell and Bill Hallahan. I remember hitting a home run against Guy Bush in Chicago and we beat the Cubs by one run. I remember hitting a home run in Chicago off Lon Warneke. I remember some important hits I had in New York, to advance a runner or to tie up a game in the late innings. I can still see where the ball landed, what the ballpark looked like, stuff like that.

"I remember a game at Forbes Field where we were trailing by one run. We had a runner on second base and when I hit a single he scored on my single. I can't think of his name, but he had two strikes and no balls on me. He threw me a high pitch, high and tight, and I got hold of it. It went out to right field. I can remember stuff like that. I remember where I used to park my car on a hill near the ballpark."

He and his son spoke about his early years in the Pacific Coast League where he played 202 games, and 199 the year before that. A normal schedule in the big leagues back then was 154 games. He couldn't get enough of baseball in his early 20s. He said it was a good league, with players like future Hall of Famer Joe Cronin, Frankie Crosetti and Dolf Camilli, and later the DiMaggio Brothers.

His son said his father was paid $9,000 for the 1938 season. "And he was already an all-star player by then," he pointed out.

Gus recalled how the Pirates were 1 ½ games out front with five games to go in the 1938 season when they traveled to Chicago to take on the hottest team in baseball in a three-game series. Gabby Harnett, a Hall of Fame catcher, was player-manager of the Cubs.

Harnett started a worn-out Dizzy Dean in the first game and got away with it as the Cubs won a squeaker. Now the Pirates' lead was down to a ½ game.

The next ballgame is a famous one in Pirates' history. The game was tied 5-5 going into the bottom of the ninth inning. Pie Traynor had brought in Mace Brown to pitch for the Pirates in that eighth inning. Brown retired the first two batters in the ninth and threw two curve balls to get two strikes on Harnett. It was getting so dark at the ballpark that the umpires agreed to call the game if it was still tied after nine innings.

Brown threw a third straight curve ball — his best pitch — but he hung it this time and Harnett hit it out of the park. Most observers couldn't see the ball sailing out into the stands. The third base umpire called it a home run. The Cubs had a 6-5 victory and first place. The Pirates lost the third game in Chicago, 10-1. When they dropped the first game of a doubleheader the next day in Cincinnati it was all over. They finished with an 86-64 record, second behind the Cubs in the final standings.

"If Mace could have thrown one more strike we might have had a chance," said Suhr. "But we had our share of opportunities to win that game, and we didn't. It wasn't Mace's fault. Oh, the memories."

Gus Suhr signs baseball with an assist from his daughter-in-law, Ann Suhr, at left, and Piratefest aide Donna Liska.

Kevin McClatchy chats with Pirates star Kevin Young at Three Rivers Stadium.

Jim O'Brien

Snapshot:

Kevin McClatchy
CEO and Managing General Partner,
Pittsburgh Pirates:

"I'd have to say that Willie Mays and Willie McCovey were my two favorite ballplayers when I was a little kid. They were at the end of their careers when I became aware of them, when I was seven or eight, but they were still huge. As you grow into different ages the heroes change. You like guys for different reasons. They may not be big stars. When I was a teenager, I liked Terry Whitfield, for instance, and a lot of people have never heard of him. He was an outfielder who played for the Giants in the late '70s, and with the Dodgers in the mid-'80s. He was a decent hitter, and he was from California. I thought he was a great player. When I was in college, I was a 49ers fan and I really liked Joe Montana and Ronnie Lott. I lived out in that part of the world (northern California) and watched them a lot. Montana was probably the coolest person under pressure that I've ever seen in sports. There was not a lot expected of him at the start. He wasn't a No. 1 draft choice. He was a third round pick. But he was so cool and so productive. He was a winner in every way."

Ron Necciai
A big man in Monongahela

"I've done well.
I can't complain."

O ne night in Ron Necciai's life dramatically changed the way he would be identified for the rest of his days. He did something in sports that no one ever did before or since. It immortalized him with serious baseball fans. He became a part of Pittsburgh Pirates folklore. He became the answer to a trivia question.

Who is the only pitcher in professional baseball history to strike out 27 batters in a nine-inning game?

Ron Necciai, that's who. That's an Italian name and it is pronounced netch-eye. It's not an easy name to spell — like Rocky Bleier in that respect — but it's a name for the ages. Ron Necciai struck out 27 batters in a ballgame!

There isn't a pitcher in baseball's Hall of Fame in Cooperstown who can make such a claim. Walter Johnson never did it. Cy Young and Christy Matthewson never did it. Burleigh Grimes, Grover Alexander and Carl Hubbell never did it. Satchel Paige, Sandy Koufax, Bob Gibson and Tom Seaver never did it. Nolan Ryan pitched seven no-hitters, but he never struck out 27 batters in a ballgame.

Kerry Wood of the Chicago White Sox created a sensation in the summer of 1998 when he struck out 20 batters in a nine-inning game. In his fifth major league start, at the age of 20, Wood tied Roger Clemens' record for most strikeouts in a nine-inning game on the major league level.

Necciai was nearly the same age as Wood when he made baseball history. On a night when the moon shone bright in the sky over Bristol, Virginia and the stars were aligned just so, Ron Necciai was untouchable. That he did it in a small minor league ballpark in Bristol rather than in Brooklyn, Boston or Pittsburgh only added to the mystique of the achievement.

On May 13, 1952, while pitching for the Bristol Twins in the Class D Appalachian League, the 19-year-old Necciai established an all-time mark by striking out 27 in a 7-0 no-hit victory over the Welch Miners at Bristol's Shaw Stadium.

Over one million professional baseball games had been played since organized baseball began in 1869 and no one ever duplicated the feat of "Rocket Ron," as he was called. It was one of baseball's greatest achievements. How come Kevin Costner hasn't played the part of Ron Necciai in a baseball movie?

For the record, it was not a perfect game. Necciai did not strike out every batter he faced. There was a groundout in the second inning and several batters reached base on errors. Seventeen of the 27 strikeouts came on swinging third strikes. One of the batters he struck out in the ninth inning reached first base when the ball hit the dirt and got away from catcher Harry Dunlop.

"All my curve balls hit the dirt in those days," said Necciai with a smile, when asked about the pitch that got away.

"That third strike really dropped and it hit the plate and bounced way over my head," declared Dunlop. "I had no chance at it."

Necciai struck out the next batter to end the game. That's how he was able to strike out 27 batters. Necciai could bring the heat. He was "a wild thing," but his prospects seemed unlimited.

Shaw Stadium is long gone and it's been a long time since there was a Class D in baseball's minor leagues, but Necciai's magical night will never be forgotten.

Before the season was over, the flame-throwing right-hander from Monongahela, Pa., was being mentioned in the same breath as Bob Feller and Dizzy Dean, by the likes of Branch Rickey, no less. Those are all Hall of Fame names. Before the season was over, Necciai would be pitching for the Pirates at Forbes Field in Pittsburgh, about 25 miles from his hometown. He was 20 years old when he first put on a Pirates' uniform for real and the world was his oyster.

He had control problems, though, little offensive support and posted a 1-6 record for the worst team in the history of the Pirates. The 1952 Bucs, managed by Billy Meyer, finished with a 42-112 record. No Pirates team ever lost more games in a single season. Meyer's uniform number (1) is one of the Pirates' retired numbers. Nobody in the organization can explain why he was so honored, except that he was popular with players, press and fans.

Necciai was drafted into the U.S. Army during the off-season, in early 1953, during the Korean conflict, even though he had ongoing physical problems. He got a medical discharge because of ulcers in April, just three months later. He rushed to get in shape for a return to playing baseball and injured the shoulder on his throwing arm. He was back in the minor leagues to rehabilitate his arm, but he had nothing on the ball. He made two brief attempts at a comeback over a three-year period, going back to Burlington and then two years later to spring training in Hollywood with the Pirates. "It didn't work," Necciai recalled, wincing at the very memory of his experience. Necciai never pitched for the Pirates again. At 22, he was finished as a ballplayer.

It was a rotator cuff injury, something routinely repaired these days, but there was no effective medical treatment back then. Necciai was just another sore-armed pitcher who could have been a big star had he stayed sound.

He had pitched in 12 big league baseball games. He had nine starts. He pitched a total of 54²/₃ innings. He had 32 walks and 31 strikeouts and a 7.08 ERA on his performance line. At the plate, he had one hit in 17 at bats. As a fielder, he had four putouts, seven assists, two errors and was involved in two double plays. And that's it. That was his big league career in a capsule.

On May 13, 1952, at Bristol Virginia's Shaw Stadium, located less than one mile from here, nineteen year-old Ronald Andrew Necciai, pitching for the Class D Appalachian League Bristol Twins, struck out 27 Welsh miners in a nine inning no-hit, no-run performance.

27 *Ron Necciai* K's

In over one million professional baseball games played since organized baseball began in 1869, no one has ever matched "Rocket Ron's" feat that special evening. It remains one of baseball's greatest individual accomplishments.

Jim O'Brien

Ron Necciai's 27-strikeout no-hitter is memorialized by plaque installed in 1999 at DeVault Stadium in Bristol, Va., about a mile from ballpark where he pulled off the feat in 1952. Author Jim O'Brien enjoyed visiting the idyllic minor league ballpark in spring of 2000.

Alex Pociask

Branch Rickey really liked Necciai and offered him a job in the Pirates organization, but Necciai was not interested.

Necciai never had a chance to realize his tremendous potential. It's understandable that he did a lot of what-might-have-been and what-could-have-been thinking. There was a period when he felt sorry for himself — why me? — but he shook off the disappointment and moved on.

Necciai got his act together and became a winning pitcher once again. Only now he was pitching sporting goods. He was a manufacturer's representative, selling hunting and fishing gear, and made a good living at it. People liked doing business with him. He had a good family and he made his mark in Monongahela, or Mon City as it's called.

He was one of 12 athletes pictured on the Wall of Fame at Ringgold High School that included pros produced by both Monongahela High School and Donora High School before the schools were merged in 1969.

He had a beautiful home in an idyllic setting at the end of a street on the outskirts of the Washington County community along the Monongahela River just over 20 miles from Pittsburgh. I had been to the homes of Pirates pitchers who had long, successful careers in the big leagues and they didn't appear to be any better off than Ron Necciai. When I visited him, on Thursday, September 23, 1999, he had been retired from business for two years, and struck me as a contented and satisfied man. There is a sweet serenity about Necciai that attracts people.

"I've never looked back, or said this could have been or that could have been," said Necciai, no doubt fibbing a little but doing his best to put on a good game face. "I've done a lot because of baseball. I say, 'You gave the game a nickel and you got a lot back.' I still get cards and letters from people who want my signature."

The Necciai kitchen contained many family photographs, especially baby pictures, and lots of cookbooks. There was a framed stitch-work sampler that read: DON'T QUESTION YOUR WIFE'S JUDGMENT — LOOK WHO SHE MARRIED.

As I was checking out the kitchen, Ron's wife, Martha, made a brief appearance. She was on her way out to meet some friends for lunch. Ron and Martha were married in 1955, and would celebrate their 45th wedding anniversary in February 2000. They were an attractive couple.

When I asked Martha for a few thoughts on her husband, she replied, "He did well with his life and he made a good life for us. He has a good reputation with his business, with people and his friends."

Necciai showed me an ink sketch of Pittsburgh's Point over his mantel. He said he won it at a celebrity golf outing at St. Clair Country Club hosted by the late Bob Prince, the "Voice of the Pirates."

He showed me a dinner program (February 10, 1967) at which Carl DePasqua was honored for what he accomplished as football

Photos by Jim O'Brien

Martha and Ron Necciai are not far from Pittsburgh at their beautiful home in Monongahela.

coach at Waynesburg College. "We had Rocky Marciano and John Michelosen and Pete Dimperio there," recalled Necciai. "Bob Prince was the emcee. It was the biggest affair this city ever saw. We were at the Elks Club in Monongahela until two in the morning.

"Bob Prince didn't charge us anything. He said he was doing it for a friend. We later held a dinner for Fred Cox (February 19, 1971), and I told him no freebie this time. He told me to send a couple of bucks to the Allegheny Valley School in his name. Bob Prince was always nice to me. He always said nice things about me."

There were other programs from sports dinners that had names familiar to sports fans, such as Jack Wiley, Steve Petro, Foge Fazio, Bill Quinter, Bap Manzini, Joe McCune, Billy Conn and Frank Pizzica. Necciai knew them all well.

At 6-5, 220 pounds, he remained a big man in Monongahela. Wherever we traveled in his hometown, Necciai seemed to know everyone. Passersby waved at him and he waved back. He was still a hometown hero. He drew a lot of smiles and small talk from people, whether he was dining at a local landmark like Lenzi's Italian Restaurant where Routes 837, 136 and 88 converge, the Mon Valley Country Club, or driving through the parking lot at Cox's Market.

Since he retired, he takes two to three long walks a day, so he's a familiar figure on the streets of Monongahela.

On a tour of the town in his automobile, Necciai pointed out the boyhood homes of professional football stars such as Joe Montana and Fred Cox. But they were long gone and he had remained in Monongahela. Necciai's family lived in the neighboring riverside community of Gallatin when Ron was born on June 18, 1932. He had job offers that would have taken him elsewhere, but he never wanted to move away from the Mon Valley. It worked for him. He had a positive glow about him, a shine to his silver hair, a glint in his bespectacled brown eyes, a great smile. He looked like a winner in every way.

"I never needed a contract on any business transaction," he said. "I never needed a witness. When things started to change in that regard I thought it was a good time to get out and take it easy."

"We've had a lot of good times together."
— Bill Mazeroski

I was nearly 10 years old when Ron Necciai struck out 27 batters in a ballgame in Bristol, Virginia. I was helping my brother, Dan, deliver the *Pittsburgh Post-Gazette* each morning before we'd go off to school. Dan was five years older than I was. We loved to read the *P-G* sports pages, starting with Al Abrams' column. He was the sports editor and featured columnist. His column was always on the left side of the first page of the sports section.

Ron Necciai talks to long-time friend Emma Jane Polonoli who lives across the street from Joe Montana's boyhood home, seen behind Necciai. Ron also points out yard behind Polonoli home where Montana used to practice throwing a football through an automobile tire hanging from a tree branch.

There are Pirates pitchers from that era whose names will never leave me. They were Murry Dickson, Bill Werle, Bob Friend, Vernon Law, El Roy Face, Paul Pettit, Howie Pollet, Paul LaPalme and Bob Purkey. So many Ps. I loved to look at their thumbnail photos and bio sketches in the *Post-Gazette's* spring training tabloid that officially opened the baseball season. We knew about Ron Necciai, as brief as his big-league career turned out to be.

The Pirates opening day lineup for the 1952 season was Ted Beard, CF; George Metkovich, 1B; Gus Bell, RF; Ralph Kiner, LF; Wally Westlake, RF; Dick Hall, 3B; John Merson, 2B; Clem Koshorek, SS; Clyde McCullough, C; and Dickson, P. Lee Walls and Ed Fitz Gerald were on the Bucs bench that year. There were two rookies from The Hill, Tony Bartirome and Bobby Del Greco. We loved them all, as bad a team as they were. If you're over 55, just reading those names can make you young again. Otherwise, this may be a history lesson.

The Pirates played at Forbes Field in Oakland in those days. That was just over four miles from our home, but it was in another world. Our dad didn't take us to games. He wasn't a sports fan. So we knew the Pirates mostly from newspaper and radio reports. Al Abrams and Bob Prince told us all we needed to know about the Pirates. We got to go to a few games each summer with the Knot-Hole Gang. A fellow named Frank Casne, whom I still run across from time to time, was the recreation director at Burgwin Field near my home, and he took us to the Pirates' games from time to time. Guys like Casne contributed much to our young lives. For 50 cents, you got a seat in right field, not far from Stan Musial, Carl Furillo and Gus Bell and, in short time, Roberto Clemente. They should have had opera seats out there.

So it was a pleasure to meet this man named Necciai. It took me back to my boyhood. I'd come across Necciai at Pirates alumni golf outings several times in the '80s and '90s and was always impressed with him. He and Nellie King stood out because they were taller than everyone else. They were also two of the nicest men you'd ever meet. If they had a Nice Guys Hall of Fame their plaques would be on display. They invited you to join them at their table before and after the golf, and always made non-ballplayers feel welcome. They were popular with Pirates from every period in the team's history. They were simply good company. Bob Friend was like that. Most of the old Pirates were pleasant fellows.

If you ever played in their foursomes you had fun. They talked to you. They had a drink with you in the clubhouse afterward. They were honored to keep company with their fans. They told you about Roberto Clemente and Ralph Kiner.

Necciai and King were proud of their Pirates heritage. Their feelings had been hurt along the way, discarded for different reasons by the organization, but they loved being a part of the Pirates' story. Sometimes ballplayers who have had short stays with ball teams treasure the association more than long-established stars and Hall of Fame members.

One of Necciai's closest friends among the former Pirates, interestingly enough, was Bill Mazeroski. "Ron and I go back a long way, and we've had a lot of good times together," said Mazeroski.

Maz knows something about having a big day in one's baseball life. He hit the home run, of course, that beat the New York Yankees in the seventh and deciding game of the 1960 World Series. It's the most significant and best-remembered moment in Pittsburgh sports history. His HR came at 3:36 p.m. on October 13.

Maz was a key member of the Pirates for 17 years, but he and Necciai had more in common than met the eye. They never forgot where they came from because they had never strayed too far from their roots. They mixed easily with the guys who paid big money to play golf at these charity-related outings. They were family men, happy to be with their wives and kids and long-time friends, never seeking the spotlight. They were simply good citizens.

They were among the former Pirates who showed up at the team's Fantasy Camp at Pirate City in Bradenton, Florida, at the end of January 2000. When I told Necciai I had met a chiropractor from Scottdale, Dan Geary, who told me how much he had enjoyed spending time with Necciai at the Fantasy Camp, he shook off the compliment by saying, "I had more fun than he did." Maz had been at a similar camp a few years earlier when one of the wannabe ballplayers hit a ball out of the ballpark, the first time that had ever happened at a Pirates' Fantasy Camp.

When the man entered the dugout after hitting the home run, Maz welcomed him, and cried out, "If you need any tips on how to live off one home run the rest of your life, I can help you."

I had interviewed Maz many times, but I had never really sat down with Necciai with a notebook and pen in hand. When I saw him at the golf outing for the Roberto Clemente Foundation at Wildwood Golf Club north of Pittsburgh on August 2, 1999, I made a note to get in touch with Necciai for my next book.

Necciai has newspaper clippings from that period pasted in scrapbooks that he brought out at my request. Seeing those clippings took me back to my newsboy days. They looked so familiar. Instead of sitting at the table in the Necciai kitchen in Monongahela, I was back in my boyhood kitchen in Hazelwood, just three blocks above the Monongahela River.

"I never had a bad day."
— Aldo Bartolotta

The small towns of Donora and Monongahela sit along the west bank of the Monongahela River, named for an Indian tribe which once populated that area.

More tons per mile are moved along this 128-mile river than any other river in the world, according to a book, The Monongahela: River of Dreams, River of Sweat (The University of Pennsylvania State Press, 1999) by Arthur Parker. The headwater of the river is in Fairmont, West Virginia. It's known as the "workhorse of American Rivers." We could walk to the mighty Mon in 15 minutes as kids and we were taught to fear and respect it. There were oil slicks along the shore that I saw as a child, and I never considered swimming in those murky waters. Necciai knew what I was talking about, and smiled knowingly when I mentioned that to him.

Donora is famous for St. Louis Cardinals Baseball Hall of Fame star Stan Musial, former Cincinnati Reds star outfielder Ken Griffey Sr. and NFL standout "Deacon Dan" Towler. Even Ken Griffey Jr. was born there, though he grew up in Cincinnati. There's a billboard on Route 51 that bills Donora as "The City of Champions." Monongahela's Joe Montana was inducted into the Pro Football Hall of Fame in July of 2000 after an outstanding career as a quarterback for the San Francisco 49ers and Kansas City Chiefs. Donora and Monongahela had long been sports hotbeds. A month earlier, Montana was inducted into a Mon Valley Hall of Fame at a dinner in California, Pa.

When I was a student at the University of Pittsburgh in the early 1960s, Fred Cox, a running back and place kicker, and two top-notch offensive linemen, Ray Popp and Ron Linaburg, all hailed from Monongahela. Necciai showed me Montana's old neighborhood, and a super market owned by Cox's relatives. He also mentioned Aldo Bartolotta, a big Pitt booster who owns and operate several super markets in that region. "He's such a great guy," said Necciai. Bartolotta tells everybody, "I never had a bad day," and Necciai likes to be around people who talk that way.

He showed me the boyhood home of Linaburg, a modest two bed-room white frame house. Linaburg wasn't an outstanding football player — he talked his way into landing the last football scholarship available at Pitt in 1960 — but he went to Pitt's dental school and became an endodontist. He was now living in Virginia Manor, a high-priced slice of Mt. Lebanon in the suburbs just south of Pittsburgh. Sports fans don't talk about Linaburg, but he, too, was a big success story in sports. Monongahela is a community that does not forget its heroes. There's a well-maintained war memorial in the downtown park that had been spruced up considerably in recent years, with some new plaques and stone work. A black marble one in the center had been unveiled about three years earlier. How many communities have war memorials that look brand new? It was a project completed by Company A, 110th Infantry, an area National Guard unit. Many community war memorials have been taken for granted, neglected and gone to seed.

The name Necciai appears on several of the bronze nameplates on the war memorial in Monongahela. Everyone from the area who served in the U.S. Armed Forces is listed, including Ron Necciai. Ron

Ron Necciai loves reunions with friend and former teammate El Roy Face at Pirates' Alumni Golf Outing at Churchhill Country Club.

Pirates' minor league coach Miguel Bonilla, at left, joins Bill Mazeroski and Ron Necciai at Pirates' 2000 Fantasy Camp at Bradenton, Florida.

pointed out the nameplates of other Necciais who are similarly honored. "You have to go to Italy to find as many people named Necciai as you'll find here," said the former Pirates pitcher.

Monongahela is a community where you can see women sweeping their porches, sweeping their sidewalks, even sweeping the street in front of their house, as I did when I visited Necciai.

One of his kids, Kirk, lives in Monongahela. His other son, Mark, lives in Lakeview, Ohio and his daughter, Susan, lives in Bradenton, Florida, where the Pirates hold spring training.

"I'll snub you like some of the current ballplayers do."
— Harry Dunlop

After I saw Ron Necciai at the Clemente Foundation golf outing, I thought about him and what he had done. I needed some facts about his 27-strikeout game. I called Sally O'Leary on the telephone. She had retired after 30 years as an assistant in the Pirates public relations office, but kept in touch with the Pirates alumni.

She was away on vacation, however, so I mentioned what I needed in the baseball press box at Three Rivers Stadium, asking Mike Kennedy of the Pirates p.r. department what I needed. This was at a Sunday afternoon game featuring Mark McGwire and the St. Louis Cardinals. I went to the game after hearing the excitement and ballpark buzz on a radio broadcast of the last few innings of the game the night before, while driving home after speaking at a sports banquet in Ellwood City.

George Von Benko, a local sportscaster, overheard me. Von Benko told me that the guy who caught Necciai's 27-strikeout game, Harry Dunlop, would be in town the next day. Dunlop was a coach with the Reds. I was already planning on catching the Cincy Reds because one of their star players was Sean Casey of Upper St. Clair.

Then I received a telephone call from Sally O'Leary, who had returned from her vacation. She called me and told me what I needed to know about Necciai. She added this note: "By the way, Ron Necciai is being honored on Friday in Bristol, Virginia —- 47 years later!"

What a coincidence, I thought. I get interested in the guy, and all of a sudden everyone is interested in him.

On Tuesday, I telephoned Dunlop at the Westin William Penn Hotel at 10:30 a.m. I had never met him before, so I told him who I was and why I was calling. He couldn't have been nicer or more helpful. We talked for 45 minutes. I made arrangements to meet him in the visiting team's dugout at Three Rivers Stadium that evening.

I'll snub you," Dunlop kidded me, "like some of these current stars do."

268

Ron Necciai was eager to show visitor the refurbished war memorial in town square in his hometown of Monongahela.

MONONGAHELA

Oldest settlement in the valley and transportation center since the days of Devore's Ferry, chartered 1775. Laid out in 1796 as Williamsport. A city since 1873. Here thousands of pioneers began the river journey to the West.

PENNSYLVANIA HISTORICAL AND MUSEUM COMMISSION

Then he told me what he looked like and promised to be on the lookout for me before the game. He was siting with Aaron Boone, one of the Reds' young infielders, when I approached him in the dugout. Boone had a big wad of tobacco tucked into his cheek.

"Here's a guy who likes to talk about the old baseball players," said Dunlop, pointing to Boone. "His dad and grandfather were in the big leagues, and he's a bit of a throwback." He introduced us. Boone had been a roommate in spring of Sean Casey, and he shared some personal observations about the Reds' sensation.

Dunlop also introduced me to Jack McKeon, the manager of the Reds. McKeon couldn't have been friendlier. Being introduced to him by Dunlop was the key. I couldn't be a bad guy if Donlop provided the introduction. Dunlop mentioned that Jack McKeon caught Neccai after he did. That happened at Burlington, North Carolina. McKeon continued to live in Burlington while managing in the major leagues. McKeon looked like a manager might in the movies. He was nice. McKeon took a seat in the dugout, pulled out a cigar and stuck it in the corner of his mouth, and talked to me.

His son, Kasey, had signed Sean Casey in Cleveland. His son was now working for the Reds. Casey had stopped at their house on the way from Richmond to Charlotte to see his girl friend. His son told him to get Casey. It wasn't long before Casey and McKeon's kid were close friends. McKeon said he felt like Casey's dad. Dunlop and McKeon couldn't say enough nice things about Casey. McKeon posed for photos with Casey. "Get me a copy of that," McKeon commanded me when I left him to return to talking to Dunlop. I was in the Reds' dugout before the game the next night as well, and McKeon greeted me the second night as if we were long-time friends. It was great that everything kept falling into place for me, that one link led to another.

"This is gonna heal."
— Ron Necciai

Necciai could not understand why his arm wouldn't come around. "You always figure you're young and you're going to get better," he said. "That was the most difficult part for me after I'd hurt my arm, to deal one day with the realization that it was never going to get better. But up until that time, it's always, 'Hey, I'm young. You know. I'm 20 years old. This is gonna heal. Young people don't stay hurt forever, they get better.' Then one day you realize that, no, maybe you wouldn't."

Because he shot across the baseball sky like a meteor, Necciai has always been an intriguing figure. He became the stuff of baseball legend like John Paciorek who went three for three in his first major league game, an achievement every rookie dreams of, and never played another game in the majors. Necciai shared a softcover book called "A Glimpse of Fame," by Dennis Snelling of Modesto, California, a member of Society for American Baseball Research (SABR).

Necciai sat out the entire 1954 season. He was watching his minor league teammates from the stands at a game in Waco, Texas in the summer of 1955, when he decided he was never going to regain the ability to blow the ball by batters.

"I just decided to hell with it. 'I give up,' I said to myself," Necciai told Snelling. "I wasn't going to stay there the rest of my life. I would sit on the bench with my teammates and work out before the games then change clothes and go watch in the stands. I decided I better go find something else.

"It was pretty tough for awhile. You're kind of lost and you want to go hide, really. You're young. You finally got to the big leagues and you've only been there a month or two and all of a sudden, your arm's gone — the thing that got you there. And you can't figure out why. You say, 'Why me? What the hell did I do?' I've never had a sore arm all that time, and I get a sore arm and it lasts a lifetime."

Just before his 23rd birthday, the dream was over.

Necciai had viewed baseball as a gift that would get him out of working in the steel mills of Monongahela and Gallatin.

During World War II the mills operated 24 hours a day, and the demand for steel brought prosperity to the area.

Working the steel mill did not appeal to Necciai. Others were motivated for the same reason to work hard in school and go to college so they could earn a living in a different way. The mills were not for Necciai, that was for certain.

"You just go in every morning at seven o'clock and you do the same thing all day until three-thirty" he said. "And you go home and you go back the next day. And that's it. It was heavy industry. You work and you either bend springs or bend axles or load them or unload them or lubricate them or assemble them. But it's all basically the same thing. I wasn't there very long. But I was there long enough to know that I didn't want to be there forever."

Necciai found a way to escape the mills when he tagged along with a friend and went to a Pirates tryout camp. He was offered a contract in 1950 as a first baseman.

George Detore, the manager of the Class D team in Salisbury, North Carolina, where Necciai was assigned by the Pirates quickly switched the kid from first baseman to pitcher after he got a look at the youngster's throws to second base on the first-short-first double play. Plus, he was slow afoot and couldn't hit a curve ball, which helped Detore make his decision.

Necciai quit the team when things weren't going well and went home to Monongahela.

"I really don't know why I did that at the time," he said. "Maybe I was homesick. Maybe I didn't think I could play ball for a living or something. I really don't know. And to this day, I still don't know. It's just one of those things you do when you're young and impulsive."

Detore taught him how to throw a drop pitch. It looked like a fastball, but broke down sharply. Necciai went to Deland and New Orleans. Then he was sidelined by ulcer problems. He was spitting up blood. Necciai had a choice of where to go next to rehab and he chose Bristol where Detore was now the manager. Bristol was located in the northwestern tip of Virginia, near the borders of both North Carolina and Tennesee. It was a Class D Appalachian League team. Necciai was there to get back in shape to move up in organization. Branch Rickey kept an eye on his progress.

Necciai loved Detore, a former minor league catcher and Cleveland Indians infielder who was like a father to him. Detore enthralled him with stories about Ted Williams who had been a teammate on the old San Diego Padres team in the Pacific Coast League.

Harry Dunlop was the catcher. He called all the pitches. So Necciai would not have to worry about what pitches to throw. He just threw to the glove. He started to come around in a hurry. He fanned 20 and 19 in back to back games.

One night, Detore brought Necciai in from the bullpen against Johnson City in the seventh inning with the bases loaded and nobody out. Necciai struck out the side and the next eight in a row. His streak of 11 consecutive strikeouts broke the 42-year-old minor league record of Harry Ables.

On May 13, 1952, Necciai had his great game. He struck out 27 batters in a no-hitter against the Welch Miners. It was the first of five no-hitters by Bristol pitchers that season. Bill Bell tossed three of those no-hitters, two of them in consecutive starts. Frank Ramsey tossed another the day after Bell's third of the year.

"I thought this was the way baseball was going to be for me," declared catcher Harry Dunlop. "I thought baseball was going to be easy."

Only four Welch batters reached base that night: one on a walk, another by error, a third was hit by a pitch, and the fourth reached base when the ball eluded Dunlop on a swinging third strike with two out in the ninth. Once again, Necciai struck out 11 in a row, tying his own mark of just a few days before, a record that had previously stood for over four decades.

In all, 17 of the 27 strikeouts came on swinging strikes, including the last three in a row. He broke the previous professional record of 25 strikeouts, set by Clarence "Hooks" Iott in 1941. Iott, by the way, lasted only two years in the major leagues and had a 3-9 career mark.

"In those days," noted Necciai, "I did have a lot of health problems and that was one of the reasons for being there. I was there on a kind of a regimen and to learn to pitch the proper way. George and Harry had a game plan in which I was to throw so many pitches at so

Ron "The Rocket" Necciai captured the eyes of Branch Rickey, the Bucs' general manager. Rickey bid goodbye to Necciai and teammate Tony Bartirome when they left for military service in early January, 1953.

many given times. They'd feed me melba toast and cottage cheese and milk between innings, that was the accepted cure in those days for ulcers. I wasn't feeling good that night and I was a little bit worried about my stomach. It was burning and I used to take these little black pills. I was more concerned with not throwing up and having stomach pains than anything else."

He almost didn't pitch that day. Detore talked him into it, saying he'd yank him if his ulcers acted up. He was a heavy smoker, which couldn't have helped his condition. Necciai said he had no idea he was writing new history that night in Bristol because of the way things were going. He was wild, as usual, and throwing the ball all over the place. There were a lot of full counts on batters.

"You also have to realize this was not 27 men in a row, which would make you cognizant of everything," said Necciai. "You hit one batter. You walk one. A guy hits a ball. I'm throwing a lot of pitches. There's action. So it's not like Don Larsen in the World Series, everybody up and down.

"There never was a point when I realized how many I struck out. I realized that I had a no-hitter in about the seventh or eighth inning when the guys and the fans started counting."

Necciai got a lot of national publicity for his pitching feat, but nothing like what would happen these days. There was no *ESPN Sports Center* back then.

There was no *USA Today*. There were no sports stories in the *Wall Street Journal*.

There was a big feature in *The Sporting News*, then the national baseball weekly. Sportswriters were calling from all over the country to interview Necciai.

In his next start, there were over 5,000 fans squeezed into Shaw Stadium, including major league baseball scout Branch Rickey Jr. Necciai did not disappoint the people who came to see him pitch.

Necciai pitched a two-hit, 24-strikeout game, including five strikeouts in one inning. That was it for him as far as playing for Bristol. He left behind some unbelievable statistics. He pitched a total of 42²/₃ innings and gave up just ten hits. He tossed three shutouts, surrendered only ten base hits and struck out 109 batters. His final ERA was 0.42. Sixty-five percent of the batters who came up against him were strikeout victims. His record at Bristol was 4-0.

Burlington, North Carolina was his next stop.

At Burlington, the Pirates' Class B team, his record was 7-9 with a last place team. He led the league with a 1.57 ERA and 172 strikeouts in his 18 appearances. He was the winning pitcher in the Carolina League All-Star Game. Necciai broke Vinegar Bend Mizell's league record for consecutive strikeouts. In 169 minor league innings between Bristol and Burlington, Necciai had averaged 15 strikeouts per nine innings.

He got a call to go to Pittsburgh in July. "I was tickled to death. I was ready to go," said Necciai. "I wanted to go. And, of course, that was home. I lived nearby, just over twenty miles from the ballpark. I was anxious to go. I wanted to go up to the big leagues and see if I could do any good."

Necciai was looked upon as someone who could help in Pittsburgh.

He and Bill Bell both came up and it created some excitement.

"I was a thrower," said Necciai. "There's a big difference between a thrower and a pitcher. I had a tendency to just go to hell. I could throw ten strikes in a row and then eighteen balls in a row."

He made his major league debut against the Chicago Cubs on August 10, 1952. He was so nervous he smoked three packs of cigarettes in the clubhouse before the game. That couldn't have been good for his ulcers.

He was tagged for five runs in the first inning. Billy Meyer stuck with him. Necciai came out of the game in the bottom of the sixth with the Cubs leading 7-3. Necciai was upset, so he volunteered to pitch in relief the next night in Cincinnati. Joe Garagiola was catching. Necciai stuck out five of the first ten men he faced in his second outing in as many days.

His next start came on August 15 in St. Louis. He got his one and only big league hit in that game. He got knocked out early, but he met Stan Musial after the game. Musial hailed from Donora, the next town up the river from Necciai's hometown. There wasn't a bigger sports hero in the Mon Valley in those days than Stan "The Man."

Musial offered Necciai some words of encouragement, and that meant a great deal to the young pitcher.

On August 24, Necciai notched his first major league victory. "My one and only," said Necciai. "That was against the Boston Braves. That's how long ago that was. Sibby Sisti was playing for the Braves. And I remember that was in Pittsburgh and Murry Dickson relieved me in the ninth. We beat them, 4-3."

When the season was over, Necciai had dropped six of seven decisions with a 7.08 ERA. He struck out 312 at three different professional levels that season.

"I was very fortunate," said Necciai. "I had a chance to play in the big leagues. And there aren't many people who ever did that. I can always say I played the game, and I won one, and I got a base hit in the big leagues, a legitimate one."

Necciai knew his baseball career was finished, but he did not give up on life. He had a good supportive family. He wasn't going to roll over and die at 23.

He has worked hard in the sporting goods business. "They won't have to hold any benefits for me," he said. "I've done well. I can't complain."

> *"Who we really are is bigger than all the attributes of the world, whether in terms of fame or fortune."*
> —Rev. Robert Aguirre

"I caught three no-hitters in 14 days."
— Harry Dunlop

Harry Dunlop looks the part of a life-long baseball guy. He still looks good in a baseball uniform. He walks tall and looks like a guy who's having a good time. He puts on a uniform and participates in the warm-up session before each game. Then he changes clothes and sits in the stands, taking notes on what he sees. In Pittsburgh, he sits behind home plate with other scouts, someone like Chuck Tanner or his old friend Ron Necciai. They usually get together for lunch or dinner whenever the Reds are in town. They are linked forever by that one night back in Bristol.

Dunlop said he met Necciai for the first time in Sacramento, California at the outset of the 1952 season. "We became friends right off the bat in spring training," said Dunlop. "It was great when we went together from Bristol to Burlington later in the year. I wished I could have gone to Pittsburgh with him, too, but I never got to the big leagues as a ballplayer."

Dunlop said he remembered going to training camps with the Pirates in San Bernardino, California and Deland, Florida. He remembers being around Pirates like Ralph Kiner, Joe Garagiola, Bob Friend, Bob Skinner, Ronnie Kline, El Roy Face ("He's a great guy," notes Necciai) and Clyde McCullough. Dunlop smiles as he mentions each of them. He has so many memories stored under that silver-gray head.

"Everybody talks about the 27 batters Ron struck out," said Dunlop: "But he struck out 24 batters in the next game. I caught that one, too. In between those games, Bill Bell pitched two no-hitters. Bell was a right-hander. I caught three no-hitters in 14 days. I thought this was going to be easy."

Bell's stay in the big leagues was brief as well. "Bell got injured the year after he came up," recalled Dunlop. "Bell suffered severe injuries in an auto accident in the winter in Florida. He was never any good after that.

"We had some great arms in those days. There were only eight teams in each league, and you had to be good just to get to Double A and Triple A. There was a backup of talent. You had to wait your turn. Mr. Rickey was trying to do something different. He was trying to build with youth.

"I remember that when Vernon Law was with our club, too, and how he was going through some arm problems. Mr. Rickey thought of making him an outfielder. It's a good thing he didn't do that. But you never know, Babe Ruth and Stan Musial started off as pitchers and were switched to outfielders."

Cincinnati Reds' instructor Harry Dunlop enjoys reunion with Ron Necciai during ballgame at Three Rivers Stadium.

Photos by Jim O'Brien

Ron Necciai, left, and his brother, Attilio, at right, flank Ron's former teammate Bobby DelGreco at Pirates' Alumni gathering at Three Rivers Stadium.

He remembered that Necciai was a first baseman in the beginning, but was switched to the pitcher's position. Necciai had been recommended to the Pirates by a barber at the Schenley Hotel a block from the ballpark in Oakland. Everyone got excited about Necciai's prospects after he struck out the 27 batters at Bristol.

"We were so young at the time," said Dunlop. "I don't think we realized that no one had ever done it. No one has ever done it since, either.

"Ron had a tendency to be a little wild. I don't know if he ever threw three strikes in a row. They didn't have a speed gun in those days, but his fast ball had to be in the high 90s. He learned to throw a curve. They called it a drop in those days. It was like a split-finger fastball today.

"It was not easy to catch him. There were probably a lot of full counts. Nobody had pitch counts in those days. No one worried about it then.

"The night of his big game, the fans started calling out from 7th inning on that he had a no-hitter going and how many strikeouts he had.

"Bristol had a pretty good-sized ballpark. When I was 18, all ballparks were impressive to me. It was easily the best ballpark in the Appalachian League. Both of us only stayed there the month of May. I didn't start the season there. We traveled together in mid-May to Burlington, North Carolina. There were jokes around the Carolina League about us being a great battery. We were both tall and skinny. We kind of went together. But he had more talent. Guys would say, 'What's going to happen when Necciai goes to the big leagues? You're not going with him.' I just got to go to spring training with the Pirates. That's the best I ever got."

Dunlop remembered that Necciai had health concerns and control problems challenging him at the same time in those early days.

"He had ulcers," said Dunlop. "He was a worrywart about things. He had to be careful about what he ate. He couldn't eat a lot of things. George Detore was the manager at Bristol. Ron was a first baseman, but he couldn't hit that well. Detore called Rickey and asked him if they could make him into a pitcher. He had a fastball and a curve ball. He was double-jointed, and he threw a baseball overhand and would snap it off, unlike anybody else.

"He was difficult for a catcher. He threw a lot of curve balls into the dirt. He was very tough on the hitters when he got the ball over. His biggest problem was control.

"He had the kind of fastball Kevin Brown has when he's on. Ron threw the ball as hard as Tom Seaver. And his curve ball was like a ball rolling off a table.

He could have been something."

> *"Whatever you can do, or dream you can do, begin it. Boldness has genius, power, and magic in it."*
> —Johann Wolfgang von Goethe

"I can't believe Maz is not in the Hall of Fame."
— Ron Necciai

We sat at his kitchen table and talked about baseball. Like most members of the Pirates alumni, Necciai was pulling for his buddy Bill Mazeroski to make it into the Baseball Hall of Fame in 2000. "I can't believe Maz is not in the Hall of Fame," said Necciai. "He's better than Phil Rizzuto, that's for sure."

Rizzuto, a second baseman and then a long-time broadcaster for the New York Yankees, was inducted into the Baseball Hall of Fame in 1994.

I mentioned to Necciai that I had recently visited in Greensboro, North Carolina, with Mace Brown, who pitched for the Pirates in the late '30s. "I think he saw every game I pitched in the Carolina League," recalled Necciai.

He said he had seen Brown in Durham in 1993 at a reunion of everyone who had ever played for the Durham Bulls. "It was the last year they were using the ballpark they used in the movie Bull Durham," noted Necciai. "I was there because I pitched for Burlington against the Bulls in 1952, and drew the largest crowd they had for a game in many years. They called me and asked me to come."

He recalled that Johnny Vander Meer had pitched for the Durham Bulls.

I was browsing through scrapbooks and talking to Necciai at the same time. I came upon a quote from Branch Rickey, who was the head of the Pirates' front-office when Necciai was in the organization. Rickey, of course, was best known for bringing Jackie Robinson into the major leagues with the Brooklyn Dodgers, breaking the color line.

"I've seen a lot of baseball in my time," Branch Rickey is quoted as saying in Murray Polner's biography of the baseball legend. "There have been only two young pitchers I was certain were destined for greatness simply because they had the meanest fastball a batter can face. One of those boys was Dizzy Dean. The other is Ron Necciai. And Necciai is harder to hit."

When I commented to Necciai about the wealth of newspaper clippings in his scrapbook, he said, "I was never into writing that much. So I sent newspaper articles back home. If my name was in the boxscore, I sent it home."

I saw the name of Harry Dunlop in one of the box scores, and mentioned the former minor league catcher who was now a coach with the Cincinnati Reds. "He caught my 27-strikeout no-hitter in Bristol, and he caught two more no-hitters by Bill Bell the same month."

He told me how Kurt Pomrenke, an attorney who was a big baseball fan in Bristol, had promoted the idea of putting a plaque at the team's new ballpark to commemorate Neccai's 27-strikeout no-hitter.

"He said that ever since he read an article about me and that game in *Sports Illustrated* back in 1987 he wanted to do something to commemorate what happened," said Necciai. "He decided this spring to do it." Necciai showed me photographs from his big day at Bristol. He was especially proud that his pal, Bill Mazeroski, along with his wife, Milene, made the trip to Bristol to witness the ceremonies. Surely, seeing Maz was as big a treat for the ballfans in Bristol as having Necciai come back to be honored.

"I've been a big fan of his for a long time," Necciai said. "We were together in Hollywood back in 1955, but we didn't even know each other in those days. It shows you what kind of guy he is that he made the trip on my behalf.

"The fans were great. Two people gave me baseballs that were used in that game, and were signed. The scorer was there, and he had the book from that ballgame. It was in bad shape."

I looked at a reproduction of the boxscore from that ballgame. Necciai had one hit and one error next to his name. Dunlop, batting cleanup, had one hit and one error.

Necciai and his family traveled to Bristol, and attended ceremonies at DeVault Memorial Stadium. A large plaque calling attention to his 27-strikeout achievement was unveiled between games of a doubleheader between Bristol White Sox and Kingsport Mets. "Something like that really comes as a shock," said Necciai. "Gee whiz. But I'm very honored."

In late April of 2000, I was traveling to see Dave Hart in Asheville, North Carolina. A buddy of mine, Alex Pociask, was driving and I was the navigator. As we were nearing the North Carolina border, I spotted a sign indicating Bristol was just ahead. I had no idea when we began the trip that we'd be driving by Bristol.

We drove off the highway into Bristol and took two right turns and we were at DeVault Memorial Stadium. Bristol was the bonus of a week-long trip down memory lane. This wasn't, mind you, the same ballpark where Necciai had pitched his memorable game, but it was where he had been honored months earlier.

I took a picture of the plaque in his honor. The ballpark was an old-fashioned ballpark. The rich red clay had just been groomed. The green grass was lush. There were two rows of billboards advertising local businesses in some places along the outfield fence. It looked idyllic, a smaller version of what the Pirates hoped to recreate at PNC Park. I thought about Ron Necciai and his special night in Bristol.

> *"Somehow everything is connected in baseball. One story, one event, always reaches back for another. You understand the season you are watching because of something that happened before."*
> —Mike Lupica,
> *Summer of '98*

Fran Rogel
Pride of North Braddock

*"Fran Rogel was the toughest man
I've ever met in the NFL."*
— Bobby Layne

T he plaintive wail of a passing train and "Amazing Grace" played on bagpipes are the sounds that stay with me. They framed an hour-long program to pay tribute to former Steelers star running back Fran Rogel in his hometown of North Braddock on Saturday, March 25, 2000. They set a funeral-like tone to what was both a celebration and something close to a memorial service.

Rogel had turned 72 in December of 1999 and was in declining health physically and mentally. He suffered from Parkinson's Disease and dementia. His family, friends and fans wanted to make sure he knew how they felt about him before it was too late. Over 50 of them showed up to share his special day.

I followed Fran Rogel into the North Braddock Borough Building, 12 miles east of Pittsburgh. His younger brother Bernie brought him there from Fran's farm in Bakerstown, about 30 miles away. Bernie helped Fran get out of the automobile, and steadied Fran as he shuffled through the glass doors.

Parkinson's is a chronic progressive nervous disease of later life that causes tremors and weakness in muscles and usually an irregular walk. Boxing great Muhammad Ali was battling the same disease. Rogel had also undergone quadruple-bypass heart surgery.

Another younger brother, Elmer, entered the hallway in a wheelchair later on. The oldest brother, Bill, begged off, saying the only way he could come would be in an ambulance. Bill would die within three months. There were five kids in the Rogel family. By the way, the family pronounces its name Rogle and not Ro-gell. And you thought Tony Dorsett was the only local running back who changed the way his name was pronounced.

There was a solid chair set out in the hallway especially for Fran Rogel. He was seated in front of a showcase that contained jerseys and caps from the glory days of the Purple Raiders of North Braddock Scott High School. The hallway was crowded with people who were fond of Fran Rogel.

Rogel wore a blue and white Penn State warmup suit and ballcap that had been sent to him by Nittany Lions' football coach Joe Paterno nearly two years earlier when Rogel was honored at a dinner at the Churchill Country Club. He seldom spoke, and only offered a word or two when he did. It was difficult to discern what was registering in Rogel's mind, but he smiled and sang and wept when appropriate. He wept when they sang his school's fight song.

281

This was a man legendary quarterback Bobby Layne once called "the toughest man I've ever met in the NFL."

Rogel was a star running back at North Braddock High, at Cal State, Penn State and with the Steelers for eight seasons (1950-1957). His retirement as a player was prompted by a back ailment. He set records that were later surpassed by the likes of John Henry Johnson, Dick Hoak, Franco Harris, Rocky Bleier and Jerome Bettis. He was the Steelers' leading rusher in five of six seasons from 1951 through 1956, finishing second to Ray Mathews of McKeesport in 1952. Rogel represented the Steelers in the 1957 Pro Bowl, along with Mathews, Jack Butler, Dale Dodril, Ernie Stautner and Frank Varrichione. Going into the 2000 season, Rogel still ranked in the Top Ten on the Steelers' all-time rushing list.

"You always knew that Fran would give you his best effort," said Butler, a four-time Pro Bowl performer, when he appeared at a tribute dinner to Rogel back on September 18, 1998. "He was a man's man, and made no excuses. He wanted the ball and he enjoyed the hitting, the harder the better. He typified our ball club back then. He was strictly an inside runner because of his power, and a guy who gave 100 percent whether it was practice or in a game."

Fran Rogel was the first pro football player I ever met in person. My father introduced me to him at Frankie Gustine's Restaurant in Oakland, just across the street from Forbes Field where the Steelers and Pirates played in those days. It was 1952 and I was ten years old.

My father hoisted me onto a barstool so I could be at eye level with Fran Rogel. He was a husky 5-11, 205 pounds at the time. He looked about 5-7 or 5-8 on his return to his hometown. I was asked to talk about Rogel at the hallway gathering, and about his role as a hometown hero. It was an easy assignment.

The Forbes Field faithful used to chant "Hi, Diddle, Diddle, Rogel up the middle!" It was often chanted to criticize the Steelers for their predictable offense. Today, they call it smash-mouth football. Joe Tucker was credited for making that chant so popular as he often mentioned it on radio broadcasts.

"He always carried the ball up the middle on first down," recalled Dan Rooney, the president of the Steelers, when asked about Rogel in late May, 2000. "A sportswriter named Bob Drum convinced our coach, Walt Kiesling, to do something else on first down in this one game. Our quarterback threw a pass for a touchdown on the first play of the game. But we were offsides and it was called back. Drum said Kiesling had the player go offside on purpose to kill the play. Fran was a fearless player, and a good man. My dad liked him a lot."

On this Saturday afternoon, Rogel was seated in a hallway at the North Braddock Borough Building that had many trophies, jerseys, dried-up and flaking footballs, photographs — so many mementos and memories. At times Rogel appeared bewildered by the all the fuss, and there was a sadness as well as a gladness about the whole scene.

FRAN ROGEL

BOBBY LAYNE

Steelers' 50 Seasons celebration lineup in 1982 was, from left to right, Mean Joe Greene, Fran Rogel, author Jim O'Brien and John Brown.

There was a framed photo of the 1937 North Braddock Scott team that won the WPIAL Class AA football title. Bill Rogel was an all-state guard on that team. They also won WPIAL football titles in 1933, 1934 and 1935. They won 42 straight football games in that era. There was a plaque commemorating the school's PIAA basketball title in 1931. They won the WPIAL basketball title in 1931 and 1943. Now there would be a new plaque on the wall, this one acknowledging the outstanding career of Fran Rogel, a hometown hero.

Two of Rogel's greatest admirers, Bill Priatko and Rudy Celigoi, organized this tribute as well as the earlier testimonial dinner. Both starred in football at North Braddock Scott in the early '50s. Priatko presided over the program, citing the highlights of Rogel's career as a player, coach and teacher. Rogel later returned to Braddock Scott as a football coach and teacher, and did the same later on at Highlands High School in Natrona Heights.

Priatko was a rookie linebacker for the Steelers in 1957, Rogel's final season with the Steelers. "Fran Rogel was the epitome of on-the-field toughness," pointed out Priatko. "He didn't know what it was to quit."

Celigoi coached the offensive line for Rogel at North Braddock Scott in the '60s. "Fran coached like he played — tough," said Celigoi. "He was a hard worker who expected the kids to be the same. And they were."

I arrived about an hour before the kickoff for the Rogel tribute and had a chance to tour some of the streets of North Braddock and nearby Braddock. I walked in some neighborhoods, drove my car through others. Like Rogel, the communities of North Braddock and Braddock had seen better days. They were still making steel at the Edgar Thomson Works of the USS Division of USX Corporation, but there were not nearly as many workers there as there were in the area's heyday. The main street of town, once one of the four busiest business strips in the Pittsburgh area, was a ghost of its former self. It was similar to so many Mon Valley and Ohio Valley communities in that respect.

I checked out the statue of General Braddock and what was once Scott High's stadium. Braddock High School used to play its home games there, too. I had toured that same stadium a few years earlier with Hall of Fame football coach Chuck Klausing. Klausing posted a 53-0-1 record in six undefeated championship seasons there in the mid- to late '50s while coaching Braddock. That remained a WPIAL record for consecutive titles.

You could see Kennywood Park across the river from there. The stadium surface had been prepared for baseball. The first time I was ever in North Braddock was as a benchwarmer with the Hazelwood Little League All-Star baseball team. We lost to North Braddock. I was 12 at the time.

Going back to North Braddock can make you young again.

Fran Rogel remains a hometown hero in his native North Braddock.

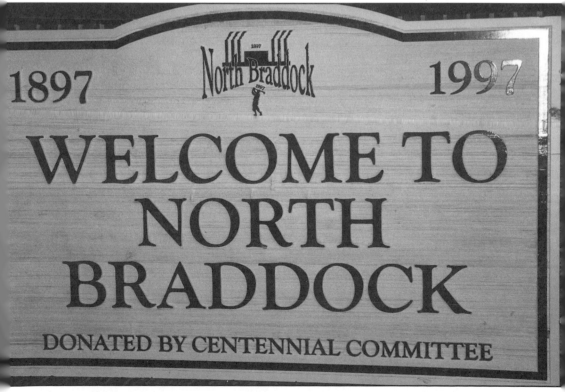

"Where'd you get that name?"

Bernie Oriss grew up just a few doors away from the home of Fran Rogel in North Braddock. Bernie's dad, Mike, was the athletic director at North Braddock Scott when Rogel was starring for Johnny Reed's ballclub.

Oriss, now of North Huntingdon, said he took the name "Francis" when he was confirmed at his church because he was such a fan of Francis Stephen Rogel. "Where'd you get that name?" his mother asked him when he told her of his choice. When he explained, his mother agreed it was a fitting name.

Bernie later became the head basketball coach and athletic director at North Braddock Scott High, and taught in the Woodland Hills School District after a merger of several schools east of Pittsburgh. He was among the many friends and fans of Rogel who showed up for the plaque unveiling at the North Braddock Borough Building.

Also seen were Ernie Gennaccaro, former superintendent of North Braddock School District and General Braddock School District, and Dr. Mike Girman, a former superintendent at Turtle Creek, West Mifflin and Frazier. Bob Garritano, who grew up in North Braddock and was now the principal at Laurel Valley High School in Ligonier, was there, too, leading the singing of Scott's alma mater and fight song "Shine, shine, Scott High will shine tonight!"

Those in attendance included Chuck Hageder, former football coach and physical education instructor for many years at West Mifflin, and George Burdell, famous at North Braddock Scott for scoring long touchdown runs all four times he touched the ball in a game against Taylor Allderdice High School.

John Varoscak, who grew up in Braddock and Rankin, was a member of Louisville's NIT title basketball team in 1958, and became an administrator in the Pittsburgh School District, was there, along with Tom Guerrieri, a former elementary school principal in the North Braddock and Woodland Hills School District. Ed Calabria, a former North Braddock football player, was there in his role as the borough manager.

Two former teammates of Fran Rogel at North Braddock Scott, Petey Paul and Dr. Fenton Mitchell of West Penn Hospital, unveiled the new plaque. An identical plaque was on display nearby at the Grand View Golf Club, on the site of a sandlot ballfield where Fran played as a youngster.

Don MacMillan played the bagpipes. Before North Braddock Scott's teams were known as the Purple Raiders they were known as the Highlanders. So there was a history to bagpipes in the school.

Also present were Joe Pekar, former football coach and principal at Baldwin High School. He also coached football at Norwin High. Jack "Beansy" Hyland, a quarterback at North Braddock High in the post-Rogel era and later a coach at Meadville, Ferndale and

FRAN ROGEL

Rochester, as well as at Edinboro College, was swapping war stories to the delight of all.

Two of his former NBS teammates, Rudy Celigoi and Bill Priatko, kept urging Hyland to tell more stories. Priatko's brothers, George and John, and a sister, Marion Campbell, came to the ceremonies to lend their support. Tony Munson, publisher of *The Valley Mirror*, was there to take photographs and witness the community event.

A grand time was had by all.

"I never forgave Rogel for that."
— Leon Hart

Fran Rogel was one of Art Rooney's all-time favorite football players. Rooney liked him so much that he named one of his racehorses after him, something he did for Elbie Nickel and John Henry Johnson as well. Rooney named one of his thoroughbreds "Ironman Rogel" in his honor.

Bill Rogel, one of Fran's brothers, had a picture of the colt standing in the winner's circle at a Jamaica, New York racetrack on April 8, 1957, according to a report by sports historian Jimmy Dunn.

Written on the bottom of the picture was a personal message that was signed by Art Rooney: "I hope the horse Ironman Rogel has a heart as big as the man Fran Rogel."

Rogel had first made his mark as a schoolboy athlete at North Braddock Scott. He was selected as a junior and senior to the All-WPIAL football team.

One game that helped establish Rogel's reputation as a hard-nosed, pile-driving running back came in his junior season.

North Braddock Scott had only one loss on its record going into the final game of the season. They were playing Turtle Creek, led by an equally impressive junior named Leon Hart. Turtle Creek came into the game undefeated.

Hart went on to win the Heisman Trophy at Notre Dame in 1947, and was an All-Pro performer, evening going both ways at times, as an end with the Detroit Lions of the 1950s. The Lions and Cleveland Browns were the best teams in that period.

The North Braddock Scott-Turtle Creek game was twice delayed by heavy rains and was played on a Monday afternoon. A reported 10,000 fans were shoehorned into the Bell Avenue stadium for the showdown. It was Rogel who bulled his way into the end zone in a 7-0 victory for the Purple Raiders.

The next season it was Rogel running for all three touchdowns in a 19-6 win over Hart and Turtle Creek.

"I never forgave Rogel for that," said Hart, who had to cancel coming to Rogel's dinner tribute after he learned that he had cancer. This news was just another acknowledgment that our sports heroes are real people, subject to the same challenges as everyone else.

Jimmy Dunn discovered in his research that Rogel had built up his legs with an exercise called "duck walking," often going the length of the field in that awkward position, sometimes with a smaller team-mate riding on his shoulders.

His coach, Johnny Reed, wanted college scouts to see Rogel's legs so they could fully appreciate the source of his strength as a runner, and why he was able to break tackles.

Whenever a college recruiter would visit Reed's office to inquire about Rogel, the coach would instruct his star back to drop his pants so the coach could eye those legs. Rogel would blush, and do as he was told. Players didn't question their coaches much in those days.

"I didn't know if they were looking for a football player or a chorus girl," Rogel was reported to have said during his senior season.

A year later, in 1946, Rogel reported to what was then called California State Teachers College. The Vulcans were a farm team for Penn State in those days due to the influx of World War II vets enrolling under the G.I. Bill at Penn State's main campus in State College.

With Rogel rushing the ball, Cal State went undefeated in 10 games and claimed the mythical State Teachers College Championship that season. Then he transferred to Penn State for his sophomore season.

He gained 615 yards for Coach Bob Higgins' undefeated squad in 1947. That included his 95-yard rushing performance against Southern Methodist and Doak Walker in a 13-13 standoff at the Cotton Bowl on January 1, 1948. He was carried off the field afterward on the shoulders of his North Braddock buddies, Fred Burdell and Bill Savko. Upon his graduation from Penn State, Rogel was an eighth round draft selection of the Steelers. It was one of the best late round draft choices in team history.

William R. Johnson
Heinz President and CEO:
"We want people who are adaptable, self-disciplined and who have an entrepreneurial outlook. Above all, we look for motivation. When I look at the most successful people I've worked with, I always see the same attributes: common sense, passion and dedication. Give me managers with those qualities and I'll give you an unbeatable team."

Deacon Dan Towler
His heroes are in the Bible

"Athletics for me was not the main show."

Deacon Dan Towler remains one of the great names in football history. It's one of those storied names you like to say slowly so it can be savored. It conjures up challenging and glorious times in a different era.

It brings to mind a boyhood collection of bubble gum cards stored in a bedroom closet. They were black and white cards, wrapped in a rubber band or gum band, as we called them. Steelers, Pirates and any players from Western Pennsylvania were particularly treasured. It was as close as most young fans would get to sports stars in those days.

In the mid-'50s, people we thought were rich were starting to get TVs in the neighborhood. A sports event on TV was a once-a-week offering at best. We'd sneak a peek through the windows of their homes as we passed by. So football players like "Deacon" Dan Towler did their thing in a far-off land. Like LA or Oz.

"Deacon" Dan Towler came out of Donora High School in the mid-'40s to star with Washington & Jefferson College and with the Los Angeles Rams in the National Football League. He was an exceptional player and an even more impressive person, and he left his mark in a positive manner wherever he roamed.

He was a big halfback for his time, at six feet, 180 pounds, and he liked to run over people. He was pleasant and well mannered in the classroom and locker room, but a ferocious competitor on the football field. He gained his nickname in middle school, first because his father was a deacon at their neighborhood church, then because Dan had a strong religious bent and, in time, became a minister.

There were far fewer teams in the NFL back then and you could memorize the starting lineups of all the teams. There was a magic to all the names, like Norm "Wild Man" Willey, Dante Lavelli, Mac Speedie and Dub Jones. Steve Van Buren, Gordie Solteau, Frankie Albert, Ollie Matson. It's fun just to say them again.

Towler came from a golden sports era — the 1940s and 1950s — when great players had great nicknames. Like "Stan the Man" Musial, a Hall of Fame baseball player from the same hometown along the Monongahela River in Washington County. Like some of his Rams' teammates, Dick "Night Train" Lane, Elroy "Crazy Legs" Hirsch and Paul "Tank" Younger. "Night Train" remains an all-time great nickname.

At Donora, Towler played for what is regarded as one of the greatest high school football teams of all time. His teammates included Arnold "Pope" Galiffa and Lou "Bimbo" Cecconi. That's when

"Deacon Dan" at W&J

Dan Towler came out of Donora to star at Washington & Jefferson College.

Donora, just 28 miles south of Pittsburgh, had its own high school, long before it was merged with Monongahela into the Ringgold School District. Towler lived a block away from Donora High School, located at the corner of Fourth Street and Waddell Avenue.

Towler was twice an all-state halfback when Donora went undefeated and won consecutive WPIAL football titles in 1944 and 1945. That team was rated No. 2 in the nation by one sports publication, second only to a Texas team led by Bobby Layne and Doak Walker.

"The Doaker" and Layne were among Towler's NFL contemporaries, along with the likes of Charlie "Choo-Choo" Justice and Clyde "Bulldog" Turner.

The Steelers in those days had terrific running backs with wonderful nicknames like Johnny "Zero" Clement and "Bullet Bill" Dudley.

Towler was one of two blacks on the football team at W&J in 1947, the same year that Jackie Robinson broke the color line in major league baseball. That is also the same year that Connellsville's Johnny Lujack won the Heisman Trophy while leading Notre Dame to a national championship.

"It was exciting when Jackie Robinson broke into baseball," recalled Towler. "It would be a while before the Pirates had any blacks. I met Branch Rickey ten years later at a Fellowship of Christian Athletes meeting and I heard him talk about those early days with Robinson. It was quite edifying. He was a role model for many of us."

Towler had done some trailblazing of his own at the academically-demanding liberal arts college in Washington, Pennsylvania. He shared a dorm room with the other black ballplayer, Walter Cooper, a halfback from Clairton who became a big success himself as an executive at Kodak Corporation in Rochester, New York. Cooper served two terms on the board of trustees at W&J.

"They had to get someone to room with me," Towler tells you with a smile.

His pioneering spirit served him well when he went to the NFL. There had been a few blacks on ball clubs in the early days of pro football, but they disappeared for some inexplicable reason from the lineups in the 1930s. Blacks came back to pro football in 1946, the year before Robinson broke the color line in baseball, and with little fuss or fanfare.

Dan Reeves, the owner of the Los Angeles Rams, signed two UCLA ballplayers, halfback Kenny Washington and lineman Willie Strode. Later, Strode gained even more fame in Hollywood as a movie actor (clashing with Kirk Douglas in a memorable gladiator scene in "Spartacus"). Paul Brown signed two blacks to his Browns team in the All-America Football Conference that same season. They were lineman Bill Willis and fullback Marion Motley. That was a breakthrough, but Towler said there were still only 14 blacks in the NFL when he joined the Rams in 1950.

292

Lester Nehamkin

"Deacon Dan" in L.A. days

From Towler family photo album.

Maury Wills of Los Angeles Dodgers meets Rev. Dan Towler

Rev. Towler meets one of his heroes, Jackie Robinson of Brooklyn Dodgers.

The Rams and Browns were two of the best pro football teams in those days, so their owners were well rewarded for their open-minded hiring practices. Willis and Motley, for instance, are both honored in the Pro Football Hall of Fame. The New York Giants had Emlen Tunnell and he's in the Hall of Fame, too.

Towler was more than equal to the challenge, on and off the field, and was a real role model. He found his heroes in the Bible, and his direction from his father and mother, William and Evelyn Towler, and a New York-bred businessman named Sam Silver who owned and operated the movie theatre in Donora during Dan's high school and college days. Sam Silver — what a great name — was a mentor for the young Towler and taught him about the world of business and how to relate to people. "Sam Silver helped a lot of young people," said Cecconi when I mentioned Silver's name to him at an Italian-American Sports Hall of Fame banquet in April of 2000. "Sam sold Pitt on giving me a scholarship because I was on the small side for football and basketball. We had quite a team. You won't find classier guys than Arnold Galiffa and Dan Towler."

Then, too, Stan Musial was the most famous hometown hero, preceding Towler by six years at Donora High School, and often returning to his old neighborhood. Musial set the standards for a lot of young men in the Mon Valley. He was one of the all-time class acts in the sports world.

When Musial retired in 1963 after 22 years with the St. Louis Cardinals, he had completely re-written the National League record book. His steadfast dedication to the game and his uncommon decency earned him the nickname "The Man," a nickname that fit him as well as his Cardinals uniform.

Broadcaster Harry Caray once said, "Stan Musial was the greatest star. Not only because of his great ability, but because of the man, the character, the soul of the man, " according to a Musial biography by Jerry Lansche. The same could be said of Towler, who was cut from the same cloth.

Towler became a minister during his pro football career, retiring from the Rams when he could have continued to play a few more years. He was offering counsel and spiritual help to college students into his 70s.

Towler was invited by his alma mater to be among alumni honored at a golf outing and dinner sponsored by the school's Pete Henry Society on August 9, 1999 at the Southpointe Golf Club in Canonsburg.

Wilbur "Pete" Henry had been an All-America tackle at W&J in 1920 and later a coach and athletic director there. He was a charter member of the Professional Football Hall of Fame. Russ Stein gained All-America honors as a lineman in 1921 and captained a W&J team that played California in the Rose Bowl. Those were the days when W&J, Pitt, Duquesne and Carnegie Tech all had nationally-respected football programs and played in post-season bowl games.

Russ and his brother, Herb, an All-American lineman at Pitt, and Pete Henry all played for the Pottsville Maroons in the early days of the NFL.

Towler was the next great football player and gentleman to grace the W&J campus. He wore No. 62, hardly a halfback's number even in those days. He left his mark at W&J. When he appeared at the golf outing and dinner at Southpointe, he still held the school record for average points per game, 16.6, with 133 points in only eight games in his junior year. Towler was named Little All-American three times at W&J in 1946, 1948 and 1949. He was sidelined with a leg injury during the 1947 campaign. He also received an honorary Doctor of Humane Letters from W&J.

There are Towler memorabilia among the school's sports artifacts on display at the Henry Memorial Center, the campus gym.

After college, Towler played for the Los Angeles Rams while attending graduate school at the University of Southern California. With the Rams, Towler gained 3,493 yards rushing in six seasons, a Rams' record that held up for two decades. He was a four-time All-Pro with the Rams and led the NFL in rushing in 1952. He eventually earned a doctorate at USC.

Towler had returned from his home in Pasadena — site of the Rose Bowl — to the same area on June 18, 1999 to be inducted into the Washington/Greene County Chapter of the Pennsylvania Sports Hall of Fame at The Holiday Inn at the Meadow-lands.

He was honored along with Dave Abraham (track & field), Barry Alvarez (football), Sammy Angott (boxing), Mark Caffrey (wrestling), Ralph Cindrich (football and wrestling), Ben Junko (cross-country and wrestling), William Knox (basketball), John Luckhardt (football), Del Miller (harness racing), Guy Montecalvo (football), John Riser (basketball), Jerry Sandusky (football), Elaine Sobansky (track & field) and Ted Vactor (football).

As usual, Towler was keeping good company.

"Donora was one of the best towns in the U.S.A."

"Deacon" Dan Towler was still a big man and a good man, at age 72, when I met him for the first time. He was robust, powerfully built, and he still walked tall, quite a contrast, for instance, to Fran Rogel, a full-back for the Steelers during Towler's NFL days. I had seen Rogel, also 72, on several occasions in recent years and he was a shadow of his former self, challenged by Parkinson's disease and dementia.

Towler's knees were balky, and stairways weren't his best friends, but his discomfort wasn't that noticeable. Towler was told to dress in a casual manner for the dinner. He arrived in an open-collared black and white print shirt. When he saw how many people were showing up in coat and tie, he had someone go back to his hotel room to secure the same for him. He wanted to dress appropriately.

If you were making a movie of his life, you'd cast James Earl Jones in the role of the contemporary Towler. He has that kind of presence. He was still a formidable figure until he offered a smile and handshake. Both were warm.

Art Rooney, the late owner of the Steelers, once shared the observation that you could tell a Pittsburgher by the warmth of his handshake. I'm not sure whether he had any scientific evidence to back that statement, but Rooney's remark came to mind when I shook the hand of "Deacon" Dan Towler.

Meeting him and shaking his hand were special. Rod Piatt, the president of the Southpointe Golf Club, let us use his office for an interview. His father, Jack B. Piatt, was responsible for developing an ambitious and attractive industrial park on rolling hills in Canonsburg. Rod's brother, Jack B. II, looked after Millcraft Industries in the same complex.

"My outlook on life came from my father," said Towler in an interview session. "That was not to be just a ballplayer, just to be a person. Athletics for me was not the main show.

"My father's name was William Lee Towler. He was from Danville, Virginia. He worked in a steel mill until he was 45. His job at the mill was as a wire drawer. Then he went into business for himself. My mother Evelyn died when she was only 48. I was 12 years old at the time she passed. She was sick for a long time. I was cared for by my sisters, Mary and Martha. I had four brothers and six sisters, and one stepbrother. So there were 11, though one died when I was young.

"Religion was always important in my family. My inspiration has always come from my faith. My father was a Biblical student. He never went beyond sixth grade, but he knew the Bible. It was his book for life. The heroes in my Bible were my heroes for life. Like Joseph and David and Solomon. They were just Biblical heroes, but they provided you with all the values you needed to cope with the challenges of the world.

"My experience, being raised mainly by my father, was different from most of the people I have counseled through the years. Usually, it's the mothers and grandmothers who raise kids, especially in the black community. There are many great mothers who carry on the show. From my experience as a minister, you're better off just having a mother if you have a raggedy father. Personally, I go for the whole family. What I've learned is that when you are looking after young people you've got to be involved.

"Donora had a lot of great athletes. I knew Ken Griffey who grew up in Donora. His son, Ken Griffey, Jr., was born there. They are still a point of pride to the community. Athletics was what made the community a community. They came out to support us in football, basketball and even track & field. Quite often, the way the town celebrated was through its teams. It was a close-knit community. It was a steel mill town, but Donora was one of the best towns in the United States.

"During that time, most of the men worked in the steel mill. It was going 24 hours a day. You'd go to work on 3-to-11 shift, or 11-7 — they called it the graveyard shift — or from 7 to 3. The big Italian and Croatian boys went to work in the mills. The money was good. I worked in the mill in the summer when I was 14, but they found out I was too young. When I was old enough, I went back to work in the mills during the summer months. I knew I didn't want to work in the mills, so it was beneficial to find out what it was like when I was still in high school."

Donora drew national attention, for something other than Stan Musial and "Deacon" Dan Towler, at the height of their popularity in their hometown.

In 1948 there was an inversion which trapped deadly fumes within the valley, and there was a killing fog for nearly a week. They still talk about that weather phenomenon which threatened the townspeople. All that smoke from the blast furnaces, galvanizing mills and zinc plant weren't blowing down the river.

Most of Donora's inhabitants were immigrants from Germany, Poland, Italy, Czechoslovakia and Russia. It was Stanislaus Musial who lived in those modest homes on Sixth Street and Marelda Avenue. That was 1139 Marelda Avenue, and the locals pointed it out to visitors as if it were a historic house. Those who knew Musial well might refer to him as Stashu, Stash and Stush.

"We lived way at the top of the hill. The last street was Waddell Avenue," said Towler, returning to his boyhood home in Donora. "We lived seven doors from the high school. I'd never leave home until the bell started ringing. I'd be there before the bell stopped ringing. I'd run up an alley and be there on time. I'd run home for lunch and wait until the bell rang again to return to school.

"None of my brothers played any sports. I learned some valuable lessons from them. They broke my father's rules and they got in trouble. But I wouldn't make the same mistakes. My father was all business, and he had no concept of how sports could benefit our family. I had no idea it would lead me where it did, but I liked sports and was good at it, and really put my heart and soul into it. I had a sense of self, and wanted to make the most of my opportunities.

"Our football coach and athletic director was Jimmy Russell. We had a great football team. Our quarterback, Arnold Galiffa, was a great all-around athlete. He was tall, really outstanding in football. He was an All-American at Army and good enough to sign with the New York Giants for a season. We had another back, Roscoe Ross, and he was the greatest high school player I ever played with. He had brushes with the law and wasted his talent. Lou 'Bimbo' Cecconi later starred as a two-way player in football at Pitt, and he was one of their best basketball players, too.

"I was fortunate to always be surrounded by good players and good people. We had a lot of great players when I was with the Rams. We had a great group of guys. Our quarterbacks were Bob Waterfield and Norm Van Brocklin. We had two great ends in Elroy Hirsch and Tom Fears. The Rams really changed pro football. We were the first team to have our helmets decorated with our team logo.

"Our other top back was Tank Younger of Grambling. He was the first player from a small black college to play in the NFL. He was a bull elephant. He came in 1949 and I came in 1950. I was the fullback in that backfield.

"We had some great defensive players, too, like linebacker Don Paul and defensive back, 'Night Train' Lane. We had great coaches, too, in Joe Stydahar, Hampton Pool and Sid Gillman. There were 14 black players in the league in 1950 and 1951, and the Rams had five. Cleveland had Marion Motley, Len Ford, Bill Willis and Horace Gillom. The Giants had Emlen Tunnell. Joe Perry was with the 49ers. John Henry Johnson was still in Canada. Those were some of the guys I remember.

"I was lucky to be able to remain involved in football even after I retired as a player. I worked with the statistics crew in the press box for all the USC, and then the UCLA games. I did that for over 30 years. I used to do them all. I was never home on weekends. I just love to watch the game.

"I've had a great life. I've been lucky to be able to remain involved with young people, work on a college campus — there's so much vitality and life on a college campus — and it all goes back to the beginning. From the outset, I had a solid base. My sisters treated me like a baby and saw to it that was I was safe and secure.

"My father set the rules. He administered the rules. He would tell you not to say something. He made you be a responsible person. Sometimes we didn't like the old man. He was tough on us at times. But you knew what was right and wrong. The kids today often don't know the difference between right and wrong. The parents work so much they often don't see enough of their kids to keep them in tow. Kids have to be taught some rules. They need to know that you can't always do what you want to do. You have to work at doing it right. It's like football. Training is hard, but you have to do it. Then you can freelance. You can improvise, just like a great artist.

"I was very, very fortunate. I visited 15 or so schools. I chose W&J. After visiting Ohio State, Pitt and Purdue, I came to the conclusion that those guys were there to play football. I wanted to get an education and be prepared for life.

"I knew that all football could do for me happened in high school. It was as good as it could get. One year we gave up only one touchdown. It was a one yard score by Altoona. This guy stole the ball from me and took the ball for a yard into the end zone.

"I got to meet and get to know Stan Musial when I was in high school. Stan was an outstanding player and an outstanding young man. He came around during basketball season and would work out with us in the gym. He'd do his off-season training with us before he'd go to spring training. He was a fair-haired boy. Every season when he came home they used to give him a new car. A fellow named Frank Pizzica owned a car dealership near Donora and he took good care of Stan. He was the Man all right, Stan the Man. I had a relationship with his mother.

"Stan's mother, Mary, worked for Sam Silver at the Harris Theater where I spent a lot of time. That's how I knew the family. Stan's father's name was Lukasz Musial.

"Sam Silver was an important man in my life. He was a great fan. He was a New York guy. He adopted me; he treated me like a son. He'd help guys get into college. Sam came to town during my junior year. I was a celebrity in Donora by that time.

"He'd let me in the movies for nothing. I'd go to his office. I was privileged to do that. He showed me how to relate to other people. The other guys were loafing, running the streets, but he kept me busy doing things.

"He gave me my first sports jacket. I never wanted to disappoint Sam. So I stayed out of trouble. If I'd done anything Sam would have heard about it and I'd have been ashamed. I was scared to do anything out of line. I didn't want anyone telling Sam I'd done something off base. Before I'd do anything, I'd ask myself, 'How would Sam feel about this?'

"When I came to California, it was a challenging place for a young man. I was making $5500 my first year with the Rams, and back then that seemed like a lot of money. The only thing that saved me in California was the discipline I'd grown up with. There were all kinds of things that could swallow you up. I was always talking to Sam, telephoning him, just like I did when I was at W&J. Sam was always there to talk to me. I had someone else I've always been able to talk to. I was lucky to always have a good partner. My partner is Jesus Christ."

"He's an interesting guy."
—John Luckhardt

One of "Deacon" Dan Towler's greatest admirers at Washington & Jefferson College is John Luckhardt, the school's athletic director and one of its prime fund-raisers. Luckhardt was responsible for returning W&J's football program to national recognition as an NCAA Division III power.

Luckhardt, a classmate of Rick Leeson on an outstanding Scott High School football team in the late '50s, was looking to the year 2000 and the new millenium. There were some impressive projects on the drawing board that included several new buildings on the Washington campus, and a refurbished football facility to be called Cameron Stadium.

There were about $5.2 million worth of projects that would greatly enhance the football environment at W&J, and that included a new building to house the locker rooms, training rooms and weight rooms to be called Towler Hall in honor of one of the school's most famous graduates.

Luckhardt coached the W&J football team for 17 seasons, compiling a record of 137-37-2, a winning percentage of .784 that places him among the all-time leaders in small college competition. After a series of health scares, he gave way as coach after the 1998 season to one of his assistants, former Steelers defensive standout John Banaszak.

He focused his activities on providing solid support for Banaszak and his staff, as well as the school at large in helping to recognize some ambitious plans on a campus-wide scale.

"We will make sure that Dan Towler is not forgotten at W&J," said Luckhardt, who played his college ball at Purdue though he would have preferred to join his Scott teammate Leeson at the University of Pittsburgh. "He represents the best of what we have to offer here, and his heritage is a point of pride to everyone associated with this school. He set a good example for all of us.

"He's a perfect model for the heritage of the program. He stands for what we want our athletic program to be about. He had a chance to go to some really big-time football programs at places like Ohio State and Illinois and even my alma mater, Purdue. He came from a Donora High School team that is still regarded as maybe the greatest from this region. And he chose to come to Washington & Jefferson College.

"He's an interesting guy. You know he got his degree here in Greek Classics. He wanted to go somewhere that stressed academics. He came to a school that had little minority representation. It's been a pattern for him throughout his life. He's knocked down a lot of walls in his time.

"He and Pete Henry are thought to be the greatest players in the history of this institution. Dan turned down some more glitzy places to come here because of what he thought was more important. And he helped establish some pretty high standards here. When I was coaching here and recruiting, I liked to boast about Deacon Dan Towler and his place in our school's history.

"Then look at what he did in the pros. They weren't getting paid a lot of money in those days, but they were still making more than the average Joe. Yet he left pro football early, at the height of his success,

Dan Towler played basketball as well as football and track & field during his days at Donora High School. He is seen in pulpit at Lincoln United Methodist Church in Pasadena, and with former W&J roommate and teammate Walter Cooper.

to go into the ministry. He continues to characterize the kind of football player and student we're looking for at W&J. It's more than X's and O's.

"Back in 1990, Towler came here for the 40th year reunion of his senior class. It coincided with the 100th year of football here at Washington & Jefferson. That 1990 team was quite a team, and it established a base for a great run we had here in the '90s. We beat Fordham and Duquesne that year and had an undefeated regular season.

"I had Towler and Walter Cooper and Bill Span speak to the team on the eve of our Homecoming game. We didn't like to keep that team too long at our meetings because they were eager to get going. Cooper, of course, was in the same backfield as Towler, and Span was the center for their team. Span became a war hero in his 40s. He was an ace in Vietnam, and he had also fought in the Korean War.

"The three of them spoke for about 50 minutes, and our guys paid strict attention to them. There wasn't any sign of restlessness among our guys. They captivated them. They really connected with our guys. They were 40 years older than our guys, but they saw the world through the same prism.

"Cooper retired as a senior vice president of Kodak. He was a chemistry major here at W&J. He set up a few foundations and he raises money for disenfranchised people all over the world.

"Some other things you should know about Towler. He was named to the all-time team of the Rams. He and Eric Dickerson were the running backs on the team. That's pretty good company. They were both pictured on the cover of the media guide going into their Super Bowl season. ESPN did a feature on Towler going into Super Bowl week."

"He has an aura about him."
—Paul Zolak

Paul Zolak was in his third year as athletic director at Bethel Park, but gained a reputation as one of the area's finest scholastic administrators when he served as athletic director for 20 of his 28 years at Ringgold High School. While at Ringgold, he started a Wall of Fame in the school hallway for outstanding sports and academic stars in the school's history.

Ringgold came into being in 1969 as a jointure of Donora High School and Monongahela High School, and five other townships, namely Carroll, New Eagle, Nottingham, Elrama and Gastonville. Donora and Monongahela remained in their own buildings for ten years before everyone was housed under one roof in a new building in 1979.

Zolak said there were some real growing pains because the schools had been such fierce rivals.

"Deacon Dan Towler was one of the first to be so honored," recalled Zolak when we spoke to him in March of 2000. "We invited him to come to one of our games (in 1990) when he was coming to W&J for a reunion of his football team there. He tossed the coin to determine the kick-off. He's quite a gentleman. He appeared very dignified; he has an aura about him."

Zolak shared a story about another one of the men pictured on one of the walls at Ringgold. That was Paul Galiffa. "He could have been recognized on either of the walls, because he succeeded in every way," said Zolak.

"He was pictured on the cover of *Life* magazine when he was at the U.S. Military Academy. He won 13 or 15 varsity letters at Army. He was a war hero, too. They tell the story about him hurling a hand grenade about 60 yards to knock out a gunnery position that had pinned down his outfit. He was a special guy, too."

"He was a role model for all of us."
—Dr. David Epperson

Dr. David Epperson, the dean of the School of Social Work at the University of Pittsburgh, joined "Deacon" Dan Towler and his wife, Roslyn, and Dan's youngest sister, Cozetta Newring, at the Washington & Jefferson dinner at the Southpointe Golf Club.

Epperson grew up in Donora and has known and admired "Deacon" Dan Towler all his life, 65 years worth. "I don't know when I didn't know him," said Epperson. "I've known him from infancy."

Epperson believes that he benefited greatly from the association. "Deacon" Dan Towler was his first sports hero and, more importantly, a role model forever. Epperson says he was eight to ten years old, in 1943-45, when he attended every home game of the Donora High School football team to root for "Deacon" Dan.

"His youngest sister, Cozetta, was a cheerleader for Donora High at the time," said Epperson. "I walked to the games. Everyone walked in Donora in those days. We didn't have cars and there weren't any sections of town where you couldn't go. There was no area, for instance, set aside for the black people, or any other nationality, to live. He grew up in the same town, and attended the same church. Our families were close. My father was his Scoutmaster. He was in the Boy Scouts for four or five years. He calls me 'the son of my Scoutmaster,' and he wanted me to be in attendance when W&J honored him.

> *"All our dreams can come true—if we have the courage to pursue them."*
> —Walt Disney

303

"When he was finished playing for the Rams in the mid-50s, they had a 'Deacon' Dan Towler Day in Donora, and my dad was the parade marshall. My dad was a deacon at the same church as his dad. We always called him 'Deaco' rather than 'Deacon.' My dad's name was Robert N. Epperson, Sr. He was also a strong and positive influence in my life."

I asked Epperson if the Sharon Epperson who is a business reporter on CNBC was any relation, he beamed and said, "That's my daughter. She went to Taylor Allderdice, Harvard and Columbia." So the beat goes on.

"Dan was very active in all sports when I was a schoolboy in Donora. He even played basketball, where he was a rough and tumble type. He was looked up to by kids as a sports hero. We were much younger than he was, and he was a role model for all of us.

"His mom died when he was young and his sister, Mary, became a big influence in his life. I think she had a lot to do with him going to college. He could have gone to the mill, as so many young men in Donora did in those days. There were always openings for good-paying jobs in the mills.

"He was a bright and able guy. He was somebody who could be emulated by all the little kids. He was very humble. When he chose to go to a school, he chose a school that had one of the best pre-professional programs in the country. Whether it was medicine or law or theology, Washington & Jefferson was a school that would prepare you. Their acceptance rate at grad programs was always high.

"I had a brother who had a bad case of whooping cough, and his mother came to our house and helped my mother, and gave my brother some treatment she knew about that helped him get better."

Epperson said that on May 1, 2000 he would mark his 28th year as dean of the School of Social Work at Pitt. "I'm the longest sitting dean in the country in social work," he said, proudly. He turned 65 in March of 2000.

"When I was in the Air Force from 1955 to 1958, prior to going to graduate school at Pitt, I was stationed in a Strategic Air Command unit at March Air Force Base outside of Riverside, California. That was about 65 miles from Pasadena, where 'Deacon' Dan had his church. He was the pastor at Lincoln Avenue United Methodist Church, an inter-racial church, and lived in the parsonage next door. I would go there on extended weekends and have the run of the house. I'd watch him preparing his sermons for Sunday delivery.

"He quit playing pro football at the peak of his ability to become a minister. He hung it up to go into what was probably the least-paying profession, but he felt that's what God wanted him to do. He has always done what he thought was the right thing to do. I've been fortunate to know him and be able to call him my friend."

"Deacon Dan" Towler, one of the fabled performers in Washington & Jefferson College history, is flanked by W & J's athletic director John Luckhardt, left, and football coach John Banaszak. Towler is joined at W&J outing at Southpointe Golf Club by, left to right, Dr. David Epperson, dean of Pitt's School of Social Work, Dan's sister Cozetta Newring and his wife, Roslyn.

Roberto Clemente
How our student became "The Great One"

*"I cried because he
looked like Roberto."*
— Manny Sanguillen

There was a stage show in Pittsburgh that fleshed out the story of the legendary Roberto Clemente, and helped introduce him to a new generation.

It was called *Clemente, The Measure of a Man*, and it examined the man they called "The Great One," and his Hall of Fame career. It was staged over three weekends at GRW Theater at Point Park College's Library Center on Wood Street in downtown Pittsburgh.

My wife, Kathie, our daughter, Sarah, and I saw it in mid-August, 1999. The show was a special treat for several reasons. Kathie and I knew Clemente as a young man — he'd been a neighbor — and Sarah and I knew Jamaal Holley, who turned in a remarkable performance playing the title role.

We had an opportunity to enjoy a reunion of sorts with two of Clemente's sons, Roberto Jr. and Luis, and one of their father's closest teammates, Manny Sanguillen, still regarded by many as the greatest catcher in Pirates' history.

Sanguillen said he was emotionally moved when he saw Holley on stage, wearing Clemente's No. 21 Pirates uniform. "I cried because he looked like Roberto," said Sanguillen. "I was struck by the resemblance, by the way he looked up there."

Sarah and I felt the same way, but for a different reason. We had tutored Holley for an hour each week when he was a 13-year-old student at Frick Elementary School near his home in Oakland.

We had volunteered at Westminster Presbyterian Church in Upper St. Clair to tutor a middle school student at the Friendship Community Church Learning Center, just two blocks from Pitt Stadium, in 1991-92, Sarah's senior year at Upper St. Clair High School.

Holley was having a hard time with his schoolwork, especially algebra, and we assisted him and another young man named Devon with their homework on a weekly basis. Algebra was always a toughie for me, as well, and Sarah usually carried the day. Sarah enjoyed the experience so much that she tutored middle school students during her four years at the University of Virginia, and returned to the Friendship Learning Center when she started Medical School at Pitt, just two blocks away.

Now Holley was a 20-year-old sophomore Creative and Performing Arts major at Indiana University of Pennsylvania. And he was up on the stage in a demanding role, mastering a great deal of

Jamaal Holley, who plays role of Roberto Clemente in stage production, is flanked by two of Clemente's three sons, Luis, at left, and Roberto Jr., and had an opportunity to meet Clemente's friend and former Pirates' teammate, Manny Sanguillen, below.

Photos by Jim O'Brien

dialogue, made even more difficult because it was to be delivered with a Latin American accent.

"I read a lot about him, and watched some film of him," said Holley. "He must have been a great man. People have such respect for him. It was an honor to meet his family and former teammates."

The way he spoke, the way he swung the bat as only Clemente could, his emotional swings, showed that Holley had, indeed, done his homework. Sarah and I shared the pride felt by his mother, who sat a few rows behind us.

I first learned of this show about six months earlier when I received a call from Wayne Brinda, the director, who asked me to review the original script submitted by Brian Kral, a playwright from Las Vegas, of all places.

Brinda called me again a few months later and invited me to attend a rehearsal at the East Liberty Presbyterian Church. When I parked my car on Penn Avenue, I looked to the left and could see the Pennley Park Apartments where Kathie and I resided when we got married in August of 1967. They were fairly new when we lived there, but now they had fallen on hard times and were being replaced, in some instances, or refurbished.

Several Pirates lived at Pennley Park, which was only a few miles from Forbes Field, and one of them was Roberto Clemente. Yes, Clemente was a neighbor, just two floors above us in the adjoining wing. We'd see him and his wife, Vera, and his first-born son, Roberto Jr. That's one of the reasons I wrote the book, *Remember Roberto*, back in 1994, when a statue was erected in his honor at Three Rivers Stadium to coincide with the Major League All-Star Game.

When Brinda introduced me to the cast, the kid who was going to play Clemente caught my eye. He looked so familiar. I thought I'd seen him play in some sports contest. It took awhile to make the connection to his school days at Frick.

For him, that was a long time ago. He had since graduated from Schenley High School, won all sorts of acting awards and scholarships, and had become an accomplished jazz musician. He was a solidly built 6-1 or 6-2, and had grown up quite a bit since we first met. The face and gleaming eyes were the same.

I shared some personal reminiscences and some characteristics of the people they were playing with the cast members. Former Pirates who were close to Clemente, such as Steve Blass, Dave Giusti, Nellie Briles and Nellie King, had offered their thoughts on the production as well at other similar developmental sessions.

I had arrived early at the rehearsal session I attended, and took advantage of the situation to walk the nearby streets. I remembered shopping there during the first holiday season that Kathie and I had shared in our first year-and-a-half of marriage. I could visualize Pirates like Juan Pizzarro, Maury Wills and Alvin O'Neal McBean playing ball with their children on the grassy knolls around the Pennley Park Apartments back in the summers of 1967 and 1968.

Sarah and her husband of a year, Matt Zirwas, coincidentally enough, were living in their first apartment and it, too, was in East Liberty, bordering Shadyside, about a mile from our first apartment. They had picked their apartment without any help or suggestions from us, yet they ended up near where we started our life together. Life goes in cycles. After attending the rehearsal, I stopped to see Sarah and Matt, both third year students at Pitt's School of Medicine back then, and mentioned Jamaal Holley. I still hadn't figured out how I knew him.

Sarah opened a drawer in a nearby chest of drawers and pulled out a photo album, and opened it to two photographs of Holley, showing him with some pro basketball scouts, when we took him to see a basketball game at the Pitt Field House. He had never seen a game there, even though he lived on the next block. He was pictured with Del Harris, who later became the head coach of the Los Angeles Lakers, and Mel Daniels, one of the early stars of the old American Basketball Association when he played pivot for the Minnesota Muskies and Indiana Pacers.

After Sarah had made the identification and our connection with Jamaal Holley, she said with a smile, "You should ask him how he's doing with his algebra."

Jim O'Brien

Dr. Sarah O'Brien Zirwas enjoys reunion with Jamaal Holley, a young man she mentored during his middle school days in Oakland.

Mo Scarry
From Duquesne to the Dolphins

"I'm still in love with the game."

Mike "Mo" Scarry could still command your attention. His brown eyes had a gleam in them, even as he neared his 80th birthday. There was something in his hawk-like look that demanded you kept your eyes fixed on his. He had been a coach most of his adult life, and he still talked like one, somebody who could teach and motivate young people to do something special.

Scarry was back at Waynesburg College, where it all began to take shape in so many ways. There were familiar faces, familiar buildings, familiar landscapes and familiar stories, so many memories, so much to be thankful for.

This was where he met and courted his wife 60 years earlier, and that alone had made it worth the trip to Waynesburg back then from his boyhood home in Duquesne.

Now he had come from his retirement home in Fort Myers, Florida. He had left coaching at age 65 back in 1985 after a great run as an assistant coach with the Miami Dolphins of the National Football League. He had worked his way to the top of his game and seen it all. He moved among giants, and contributed to their success. Now it was his turn to take a bow.

He had already been selected to the NAIA Hall of Fame in 1964 for what he accomplished at Waynesburg. This was even more satisfying, being honored by his old school.

It was Saturday, September 11, 1999, and Scarry was sitting in the lobby of the Stover Campus Center, a red brick, multi-purpose showcase facility that had opened only a year earlier. Scarry wore a dark blue suit, a well-starched white dress shirt and a pale yellow, gold and blue paisley tie. His sisters, Sally and Mary Catherine, were the first to show and embrace him.

He was waiting for other family members to join them before going upstairs where he would be feted at a brunch that preceded a football game between the Waynesburg College Yellow Jackets and the Manchester (Indiana) Spartans. Waynesburg is a member of the NCAA Division III and Presidents Athletic Conference.

At halftime ceremonies, the new press box at John F. Wiley Stadium would be named in honor of Michael M. Scarry. M. was for Maurice, but whisper that, please. "I don't think I've changed much," said the man of the hour. "I'm still just Mo."

If so, Mo was moved by this tribute. "I can think of Lou Gehrig saying, 'I'm the luckiest guy in the world,' and right now I'm the luckiest guy in the world," he said during his remarks, paraphrasing the retirement speech of the Yankees "Iron Horse" after Gehrig learned he was terminally ill.

Mo Scarry is honored at Waynesburg College by friends and family, including former teammate Jack Wiley, and Mo's sisters, Sally, at left, and Mary Catherine.

Photos by Jim O'Brien

The party would regroup for a dinner at the Stover Campus Center, a real point of pride for President Timothy R. Thyreen, who hosted the day's events. It was a sunny day, with temperatures in the mid-60s, warm for September. It was the sort of day school administrators pray for when planning such events.

John F. Wiley, better known as Jack Wiley, a teammate and fellow lineman on the 1939 and 1940 Waynesburg College football team, was among the first to greet Scarry when he arrived on campus. Scarry and Wiley were among the most admired athletic figures ever to grace the charming 12-acre tree-lined campus, located 50 miles south of Pittsburgh.

The 1939 team, by the way, played in the first college football game ever televised, a contest with Fordham at Randalls Island in New York City. NBC televised the game even though there were only a few special TV sets in the New York area that could pick up the telecast. That's part of the sports lore of Waynesburg College.

Scarry had seen a lot with those deep-set, penetrating eyes. He had been a standout football and basketball player at Duquesne High School and Waynesburg College. He later coached both sports and served as athletic director and trainer — all at the same time — at Waynesburg College. He had worked hard and paid his dues to earn this tribute.

After playing pro football in Cleveland for three years, he coached at six different colleges over an 18-year period, and worked for three different teams in the NFL over a 22-year span. He served the last 16 as an assistant coach on Don Shula's staff at Miami. The Dolphins went to the Super Bowl five times when Scarry was on Shula's staff, and won back to back titles in 1972 and 1973. Scarry helped Shula become the winningest coach in NFL history and felt proud when Shula was inducted into the Pro Football Hall of Fame in 1997. I recall spotting Scarry in the crowd at Canton during those ceremonies. He was also there when Bob Griese was similarly honored.

Scarry turned out some great defensive lines and was regarded, along with Bill Arnsparger, as one of the architects of the Dolphins' "No-Name Defense." The highlight, says Scarry, was the 1972 season when the Dolphins went 17-0, the only undefeated team in NFL history.

When I was covering pro football (1969-1982) at *The Miami News, The New York Post* and *The Pittsburgh Press*, Scarry was someone I could count on for an easy interview. He was especially cordial and cooperative after I reminded him that my mother-in-law, Barbara Stepetic Churchman, grew up in Duquesne, as did her brothers, Tom and Mike Stepetic, and three of her brothers-in-law, Sam Carr, Steve Volk and Lou Goldman. Scarry said he recognized those names. Scarry didn't think most sports writers knew much about football, but even a sports writer couldn't be that bad with such connections in his hometown.

Then, too, our fathers had both been machinists at mills in the Mon Valley, mine at Mesta Machine Company in West Homestead, his at U.S. Steel in Duquesne. Both were located within a few miles of each other along the Monongahela River.

He had humble beginnings. When I asked him for photographs of his early days, he said, "We don't have any. We didn't have a camera."

Scarry could speak on a first-hand basis about great quarterbacks like Otto Graham and Dan Marino, and great coaches like Paul Brown and Shula. Scarry was never a marquee name, but he was one of those hard-working guys who were, indeed, the heart and soul of sports. He could also tell you about a lesser-heralded quarterback, Harry "The Golden Greek" Theofiledes of Homestead, whom he thought should have fared better in the NFL ranks. They worked together with the Redskins in Washington. "He had great athletic ability; I was always rooting for him because we came from the same area," said Scarry.

Though he led a nomadic existence before he joined Shula's staff in Miami, Scarry never forgot where he came from.

He has looked at life in football from every conceivable level, including a one-year (1953) stay at Loras College in Dubuque, Iowa. "It was a small Catholic college," said Scarry with a smile, "and everyone, including the coaches, had to take a vow of poverty."

No matter where he worked, Scarry considered himself "a Pittsburgh guy," and boasted he was a life-long admirer of Art Rooncy and his Pittsburgh Steelers. Scarry sprinkled his conversation with mentions of Pittsburgh sports broadcasters such as Rosey Rowswell, Bob Prince and Joe Tucker.

Scarry kept searching for paydays at college and pro posts to support his large family. He and his wife, Elizabeth, or Libby as he liked to call her, had met during their schooldays at Waynesburg College. They were married January 27, 1943 after a three-year courtship. They had eight children, five boys and three girls — Sally Beth, Mike, Patricia, Tom, Maggie, John, Jim and Dennis. Libby and five of their children came to Waynesburg College for Mo's big day. The others were unable to attend.

Scarry once bought an old taxicab to drive his family around in. "It was like one of those limousines at the airport," said Scarry. "You'd throw the kids in the backseat and take off."

There were times when Scarry almost walked away from sports, one of those down spells, ironically enough, came right before Shula called and asked him to be one of his first assistants in Miami in 1970. Scarry had spent the previous season as a scout for the San Francisco 49ers, which put him on the road a lot. He tired of his gypsy life. He didn't have the heart to leave the game, however, as much as he might have loved to spend more time with his wife and family. "I'm still in love with the game," he said, explaining why he stayed.

"The people in Waynesburg care."
—Mo Scarry

I went to Waynesburg College with a neighbor and good friend, Bill "Woody" Wolf. He was a proud alumnus of the school. He was a tough, hard-nosed lineman during the same four years (1951-54) that Jack Wiley was the head football coach of the Yellow Jackets.

Wolf went to Waynesburg after playing at Bridgeville High School, where teams coached by Bob Hast and Tiny Carson won back-to-back WPIAL Class B football championships in 1948 and 1949, winning 25 straight games in one torrid stretch going back to the 1947 season.

Wiley, Class of 1941, had returned to Waynesburg College after playing five seasons (1946-1950) as a tackle with the Pittsburgh Steelers. Wiley had a 33-man squad and an all-volunteer coaching staff during his stay at Waynesburg, yet the Yellow Jackets played the likes of West Virginia, Virginia Tech and Bowling Green. Those who played for him proudly call themselves "the Wiley-men."

When Wiley left Waynesburg, he joined John Michelosen as a line coach at the University of Pittsburgh for many years. I was a student at Pitt in those days, and got to know Wiley. We had met and talked at get-togethers through the years. He observed that now we both had gray hair. He was always a class act. He was well respected and regarded as a great recruiter, responsible for convincing Mike Ditka, among others, to come to the Oakland campus.

"I got Ditka out of Aliquippa and Jim Cunningham out of Connellsville and Dick Haley out of Midway," said Wiley. "I took them out of Joe Paterno's pocket."

Wiley got out of football in the early '60s to take a sales position with Balfour, a jewelry company known best for class rings, so he could spend more time with his family. Wiley was a born salesman.

He remained close to Waynesburg College, and served on its board of trustees. He was awarded an honorary doctorate degree there for his accomplishments and service to the college and community.

"Jack Wiley has meant a great deal to this college," said President Thyreen at the brunch at Stover Hall. "We want everything to be the best it can be for the students, and that was what Jack Wiley wanted, too."

Waynesburg College was marking its 150th anniversary in 1999. The college and the community in which it is located are named after Revolutionary War hero, General "Mad" Anthony Wayne. Waynesburg is an hour's drive south of Pittsburgh, in Greene County, in the southwestern corner of Pennsylvania. In one of the school guidebooks, there was a line that cited Waynesburg "for its beautiful setting, for its spirit of determination and success, for the friendly atmosphere of the campus and the community, or for its Christian approach to life."

It's a Presbyterian-related college of about 1,500 students in a close-knit town of 5,000 people. "It was warm to me as a student and later as a coach," said Scarry. "I always felt safe and wanted. It's the people. The people in Waynesburg care. The professors care. They wanted you to do well. They helped you any way they could. The townspeople were great."

Wiley would agree with Scarry's assessment of what made Waynesburg special. Wiley said he grew up on a farm 22 miles west of Waynesburg. "My dad raised cattle," he said. "I milked cows every morning before going to school. We sold all the cattle in 1953, and got out of the farming business."

He always had a special affection for Scarry. "He's like a brother," said Wiley, who came to Waynesburg for the special weekend from his retirement home in Clearwater, Florida. "I introduced him to his wife. She once sent me a card on their wedding anniversary in which she wrote, 'Look what you got me into!' She had gone to school with my sister. We hated to lose them when Mo was coaching here, but he had a chance to go with his friend Otto Graham and be a coach with the Washington Redskins for twice the money he was making here. He had to go."

Scarry said his wife, Libby, lived in the same home in Moundsville, West Virginia all her life until they got married. "She was used to a sense of permanence," he said. "She figured I'd get a coaching job and just stay there. Little did she know what kind of a ride I was going to take her on. For awhile, I went wherever I could get a job to stay in football and feed my family. It wasn't until I got to the Dolphins that I found a permanent home."

When it was Scarry's turn to talk at the brunch, he bounced from one topic to another, as his mind raced with so many memories.

"Jack Wiley played tackle and I played linebacker, and once in a while he let somebody slip through so I could make a tackle, too," said Scarry.

"I couldn't sleep last night, thinking about today. I'm flabbergasted. This is one of the nicest things that ever happened to me. I never thought they'd do anything like this for me. It (the press box) will be there for quite a spell, so it'll be nice to be remembered that way.

"I thought about the first day I ever walked on this campus. It was 1939 and I walked into Coach Wolf's office. I came here to play basketball. He asked me if I played football, and I said I had. 'What did you play?' he asked me. I told him, 'Whatever the coach needed I was there.' That's how my football career started at Waynesburg College. Frank Wolf was from McKeesport, so we had some common links. I was still 5-9, 155 pounds when I got here. Over the next three years I grew to be 6 feet, 185 pounds. I grew like a weed once I got here.

"I remember I had an appendicitis attack on New Year's Eve of my freshman year. I went to the hospital here. Everyone took such good care of me. The townspeople were always good to me; they cared about me. When I came back to coach here it was more of the same.

"I met my wife here 60 years ago. We loved to dance. We danced up a storm at Walton Hall (a women's dormitory in those days). That was our entertainment."

"They wasted a great opportunity."

Michael Maurice Scarry was born on February 1, 1920. He grew up on the outskirts of Duquesne, on a patch that would later be part of West Mifflin. Dave Parker was his football coach at Duquesne High, Bill Lemmer was his basketball coach. His high school varsity seasons were 1936, 1937 and 1938

"When I grew up in Duquesne it was Depression time. Everyone was close. The mills were down, no one was working. We played softball. We didn't have enough money to buy baseball equipment.

"My dad had been a machinist at U.S. Steel at the Duquesne Works. He left the mill and taught the machinist trade in the vocational section of Monessen High School. He coached football and basketball at Holy Name High School in Duquesne at the same time. Then the Depression came along and knocked out Catholic high schools. He coached the football team at a junior high in Monessen for the rest of his life. As a kid, I'd go to all his games and practices.

"We lived on Crawford Avenue near an old German cemetery. There were a bunch of homes built by the mill. It was like an annex. Two guys from Duquesne, Rags Radvansky (1936-38) and Miles Zeleznik (1945-46) played basketball for Doc Carlson at Pitt. I admired them both. They both came back to the community as coaches and administrators. They stayed the course. A lot of guys from our area went to school, but dropped out and came home. They wasted a great opportunity to accomplish something.

"I didn't go to college right out of high school. I was only 5-9, 155 pounds. I thought I'd work in the mill for a year to get bigger. My older brother was at Duquesne University. His name was John or Jack. After I worked in the mill for a year I was more eager to go to college."

**Nick Buoniconti, Captain,
Dolphins' No-Name Defense
At Mario Lemieux Celebrity Invitational,
June 10, 2000:**
"Mo Scarry had the ability to take guys with raw talent, like Bill Stanfill, and teach them techniques that would serve them well the rest of their careers. He was low-key. He could get fiery at times, but that wasn't his style. Guys loved him. They really played for him. He was a great coach, and a good man, and he motivated people."

"Shula ran a tight ship."
—Mo Scarry

I went to work for *The Miami News* in 1979 and was assigned to cover the Dolphins for their final year in the American Football League. George Wilson was in his fourth year as the head coach. He was the only coach the Dolphins ever had.

Wilson wasn't big on discipline, for himself or his team. He was a colorful character, a hard-drinking throwback to a more innocent let-your-hair-down era. He could laugh at himself. The players loved him. They loved him to death. The team finished 3-10-1 in Wilson's swan song.

I recall being at a season-ending dinner for the team where one of his players said from the podium that if he were going down a dark alley at night he'd want to be accompanied by George Wilson. "What were you going to do," a teammate in the audience said in a stage whisper, "empty garbage cans?"

So Wilson didn't command respect throughout the ranks. Club owner Joe Robbie realized that Wilson wasn't the answer to his needs. Robbie hired Don Shula away from the Baltimore Colts to come to Miami to replace Wilson.

Shula had come with mixed emotions. He had broken into pro coaching as a defensive coordinator on Wilson's staff in Detroit. I covered the press conference where Shula was announced as the new coach, and then left Miami in favor of New York where I would work for *The New York Post*. There was too much going on in New York to second-guess the decision to leave Miami, but I did miss out on a spectacular run by the Dolphins. It might have been fun.

The Dolphins finished 10-4 in Shula's first season. He had them in the Super Bowl a year later. The following season they went 17-0 and won it all. It was an unbelievable turnaround.

Many of his star players had been with Wilson's edition of the Dolphins, beginning with Hall of Famers like Larry Csonka, Bob Griese and Larry Little. Jim Kiick, Mercury Morris, Nick Buoniconti, Howard Twilley, Norm Evans, Doug Crusan were holdovers from the offensive unit, and defensive stalwarts who had played for Wilson included Dick Anderson, Manny Fernandez, Bob Heinz, Bill Stanfill and Lloyd Mumphord. Larry Seiple stayed on as the punter.

How could they have been so bad with Wilson and so great with Shula? The team added the likes of Paul Warfield, Marv Fleming and Jake Scott to the starting cast and became one of the powerhouses of pro football.

Scarry coached the likes of Fernandez, Heinz, Stanfill and, later on, Vern Den Herder, A.J. Duhe, Bob Baumhower and Doug Betters,

In 1983, for instance, both Betters (AP) and Baumhower (*Pro Football Weekly*) were selected as the NFL's Defensive Player of the Year.

Scarry, a demanding individual, coached some of the NFL's best linemen in the 1970s and 1980s. The Dolphins were consistently among the league leaders in several defensive categories. They had the most shutouts (14) in the 1970s when the Dolphins, Steelers and Raiders ruled the league.

"You love the guy in a sense, but you don't always like him," said Betters during his playing days under Scarry. "He tells it like it is. He's from the old school."

I shared a story with Scarry about an experience I had as a rookie reporter. This happened at the team's training camp at a private boys school in Boca Raton, Florida. One day I was interviewing Ernie Hefferle, the offensive line coach. He was from Herminie, Pa., had played at Duquesne University and had coached Mike Ditka, "Mean" John Paluck and Joe Walton at Pitt.

Hefferle was complaining that his offensive linemen were opening holes, but that the Dolphins' running backs were too slow and weren't getting into the holes fast enough. His observation was, of course, an off-the-record remark. He was talking to me in his room at Boca Raton. The walls were paper-thin.

John Idzik, the backfield coach, was in the adjoining room. As I was leaving Hefferle's room, I heard a "psst, psst" sound. I looked to my right and spotted Idzik at the door of his room. He waved me to his side. "That's a bunch of bull," said Idzik in a whisper. "The line is not opening holes for our backs."

I thought about that exchange on many occasions when both the running backs and linemen in question that day were inducted into the Pro Football Hall of Fame. Scarry smiled when I related the story.

"Don Shula and George Wilson were good friends," said Scarry. "Wilson's the guy who gave Shula his first job in the NFL. It's a shame he lost his job. The attitude about what was expected of everyone was established early. There was no way you'd be around Shula and feel like you were on a losing team. Don was so upbeat. He knew personnel. He could get the most out of a guy like Griese. The nucleus was there, we made some good additions, and our staff was solid. Shula, like a lot of us who played for Paul Brown, was highly-organized. And he ran a tight ship."

"A lot of Paul Brown rubbed off on all of us."

Scarry played pro football in Cleveland in 1945, 1946 and 1947. "I was one of the original Browns," said Scarry. "I played for the Cleveland Rams my first year, and we won the National Football League championship. The Rams left town in favor of Los Angeles after my rookie year. That's when Paul Brown started the Browns in the All-American Football Conference. I was one of several players who stayed rather than relocate in Los Angeles. It wasn't a big deal back then. It was reported in the newspapers, but then it was over.

318

"When I played for the Rams, we had one head coach and three assistants, who were all part-time. Paul Brown had the first full-time staff in pro football. He was a brainy sort and he established the blueprint for so many coaches who came after him."

One of those, of course, was Chuck Noll, who played both ways for the Browns. Noll would come to Pittsburgh and lead the Steelers to four Super Bowl championships in the 1970s when they were known as the "Team of the Decade." Shula also played defensive back for the Browns, and gained the basis for his own coaching philosophy.

"When I was with the Browns, we never practiced more than two hours," said Scarry. "Usually, it would be about 1½ hours. It was like going to a seminar. We had a lot of meetings. You knew what you were going to do. A lot of Paul Brown rubbed off on all of us

"Shula was simply an honest roll-up-his-sleeves hard worker. He didn't lie. He would tell you how things were. He was a delight to work for."

"I knew Marino because I'm a Pittsburgh guy."

Mo Scarry was with the Dolphins when they drafted Dan Marino in 1983. Marino was the 27th player picked on the first round and the sixth quarterback, behind John Elway, Todd Blackledge, Jim Kelly, Tony Eason and Ken O'Brien. The Steelers passed him up to draft a defensive lineman named Gabe Rivera of Texas Tech. Rivera was injured and left paralyzed in an auto accident on the North Side, not far from Three Rivers Stadium. Police said he was drunk when he drove his car into an oncoming car, driven by a staunch Steelers fan who escaped relatively unharmed.

Did Scarry remember the day the Dolphins drafted Danny Marino?

"Yes," said Scarry. "I knew Marino because I'm a Pittsburgh guy. He was such a great athlete. I didn't believe we'd get to draft him. We didn't think he'd be there when our turn came. Chuck Connor was our scout in that region — he's a Pittsburgh guy, too   and he was high on Marino. Connor is now with the Atlanta Falcons.

"When our turn came, we couldn't believe he was still on the board. As our turn got closer and closer, somebody said aloud, 'What if Marino's up there it's our turn to pick?' And Connor said, 'If Marino's up there we've got to go for him.' Shula nodded in agreement."

> *"I didn't for a moment think I wasn't going to make it. Certainly, at times you lose confidence, but I always believed there was a place for me."*
> —Actor Nathan Lane

319

"Assistant coaches seldom get the credit they deserve."
— Don Shula

Mo Scarry was honored at a banquet by a Dolphins' booster group in November, 1986, about a year after he had retired. Otto Graham was there, and was a featured speaker. Scarry had centered for Graham for two seasons (1946 and 1947) in Cleveland, and started his pro coaching career as a member of Graham's staff at Washington from 1966-1968. They gave way to Vince Lombardi. After one year as a scout with the San Francisco 49ers, Scarry joined Shula's staff in Miami in 1970.

Shula shed tears talking about Mo Scarry. They were that close, and had that kind of special relationship. That stone jaw that gained fame long before Bill Cowher became coach of the Steelers, and drew attention to his jutting jaw, didn't look so formidable when Shula spoke of his long-time assistant.

"A lot of credit goes to the assistant coaches I had, guys like Monte Clark and Mo Scarry," said Shula. "They were willing to work morning, noon and night for very little recognition. Those are the kind of guys who made this the game it is today.

"Assistant coaches seldom get the credit they deserve for devoting their lives to the game. If they ever start a Hall of Fame for assistant coaches, Mo Scarry would have to be one of the first ones inducted."

Shula first met Scarry when Shula was a senior at John Carroll College in Cleveland, and Scarry was the basketball coach across town at Western Reserve. Shula and defensive back Carl Taseff, who later played with the Baltimore Colts, became friends with Scarry. "He was our idol," said Shula.

Scarry expressed his gratitude when it was turn to talk, directing many of his remarks at the men he had coached during his distinguished 16-season stay with the Dolphins. He was a proud, hard-working, sometimes smiling and sometimes gruff guy.

"I felt blessed to work with a man like Don Shula and the staff that we had," said Scarry. "I enjoyed every minute of it. To me, coaching was pure joy. I've got a million memories. Every time I stepped on the field with the guys, I had a good time. Working with the guys is what it's all about anyway.

"You're not working with clones. You're working with people," Scarry continued, explaining his approach. "You're constantly teaching.

"You had to be willing to work and pay the price, but I was fortunate that I was able to work with good people, people who wanted to learn and get better and were interested in improving themselves.

"Basically, coaches are teachers. Most people don't consider coaches as teachers, but that's what we are. You try to motivate your

320

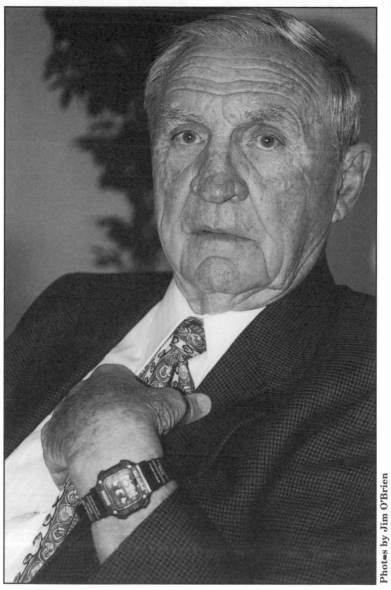

Michael "Mo" Scarry returns to Waynesburg College.

players, and try to help them not only improve on their techniques and fundamentals, but provide a little input into how to live and how to get along with people.

"Communications is one of the most important things we have, whether it's in sports or between neighbors. As long as you have an open line of communications, you always have a chance. I was fortunate. I had good people and we had good communications. When you have that combination, you're going to be successful."

Looking at his wife, Libby, prompted Scarry to share another thought about his demanding profession.

"I've been in football since 1933 and coaching since 1946," said Scarry. "Wives should get special attention for putting up with any of us in the coaching profession. On the other hand, football has provided a nice life for our family."

"We were sort of bad guys."

He left Waynesburg in his junior year to enlist in the Army. He served as an infantry officer in North Africa during World War II. "I spent a lot of time praying that I'd get back home," he said. When he came back home he decided to go into pro football immediately and went to Cleveland. Scarry captained the Cleveland Rams when they won the NFL championship in 1945. He went to night school at Western Reserve, where he completed his college studies and earned his degree. During the off-season, he coached the basketball team at Western Reserve. Pro football players did that sort of thing in those days, finished their college studies or went to graduate school, and supplemented their modest incomes with off-season jobs.

Following their championship season, however, the Rams left Cleveland in favor of Los Angeles. Scarry stayed in Cleveland, as did several of his teammates. "We were sort of bad guys because we jumped to the other league," he said, "but for the most part it was no big deal."

Scarry served as captain of the Browns for two seasons (1946-1947) in the old American Football Conference.

Scarry was injured at mid-season in 1947, and that opened the door for Frank "Gunner" Gatski at center. Gatski was good, and much bigger than Scarry or most other pro centers. Gatski was so good, in fact, that he became a Hall of Fame player.

Following the 1947 season, Scarry was offered a job as head football coach at Western Reserve, and he accepted it.

He began an 18-year college football coaching career at Western Reserve (1948-49), Santa Clara (1950-52), Loras (1953), Washington State (1954-55) and Cincinnati (1956-62) before becoming head coach at Waynesburg (1963-65). His Yellow Jackets posted a record of 17-8-1, including two West Penn Conference titles, and he recruited and developed the Waynesburg squad that went unbeaten and won the NAIA championship under Carl DePasqua in 1966.

Scarry was Coach of the Year in NAIA District 30 in 1963, and won similar honors that year from The Pittsburgh Press and the Pittsburgh Curbstone Coaches. In 1969 he was named to the Waynesburg College Hall of Fame for both football and basketball.

His wife and family had to be flexible, right from the start. Following the 1950 season, Libby was putting up wallpaper in Cleveland and Mo came home and told her he was going to Santa Clara.

"I just learned if you roll up your sleeves and go to work you can usually get what you want," said Scarry. "I learned that right after high school when I went to work at the mill in Duquesne. I spent a year shoveling, cleaning track and acting as the greaser's helper rolling steel. It was dirty work.

"I also learned that you had to roll with the punches. You didn't always get your first choices, but you had to recognize there were options, that there were other opportunities to pursue your dreams. One door closes and another one opens up. Coming up, I had always wanted to go to Notre Dame and play for the Pittsburgh Steelers because I'm an Art Rooney man all the way. Neither of those happened. And maybe that was for the best."

Rod Thorn
The Prince of Princeton

"My parents always told me to be polite."

He had a strange shot that set him apart from the pack. Rod Thorn had a two-handed over-the-head jump shot back in the early '60s. He was a 6-foot, 4-inch, 180-pound guard, a raw-boned fellow with wide-set shoulders — as if he'd swallowed a coat hanger — and he was just easy to follow on the floor. He was simply better than just about every one he played against. He demanded your attention.

In my teen years, I had read about Rod Thorn in *SPORT* magazine, and knew about his talent and triumphs and trials before I ever saw him in action. He was an intriguing individual. He came to WVU as an outstanding student, a highly recruited basketball and baseball star, a humble and polite ballplayer who impressed everyone with his good manners. It was "Yes, sir," or "No, sir," to every one who spoke to him. Trying to meet everybody's expectations put a lot of pressure on him, however, and it nearly undid him.

Seeing him play for West Virginia University at the old Mountaineer Field House in Morgantown early in 1962 and talking to him in the locker room afterward was one of the big treats of my student days at the University of Pittsburgh. The atmosphere at Mountaineer Field House was just so much more exciting than the atmosphere at the Pitt Field House. Clippings of my columns remain in the Thorn file in the WVU sports information office, which rekindled some fond memories.

He wore No. 44, just like Jerry West and Joe Stydahar, two other West Virginia legendary athletes. In fact, he wore No. 44 back in high school, before West wore that number at West Virginia University. West, Stydahar and Thorn were, coincidentally enough, the only three WVU athletes ever to wear that number in basketball. Thorn was the last to wear it, back in 1963.

When I returned home to Hazelwood, where I lived while attending Pitt four miles away, I would mimic Thorn's two-handed over-the-head jump shot while playing H-O-R-S-E. We'd play this game at the hoop on the telephone pole in front of our home. H-O-R-S-E was a game you could play with one friend, or a few friends. You would shoot the ball a certain way — a jumper or a hook — and the next shooter had to shoot the same shot from the same spot if you were successful or, if you missed your shot, take whatever shot they desired. If they made their shot, the next shooter had to make the same shot or pick up a letter.

324

Photo from West Virginia University sports information office

Rod Thorn is flanked by teammate Jim McCormick, at left, and West Virginia University coach George King.

Photo from Doug Huff collection

Three of WVU's all-time basketball performers are pictured, left to right, with Jerry West, Coach Fred Schaus and Rod Thorn.

If you made a shot and they missed it they would pick up an "H" or and "O," etc., until someone spelled H-O-R-S-E. The first one to do so would be eliminated from the game. You'd holler "Rod Thorn!" and heave up a two-handed over-the-head jumper. Or "Wilt Chamberlain!" and toss up a looping hook shot. You'd holler "Dolph Schayes!" and toss up a two-handed set shot from way out. It was a make-believe world.

We used to see these guys on TV once in a while, so we knew what they looked like, and we knew their favorite shots. Nobody hollered "Elgin Baylor" because nobody I knew could do what the acrobatic Baylor did routinely.

Thorn even had a name for his two-handed, over-the-head jump shot. He called it "the Thunderbolt." He said, "I used to shoot one-handed, but I was a little weak in high school, and couldn't reach the basket from outside. So I started using two hands."

Rod Thorn remains one of the great names in West Virginia University basketball history. Photos of him and mentions of him can be found throughout the current team's yearbook. When Thorn was playing, his name would be mentioned in the same breath as earlier WVU All-Americans like Mark Workman, "Hot Rod" Hundley and Jerry West. His name remains in the record books with those all-time great performers, along with later WVU stars such as Ron Williams, Wil Robinson Jr. and Greg Jones. Thorn scored 44 points in an NCAA Tournament game against St. Joseph's in a losing cause in 1963.

He was a freshman when West was a senior during a golden era in West Virginia basketball. There was always a lot of excitement when the freshman team had a scrimmage with the varsity. Jerry West was Rod Thorn's idol. Trying to fill West' shoes the next year proved a difficult task for Thorn. He made quite a comeback the following year, however, to make his own mark on the Morgantown campus.

As a junior, he became the first backcourtman in college history to lead his team in the four major statistical categories. In fact, only two other players ever achieved this grand slam, namely Oscar Robertson and Jerry Lucas, to show you the kind of company Thorn was keeping.

He was the 1963 Southern Conference Athlete of the Year, a member of two NCAA basketball teams and three NCAA baseball clubs at West Virginia. Thorn was an All-America basketball player in 1962 and 1963. His greatest thrill was leading West Virginia to the 1962 Southern Conference crown.

From 1961-63, Thorn scored 1,785 points (No. 5 all-time going into the 1999-2000 season) and had 304 assists. He led the Mountaineers in scoring, rebounding, shooting-percentage and assists for two seasons.

In 1963, Thorn was a first round draft pick of the Baltimore Bullets. He was chosen right after the Detroit Pistons made Jimmy

Walker the top overall pick in the draft. Thorn went on to play with Detroit, St. Louis and Seattle during an eight-year pro career, averaging 10.8 points per game. He became an assistant coach under Lenny Wilkens at Seattle in 1971.

He was inducted into the WVU Sports Hall of Fame in 1992.

Thorn enjoyed a successful career as a player, coach and front office executive in professional basketball. The 1999-2000 National Basketball Association season was his 37th year in pro ball, and his 14th as vice-president and director of operations for the NBA, one of Commissioner David Stern's most trusted lieutenants. He seemed well suited for this executive position. Thorn had a tough job. He was like the assistant principal in high school, in charge of discipline. He was responsible for the referees and the conduct of the players. Thorn dealt out fines and suspensions for misdeeds.

When I spoke to him, in mid-May, the NBA was in the midst of its championship playoffs. Thorn was busier than ever. Only a few days earlier, he had to fine and suspend Philadelphia's Matt Geiger and Indiana's Reggie Miller. He had to set them down for one game in the playoffs, a fifth and final game in their series, not an easy decision. Geiger had flattened Miller with a flagrant foul and Miller had gotten off the floor and tossed a punch at Geiger.

Often overlooked is that Thorn served for seven seasons as general manager of the Chicago Bulls before, at age 44, joining the NBA's front office in New York. During that stretch, the Bulls had only one winning season.

His greatest moment with the Bulls was when he picked Michael Jordan of the University of North Carolina in the 1984 college draft, with the third pick in the first round. Six months after signing Jordan, Thorn was fired. Jerry Reinsdorf had become the Bulls' owner only a few days earlier and he brought in Jerry Krause to run the club.

"I'm always happy to have my name associated with Michael Jordan," said Thorn. "Jerry Krause has done a great job for the Bulls."

Working for the league has probably been better for Thorn's health. "When you're with a club, you have tunnel vision," he said. "You only see your team's side of the issue. You get all wrapped up in the game. But when you work for the league, you don't care who wins. And you don't get that nervous feeling in the pit of your stomach."

Rod was within a week of his 59th birthday. He and his wife, Peggy, had a 25-year-old son, Jonathan Jared, and 20-year-old twin daughters, Amanda and Jessica, and they had a home in Rye, N.Y.

Jared had played basketball at and graduated from West Virginia Wesleyan University and had gained a master's degree in physical education at his dad's alma mater in Morgantown. He was coaching and teaching at Tavares High School, just north of Orlando, Florida. The twins, who would be 21 in July, were both juniors at Georgetown University. They were both majoring in Spanish and doing international studies. They were living in Spain for the spring-summer session, Jessica in Madrid and Amanda in Salamanca. Their parents were proud of the Thorn kids.

"When I think of the Nets, I always think of you."

Rod Thorn and I shared some special times. In addition to being college contemporaries — he was a year ahead of me at the rival school — we worked together and traveled in the same circles as adults. Thorn was twice an assistant coach to Kevin Loughery with the New York Nets, the first time (1972-74) in the American Basketball Association, and the second time (1976-78) in the NBA. The Nets were one of my main newspaper assignments, along with the New York Islanders of the National Hockey League who shared Nassau Coliseum as a home base in Uniondale. We lived about five miles away in the south shore community of Baldwin. "When I think of the Nets and the ABA, I always think of you," said Thorn. We hadn't talked in a long while and we were talking fast, trying to catch up.

Thorn was a good guy, an intelligent individual who was good company. He had a great sense of humor, and easy laugh. He was intense on the sideline, too intense for his own good, as it turned out, but carefree and fun away from the court. He was one of my all-time favorites from my days on the newspaper beat. He and Loughery liked to wear those awful polyester suits of the '70s, that we thought were so cool at the time.

I remember the time he and Loughery brought several ballplayers to a free clinic in our community. I remember the time Thorn brought Billy Paultz, Billy Schaeffer and Mike Gale to the cul-de-sac in front of my home and did a clinic for the kids in our neighborhood. Billy Smith, a goaltender for the Islanders, also participated in that two-sport clinic. Smith went on to play goalie for four Stanley Cup champion teams on Long Island and is now enshrined in the Hockey Fall of Fame in Toronto. I have a picture of Thorn and Paultz holding my daughter, Sarah, about 18 months old, in their arms.

We enjoyed some fun family picnics in the backyard of Loughery's Long Island home. I can still see Fritz Massmann, the team's trainer, passing out beer from an ice-filled tub. Fritz preferred Vodka and cranberry juice. I can see Larry Kenon and Super John Williamson, Bill Melchionni, Billy Paultz, Rich Jones, John Roche all having a good time.

Legendary sports writer Jimmy Cannon thought he was close to Joe DiMaggio, one of the shyest people he ever met in the public eye. But Cannon thought that any sports writer who thought sports performers genuinely befriended them were fools or dupes. In

Cannon's jaundiced eye, sports performers merely suffered the company of sports writers. In the company of their peers, coaches and athletes, they spoke critically of sports writers. They viewed them as pests at best. I have only seen and spoken to Thorn briefly on perhaps two occasions in the 21 years since I left New York and returned home to Pittsburgh, so our friendship was no doubt based on our working relationship.

It was thought to be best to keep one's distance from the people one covered in sports, so there wouldn't be any conflict of interest, so you could write about them with a critical and honest eye. Friendships could bring about problems, hints of favoritism or dishonest reporting.

Even so, it was difficult not to be arrested by the charm of Loughery and Thorn. They were family men, both down to earth individuals and fun to be around.

"The papers here seemed to have hired you."
—Harry Weltman, General Manager
ABA's Spirits of St. Louis

Thinking of Thorn brings up the best of memories. I was covering pro basketball for *The New York Post* and *The Sporting News* and traveled with the Nets for nine years. Julius "Dr. J" Erving was the star the first time around and Nate "Tiny" Archibald was the star the second time around. I socialized and played tennis with Loughery and Thorn, the first time I'd permitted myself to get close to coaches or athletes as a sports reporter.

Most ABA people were cooperative with the media as they were desperate for attention and recognition.

When I was covering the Nets, Loughery and Thorn routinely played tennis with another sports writer, Doug Smith, who was covering the Nets for *Long Island Newsday*. Smith covered tennis for *USA Today* during the past two decades.

I thought Smith enjoyed a tremendous advantage in getting information about the Nets because he was able to spend more time with the coaches, and talk to them more casually away from the court. They'd play tennis for two hours and then sit around and have a few drinks and snacks afterward and talk about basketball.

I asked Smith, who had played varsity tennis on the college level at Hampton (Va.) Institute if he would teach me how to play tennis. He knew Arthur Ashe on a personal level. He told me to bring a racquet with me on the next road trip with the Nets. The first stop was Lexington, Kentucky, where the Nets were playing the Kentucky Colonels in a game that was farmed out to the University of Kentucky campus facility. The Colonels' starting lineup had two UK alumni, Louie Dampier and Dan Issel. I had an opportunity to sit with and interview legendary coach Adolph Rupp, who attended the game.

The day of the game, Smith called me in my hotel room and asked me if I had my tennis racquet. I told him I did. It was a wooden framed racquet, so you can appreciate the time period. He said, "Good, we've got a match today." My jaw dropped. A match? We were going to team up, I was told, against Loughery and Thorn, two former pro basketball players and terrific athletes.

Loughery was 6-3 and had played for the Baltimore Bullets. He and the 6-4 Thorn were teammates in Baltimore for a few years. I had never played a real tennis match in my life. Talk about learning under fire. Eventually, I would be able to hold my own and compete with these guys when teamed with Smith, who was clearly the best of the bunch. And now I, too, was getting to talk with Loughery and Thorn on a more frequent basis.

I remember going to Kutsher's Country Club in the Catskills one summer for the annual Maurice Stokes Memorial Game. I went out with Loughery, Thorn and one of their good friends, Billy Cunningham, to play tennis around midnight. The courts were closed and there was a lock on the gate. We all climbed over a ten-foot high screen fence to play a few games on dimly lit courts. They were all coaches, but they still had a lot of little boy in them, too. Cunningham has since been inducted into the Basketball Hall of Fame.

When I talked to Thorn on May 17, 2000, he told me he was no longer able to play tennis because of old knee and foot injuries.

I gave Thorn a boost in his career, lining him up for his first head coaching assignment. Following his second year with the Nets, Thorn and his wife, Peggy, invited my wife, Kathie, and me to their apartment at Woodbury, Long Island for dinner. We had a baby-sitter look after our daughter, Sarah, when we went out that evening.

A sportswriter from the *St. Louis Post-Dispatch* called me at my home that night, and the babysitter gave him the telephone number at the Thorn residence where he might be able to reach me. During dinner, the phone rang and Peggy Thorn answered the call and announced that it was for me. The sports writer called me to ask me if I knew anything about who was being considered for the coaching position with the ABA's newest team, the wonderfully named Spirits of St. Louis.

He was calling me because I had been writing a column about the ABA for six years for *The Sporting News*, which was headquartered in St. Louis. The Silna Brothers, who were in the garment business in New York City, were the owners of the St. Louis franchise. They had hired Harry Weltman to run the basketball operation.

I had no idea what coach Weltman was after. But I told the writer, "I hear they're interested in Rod Thorn."

It made sense, as far as I was concerned, so let's run it up the flagpole to see how it flies. The sports writer in St. Louis agreed that it made sense. Thorn was a top assistant to Loughery on one of the ABA's best teams, for starters. Better yet, Thorn had played for the St. Louis Hawks for nearly two seasons in the mid-60s, and had been a popular ballplayer.

I told the writer I would contact Thorn and have Thorn call him. Thorn took time out before we had dessert and called the sports writer in St. Louis and told him he hadn't talked to anyone about the coaching job, but that he would be interested if such an offer was forthcoming. So the sports writer did a story about the possibility of Thorn returning to St. Louis as coach of the new ABA team.

Thorn later told me he got a telephone call from Weltman, who invited him to come to St. Louis to talk about the job. "I'll be honest with you," Weltman told Thorn. "I hadn't really thought about you, but the papers here seem to have hired you already."

Thorn took the job and coached the Spirits for two seasons. Over the course of those two seasons, the Spirits had tremendous talent, but never good team chemistry. For whatever reason, Thorn couldn't get these guys to play to their awesome potential.

Thorn remembered my role in his going to St. Louis. "Thank you," he said. "I remember past favors."

At one time or another, the Spirits' lineup included Marvin "Bad News" Barnes, Freddie Lewis, Maurice Lucas, Moses Malone, Caldwell Jones, Ron Boone, "Fly" Williams and Gus Gerard.

There was talent everywhere. Broadcasting the Spirits' games was a relative newcomer to radio named Bob Costas. Of course, in time he would become one of the most celebrated sports broadcasters in the business. The American Basketball Association was struggling for survival during those two seasons the Spirits were in the league. At season's end, NBA Commissioner Larry O'Brien and ABA Commissioner Dave DeBusschere finally succeeded in a merger of sorts.

Four teams from the ABA were blended into the NBA. They were the Indiana Pacers, New York Nets, Denver Nuggets and San Antonio Spurs. Folded were the Kentucky Colonels, Virginia Squires and Spirits of St. Louis. Players from the latter three teams were distributed to the incumbent NBA teams in a special dispersal draft.

"You don't have to compare him to anyone."
—Fred Schaus

The first time I saw Rod Thorn up close was at the old Mountaineer Field House in Morgantown. That facility was fantastic for basketball. It was like a smaller version of the old Madison Square Garden, seating about 6800. It was a two-tiered building, and the upper level of seats extended out to the sideline. The press box was located in the front row of the second level, right above the benches where the ballplayers from both teams were seated. It was like watching a show from an opera box.

I have come across a column I wrote for *The Pitt News* about Thorn after that January 21, 1962 game in Morgantown.

It went like this:

A button-down shirt collar seemed to be choking the almond-shaped Adam's apple on Rodney Thorn's neck. He spoke fluently, however, despite the harsh pressure on his esophagus.

Rod Thorn was dressed strictly Ivy League. Why not? He's a Princeton man. Princeton, West Virginia, that is. Rod's not acclaimed for the cut of his dress clothes, however, but rather for the skills that he displays when wearing a flimsy nightshirt for the West Virginia University basketball team.

Playing as if he had been living on Benzedrine, Thorn personally beat the visiting Panthers, 88-78, at the notorious Mountaineer Field House. Running with an odd-looking, stilted motion, his bony shoulders bobbing up to his big ears like bicycle pedals, Thorn slid past the fastest of the Panthers. He shot over the outstretched hands of their tallest men, and padded his 25-points per game scoring average with 30 points, his seventh 30-plus point game of the season.

Like Janus, he could look two ways at once, often did and hit five teammates for quick, easy scores. Now he was sitting in front of his locker in the Moutaineers' clubhouse.

He has wiry blond hair, something like Danny Kaye's, and a slight cleft in his chin. He is a strong candidate for All-American honors. He's only a junior. He was also considered last year, but didn't make the grade.

Does this status affect Thorn? "Last year it bothered me," said Thorn. "But now if I'm good enough I'll make it."

Rod is a good student — B plus average — and he's serious about his studies. He's serious about his basketball, too, and last year these two aspirations had a fierce rivalry, tugging away at the soul of Thorn. Other sportswriters would have you believe from their accounts that Thorn cracked under the pressure. He merely dropped out of school to ease the tension.

"This year it doesn't occupy a place in my mind," he said. "Last year I let it get the best of me, a lot worse than I should have. The sportswriters exaggerated it a bit, that Freudian idea.

"Lotta ballplayers have troubles like mine — some probably worse. I just couldn't cope with the situation," he said.

"This year if I'm not good enough, I'm just not good enough," he said.

This year we was good enough to make the all-tournament team in the Los Angeles Classic along with the likes of Ohio State's Jerry Lucas and John Havlicek, Purdue's Terry Dischinger, Utah's Billy "The Hill" McGill, and Southern Cal's John Rudometkin.

"That Lucas is the greatest ever," Thorn offered. "What a team player. Dischinger didn't even seem like he was out there even though he scored 32 points against us."

Thorn scored 32 points himself in that game with Purdue. He scored 31 against Billy McGill and Utah, 30 against arch-rivals Pitt and Virginia Tech, and 29 against Villanova. He had 38 against Furman.

When he was in Los Angeles, Thorn naturally drew some comparisons in the LA newspapers to Jerry West, a star performer for the NBA Lakers. How does Thorn feel about such comparisons?

"It's something that's going to happen," he said. "I overlook it. I think that West is the greatest his size in the game. I've tried to copy some of his best moves. I don't worry about being as good. It's almost impossible to be as good. I've a long, long way to go. Those sportswriters just have to have something to write about. Now I just want to do my best."

Mountaineer coach George King shuns comparisons. "Rod's performances rate with themselves," commented King, who succeeded Fred Schaus as the WVU coach when Schaus left the college ranks to coach the Lakers. "You don't have to compare him to anyone."

There is a lot of fantasy connected to the tales of Rod Thorn, except those of his basketball prowess. He's not a hillbilly, either. "I think our state sorta has a reputation for being backward," said Thorn. "They figure we're a bunch of guys from small towns in hills and backwoods. It's just natural."

So was Thorn.

Only the year before, as a sophomore, Thorn had two of his worst games against Pitt, and the memories stayed with him.

"My parents wanted me to make good grades," recalled Thorn, "and a point where it got real bad was when we played Pitt in January at Pittsburgh. Night before I stayed up all night and studied for an 8 a.m. exam.

"I had never made a C in my life. I didn't want one. I was afraid I'd go to pieces. I've got so much hypertension I can stay on top for a while. It didn't bother me on the test, but that night I couldn't dunk the ball during the warm-ups. It was the first time that had happened since I was in high school. I didn't tell the coach how I felt because once the game started I thought I'd still have a good game in me.

"I scored eight points and was terrible. Instead of just forgetting it, I had the rabbit ears. From the stands, I heard, 'You couldn't hold West's shoes.' I thought I was losing what ability I had. You can't ever afford another game like that one I told myself after it was over."

Thorn couldn't sleep nights after that, and he missed three games. "I wasn't that physically sick," Thorn said. "What was really the crux. I was so far behind in school and I didn't give a damn.

"The game after one I sat out was four days later against Pitt at home. I based all my hopes on redeeming myself that night. I'd been in bed for nearly a week. I was down to 167 pounds (from 178 prounds). Still, beating Pitt was my goal. On the opening center jump, the ball was tipped to me. I started down the floor and fell on my face. I took four shots and made six points. Then I came down on the side of another player's foot and hurt my ankle. It was another nightmare."

That's why Thorn took such great satisfaction from scoring 30 points against Pitt in a victory at Morgantown.

"I shot a basketball almost every day."

Rodney B. Thorn was born May 23, 1941 in Weirton, but grew up in Princeton, at the southeastern end of West Virginia. His father, Joe Thorn, was a cop who became the police chief in Princeton. His mother, Jackie, was a schoolteacher. She taught at Thorn Elementary School on Thorn Street, both named after Rod's ancestors. Rod's great uncle, Arthur Thorn, was president of what became West Virginia Tech.

Joe Thorn was with the Marines when they invaded Iwo Jima. He was severely wounded and, for a time, reported missing in action. Joe had been a good athlete in his day, good enough to get as high as Triple A in the St. Louis Cardinals organization. He trained his son to become a big-time ballplayer. Joe and Jackie Thorn wanted their son to become a doctor while he was at it.

The Thorns had their only child shortly before Joe became a soldier in World War II. When Joe returned from the war, his son was four years old. "I raised my son to be what I never was — a great athlete," said Joe.

When Rod was growing up, his dad required that he practice basketball or baseball at a certain time every day. "He played for me," the father recalled. "I treated him like everyone else. If you didn't pass to the man who had the good shot, you sat down on the bench."

Rod recalled those early days. "Dad got me so interested in basketball," Rod said, "that from eight to 12 years old I shot a basketball almost every day of my life. I often swept the snow off our neighbors' asphalt driveway who had a basket set up for his son. Mr. Walter Burton — who was the main attorney in town — was real good about it. He only chased me home when it got dark or he had company."

That's when Rod developed his overhead, two-hand shot. He began by balancing the ball with one hand and pushing the shot with the other. Then he began to supply the push with both hands.

Rod practiced for long hours at the Thorn Elementary School where his mother taught. "It got so I hated it," said Thorn, "but my dad kept telling me, 'Someday you'll thank me for this,' and he was right. I played on an organized team when I was six years old."

In four seasons at Princeton High School, where he was coached by Buster Brown, he averaged 27.6 points while playing only 26 minutes a game.

Nearly 100 colleges contacted him about coming to play for them. He considered Kentucky and Duke before deciding on West Virginia. He sat in Governor Happy Chandler's box at the Kentucky Derby with Adolph Rupp whispering sweet nothings in his ear. The West Virginia

From West Virginia University sports information office

Rod Thorn was a point of pride to his father, Joe Thorn, and community of Princeton during his basketball and baseball playing days at West Virginia University.

Jim O'Brien

legislature passed a resolution declaring Thorn as one of the state's natural resources and urged him to attend a school within its borders.

Thorn thought that being put in the same class as West Virginia's coal mines was flattering. "That was a nice gesture," he said. Thorn liked the Duke campus and its medical school, but decided to attend West Virginia because he had "too many loyal Mountaineer people behind me to go anywhere else."

He was quite a prospect. In addition to his heroics in sports, Thorn had all A's and three B's for his classroom efforts in four years at Princeton High School. He graduated fourth academically in a class of 220. He even sang in the school choir.

He led the WVU freshman basketball team to an undefeated season and he batted .500 for the varsity baseball team. He was sixth in the class academically, but fretted that he could have finished higher if he had worked a little harder. After the season, *Newsweek* magazine reported, "When All-American Jerry West graduates in June, West Virginia will be ready to replace him with Rod Thorn, a freshman. The Mountaineers insist that Thorn is as good a basketball player as West was at the same stage."

He became a good friend of backcourt teammates Jim McCormick of New Moundsville and Gale Catlett of Hedgesville, near Martinsburg. They have kept in touch through the years. Catlett would become the coach at his alma mater for the 1978-79 season and would still be at the helm for the 2000-2001 season.

At age 19, young Thorn was almost burned out by his parents' expectations, and those of every one who followed his career. He had difficulties on and off the court all year long. After his sophomore season, he dropped out of school. "I was physically and mentally exhausted," he explained at the time.

"I was so sick mentally that I thought I was sick physically. Finally, I called Dad and told him to come and get me. I just sat and stared out the window all the way home."

He came back, but switched his major from medicine to law, and decided not to worry so much about his studies. "I've changed," he said at the time. "I don't get as worked up any more over my test scores anymore. The classroom pressure isn't as great."

Rival fans called him "Psycho" and "Bugs," but Rod refused to be rattled. "No more hysterics," he said. "No more punching the lockers. If I had a bad night, well, I just had a bad night."

Virginia Tech's Chris Smith played against Thorn in a Charleston, West Virginia summer league. "One time he fouled me," Smith related, "and he said, 'I'm sorry, Mr. Smith, sir.' I didn't know whether he was being sarcastic or what. But, when he kept calling me 'sir,' that was too much."

Thorn smiled brightly when Smith's story was related to him. "They rib me all the time about that 'sir' business," he said. "But, well, sir, my parents always told me to be polite. It never hurts to call anybody 'sir,' particularly when they're older than you are."

While Thorn is regarded as one of WVU's all-time greatest, it's not that well known that he obtained his collegiate degree, in political science, at the University of Washington in 1972, while he was playing for the Seattle Supersonics.

"I've been blessed."

Rod Thorn thinks he's been fortunate to make a living doing something he enjoyed doing. "It's been great," he said over the telephone from his office at the Olympic Tower near St. Patrick's Cathedral in mid-town Manhattan. "This job gave me a chance to play a role in how the rules of the game are administered. I've been part of a league that, up until this year, has been on the rise and been enormously successful. Our ratings and attendance are down now in the wake of the retirement of Michael Jordan. So we have our work cut out for us. I've been associated with USA Basketball, and serve on a committee there. I've helped pick players for the Olympic Games and for world competitions. It's provided me with an opportunity to enjoy a good life style for my family. I've been blessed.

"I've been very fortunate. I've been working with a great leader in David Stern, who has done so much to advance this league on an international basis. He came after Walter Kennedy and Lawrence O'Brien and he took this league to another level. As a ballplayer, I was just a journeyman player, but I met and worked with a lot of great people along the way and the connections helped me to continue to work in pro basketball in one capacity or another. I was fortunate to be an assistant coach at Seattle in the NBA and in New York in the ABA, to be a coach in St. Louis in the ABA. I've had a lot of interesting experiences on different levels. The totality of those experiences has really helped me in my current position. I have a good understanding of owners, front-office officials, coaches, players and rules. I know what their life is like, what the demands are on them. I know what you need to know to enhance the product and our sport. It's been a fun ride."

At the outset of June, 2000, it was announced that Rod Thorn was leaving the NBA office to become president of basketball operations for the New Jersey Nets. He had accepted the same job a year earlier, changed his mind, and decided to stay with the league office. The league doubled his salary, from $400,000 to $800,000 a year. The Nets did much better this time around. He signed a five-year contract for a reported $10 million. Yes, that's $2 million a year. The Nets had the No. 1 pick in the upcoming NBA draft. If only Thorn could draft Michael Jordan again. "I had been offered similar positions in the past," said Thorn. "I couldn't turn the money down this time. I was looking for a new challenge. I'm back on the firing line again." He would no doubt get reacquainted with "that nervous feeling in the pit of your stomach."

337

Tunch Ilkin
Wants to coach his kids

"Sometimes I sound like Myron."

Tunch Ilkin always considered himself a team player. During his 13 seasons as an offensive tackle with the Steelers, he served as a team captain and player representative. He was a Pro Bowl participant in 1989 and 1990.

In early February of 2000, Ilkin turned down an offer from Bill Cowher to join his coaching staff and help tutor the Steelers' offensive linemen. "I knew six months earlier that he was going to offer me a job," said Ilkin, "and I prayed to God all that time to help me make the right decision."

It was a tempting offer, and Ilkin came close to saying "yes," but in the end he decided it would be better to continue doing what he's already doing. Coaching football on the pro or college level is an all-consuming proposition. The hours are unreal. It leaves little time for anything else.

Ilkin was putting his family first, not his own "need for personal validation," as he put it. So Sharon, his wife of 18 years, and the kids, Tanner, 14; Natalie, 11; and Clay, 8, would be seeing more of their husband and father, respectively.

"When I visit schools or churches in the community," said Ilkin, "I am often identified as Tanner's dad, or Natalie's dad or Clay's dad, and that's enough for me."

Ilkin would continue to be involved with the Steelers in a media role. He was about to begin his third year as an analyst on the radio broadcasts, teamed on WDVE-FM with Bill Hillgrove and Myron Cope. "My wife says I'm starting to talk too fast, and that sometimes I sound like Myron," kidded Ilkin. "That comes from keeping company with him all season. It's a real blast."

He also was doing pre-game and post-game shows on Steelers football with Sam Nover at WPXI-TV. Similar work led to network opportunities for two of his former teammates, Mark Malone and Merril Hoge. Ilkin has had a few chances to do network analysis as well. He also did some consultant work on offensive line techniques with NFL teams and at summer training camps.

This would keep Ilkin involved with the game and environment he enjoys, yet allow him time to continue to coach his kids' teams in Upper St. Clair, and maintain a strong commitment to his church and related activities.

"I'm glad he decided to stay with us for selfish reasons," said Hillgrove. "Cope and I can handle most things, but Tunch gives us a different dimension. He knows what's going on on the sidelines — he's been there — and he doesn't miss anyone moving too soon in the line.

Craig Wolfley and Tunch Ilkin have been close as Steelers teammates and radio and TV analysts in Pittsburgh.

He picks up on those infractions before the officials identify the culprit.

"He's solid. He's still the same person he was when he was playing, only a little more into his Christian faith. He can still do some coaching on a consultant basis with ballclubs, and still be around the game. He's just a joy to be around. I know he was tempted, but I remember that he turned down an opportunity to do more network stuff because he didn't want to be on the road so much.

"He told me he was in a hotel room in Green Bay one Saturday to do a TV game that weekend, and his son was playing soccer in Upper St. Clair and that's where he wanted to be. Working with the Steelers, he's not on the road all the time. He knows what's important and he has his priorities in order."

Ilkin was born in Turkey — "that's how I got that funny name" — and came to America as a Muslim. He became a Christian during his early years with the Steelers, inspired by teammates who had a strong religious commitment. He grew up with the Koran, but can now recite Biblical passages as casually as the Steelers' lineup.

"The Bible is our playbook for life," Ilkin is fond of saying.

Ilkin played for the Steelers from 1980 through 1992, even though he was cut at his first camp at St. Vincent College. He went home to Chicago, worked at a health club and stayed in shape. When injuries piled up in the Steelers' offensive line, Chuck Noll called Ilkin back and he made the most of his second chance opportunity.

He weighed only 265 pounds when he started at right tackle for the Steelers, but his blocking techniques enabled him to fend off opponents who outweighed him by as much as 50 pounds. His teaching is unique because he applies martial arts techniques to blocking an opponent. He's a good friend of former roommate Craig Wolfley, one of those who led him to becoming a Christian.

"He's really wrestled with this decision," said Wolfley. "At one point I thought he was going to do it. Knowing Tunch, I believe he made the right decision. This way he can remain involved, but not turn over his entire life to football."

Ilkin and Wolfley, who owns a martial arts studio in Bridgeville, often appear together at church-related seminars. Wolfley began working as an analyst on Steelers football on Pittsburgh's ESPN Radio during the 1999 season, so he and Ilkin compare notes in their preparation.

Ilkin played one season for Cowher, then signed with Green Bay as a free agent when it became obvious that Leon Searcy was ready to succeed him. Ilkin played two years for the Packers, then retired. He remained in Pittsburgh. "I've bought only one house in my life and I still live there. I came a year after the Steelers won the Super Bowl for the fourth time and left before the Steelers went back to the Super Bowl. So I have no Super Bowl ring."

His mother, a beautiful woman who was once Miss Turkey, was living on Mt. Washington

On Saturday, February 19, 2000, Ilkin was the featured speaker at the 5th Annual South Hills Fellowship of Christian Athletes Sports Awards Breakfast. He delivered a powerful message to teens and their parents and sponsors at Christ United Methodist Church in Bethel Park.

Ilkin is a good man, to begin with, and he's become quite the preacher. He doesn't believe young people should look to sports for role models, yet he sets a good example for everyone. He's well grounded, personable, and a real teddy bear. He had an encouraging word and a hug for the 11 young men and women who received awards.

He said it was disheartening to hear so much negative news of late regarding the personal behavior of pro football players and other athletes. Two have been accused of murder; some have died in auto mishaps; others have been cited for drug-related activity.

"There's too much ego in sports these days," said Ilkin. "I hate it when you see guys calling attention to themselves on every play. They make a simple tackle or they gain five yards and they're running around waving their arms and pointing to themselves. It drives me nuts. Hey, that's what you're getting paid to do. It's the me-me-me generation. We had a coach, Chuck Noll, who used to tell us, 'Look like you've been there before.'"

Ilkin has been there before. He's played with and against the best, and he would have much to offer as a coach. When he attended the funeral services of former teammate, Steve Furness, age 49, a week earlier it only reminded him of the "brevity of life."

"Back in May," said Ilkin, "I stood next to Steve Furness at the funeral for Steve Courson's wife. Now I was standing next to Steve Courson at the funeral for Steve Furness."

Ilkin wants to make the most of his time on earth. "My wife and children are the most important people in my life," he said, "and it's them I have to look after and mentor."

Jim O'Brien

Tunch Ilkin teams with Bill Hillgrove on 2000 NFL draft coverage for ESPN Radio (1250).

Dave Hart
He wouldn't stay down

"I thought I was a winner when I came to Pitt."

Dave Hart was a waist-gunner in a B-17 bomber that flew 30 missions in Europe in World War II, and he coached the University of Pittsburgh football team for 30 games in the late '60s. It's a toss-up as to which of those 30 outings was the most perilous period in his life. He survived both and went on to become one of the most successful and respected college athletic administrators in the country.

He had rewarding runs as athletic director at Louisville and Missouri, and as the commissioner of the Southern Conference before retiring in 1991.

It's quite a comeback story. It's a study of persistence, determination, drive, hard work and a hell bent belief in one's ability to do a job right that enabled Hart to succeed. Hart was more than a survivor. He was a sharp cookie, honest and he hustled for financial support.

"My goal was to make money and keep the programs clean," said Hart.

Lessons learned about the rewards of hard work and proper respect for others in his hometown of Connellsville, and later in Latrobe, Johnstown and Pittsburgh enabled Hart to have what it takes to overcome so many defeats and disappointments during his Pitt period. His 3-27 record at Pitt was a dismal failure, for sure, and it could have derailed him for good. He bounced back, however, and resumed his winning ways.

His Pitt experience is still an embarrassing blemish on his record. When he was interviewed for a front-page story in *The Wall Street Journal* in October of 1981, the writer pressed him to talk about his three-year record at Pitt. Hart blanched and said, "You're not going to put that in the paper, are you?"

There have been plenty of stars to cover up the scars.

He earned a distinguished Flying Cross and Air Medal with Oak Leaf Clusters for his World War II efforts. A waist gunner sits behind a rapid-fire gun at an open door in the center of the airplane. If you saw the movies "Memphis Belle," "12 O'Clock High" or "The Tuskeegee Airmen" you get the picture. It's hazardous work. According to information offered by World War II historian Joseph Ambrose in a CNN report, anyone who flew more than 20 bomber missions "statistically shouldn't have survived that."

Hart has several Hall of Fame credits and has won countless awards for his athletic achievements. When he was fired at Pitt after the 1968 season it would have been difficult to envision the string of successes that lie ahead for Hart. His prospects didn't look good. "I

Dave Hart and Pitt Athletic Director Frank Carver meet with Navy brass.

Curbstone Coaches lineup on January 10, 1966 includes, left to right, former Glassport High School and Pitt quarterback Kenny Lucas, Steelers running back Dick Hoak, Aldo Pallone, Dave Hart and Tony DeNunzio. Pallone and DeNunzio were Jeannette businessmen and friends of Hoak who promoted annual Steelers game in their Westmoreland County community.

1966 Pitt coaching staff includes, kneeling left to right, Walt Cummins, Dave Hart, Bill Neal, Leeman Bennett and, standing, Frank Cignetti, Dick Bestwick, Bill Lewis, Steve Petro and Jim Royer.

was just hoping I could get a job," recalled Hart. "Art Rooney called me and said, 'I'd like to see you with the Steelers.' He said he would speak to his son, Dan, but I never heard back from them."

No one tells this comeback story as well as Dave Hart.

"I was too young to be scared or realize what a dangerous assignment I had when I was in the Air Force," said Hart. "We were all so young; I was just a teenager. I saw some planes go down. I was in some sticky situations. We went over Berlin once where they had strong anti-aircraft installations.

"Some times we couldn't drop our bombs because there was cloud cover, or haze, and we couldn't see our targets. We couldn't come back and land with those bombs on board, so we had to drop them in the Adriatic Sea, for instance. There has to be a lot of bombs at the bottom of a lot of oceans and seas and lakes over there.

"The Pitt experience was different, of course," continued Hart. "But I was so upset and so distraught after I was fired with a year to go on my contract at Pitt that my family was really worried about me. I was heart-broken and depressed. Looking back, those challenges and heartaches toughened me for what lie ahead."

"I always tried to surround myself with winners."

Hart has always believed that athletics was a classroom where one could teach or learn proper values. He thought it taught him discipline, sacrifice, pride and motivation, all essential to success in sports and in business, and he did his best to pass along the knowledge he acquired along the way. That's the way it works. The baton is passed from one generation to the next.

"I thought I was a winner when I came to Pitt," allowed Hart. "That stretch shook my faith, for sure, but I'd like to think that I turned out to be a winner after all. And I always tried to surround myself with winners. They make you look good."

With that comment, Hart flashed a smile, and it was a winning smile. He was sitting across a table during a breakfast interview session at TGI Fridays, adjoining the Quality Inn at Biltmore in Asheville, North Carolina. We talked a total of five hours at dinner and breakfast sessions at TGI Fridays and in the lobby of the Quality Inn over two days, Monday and Tuesday, April 24 and 25, 2000.

There was a steady rain both days, with temperatures in the low 50s, so Hart didn't have to give up a game of golf or tennis at his club to join us. He warmed to his company and his story as soon as he sipped some steaming coffee.

Dave Hart, retired and a month away from his 75th birthday (May 25, 2000), remained an engaging guy, full of great grins, gleaming brown eyes and a positive outlook. He was animated and enthusiastic about every topic. He was keeping busy, serving as a consultant

344

to the athletic department at University of North Carolina at Asheville, was active at his country club — he had served as president a few years earlier — and involved with other community activities. He had been a consultant for U.S. Airways. When he left us the second day, Hart said he was going over to the UNC campus where he was assisting in a screening process to hire a new athletic director.

He also said he was scheduled to have back surgery later that week. "Just some old spurs that need to be removed, stuff like that," he said. I called him on the telephone a few days after his surgery and he said he was feeling good, recuperating at home.

I learned during my visit that Hart was an orphan — there's a phrase you don't hear anymore — and some other aspects of his life I hadn't heard or read about before. He said the social worker from the foundling home in Pittsburgh told his adopted parents in Connellsville that she thought he had come from a family in the Glenwood section of Pittsburgh. He was placed after a short stay at the Salvation Army's Booth Memorial Hospital on Pauline Avenue in Pittsburgh. He was born May 25, 1925. Glenwood was where I grew up, a mill town and railroad community at the southeastern end of the city, bordered by Hazelwood, Hays, Homestead and the Glen-Hazel Projects. Hart didn't know his birth parents. It struck me that I may have known his parents. They might have been neighbors, or people I knew as a young man.

I lived 23 of my first 25 years on Sunnyside Street in Glenwood. My father, Dan O'Brien, was born on a couch on that same street. I spent my first five years in that house where my father was born. Then we made a big move to the other side of the street to a rowhouse that had one more bedroom. We went from 5410 to 5413 Sunnyside Street. My father's first job, at age 15, was at the Baltimore & Ohio Railroad, located a block away between our home and the Monongahela River. My maternal grandfather, Richard Burns, had been the yardmaster at the Glenwood Yard of the Baltimore & Ohio Railroad. Hart worked there in the summer during his student days at St. Vincent College in Latrobe.

I didn't realize what common beginnings we shared until I visited Dave Hart in Asheville. I first met him when he came to Pitt as the head coach after John Michelosen was fired following the 1965 season. We both did sports commentaries on WEEP Radio (1080) for the late Roger Willoughby Ray, who was the general manager of the station. Hart followed me in that role.

I had gotten an early out (by 81 days) from a two-year stint in the U.S. Army to attend graduate school in 1966 at the University of Pittsburgh, from which I had graduated in 1964 with a degree in English (writing emphasis). Beano Cook, then the sports information director at Pitt, and I had started a tabloid newspaper called *Pittsburgh Weekly Sports* in 1963.

I resumed editing the paper, and writing many of its stories, when I got out of the Army. One of the last stories I wrote was when

Pitt hired Carl DePasqua, a former Pitt football player and a former assistant on Michelosen's staff, to succeed Hart. Frank Carver, the athletic director, pulled the plug on Hart with one year remaining on his four-year contract. Hart felt betrayed. He thought he was on the verge of turning the program around.

I recall walking with DePasqua as he left the Pitt Field House and walked across Allequippa Street to Trees Hall for the press conference to announce his appointment. He looked like a man walking the last mile. Trees Hall was a strange setting to announce a new head coach. The words posh and Trees Hall have never appeared prior to this in the same sentence. Pitt had tried in vain to hire some big-name coaches from out west, like Frank Kush, Lloyd Eaton and Dee Andros, but all turned down the offer. So Pitt called on DePasqua, who was coaching at Waynesburg College where his first team had won an NAIA championship in 1966. Soon after this development, I moved to Miami to cover the Dolphins in their last season (1969) in the American Football League for *The Miami News*.

So Hart and I had a history. We had both grown up in western Pennsylvania as Pitt fans — he remembered as a youngster seeing Marshall Goldberg play for the Panthers against Wisconsin at Pitt Stadium; I remembered seeing Joe Schmidt against Iowa in the 1952 opener at Pitt Stadium — and we both went on to work for the University of Pittsburgh. Hart earned a master's degree in education from Pitt in June, 1959.

I initially knew him during one of the most difficult and discouraging periods in his life. Even so, I liked Hart from the start, and was often accused of misjudging his ability back then. He convinced me he could get the job done at Pitt. I wrote a lot of upbeat stories about him in *Pittsburgh Weekly Sports*. Hart could sell you on anything. I saw him from time to time after he was dismissed. He served one year as a scout for the Dallas Cowboys, three years as assistant to the president, Charles Sewell, at Robert Morris College, then six years as athletic director at the University of Louisville, eight years as athletic director at the University of Missouri and, finally, five years as commissioner of the Southern Conference. During his stint as commissioner, Hart moved the league offices from Greensboro to Asheville. He chose to remain there. A visitor to Asheville could easily appreciate Hart's love for the area.

"I've been lucky to have two great wives."

Asheville is a beautiful town in the western mountains of North Carolina. George Vanderbilt fell in love with the mountains and built a palatial home there in 1895. It's called the Biltmore Estates. I toured a portion of the 250-room French Renaissance-syle chateau, billed as "America's largest home," with its formal gardens, walking trails, winery and restaurants after I had completed my interviews with Hart. He didn't want me to leave without seeing the impressive tourist attraction, and he even provided complimentary admission passes. Hart still had connections.

There's a rambling Victorian structure on North Market Street that is the boyhood home of author Thomas Wolfe, immortalized in his autobiographical novel "Look Homeward, Angel."

Hart and his wife, Earlyn, live in the beautiful Beaverdam Run Condominiums in North Asheville. The Harts were even pictured in a promotional flyer about the community. They enjoyed the tennis courts there as well as at their club. She shared his enthusiasm for sports and education.

Hart recalled a weekend when he and Earlyn were traveling together and he introduced her to Roger Staubach and Johnny Unitas, two of the all-time great quarterbacks, at two different venues. "She seemed impressed," he said with a lopsided grin. "Hey, that was quite a parlay."

He had served for five years as the chairman of a highly successful fund-raising celebrity golf tournament on behalf of UNC-Asheville, and learned in late May of 2000 that henceforth the event would be named in his honor. The Southern Conference had earlier established a scholarship in his name. So Asheville was definitely agreeing with Hart.

I remembered that a former next-door neighbor of mine in Upper St. Clair, an advertising/public relations executive named Boris Weinstein, once whispered the word "Asheville" to me during a backyard discussion. "It's my secret city," Weinstein said. "I don't want the world to know about it."

Since Hart retired, the Southern Conference returned its headquarters to Greensboro, but he chose to stay in Asheville. That's understandable. The views are spectacular from so many high points, and the pink and lilac azaleas, white dogwood and red, yellow and burgundy tulips colored the landscape. Asheville is an awesome scene.

It's kept the smile on Hart's face. So has Earlyn, whom he married in 1983. They moved from Columbia to Asheville in June of 1986. His first wife, Patti, was with him for 36 years. She died of a stroke at age 56. He and Patti knew each other from their grade school days in Connellsville and were married in 1946 at Athens, Georgia when he returned to the University of Georgia following a three-year stint in the Air Force. They had three sons, Dave Jr., in Tallahassee, Florida; Dick, in Palm Harbor, Florida; Danny, in Louisville, Kentucky; and a daughter, Candy, in St. Louis. "I've been lucky to have two great wives," said Hart.

Hart believes he has been lucky in a lot of ways. "The harder you work the luckier you get," Hart said, repeating a phrase he heard early in his life. "Branch Rickey once said, 'Luck is the residue of design.' I was lucky to have the people who supported me along the way."

His good luck or good fortune began when the childless Hart couple of Connellsville took him in and adopted him as a baby. It continued when he enlisted in the military service, when he went to the University of Georgia and when he transferred to St. Vincent College in Latrobe.

When he graduated from St. Vincent College, he became one of the most successful high school football coaches in the history of Pennsylvania, first at Hurst High School in Mt. Pleasant, not far from the St. Vincent College campus, and then at Johnstown High School. He had a 21-7 record at Hurst High School (later Mt. Pleasant High School), and posted a 63-12-2 record at Johnstown High School. His Trojans were undefeated in 1958 (11-0) and 1959 (10-0). The 1958 team won the WPIAL title.

"Al DeLuca, the coach at St. Vincent took me to meet all the members of the school board at Hurst and I had a chance to talk to them individually before they selected a coach," recalled Hart. "When the Johnstown job came open, I did the same thing on my own. I contacted all the board members to express my interest in the job. Some of them were good about it, some didn't like the idea of me doing that. They thought I was pushy. Hey, I was selling myself to them. I wanted that edge. I wanted them to know what I had to offer. I wanted the job."

He coached in the Western All-Star Game and the Big 33 All-Star Game in Hershey in 1959. He remembers not permitting Joe Namath, a quarterback from Beaver Falls, to play in the Big 33 game because Namath reported late for practice because he chose to stay back in Beaver Falls to play for his school's baseball team. He had told Namath before he reported that he could come but that he would not play. Hart was inducted into the Pennsylvania High School Coaches Hall of Fame at ceremonies in Hershey in July of 1997.

His success at Johnstown landed him assistant coaching positions at Kentucky (1962-1964) and then the U.S. Naval Academy (1964-1966). He was at Navy when Roger Staubach was an All-American quarterback for the Midshipmen. Then Hart interviewed for and gained the head coaching assignment at Pitt in 1966.

"I was a hot commodity," said Hart. "The Maryland and West Virginia jobs were also open. They were interested in me. I went in to see Rip Miller (Navy's assistant athletic director). He said he would help me. He wanted to know which of the jobs I was most interested in. I told him Pitt. He said, 'Are you sure?' He was very tactful. He said, 'Is that what you want? Are you going in with your eyes open?' I guess he was trying to tell me something."

Hart's record at Pitt was 1-9 in each of his three seasons. His teams were outscored by 1,014 to 270 over those three seasons, or by an average score of 34-9. His Panthers lost all three of their games to Notre Dame by a cumulative score of 134-7. The scores were 40-0, 38-0 and 56-7. That last game, November 9, 1968, was the low point for Hart and Pitt football followers. Notre Dame coach Ara Parseghian

Dave Hart and his wife, Earlyn, love to play
tennis near their home in Asheville, North
Carolina. Dave is pictured at Pitt Stadium in
1966 and at Quality Inn at Biltmore in 2000.

permitted the officials to let the clock continue to run after out-of-bounds plays and incomplete passes to ease the pain. It was embarrassing.

Hart's days at Pitt were numbered after that fiasco. His successor, DePasqua, was a disappointment as well. DePasqua posted records of 4-6, 5-5, 3-8 and 1-10. Many thought DePasqua did better in the beginning because he had inherited Hart's players. DePasqua distanced himself from Pitt after he was discharged and was bitter about his experience. I always liked DePasqua and felt badly that his experience at Pitt didn't have a happier ending.

"He had a terrific personality."
— Vic Surma

Hart revealed that he was responsible for recommending to Pitt officials that they hire Johnny Majors, then the head coach at Iowa State. "Majors wanted no part of the job," recalled Hart at our Asheville meeting. "He sent his brother, who was an attorney, to Pittsburgh to hear what Pitt had to say. John didn't even come in for an interview, at first, when they wanted to talk to him."

I had never heard that before. I mentioned to Hart that, along the same line, it was Foge Fazio who recommended Mike Gottfried for the Pitt head coaching position. When Gottfried got the job, ironically enough, he bristled when anybody in the Pitt family referred to Fazio.

Majors turned things around at Pitt. He brought in about 85 new players his first year, and Pitt beat Arizona State in the Fiesta Bowl to end the season. His records in four years were 6-5-1, 7-4, 8-4 and 12-0. His 1976 team won the national championship and his star player, Tony Dorsett, won the Heisman Trophy as the outstanding football player in the country. His Panthers beat Notre Dame all four years. It was payback time. Dorsett set rushing records against the Fighting Irish. They brought out the best in TD.

"Johnny Majors was a great coach," said Hart, "and he had Tony Dorsett on his side."

There were times, during his Pitt experience, that Hart felt he had no one on his side. In truth, a lot of people liked Dave Hart, despite his record in Oakland. He was just a likable guy, a born salesman. He could recruit, but Pitt had stricter standards in those days — a demanding 1,000 SAT minimum score and a two-year foreign language requirement that had proven a nightmare for Michelosen as well at the end of his Pitt stay. It was tough for him to get the good players he needed. But Hart brought in some good ones during his stay.

Hart inherited Jim Flanigan of West Mifflin, his best player, who went on to play linebacker for the Green Bay Packers and New

350

Orleans Saints, and some stellar performers like Tom Mitrakos of Penn Hills and Bob Longo of Baldwin.

To their credit, he and his staff landed the likes of Harry "Skip" Orszulak of West Mifflin, Rod Fedorchak of Monongahela, Lloyd Weston of Westinghouse High School in Pittsburgh, Denny Ferris of North Catholic, Jack Dykes of Kiski Area, Dave Havern of Montour, Tony Esposito of McKees Rocks, and Ralph Cindrich of Avella. They also had Charlie Hall, Bryant Salter, Dave Garnett, Bill Pilconis, Bob Kuziel, Joe Carroll and Henry Alford, who would be selected, along with Cindrich, in the 1971 and 1972 NFL drafts. Salter came to Pitt primarily for track & field and was a walk-on for football.

Hart still talks about the ones that got away. He mentioned that he thought he had a chance to get Jack Ham and Franco Harris, but lost them both to Joe Paterno and Penn State. I remembered Hart telling me when he was at Pitt about how close he'd come to getting this outstanding running back out of Mt. Holly, New Jersey. At the time, I thought the kid's name was Frank O'Harris. Hart thought he had a shot at Ham, a Johnstown kid. He thought he had a shot at Vic Surma, an All-American lineman at Mt. Lebanon, where Hart lived while he worked at Pitt. Surma also went to Penn State. He lettered three years and was a starter at offensive tackle for two years.

Surma, now a successful dentist with a practice in Mt. Lebanon, lives in Upper St. Clair, about a half-mile from my home. He remembers Hart well.

"He lived a few streets from our home, and I spent a lot of time at his place," recalled Surma. "He was a great guy; he had a terrific personality. He was always a first-class guy with me. I had a great visit at Pitt. He had all these young dynamic guys on his staff and they tried to talk me out of Penn State, which had a lot of older coaches. I had a blast at Pitt. Rod Fedorchak, who is a dentist now, hosted me when I was at Pitt. They took me to a Penguins' game; it was my first National Hockey League game. I met some terrific young ladies. Hey, I was 17 and I was in heaven. I was all set to go to Pitt, but my dad put the kibosh on that because he didn't think they could turn things around. Now I'm glad he did what he did. Penn State was the right place for me. Pitt brought in a real ballyhooed group of recruits that year — like Cindrich and Weston — but we beat then when they came up to Penn State for a freshman scrimmage. That sort of set the tone for things. I roomed with Jack Ham my freshman year at Penn State. Franco came the next year. Now they're both in the Pro Football Hall of Fame."

Cindrich, a highly successful sports attorney/agent who lives in Mt. Lebanon in a magnificent home previously owned by Mario Lemieux, but has his own office complex in Carnegie, recalls Hart fondly. "He recruited me and he's the reason I went to Pitt," said Cindrich. "He got 13 of the Big 33 players the year I came, and that was more than anybody else got from that group. He could recruit, that's for sure. He looked you in the eye when he spoke to you and you always knew where you stood with Coach Hart. You always knew that the University, at that time, wasn't behind his program. He was dealt a losing hand. Under the circumstances, he did the best he could do. The same was true for his successor, Carl DePasqua. It wasn't until the University changed its whole approach when they brought in Majors that we had a chance to be a winning program. They opened the doors wide for Majors. When you look at Hart's coaching staff and what they did later on, it's a great success story. Even if Hart had the other year at Pitt, though, it wouldn't have changed things. It wasn't close. They couldn't have won the way things were at the time. You have to have more than good coaches and recruiters to win in major college football. You have to have all the resources and everything in place."

Pitt came this close to dropping its football program on a major college level after DePasqua's disappointing period. Chancellor Wesley Posvar's top aide, Dr. Jack Freeman, voted to give up the ghost. This was all debated behind closed doors and was a hush-hush affair. In the end, Pitt officials decided to give it one more go and hired Majors to turn things around.

"Dave is one of the great guys I know."
— Dick Bestwick

Hart's first coaching staff at Pitt included several men who would become head coaches later on, Frank Cignetti (West Virginia and Indiana University of Pennsylvania), Dick Bestwick (Virginia), Bill Lewis (East Carolina and Georgia Tech) and Bill Neal (Indiana University of Pennsylvania). Leeman Bennett became the head coach of the Atlanta Falcons in the National Football League, and Jim Royer became the player personnel director of the New York Jets. So Hart had assembled a good staff. They were just all so young, and didn't have the kind of support needed to realize their dreams.

Jim Kriek, former sports editor of the *Connellsville Courier* in Hart's hometown and more recently a stringer for the Uniontown *Herald-Standard*, has long been a booster of Hart as "the good and respectable man he's always been."

Missouri became known as "The Cradle of Athletic Directors" when Hart was there. During his eight years on the Columbia campus, eight different assistant athletic directors went on to become Division I athletic directors. One of those was Dick Bestwick, originally from Grove City, who was on his first coaching staff at Pitt. Bestwick became the athletic director at the University of South Carolina, and later served in the athletic department at Georgia.

"Being AD is one of the toughest jobs on campus," observed Hart. "But I would do it all over again. It's the greatest job in the world. An AD's job today, however, is more like a corporate CEO."

Dave's oldest son, Dave Jr., became the athletic director at East Carolina University and then Florida State University, and has been sought after by many schools, including Pitt and Alabama, his alma mater. He was the president of the National Association of Athletic Directors at the time of my visit to see his father. Dave Hart's grandson, Ricky, was following in the footsteps of his father and grandfather. He was working in promotion and marketing in the athletic department at the University of Oklahoma.

His boss was Joe Castiglione, who had worked for and succeeded Dave Hart at the University of Missouri. Ricky had worked in the athletic department during his student days at the University of North Carolina at Chapel Hill. "They had a picture of the three of us in the athletic directors' publication," said Dave Hart. "We might be the first family to have three generations in college athletic administration."

When Dave Hart Jr. was at East Carolina University, he hired Bill Lewis in 1989 to be the head football coach. Lewis had been an assistant on his father's original staff at Pitt over 20 years earlier. Three years later, the Pirates had their finest football team ever. After losing their season opener, they won 11 straight games, including a victory over North Carolina State University in the Peach Bowl.

Two of Hart's grandsons are seeking to become major league baseball players. They are the sons of his second son, Dick, who played defensive back in the late '60s and early '70s for Bobby Bowden at West Virginia University. Dickie graduated from Florida Atlantic University where he played baseball for three years. He's an infielder playing for a Class A team at Boise, Idaho in the California Angels system. Chris, a first-team catcher for Florida State University, broke his leg sliding home against Florida in the 12th game of the 2000 season and was being red-shirted.

Dick Bestwick, who retired in June of 2000 as an assistant to athletic director Vince Dooley at the University of Georgia, recalls those early days in Pittsburgh and when he later served on Hart's staff at the University of Missouri. "Dave is one of the great guys I know and I love him dearly," said Bestwick, who would soon be 70 and had 18 years in college athletics on his resume. "He was a class guy and he brought in good people to work with him wherever he went. Howard 'Butch' Weyers, the guy who came to Pitt when I left, is the real success story of that group of coaches. He has his own huge company (insurance, I think) in Lansing, Michigan and is a multimillionaire. As a native of Greenville and a well-to-do Thiel grad, he is a member of the Thiel governing board. Where Dave really had people go on to success would be in his administrative career. I've played some small part in that, too, but it is amazing how that chain has expanded over the years."

From Michelosen's staff, Hart inherited Steve Petro, Walt Cummins and Bob Timmons, and he has fond memories of all of them. "They were all devoted Pitt people, and they were all good guys," Hart said. "They all taught me something."

Hart, by the way, had a lot of respect for Michelosen, and still believed Pitt was wrong to fire Michelosen when they did, following a 3-7 season in 1965. After all, the Panthers had posted a 9-1 record in 1963. Hart had little respect for Frank Carver, who hired and fired him and Michelosen. He didn't think Carver did much to help his coaches be successful. Carver was a calm, conservative sort and even his biggest supporters believe he was better suited to be an AD at an Ivy League school. ADs back then didn't have to do what ADs have to do today. I asked Hart what he would do as an athletic director if his football coach compiled three straight 1-9 seasons. Suddenly, those brown eyes were fixed on mine. He paused a few seconds, and said, "I'd probably have to fire him."

Hart had big plans at Pitt, but somehow he couldn't pull them off. He wanted a live mascot, for instance. During his days as an assistant coach at the University of Kentucky, he had seen the caged tiger at Louisiana State University. Someone would rattle the tiger's cage at the outset of the home contests and the tiger would roar over a loud speaker to get the crowd fired up.

"The crowd would chant 'Tiger bait! Tiger bait!' If you're up there with the opposing team, it shakes you up," said Hart.

When Hart was at Johnstown High School, the team's nickname was Trojans. A farmer gave Hart a gentle old workhorse, a brown one. Hart dyed the horse black and blue (Johnstown's school colors) and dressed up a rider in a helmet and imitation armor to look like a Trojan warrior. The rider carried a spear, "and when he'd take off and come up that field before the game, the fans would go crazy," Hart said.

After Hart expressed a desire to do something like that, the Beaver Valley chapter of the Golden Panthers purchased a panther cub for him. It had to be housed at the Highland Park Zoo. It wasn't permitted to be at Pitt Stadium during games. Insurance policies for Pitt Stadium didn't cover having wild animals on the sidelines, even in a cage. This was hardly what Hart had in mind.

He said he learned something from every experience. In his one year as a scout with the Cowboys, for example, he looked up to Tom Landry, the coach of the Cowboys. "He was a really high class act," said Hart, "and he tried to teach his players how to live, how to behave and how to act."

Of his short stay as an assistant at the University of Kentucky, he recalled how Adolph Rupp, the Wildcats' legendary basketball coach, was treated like a god. "I remember being told never, never use Adolph Rupp's No. 1 parking slot, even if you know he's going to be away for a month," said Hart. "I never did, nor did anyone else."

"Thank you for the indelible mark you left on my soul."
— John Kasay

Hart treasures correspondence he has received from former players and colleagues from his high school and college days. One of his favorite letters came from John P. Kasay who became an assistant football coach and then an assistant athletic director at the University of Georgia. Kasay's son, John, Jr., was a superb left-footed place-kicker at Georgia and with the Carolina Panthers of the National Football League.

Kasay wrote a hand-printed four-page letter to Hart following a 1970 reunion of Hart's players at Johnstown High School. There were 52 of Hart's former players who showed up for the reunion.

It read in part, "The memories that you left behind in the minds of those you coached are vivid. The period of eight years that you coached in Johnstown, the world for us was aglow. The pride that you injected into a rag-tag bunch of blue-collar guys year after year was unreal. Our expectations and desire exceeded our ability.

"One comment was made the morning after (at the reunion), while we were sitting in the office of the motel. 'Do you remember, guys, the day after we returned from camp?' someone asked. I sure do. We would walk through the streets with our duffel bag on our shoulder, or a suitcase in our hand, swelled with so much pride we thought we would burst. Someone else remarked that it was like returning home victorious from some foreign war. There is a recollection of all the younger boys from the school crowding around us, touching the Trojan T-shirt, wanting to know all that went on at camp. Each one of them wanted to be in our shoes someday.

"I think that championship teams were a combination of talent, dedication and unusual commitment. I played on an SEC championship team, coached five more, plus a national championship team. It held true with those teams and with our 1958 WPIAL championship team at Johnstown. It was great to see so many guys return from that '58 bunch

"I believe that Bobby Bambino would run through a brick wall for you this very day. I wish you could have seen the affection for you in his eyes. Coach, I always believed that high school coaches have more influence over a young man's life than at any other level of coaching.

"I want you to now that the boys you coached sure have turned into one hell of a good bunch of men. We all thank you, and I personally thank you for the indelible mark that you left on my soul. Johnstown is a much better place for having you pass through, not in bricks and mortar, but in character. Every time I head into Connellsville or Johnstown, you are the first thing I think of. I am extremely proud to have been a part of the Hart Years in Johnstown."

"(They) never saw the water coming, they only heard it."
— David McCullough, Author
The Johnstown Flood

By coincidence, I was in Johnstown on Easter Sunday, April 23, 2000, the day before I visited Hart in Asheville. My wife, Kathie, and some friends had gone to Arizona that Saturday for a week's vacation. I was planning on taking a trip to the Carolinas with my friend, Alex Pociask. His wife, Sharon, had invited my wife to join her and some other friends on a trip to Scottsdale.

My daughter, Sarah, and her husband, Matt Zirwas, invited me to join them for an Easter Sunday dinner in Johnstown, where his parents and his sister, Marsha, and her family were living. We were also celebrating Matt's 26th birthday. He and Sarah were just a month away from completing their studies at the School of Medicine at the University of Pittsburgh. We were so proud of them.

We went out to dinner at Lino's Restaurant & Trattoria in the Westmont section of the city. While waiting to be seated, I spotted Jerry Lino Berteotti in the lobby. It turned out that Berteotti, who had been a standout baseball player at Upper St.Clair High School and at Pitt, and had a brief pro baseball career in the Dodgers organization, was running the restaurant. His father later told me the restaurant was named for Jerry and his grandfather.

Bertiotti was living upstairs of this Italian restaurant. It had some of the same sports photos on display on its walls as his family's other restaurant, Pizzaz Pizza Restaurant & Saloon on Rt. 19 in McMurray, where my wife and I went to dinner about once a month. Jerry's sister, Missie, was a pro golfer of note. She was pictured with Arnold Palmer in both restaurants, and Jerry was pictured with former Dodgers manager Tommy Lasorda.

Matt's father and mother, Tom and Shirley Zirwas, knew the Berteotti family from their respective early days in the Bridgeville area. Tom had told me that on the way to the restaurant. There are still lots of Berteottis in Bridgeville.

We visited the Johnstown Inclined Plane, hailed as "the steepest vehicular incline in the world" in the Guiness Book of Records. There was quite a striking view of the city below. It was the Conemaugh Valley of the Alleghenies. I could see Point Stadium directly below. That's where the Johnstown Johnnies baseball team plays its home games in the independent Frontier League. Tom told me they were installing bleacher seats in the outfield that had been removed from Pitt Stadium. That news did nothing for my spirits.

To the right was the Cambria County War Memorial Coliseum, home of the Johnstown Chiefs of the East Coast Hockey League. I remembered going there as a freshman at Central Catholic High School to root for the Vikings varsity basketball team in a post-season

season tournament back in 1956. Central Catholic had a terrific team, with six future college players in the lineup (George Patterson and Jim Miller at Toledo, Paul Benec at Duquesne, Dink Larkin and Jim Foley at Pitt, Chuck Dees at LaSalle). I remembered how Central blew a lead in the late going and lost a heartbreaker to Bishop McCort in the western Catholic Class A finals.

Two others, John Mitchell (Penn State) and Tim Grgurich (Pitt) were on the jayvee team at Central Catholic that same year. The freshman team included "Sudden Sam" McDowell, later an All-Star pitcher with the Cleveland Indians. Chuck Rutter, who would become the athletic director at Seton-LaSalle High School, was a member of the basketball and baseball teams at Central.

"You brought back a dark day in my athletic career," recalled Rutter, a junior on that team, when I called him later to check on the details of that defeat. "We had two inbound passes under their hoop intercepted and they scored two field goals in the last six seconds to beat us by a point. We had the game won. It was a killer."

"Mouse" McCullough was the manager for the varsity and jayvee teams. He would work in the equipment room for the basketball program at Pitt for the next 40 years.

I could see all their faces from the viewing deck near the Johnstown Incline. I could see movie actors Tom Cruise and Paul Newman. Cruise was the star safety in a 1983 movie "All The Right Moves," about a high school football team in Johnstown. Newman was a tough hard-hitting minor league hockey player-coach in a 1977 movie, "Slapshot," filmed at the Cambria County War Memorial Coliseum. The latter decried the violence in hockey, as displayed by a sleazy minor league team.

"All The Right Moves" featured a newcomer named Lea Thompson as Cruise's girlfriend, and a hard-nosed coach played by Craig T. Nelson, which led to a long-playing TV sitcom role in "Coach." It was about student sports stars fighting to get out of a dying Pennsylvania mill town to enjoy a better life.

I thought about another McCullough, David McCullough, a Pitt alumnus, who wrote a prize-winning book, "The Johnstown Flood." There were photo displays in the lobby of the Johnstown Incline and at the lookout nearby showing what happened below when that flood devastated the Cambria County community on May 31, 1889. Heavy rainstorms resulted in a dam giving way. An estimated 20 million tons of water roared down the mountains, a wall of water, 70 feet high in some places, smashed through Johnstown. The flood killed, in a matter of minutes, over 2,200 men, women and children in one of the worst disasters in U.S. history. It was a real scandal, as some of the area's bluebloods were blamed for altering (and weakening) the structure of the dam to suit their pleasure boating needs. They were aware of what they'd done and could have reinforced the dam at a minimal cost if they had chosen to do so. I later toured Grandview Cemetery where hundreds of plain marble headstones mark the graves of the flood's unknown dead. It resembled one of those gravesites for American soldiers in Europe.

"Most of the people in Johnstown never saw the water coming; they only heard it," wrote McCullough at the start on one chapter in his book about the tragic destruction, "and those who lived to tell about it would for years after try to describe the sound of the thing as it rushed on them."

I could see Steve Petro, known as "The Rock," who came out of Johnstown to play for Jock Sutherland at Pitt and later served as a coach and assistant to the athletic director at his alma mater. Petro was one of the most popular and revered figures in Pitt athletic history, as far as the ballplayers and alumni were concerned. Petro often spoke with great pride about Johnstown during his long stay at Pitt. I could see Jack Ham and Pete Duranko who came out of Johnstown to star, respectively, at Penn State and with the Pittsburgh Steelers, at Notre Dame and with the Denver Broncos.

I could see Dave Hart, who I would be seeing the next day in North Carolina. Hart had worked wonders during his days in Johnstown. I wondered how I should happen to be in Johnstown the day before I was to see Dave Hart once again.

"John Woodruff used to run by my house."
— Dave Hart

Hart graduated from Connellsville High School in 1943. He and Johnny Lujack were the starting halfbacks on Connellsville's undefeated football team in 1941.

Lujack was a senior in Hart's junior year. They both lined up on occasion at tailback and took turns throwing the ball. The quarterback was strictly a blocking back in Connellsville's offensive scheme. Hart starred for another undefeated team there in 1942. "We had two undefeated seasons in succession," said Hart, "and we had only 13 points scored against us."

Hart was a sprinter on the track squad (10.4 seconds in the 100 yard dash) and a starter on the basketball team. Lujack was a star in those sports as well. Lujack would lead Notre Dame to a national championship and win All-American and Heisman Trophy honors in 1947. I had last seen them both in Connellsville on September 16-17, 1994, at a 50th anniversary reunion of the '44 Cokers.

"I grew up in the Catholic school system in Connellsville," recalled Hart, reciting an example of his good luck. "I went to Immaculate Conception High School and went out for football as a freshman. Earl Trump was the coach. He was a Georgetown graduate.

They dropped the sport during my first year and sent the uniforms to Boys Town. Trump came to my parents and told them, 'Your son has ability. I recommend you transfer him to Connellsville. He should be playing ball somewhere.' Lujack went to Immaculate Conception, too, and he transferred. Five of us were starters that year at Connellsville and the team went 6-4."

"Lujack was always a class act," said Hart. "He was our class president. He carried himself well. He was a point guard on our basketball team. He threw the javelin in track. He was a shortstop in baseball. He was a four-sport letter-winner at Notre Dame. When I came back from the military service, I thought of transferring to Notre Dame. I had originally been recruited at Connellsville by Frank Layden, the Notre Dame coach. I talked to Lujack about it, and he was telling me he didn't think he'd be starting at Notre Dame. They had so many great players in those days. If Lujack couldn't start, I didn't think it would be the right place for me."

I asked Hart if, in his youth, he had been aware of Connellsville native John Woodruff, the Olympic gold medal winner in the 800 meter run in the 1936 Olympic games. Known as "The Hitler Games." Hart smiled and said, "John Woodruff used to run by my house when I was growing up. I've always been a big admirer of John Woodruff."

Hart entered the University of Georgia on a football scholarship in the summer of 1943. He was a first team tailback as a freshman, only to be called into the U.S. Air Force two weeks before the opening game. Dave had enlisted in the Air Force at the age of 17 in the spring of 1943. Almost all of the players on that Connellsville championship team enlisted in the military service. Connellsville historian Bart Mallory pointed out that every branch of the military service was represented by the backfield and an assistant coach from the 1941 Connellsville High School football squad: quarterback Alfred Bieshada (Marines), right halfback Lujack (Navy), fullback Wally Schroyer (Army), left halfback Dave Hart (Air Force) and assistant coach Edward Spotts (Coast Guard). Bill Feniello lent me photos of those players from his personal collection. His big brother, Gary, had been a lineman on that team.

Connellsville Coker teammates Hart and Bill Sohonage served in the Air Force together and both saw combat action in the European Theater of Operations, including the famous bomb runs to Hitler's number one concern, the heavily-fortified Ploiesti oil fields of Romania. Hundreds of American airmen lost their lives on those missions. One time their airplane was forced to land in Russia. On another bomb run, Hart lost his oxygen due to an equipment failure, and Sohonage shared his oxygen with Hart — taking turns with Sohonage's air supply — until the plane landed safely at their home base in England.

While with the Air Force, Dave returned to the University of Georgia and was a member of the 1946 undefeated Bulldog Sugar Bowl championship team. Charlie Trippi was the star running back on that team. "Joe Geri, who would go on to play for the Pittsburgh Steelers (1949-1951), was playing behind me," recalled Hart. After a knee injury held him back in 1947, Hart transferred to St. Vincent College, close to his hometown in southwestern Pennsylvania.

"I didn't see a big future playing behind Charlie Trippi," said Hart.

He was the starting halfback on the Bears' 1948 and 1949 teams and was the co-captain of St. Vincent's undefeated team of 1949 that won the Tangerine Bowl (now called the Citrus Bowl) at season's end. "We gave up only six points all year," said Hart, "and that was the lowest of any college team in the nation."

When Hart reflects on his roller coaster ride through college athletics, he points to his experience at Robert Morris College for providing the springboard to his eventual success.

Hart supervised athletic development, public relations and placement. "It was the best thing that could have happened to me," said Hart. "I learned how to raise money, and the stuff you needed to know in athletic administration. Those were three of the greatest years of my life. When I was in coaching, I thought I was ready to be an athletic director. I wasn't. I learned how to do that at Robert Morris. Charlie was great to me, but he was not very happy when he heard I was going to leave. He was cool to me after I told him of my decision. He didn't want me to go."

Hart left for the University of Louisville to become the Cardinals' director of athletics. "I received some great recommendations for the job from such people as Homer Rice and Joe Paterno," said Hart. "Imagine Joe Paterno recommending me after I'd competed against him at Pitt."

In truth, Pitt didn't offer much competition to Penn State in Hart's three seasons. Pitt was as overmatched against Penn State as it was against Notre Dame in those difficult days. The Panthers lost all three games to the Nittany Lions, by scores of 48-24, 42-6 and 65-9. Those meetings with Penn State were always the last game of the season, and the third one was Hart's last outing in his three years at Pitt. That 65-9 score was the most lopsided in Hart's three seasons, topping the season opener at UCLA that the Panthers lost by 63-7.

Hart's three victories, by the way, were over West Virginia (17-14), Wisconsin (13-11) and William & Mary (14-3). It's intriguing that he got his three Ws against teams whose name began with a W.

"I had my fill of it," said Hart. "I was so broken-hearted and depressed that things just fell in on me.

"After I lost my job at Pitt, I was offered several jobs as an assistant coach on the college level, but I didn't want to step down. Joe Restic offered me a job on his staff at Harvard, for instance. I really didn't feel like coaching. I thought I should get into administration work. I went to Chancellor Posvar at Pitt to see if he could help me. He said, 'I'll talk to someone to see what we can do.' He thought I might have to start at one of the state schools, like Clarion or Slippery

Dave Hart during his Pitt coaching days

Dave Hart during his U.S. Air Force training days in 1943

From the Hart family photo album

Dave Hart and one of his assistant coaches during his Pitt stay, Steve Petro, greet Jeff Barr, a quarterback candidate from Canton, Ohio.

Rock. I got a call from Bob Miller, who was in the laundry business and was a member of the Golden Panthers. He had been a big supporter of mine during my Pitt stay. He said, 'Charles Sewell wants to talk to you about coming to Robert Morris.' They were a junior college at the time, but they went to a four-year program while I was there. Bob Miller said they'd pay me what I was getting paid ($18,000) to coach at Pitt. And I was drawing one more year on my salary at Pitt. I wanted to stay in Pittsburgh. My son, Dickie, was the quarterback and captain of the football team at Mt. Lebanon High School. At first, I didn't have much to do, and I was really down in the mouth. I was sitting in my office, getting nothing accomplished, and feeling sorry for myself. I didn't think it was the right job, and I was thinking of quitting. Sewell could see that I was down in the dumps, and he talked to me about it. He started giving me specific assignments and I got busy. He pointed me at the right people. I got good at getting money for the school.

"One time, I had Mrs. (Teresa) Heinz sign a check for Robert Morris in her chauffeur-driven car in the amount of $75,000. We were sitting in the back seats and she just handed me the check. Charlie Sewell thought I was the greatest after that.

"I started going to the Duquesne Club all the time. That's where all the corporate leaders and rich guys went to lunch. It was a place I'd never been to before that. I didn't know a darn thing about fund-raising until I got to Robert Morris. I learned how to write proposals, how to get grants.

"I was grateful. When I got to Louisville, I put Robert Morris on our basketball schedule. Our basketball coach, Denny Crum, asked me what Robert Morris was doing on our schedule, and I told him why I was doing it. He went along with it. It was a good payday for Robert Morris to come to our place, and to play at Freedom Hall. It was my way of paying back Robert Morris for what it meant to me."

Hart doesn't forget old friends. Loyalty is one of his qualities. "When I first came to Pittsburgh to coach at Pitt," he recalled, "some guy hit my car my first week there. Bill Baierl, the automobile dealer, heard about it and lent me a car. I think it was the first courtesy car in the athletic department at Pitt. He's been providing cars for coaches for 40 years. The car I'm driving now is one of his cars. I bought it from Bill Baierl because he gave me a great deal."

Hart had arrived at the Quality Inn in a 1996 diamond white Cadillac Sedan Deville. When I later told Bill Baierl about my meeting with Hart, he said, "That's how I started giving cars to Pitt, and then I got my fellow car dealers providing cars as well. After I was loaning out three cars, I needed to get others involved. It's turned out to be a real good program for Pitt."

Hart also treasures a card he received from the late Leo "Horse" Czarnecki, a legendary character on the Pitt sports scene during his long stay as the director of the ground crew for the athletic department. It reads: "Your name should be Mr. Heart for what did you did and tried to do while at Pitt with a box lunch budget and a steak schedule."

Looking back at Hart's difficult days at Pitt, Pittsburgh sports columnist Bob Smizik once described Hart as a "hard-working, hard-driving enthusiastic salesman who recruited well and won friends and supporters for Pitt."

It turned out though that Hart was better suited to serve as a sports administrator. He was the perfect commissioner.

"Being a commissioner is the best job of all in college athletics," he reflected. "You don't have to please parents or alumni. There's no fund-raising. You don't have to worry about what the players are doing when they're not practicing or playing. You don't have to hear the coaches complaining about this or that, how they're not getting the publicity they deserve. I didn't walk out of my office and have people telling me to get rid of coaches. I didn't have any coaches. You don't see too many conference commissioners giving up their jobs."

Jim O'Brien

Dave Hart, nearing 75th birthday, visits Pittsburgh friends at Quality Inn at Biltmore near his home in Asheville, North Carolina.

Myron Cope
Closes out Steelers yoi-ful season

"I've seen things I've never seen happen before."

Myron Cope came into the large white tent that is called Cope's Cabana twirling his signature Terrible Towel. He had a smile on his face, and was flanked by two handlers, as he hustled his way through the cheering crowd that chanted his name. Cope! Cope! Cope!

He entered the fray like the boxer he'd been in his teenage years in Squirrel Hill, set to do battle with first-time callers and the hundred or so masochists who came to hear more Steelers' talk following the final game of the 1999 season, one of the most dismal seasons in Cope's 30 years as an analyst-color man.

Cope wore a Steelers jersey with COPE and No. 30 on it. As if he needed his name on his jersey. Cope may be the most recognizable figure associated with the Steelers in this city.

He's lived those 30 years in the South Hills, first in Scott Township, most of it in Upper St. Clair, and during that same year he had moved to Mt. Lebanon. Just because the Steelers had a bad game and a bad season, their second consecutive stinker, didn't mean Myron Cope had to have a bad show on WDVE FM. That station and the Pittsburgh Brewing Company sponsored Cope's Cabana. Dan McCann, a retired executive from the brewery, and his wife, Rose, had ringside seats. They invited me to join them.

Cope's Cabana was located outside Gate D of Three Rivers Stadium. It stood right up against the statue of Steelers' owner Arthur J. Rooney — there was a crushed I. C. Light can under Mr. Rooney's right leg — and the fence that surrounds the site of the stadium being built for the Steelers and Pitt Panthers. Fans pay a $10 cover charge that gets them two Iron City or I.C. Light drafts, soda pop if they prefer, and some potato chips and popcorn.

They provide a live audience for Cope's post-game radio show. They get to watch Myron smoke cigarettes and sip something from a little plastic container as he rants and raves and has a helluva good time talking about the issues of the dreary day.

The 47-36 loss to the Titans had a little of everything in it, sensational once-in-a-lifetime plays for the second Sunday in a row, sandlot action most of the way, and some shameless showboating by the Steelers after scores by players who forgot they were still trailing on the scoreboard.

It had been a long day already, with a 4:15 start, an endless game capping a 6-10 season, yet these Steelers' fans came, mostly just to keep company with the beloved Myron Cope. What could he say to ease the pain?

Myron Cope at work in broadcast booth at Three Rivers Season for 1999 season finale with Tennessee Titans and, later, doing post-game show from Cope's Cabana.

Cope was more than equal to the challenge. "How does Myron Cope keep his enthusiasm through all this?" a drunk asked me at half-time of the Steelers' season-ending game with the Tennessee Titans. How, indeed? But he does. That, more than the Terrible Towel and all those familiar phrases — yoi and double yoi! — was the secret to his success. He was responsible for starting the trend of towel-waving that is evident everywhere in sports these days.

Myron always comes to play. "This is the place to close out the 1999 season," he said smugly. It was fitting that the season had stretched into 2000, the new millennium. The Y2K bug didn't knock Cope out of commission. He was still ticking.

A journalist at heart, Cope kept studying the post-game statistics during commercial breaks, but he didn't need the numbers to sum up what he'd just seen. He referred to what he'd witnessed as "this masterpiece of a game," and then as "stinking to behold" and summed it up as "a dreadful season."

He started out by pointing up something I'd been saying for the hour or so since the game ended. "I've seen things I've never seen happen before." He asked if anybody had ever seen the Steelers kick off from the $7\frac{1}{2}$-yard line before?

Two major penalties had pushed the Steelers back there after an on-side kick attempt. It was a strange-looking scene as they set up to kick again.

Many fans stayed away from Three Rivers Stadium for the final two games of the season. They missed seeing plays in both games — the upset win over the Carolina Panthers and the loss to the Titans — they might never have an opportunity to see again.

You have to watch enough bad football to appreciate good football. The 1999 season not only marked Cope's 30th in the broadcast booth at Steelers' games, but he would be turning 71 in January. He had seen his share of Steelers' football. In his early years, the Steelers weren't very good.

They had a reputation for competing hard, but coming up too often on the short end. This season was one of the worst in all ways in Cope's 30 years at the microphone, and no one knew that any better than Cope.

He tried to point out some good things — like the inspired play of a local kid, Jim Sweeney, in his 16th and final NFL season — and he had some positive things to say about the Steelers. He also said the front-office folks better realize they had lots of needs to fill if they were going to get better the next year.

Cope kept talking. He kept smoking. He kept drinking. He kept smiling. He dazzled the crowd, especially when he cut off a caller, something he rarely does. "Don't hold your breath," he warned the wise guy. They chanted his name once more. They were celebrating at Cope's Cabana. It was unreal.

Myron Cope presents award to former Steelers star linebacker Andy Russell, and joins former Pirates pitchers El Roy Face and Bob Friend at annual Sports Night at Thompson Run Athletic Association in West Mifflin.

"Hot Rod" Hundley
Always the clown

"Nothing could match getting that degree."

"Hot Rod" Hundley has always done it his way. He played basketball and life to entertain the crowd. He was always looking for a laugh, a smile, attention, adulation, admiration and acceptance. He wanted everyone to love him. Frank Sinatra sang his songs. Hundley was always seeking the spotlight.

He was Pete Maravich before Pete Maravich, just as Connie Hawkins likes to say that he was Julius Erving before Julius Erving.

That's why Hundley's behavior as he was about to receive his degree at West Virginia University, at long last, was so striking. It was so out of character, for those who had known him during his early years. Hundley went back to the Morgantown campus on May 14, 2000 to receive his bachelor's degree — 43 years after he had left school in pursuit of a professional basketball career.

One of the school's most famous basketball players — right up there with Mark Workman, Jerry West, Rod Thorn, Ron Williams, Wil Robinson et al — was finally finishing what he had started in 1953. His decision to do so was inspiring others who had come up short on credits to claim a college degree to do the same. Hundley would tell them it was worth the effort.

"I'm 65 years old and I'm supposed to be getting Social Security," Hundley told Danny Wells of *The Charleston Gazette* before the big day, "but instead I'm getting my degree. I think it's the best thing that ever happened to me. I made the all-state team in high school, the All-America team in college and the NBA All-Star team, but nothing would match getting that degree. I'm all excited about it."

Hundley had gained the necessary credits to complete his college requirements through correspondence courses, documenting his professional broadcasting career and what he had learned on the job to satisfy a degree-completion program outlined for him by school officials.

Pittsburgh sports broadcaster Bill DiFabio followed Hundley about the campus for seven hours on graduation day to do a TV report. "He was nice to everyone," recalled DiFabio. "He was nervous, though. He said he wanted to make sure he said the right thing. At the same time, he didn't want to upstage the seniors who were getting their degrees that day. He was worried about how it would go down."

It takes some of us longer to grow up than others. As a freshman at WVU, Hundley upstaged the seniors, as well as the juniors and sophomores, on the varsity team. Basketball fans filled the old Mountaineer Field House to watch Hundley and the WVU freshman team — he was the best show in town — and many of the fans left

"HOT ROD" HUNDLEY
"Voice of the NBA's Utah Jazz"

before the varsity game got under way. Throughout his 25 years as "the voice of the Jazz," going back to their Pete Maravich days in New Orleans, and earlier broadcasting gigs with the Los Angeles Lakers and Phoenix Suns, Hundley had never worried about what he said. He never worried about offending anybody. He's nearly as popular in Utah as Karl Malone and John Stockton, the stalwarts of the Jazz, and the team's long-time coach, Jerry Sloan. He's a glib guy who knows his basketball, and still takes advantage of a lull in the action to entertain the crowd with some comic relief. Hundley has homes in Salt Lake City and in Phoenix. To hear Hundley, he never really had a home before he went to West Virginia University.

"I love West Virginia," he says. "That's where it all began. I'm grateful for the folks who stuck with me, and helped me find the way."

WVU officials were eager to work with Hundley to get him his degree. School President David Hardesty told Danny Wells of *The Charleston Gazette*, "Hot Rod is one of the great athletic and broadcasting talents ever to come out of West Virginia and we're very happy to reclaim him as a degree-holder at the university. His degree is based on his lifetime of achievement in the broadcast industry. We're very, very happy that he is being recognized for his work. He is a wonderful person. He visits the campus and talks to the students and faculty. He always gives very inspirational and heart-warming talks about West Virginia and Charleston."

Hundley had first discussed the idea of getting his degree, at long last, with Dana Brooks, the dean of the department of physical education.

"I always wanted to get my degree," Hundley said. "Sam Huff and Freddy Wyant (former WVU football stars) went back and got their degrees. It's never too late. I wanted to do it."

"It's a wonder Hundley survived his childhood."

As a ballplayer, Hundley was a hot dog, a ball-handling wizard who liked to put on a good show. He had a great jump shot and could score with the best of them. But if the Mountaineers had a big lead on someone, Hundley would have his way, performing ball-handling tricks. He might pass the ball or dribble it between his legs, let the ball roll up his arm and across his shoulders and across his other arm. Given the same freedom as ball-handlers enjoy in basketball today — does anyone get called for palming the ball anymore? — Hundley would have been even more dazzling.

The closest act to Hundley's in the NBA these days belongs to another native West Virginian, Jason Williams, the zany point guard for the Sacramento Kings. Williams comes from Nitro, West Virginia, not far from Hundley's hometown of Charleston. Williams and Randy Moss, now an All-NFL receiver for the Minnesota Vikings, were quite a 1-2 combination on their high school basketball team. Nitro is a small industrial town that can be seen from the highway, with plumes of smoke shooting skyward, as one is heading for Charleston. It's next door to East Bank where Jerry West played his high school ball (Class of 1956). In fact, Jerry's No. 12 jersey from his Pioneer playing days is still on display in the East Bank High School gymnasium.

In Hundley's heyday at WVU, during a timeout, or as he readied to shoot a free throw, he might spin the ball on his fingertip. Some of his passes would bounce off the hands of unsuspecting teammates. Some writers praised him. Others were critical of his shenanigans. His own coaches usually defended his antics publicly while cautioning him in the clubhouse to limit his light-heartedness on the playing floor. Opposing coaches would often say they were glad they didn't have to deal with a star that didn't take the game more seriously.

There were stories about how Hundley shot hook shots for free throws, scoring a field goal while shooting with one knee on the floor, and how he had left the court to go to the concession stands during a game. No doubt, he bought a hot dog with lots of mustard. Legendary sports broadcaster Jack Fleming recalls how Hundley once hung from the hoop and scratched his belly like a chimpanzee during a game with Rutgers.

Two of Hundley's idols were Goose Tatum of the Harlem Globetrotters and Bob Cousy of the Boston Celtics, two of the most renowned ball-handlers in the sport. Two of his non-sports idols were Marlon Brando and Jimmy Dean. That tells you all you need to know about the young Rod Hundley. Brando and Dean both played the part of cool, mumbling rebels in movies during that era. So Hundley, following the lead of these handsome young men was simply hell on wheels. His nickname "Hot Rod" suited him perfectly.

It's no wonder he wasn't disciplined. It's no wonder he was looking for laughs and love in all the wrong places.

He had a wretched childhood in Charleston, an impoverished, bleak early life right out of a Charles Dickens novel. He has detailed his difficulties in two books, *Clown*, with Bill Libby back in 1970, and *You Gotta Love It, Baby*, with Tom McEachin in 1999. Libby was a free-lance sports writer with a regular byline in *Sport* magazine. Libby also wrote a book on Jerry West. McEachin covers the Jazz beat for the *Ogden* (Utah) *Standard-Examiner*. Anybody who has read either or both of those books, or knows about Hundley's upbringing, can better understand his style and guile, and the roots of his public persona.

Hundley missed an NBA playoff game between the Jazz and Portland Trail Blazers in order to accept his degree which indicates how important this was to him. This is a man who missed fewer than five games in 25 years. He missed one game to receive an NCAA award at the 1982 Final Four. He missed a game to attend the funeral of his mother. He also attended his father's funeral, but that was in between his ballplaying and broadcasting days in the NBA when he was working for Converse and living in Greensboro, North Carolina. In the end, he had made peace with both of his parents. He forgave them for their shortcomings and for abandoning him as a child. It's a wonder that Hundley ever survived his childhood, let alone live long enough to gain a college degree.

When he became a star basketball player his parents were proud of him. They had photos and clippings of him on display in their respective homes. They would have been proud, most likely, to see him get his degree from WVU as well. Hundley can only wonder about that. It hurts to think too much about what might have been. His good humor has helped Hundley get through the bad times.

During his six years as a ballplayer in the NBA, and later as a broadcaster with NBA teams for nearly 30 years, Hundley had a reputation as a free spirit and someone that stayed up late at night and had a good time.

I recall Hundley holding court in the lobby of a hotel in Houston on February 11, 1989 — I had to look up the date — the day before the NBA All-Star Game there. Basketball people and members of the media surrounded him. He was there as the TV and radio voice of the Utah Jazz.

"My daughter was going out on a date with John Havlicek's son," Hundley told his audience. "So I gave her a little father-daughter talk about how to handle that. I told her, 'Look, if he tries anything, let him!' Can you imagine the genes at work there? Hot Rod and Hondo! A union of our children could produce such a great basketball player!"

Anything for a laugh, even at his daughter's expense.

Time passes. People change. As he prepared for his graduation day at Morgantown, Hundley said he had another reason to be excited about the month of May. "My daughter, Jennifer, is having a baby at the same time."

Hundley had three daughters: Jennifer, 37; Jackie, 34; and Jennifer, 29. He and his second wife, Florence, were proud of all of them. Hundley has tried to become a better, more attentive father in recent years. He finally recognized that he had been selfish when they were young, and too often away from home, doing his own thing, looking for a good time. In short, he had been like his father.

His dad was a drunk, in Hundley's own accounts, who frequented bars and pool halls around Charleston. He never saw much of him. His dad started showing up when Rod became a basketball star. That happens with a lot of young sports stars. There were times his father showed up drunk and embarrassed him. Rod chased his father away from time to time, then cried when he got to his room.

"Hot Rod" Hundley has been a howl during his days with the Utah Jazz and Los Angeles Lakers and with West Virginia University.

"I was always on the outside looking in."

He was born Rodney Clark Hundley on October 26, 1934 in Charleston. "I never had a family and I never had a home," he says in his latest book, *You Gotta Love It, Baby.* "I never even had a childhood, really. I bounced from one place to place since I could remember. I never had anyone or anything."

"I never knew my folks, not as a kid," Hundley said in an earlier interview. "My dad was a meat-cutter by trade, so everyone called him Butch, short for Butcher. Cora was my mother's name. They were divorced when I was about six months old. My mother didn't earn enough to support me, so she turned me over to a couple, who must have been in their 50s, George and Mamie Sharp. My mother moved to Washington, D.C. where she could get a job. She was a waitress most of the time. I was probably four or five, I'm not sure, when she left town. She just knocked on these people's door one night and asked them to take care of me. She'd come back once in a while to see me, but not that often.

"This was during the last days of the Depression, so money was hard to come by. The Sharps were poor people and they lived in the slum section of the city. He was a bottle-washer at an ice cream plant. He never made much money, so he couldn't give me much. But they treated me like one of their own. I had my three meals and a place to sleep. It was a small house and I used to sleep in a cot behind a curtain under the stairs. Damn, it used to get real cold down there. I was always cold, or it seemed that way anyhow. I know there were a lot of nights when I cried myself to sleep."

The Sharps lived within two blocks of a city playground and Thorn went there all the time to play basketball. Then he started playing basketball at the YMCA as well.

"I lived on that playground and in the YMCA gym," said Hundley. "It didn't take me long to see that I was going to be the best player there. I put it in my mind that I could get out of my situation by excelling at basketball. I taught myself how to play basketball. I always thought the best way to get better was to play against better players.

"In junior high and senior high school," said Hundley, "I'd go down there and play with Mark Workman, and George King and great players like that. The competition was really difficult because if you lost you had to sit out an hour before you got a chance to play again."

Hundley stayed out late, didn't study much in school, and frequented the pool halls of Charleston when he wasn't playing basketball. He did some drinking, anything to have a good time. He became too much for the Sharps when he was 16 and they turned him out. He moved in with a high school friend, Tommy Crutchfield. His mother, Mrs. Ida Crutchfield, owned a boarding house hotel and she gave Hundley a room there. There were older men staying there, paying $2 a night for a room, some of them bringing women to their rooms late at night. Hundley used to enter and leave his room by way of a fire escape.

He was strictly on his own most of the time. He had little direction or guidance, unless someone was coaching his team in a basketball game. He was a bit of a loner, feeling strange because his classmates had real moms and dads and homes to call their own.

"I used to look at those kids with families, real families, and it was like they were in another world from me," he said. "I wanted to belong very badly, but I didn't and I knew it. I never fit in. I was always like a round peg in a square hole, always on the outside looking in."

In junior high school, he set state scoring records of 441 points for a season and 37 points for a game, while averaging 20 points a game. In high school, he broke the state's four-year scoring record in three years, averaging more than 30 points a game.

"He was a free spirit."
—Jack Fleming

He had problems in college. He always had to go to summer school because he flunked so many classes. Twice, he almost left school. Red Brown talked him into returning.

Hundley averaged nearly 25 points a game in his three-season college career. Six times he scored 40 or more points in a game. The team ran a fast-break offense under Coach Fred Schaus, with Hundley leading the way. They were a high-scoring team and they won the Southern Conference championship three times, something they hadn't done before.

He got married during his junior year at WVU, but that lasted less than three years. There were no children from that marriage.

"He was a free spirit, no doubt about it," said Jack Fleming, the long-time Voice of the Mountaineers. "They had trouble getting him to class. On one occasion, we went to Davis & Elkins, and we came back in a snowstorm. We were out all night. Hundley showed up for an 8 o'clock class the next morning. He would do things like that just to confound people."

Schaus scolded him early on about his showboating, but put up with it when Hundley used better judgment. "Some thought he was a clown and that's all he did, but he was a heckuva player," said Schaus. "Almost all the way he was considerate of other players and coaches and used common sense not to overdo the antics with the wrong people. He used good judgment."

Hundley gave himself credit for that as well. "I never jeopardized a game. If the score was tied, I wasn't going to clown around. I only pulled that stuff when we were ahead.

"Basketball was just a game, and I always had fun. I wanted to win and I tried hard but it wasn't the end of the world if we lost. Compared to everything else in life, this was easy. This was my security in life."

"Hot Rod" Hundley was one of the first college basketball players I became aware of as a 12-year-old sports fan. The Steel Bowl in 1954 was the first college basketball I ever saw in person. Pitt, Duquesne, George Washington and Wake Forest comprised a four-team field for the holiday season tournament.

Corky Devlin of George Washington and Dick Hemric of Wake Forest were two of the top stars in that tournament. I had a board basketball game at the time that employed a ping pong ball. I used to have each of the five spots on the floor designated as one of the players on those Steel Bowl teams. I kept statistics.

That was during "Hot Rod" Hundley's sophomore season at West Virginia and he was a well-publicized player, right from the start. His files in the sports information department at West Virginia University are jam packed with copies of newspaper and magazine stories about his heroics. Hundley has his own collection of clippings and mementos from his playing days.

There were three daily newspapers in Pittsburgh in the mid-50s. Hundley was hailed by Al Abrams in the *Post-Gazette*, by Roy McHugh and Carl Hughes in *The Pittsburgh Press,* and by George Kiseda in the *Sun-Telegraph*. Abrams, his paper's sports editor, wrote of Hundley: "Call him clown, master showman, superb player or what you will, West Virginia's Hot Rod Hundley is box office dynamite." Hundley, it was written, was the main reason for 3,950 fans showing up at the Pitt Field House, whereas a thousand or less fans were usually there for the Pitt games.

Hundley had been a high school hot shot at Charleston High School, setting all sorts of scoring records and gaining all-state status three straight seasons. Robert "Red" Brown recruited Hundley to WVU, but gave up coaching the basketball team when he became athletic director. He turned over the job to Fred Schaus, a former WVU star who had played in the NBA.

"He was the best prospect I've ever seen," said Brown back then. "Certainly, he's the best prospect ever to come out of West Virginia."

During his freshman season at West Virginia, Hundley was tabbed "the best basketball player in the country" by Chuck Taylor, a sporting goods ambassador and a prominent authority on the game.

He would become the most colorful and controversial college basketball player in the country. He drew large crowds everywhere. Fans were eager to see him in action, wanting to see his shooting and ball-handling skills, even more so to see what he might do next.

There were a lot of great college basketball players during that period. The All-America lists in the mid-50s included Tom Gola of LaSalle, Dick Ricketts and Sihugo Green of Duquesne, Bill Russell and K.C. Jones of San Francisco, Dick Garmaker of Minnesota, Robin

Freeman of Ohio State, Dick Hemric of Wake Forest, Don Schlundt of Indiana, Tom Heinsohn of Holy Cross, Darrell Floyd of Furman, Bill Uhl of Dayton, Lenny Rosenbluth of North Carolina, Charlie Tyra of Louisville, Jim Krebs of SMU, Jack Twyman of Cincinnati, Wilt Chamberlain of Kansas and Elgin Baylor of Seattle.

Hundley was good enough to gain first team All-America honors as a senior. He was the first pick in the 1957 NBA draft, taken by the Cincinnati Royals. The Royals then traded him to the Lakers for Clyde Lovellete. He played six seasons with the Lakers, three of them in Minneapolis and three in Los Angeles.

"I heard it on my car radio," recalled Hundley. "I stopped at a pay phone and called the owner of the Lakers. I asked for $11,000 and he offered $9,000, and we settled on $10,000."

Elgin Baylor joined the Lakers a year after Hundley did. When the Lakers moved to Los Angeles they were joined by Jerry West. The Lakers new coach was Fred Schaus, who had coached Hundley and West at West Virginia. When West was at East Bank High School, Hundley attended several of his basketball games and helped sell him on staying in state to play at West Virginia. Hundley told him he'd be big at WVU.

Hundley had a few good years with the Lakers, good enough to get named to two All-Star Games. He averaged 12.8 points during the 1959-60 season, the team's last in Minneapolis, and 11 points during the 1960-61 season, the team's first in Los Angeles. He averaged 4 points a game in 1962-63, his last in the league. Over his six years, he averaged 8.4 points. Keep in mind that two of his teammates, West and Baylor, were among the league leaders in scoring.

All in all, with all the ups and downs in his life, Hundley has done all right for himself, and he turned out to be a good citizen.

"I've done pretty well with my life," he said. "I owe it all to basketball and the start I got at West Virginia."

Frank Sinatra
"An American Legend"
"Sometimes I sang for nothing or a sandwich or
cigarettes — all night for three packs.
I worked on one basic theory: Stay alive and
get as much practice as you can. To learn more
about the trade, I would hang around clubs
after I performed and ask any established
vocalists who were there about their methods.
I wanted to learn how to do it right."

Andy Beamon
Building a football stadium

"This is my baby."

A former University of Pittsburgh football player is overseeing the construction project to build a new stadium on the North Side where the Steelers and Panthers are to begin playing in the 2001 season.

Andy Beamon positively beams — what else? — when he leans back in his chair in his temporary office across the street from the construction site and speaks about his exciting assignment.

His title is general superintendent for Hubert Hunt & Nichols — Mascaro, according to a fresh-minted business card. He is a senior vice president for Mascaro Construction, headquartered less than a mile away. His boss is Jack Mascaro, who holds undergraduate (1966) and graduate (1980) degrees in Civil Engineering from Pitt. Beamon has a B.S. in Civil Engineering, Class of 1968. Both Beamon and Mascaro keep pinching themselves to make sure this isn't just a dream.

Their North Side firm is working in conjunction with Hubert Hunt & Nichols of Indianapolis to build the $250 million dollar, 65,000-seat stadium. It's one of the biggest construction projects in Pittsburgh, and along with PNC Park — the future home of the Pirates — and the expansion of the Convention Center, a symbol of the revitalization of the city. The 1,500,000 square foot stadium will have 6,600 club seats and 120 luxury suites among other amenities.

Beamon points to a large color photograph pinned to a bulletin board overhead. It's an aerial shot of the work site between Three Rivers Stadium and the Carnegie Science Center. It looks, at first glance, like an overhead photo of an archaeological dig, but upon closer inspection shows the outline of a football field, the beginnings of a stadium.

"I've seen a football stadium here since September," Beamon said. He spoke to me enthusiastically about pile caps and grade beams, steel, milestone schedules — certain aspects of the construction have to be done by certain dates — and nervously tapped away on the lap-top computer he uses to communicate with others working on the project.

Beamon is a busy boy. He arrives at 7 a.m. each workday and usually doesn't get out of there until 8 p.m. He admits to driving by, just to survey the scene, even on so-called off days. The site, unsightly as it appeared to the average citizen in the initial stages of construction, has become a magnet in his life.

Beamon has studied the blueprints and artist renderings and the scale model of the stadium enough to be able to easily envision the final product. When he stands over the glass-encased white model of

Photos by Jim O'Brien

**Andy Beamon
looked after
construction
of Steelers
stadium
from the
beginning.**

the stadium, he looks like a proud father looking at a newborn in the viewing area of a hospital maternity ward. Beamon is one of a chosen few who can proudly say of the stadium project, "This is my baby."

It's Beamon's responsibility to see that everyone is doing what they're supposed to do to get it built the right way, and to do whatever it takes to keep everyone busy so it is erected according to plans. Construction should be completed by August of 2001. Both the Steelers and Panthers are scheduled to open their 2001 season in the new stadium. Both would play the 2000 season in the final year at Three Rivers Stadium.

It's an exciting challenge. Imagine having breakfast in the morning, knowing you're going to work to help build the new state-of-the-art stadium for the Steelers and Panthers. Imagine being able to eat breakfast, or keep it down, with that kind of daily challenge. Beamon smiles through the stress.

"It's a big deal," he acknowledged. "It's terrific for the city. It will make a big impact. The Steelers wanted the best possible football stadium. It will work for Pitt, too, if Pitt puts a good team on the field."

Beamon, age 53, doesn't wear a business suit to work. In December and January, during our visits, he looked more like a man who was going ice fishing. His balding head and beefy cheeks were rosy before he even went out in the cold. He looked comfortable, however, in a plaid flannel shirt and khaki slacks. Construction helmets and boots were nearby, also staples of his winter wardrobe. There are also hardhats on the shelf that bear the imprinted names of Dan Rooney and Art Rooney II and other high-ranking Steelers officials. There were times during the winter spell when the construction site looked like an Alaskan tundra plain. It was hard to imagine any work getting done on such difficult days — snow swirling in soft mists about the site and blotting out the blue-gray sky at times and the cold numbing to the skin sometimes at the start and finish of the work day — but fast-approaching deadlines demanded that work continue in earnest. The calendar on the wall of his office was unforgiving.

"The Steelers are supposed to play two pre-season games here in August, 2001," added Beamon. "No, I'm not nervous at all. I'm more excited than anything. I'm very optimistic, very confident. We have a great group of workers here. We'll get it done right and on time."

A few weeks later, in late January, I spoke to him at 7:30 a.m. one day when temperatures dipped to 11 degrees. It felt worse with the wind whipping in from the three rivers. "We won't be working today because it's just too cold," said Beamon. "Such days are built into the schedule projection. This is one of those days you get your office cleaned up."

As a boy in Port Vue, just outside of McKeesport, Beamon remembers riding around Pittsburgh in his father's automobile, Edward Beamon proudly pointing out projects he'd worked on as a surveyor for Michael Baker Jr. in Rochester, now Baker Engineers. One of the jobs his father liked to point out was the Fort Pitt Tunnel.

Beamon looks forward to a day when he takes his grandchildren for a similar ride, perhaps through the Fort Pitt Tunnel, and he will be able to point out the stadium he helped to build. "Yeah, this will be the one they'll point out to their kids as well," said Beamon. "I'll be able to show them something that means so much to Pittsburgh. I'll be real proud of it, and my involvement in this project."

He and his wife, Shirley, have 26-year-old twins, Anne and Emily, and a 21-year-old daughter, Sara, a junior at Washington & Jefferson College. They are among his biggest fans and share his pride in this project.

"We were all excited when we learned that his company got the project and he would be working on the stadium," said Shirley, who hails from Liberty Boro and says they were high school sweethearts. "We're a football family, for one thing. Andy has built many good projects, like schools, office buildings and bridges, but this is one that everyone will know and talk about. We're thrilled to death and so happy for him.

"Someday our grandchildren will be able to come across the Fort Pitt Bridge and say that their great-grandfather worked on the tunnel project, and point to the new football stadium and say their grandfather helped build that. It will be a real monument to everyone involved with the project."

Beamon has many boosters in the industry, beginning with his boss, who say he is more than equal to the challenge. "He's a good man and he knows what he's doing," said Mascaro, sitting behind his handsome desk at his year-old headquarters on Manchester's Reedsdale Street. "That's why he drew this responsibility."

"He brings the same sort of tenacity and aggressiveness he must have brought to playing football for John Michelosen and Dave Hart at Pitt," allowed Louis Astorino, an architect who is working on PNC Park for LD Astorino Associates LTD and has worked on projects with Beamon in the past.

"I'm happy to see a good Pitt man looking after an important project like this," said former teammate Frank Gustine Jr., a mover and shaker in the Pittsburgh commercial real estate market. "I share Andy's pride. I've always been impressed with his attitude and work ethic."

Gustine had strong emotional ties to Pitt Stadium and to Oakland, where his father, Frank Sr., a former Pirates ballplayer, owned and operated a popular restaurant on the Pitt campus for over 30 years. "I still believe this move to a new stadium is critical to a turnaround in Pitt's football fortunes," said Gustine. "I'd feel the same way if our family still had the restaurant in Oakland."

These guys are all friends. They share similar roots and a hometown pride. They show up at the same Christmas parties. Mascaro can't stop smiling since Dan Rooney, the president of the Steelers, and Art Rooney II, vice president and heir apparent, picked him to be a part of the construction project team. In a separate project,

Mascaro and his three sons, Michael, Jeffrey and John C. Jr., are all personally involved with building practice, workout and sports medicine facilities for UPMC, the Steelers and Pitt on the city's South Side.

Mascaro has become a public relations man for the Rooneys. "They are Pittsburgh," he is fond of saying. "I'm proud to be working on something so important to Dan Rooney and his team."

Another local construction firm, The Massaro Company in O'Hara Township's RIDC Park, was one of the final three in the competition for the plum assignment. Owner Joe Massaro and his three sons would have felt the same sense of pride as the Mascaro family in working on such an important Pittsburgh project.

Jack Mascaro commissioned Doug Cooper, a professor of architecture at Carnegie Mellon University, to create murals in the lobby of his construction company that show the new stadium with the city's skyline in the background. There is an intriguing rendering in the foreground, a scene from the hilltop village in Italy where Jack's father came from, blending in somehow, a walkway leading from the village to the grand concourse at the top of one end of the stadium. It's an awesome vista, one that expresses Mascaro's heartfelt feeling about the personal meaning of this project. For him, this project began in his father's hometown in Italy. Rooney has the same regard for his family's roots in Ireland.

Asked about the significance of this prized assignment, Mascaro commented, "It's both an honor and privilege to be part of the construction team that is building the new stadium, which is one of Pittsburgh's largest construction projects ever.

"The Steelers are Pittsburgh, and being part of this new football stadium, which will be a permanent landmark of our city's landscape, is very special. We have a passion about Pittsburgh and the Steelers. It's exciting to have a major role in Pittsburgh's current renaissance, and I am particularly happy that the Pitt Panthers will be playing there, too!"

Beamon, of course, shares Mascaro's excitement over what they are doing. "I could never do another job, and I'd be satisfied," he said. "I'd be happy I did it."

It began with Beamon reshaping what used to be the Miller Printing Plant into a field office for his staff. Fans who once parked their car in that vicinity may recall the Miller Printing Plant, just across the street from the Steelers' grass practice field. It will be leveled when the stadium is completed. The Steelers practice field would soon be converted into a parking lot. "I take personal pride in this project," he said, "setting this place up, and getting the office ready to go. Doing the earthwork. Now the actual construction is underway. The foundation has been laid. Now we're building up to the sky.

"You watch everything like it's your own. The Steelers have been terrific. They make you want to do a good job. You want to please them. They make you a part of the team. It's special."

Photos by Jim O'Brien

Andy Beamon and his boss, Jack Mascaro, are so proud of football stadium project on the city's North Side, not far from Mascaro Construction Company.

When I asked Beamon about how things were progressing, he calmly offered, "We're just about on schedule."

"Football wasn't an end all."

Andy Beamon was a part of some of Pitt's sorriest football teams. "Bill Kaliden recruited me to Pitt," said Beamon. He came to Pitt in John Michelosen's last two seasons, when they went 3-5-2 in 1964 and 3-7 in 1965. Then Dave Hart came in and Beamon was there for two of those three consecutive inglorious 1-9 seasons before Pitt pulled the plug on Hart.

Beamon was the starting center in his junior year, but he was sidelined his entire senior season because of a series of concussions. Beamon came to practice every day and centered the ball, though, even if he wasn't permitted to scrimmage. "I centered for the quarterbacks, but there was no contact work," he said. "The doctors wouldn't let me." He showed up for work every day; he thought he owed Pitt that much for his scholarship.

"John Michelosen probably cared more about you as a person and getting your education than he did the football aspect of the program," observed Beamon. "Football wasn't an end all. Take a look at how many dentists, doctors, lawyers, teachers and business people came out of the program in that period. It's a pretty impressive group. Many of them were there for the Varsity Letter Club dinner on the eve of the final game at Pitt Stadium. That made it special."

He mentioned teammates like Dr. Bob Bazylak, another McKeesport High School product, and Dr. Jock Beachler of Mt. Lebanon. "When I first came in, our starting center was Fred Hoaglin from East Palestine, Ohio, who had a long career in the NFL and is still a coach there," said Beamon. "So there were good people, and some outstanding players, in the program. We just didn't have enough talent."

Everyone learned something positive from what appeared to be a negative environment. Hart himself went on to become a successful and respected administrator at Robert Morris, Missouri and Louisville, and as commissioner of the Southeastern Conference before retiring in Asheville, North Carolina.

All of Hart's assistant coaches from his first season went on to become head coaches or to hold successful pro positions. "We had a lot of good people, but we weren't a very good football team," recalled Beamon. "But most of my teammates have been successful in life."

He saw many of those teammates at the final game at Pitt Stadium in late November. He was among the nearly 400 letter-winners who walked across the field at halftime of Pitt's exciting victory over Notre Dame in the finale.

"I have mixed emotions about the Pitt Stadium situation, like so many others," he conceded. "When I walked down on the field at half-

Artists' renderings of Steelers stadium, above, and PNC Park below offered excitement about new landscape on city's North Side.

time, I said of the decision to level the stadium, 'This is a mistake. This is bad.' But when I went back to my seat to rejoin my wife it took me forever to get there. I didn't reach my seat until the start of the fourth quarter. There's no room to get around. The stadium is too steep; it's really an outmoded facility. It was great to see it filled for the last game, but it only pointed up all its inadequacies. The seats are so uncomfortable. It's outlived its useful life. I knew then that this is something that had to be done. It would have taken a lot to fix it up. Pitt's going to have a great place to play football, as fine a stadium as there will be anywhere in the country. It should help them improve the program."

I asked Beamon if he had gone out to Oakland to see Pitt Stadium since the bulldozers began ripping out the stands and cement bowl. "No," Beamon came back. "I'm avoiding it."

"We think he does just a superb job."
—Steelers' owner Dan Rooney

Andy Beamon is a "Pittsburgh guy," as the late Art Rooney liked to dub such locals. Beamon was born on the South Side, at St. Joseph's Hospital. He grew up in Port Vue. He played for Bill Lickert's Little Tigers in McKeesport for two years. He played at Port Vue Liberty Junior High School, now part of the East Allegheny Area School District. His coach there was Dan Giger, who had played for Duke Weigle at McKeesport High School.

That was Beamon's next stop. His coaches at the high school were Weigle, Ding Schaeffer and Dick Bowen, a former Pitt quarterback. Beamon played tackle for the Tigers as a sophomore, center as a junior, and center and linebacker as a senior.

He's come a long way since those humble beginnings. He was now living in Elizabeth Township, not far from his hometown. He likes it that way.

Beamon believes the Rooneys liked the idea of doing business with a local firm like Mascaro Construction. There was a sign on the building beside the one where Beamon's office was located that showed that Bryan Mechanical of Neville Island was a subcontractor on the project. The firm's owner, Miles Bryan, was a teammate in the same backfield at North Catholic High School as Dan Rooney once upon a time.

Two other local firms, Sauer Heating & Air Conditioning of Ross Township and SSM Industries Inc. of Manchester, are working with Bryan Mechanical on the plumbing, heating and air conditioning.

"Most of the major contracts are with Pittsburgh companies," said Beamon. "That's the way Mr. Rooney wants it. Hirschfeld Steel of San Angelo, Texas is providing the steel, but Century Steel of West Mifflin is erecting it."

Photos by Jim O'Brien

The view from Allegheny Club was always awesome, as it was for 1999 Steelers' season finale when snow covered the turf in late going.

Beamon mentioned the OAC meetings. OAC stands for Owner, Architect and Construction Manager get-togethers. "We just had one this morning," said Beamon during our mid-morning visit. "The Rooneys participate. Art attends most of the meetings, and Mr. Rooney comes at least once a month. He calls in from time to time. He wants to know how it's going. We have a contract to get aerial photographs for progress reports, but Mr. Rooney flies over the site in his own plane, and takes his own pictures as well. He also takes photos of PNC Park. He's such a fan of this city.

"We also have meetings with people involved in the Pirates' ballpark project because we have to do some things in concert. We have a labor agreement on the two projects that assures us that there will not be any work stoppage. Dick Corporation is building PNC Park and I have some great friends there."

Before Beamon came to Mascaro Construction ten years ago, he previously worked at Dick Corporation and with Mellon-Stuart, so he is well known and respected in the industry. He's worked on projects out of town, in places like Atlanta, Harrisburg, Waynesburg and Scranton, but he can point with pride at the Ironworkers Building in the Strip District which he worked on in the '70s.

"I've worked on some important projects in Pittsburgh, but this is the best one, and working with Mr. Rooney and his family makes it even more special," said Beamon.

"He cares a great deal about this project. Most of all, it's really his baby. We had a catered lunch for our workers right before Christmas. Mr. Rooney came and he addressed everyone. He offered best wishes for the holiday season. He talked to all the workers. He told them what a great job they were doing. He was just terrific with us. He told them he was proud of what they were doing. He said he wished his football team were doing as well as they were. He told them the significance of what they were doing, and how important it was to Pittsburgh.

"He said he hoped the new stadium would have the same kind of impact on his team that moving into Three Rivers Stadium in 1970 had on the team. He signed autographs for anyone who asked. He was a big hit. It meant a lot to everyone."

Dan Rooney has a high regard for Beamon as well. When he talks about Beamon, it's like he's talking about an old friend. "He's a terrific guy, a special guy, a quality person, the kind of person it's easy to be around and talk to," said Rooney. "He's very, very capable. We think he does just a super job. And Mascaro is doing a great job working on the UPMC practice site on the South Side. We're very pleased."

> **"You can be young without money,**
> **but you can't be old without it."**
> —Tennessee Williams

388

Views of Three Rivers Stadium during Pirates last summer there in 2000.

Photos by Jim O'Brien

"Through the lean years I was there."

Andy Beamon goes back a long way with the Steelers. He remembers going to games with his older brothers, Jack and Ed, at Forbes Field in the '60s. "I was a Steelers fan since I was a kid," he said. "I remember Bobby Layne, Ed Brown, Ernie Stautner, Fran Rogel, Buddy Dial and John Henry Johnson. Ray Mathews' mother lived two doors from me as a kid. When I went to Pitt, they were playing at Pitt Stadium. Through the lean years I was there."

Beamon said he and three of his friends bought season tickets for the Steelers in 1969, the first season with Chuck Noll as the head coach and the team's final season playing at Pitt Stadium. They moved to Three Rivers Stadium in 1970. He remembers how he and his Brentwood buddy, Joe Tain, got their tickets when the Steelers went to the Super Bowl after the 1974 and 1975 season. "I remember we slept out on the sidewalk outside the stadium overnight in order to have a good position at the ticket line for the Super Bowl," said Beamon. "Now I have ended up with all four tickets. My three buddies went their own way and I picked up their tickets. When they close it down next year I will be there in my same seats. Most of the people around me are the same people who were there when I first got them.

"They are field boxes, between the 30- and 40-yard lines, on the visitors' sideline. It's by third base for baseball. You come out of the tunnel and our seats are right there. I was in a position to get better seats in the new stadium, but I want to keep the same seats. No one knows yet their exact seat locations. I have a pretty good idea where they should be. There are going to be so many great seats in this new stadium. I didn't want to be in any luxury box. I'll be happy holding onto the same seats. Somehow I think I'll feel even better about being in those seats in the new stadium. I can't wait."

Jim O'Brien

View from Mt. Washington when football stadium and baseball park were in early stages of construction during fall of 1999.

Joe Luxbacher
A Man For All Seasons

"I love soccer.
I love being around the game."

<p>

*T*his was a Saturday in September of 1962, an open date for the football team at the University of Pittsburgh, and Beano Cook had come to his office at the Pitt Field House early to catch up on some work. Cook was the sports information director at Pitt, at least that was his job description. Cook moved to the beat of a different drummer. There was no other SID quite like Cook in the country.

He had to write a feature news release that day on Pitt's star running back, Paul Martha, a junior from Wilkins Township who was one of Cook's favorites. He would be successfully promoting him for All-America the following season.

Cook, better known today as a college football analyst for ESPN, was departing the Pitt Field House when he came upon a gathering of people just inside the doors near the corner at Allequippa and Darraugh. An injured soccer player had been helped across the street from Trees Field where the soccer team played in those days.

Now the soccer player was lying on the concrete floor in a corner of the Field House, his teammates, friends and family gathered around him. His coach, Leo Bemis, and a trainer, Roger McGill, were tending to him. Beano Cook poked his head into the huddle, and asked who it was. He was told it was Jerry Yospin. He was also informed that Yospin had suffered a broken leg. "Better him than Paul Martha," cracked Cook to no one in particular as he went on his merry way.

When Cook came to work on Monday morning, his secretary told him he was to report immediately to his boss, Frank Carver, the Pitt athletic director.

Bemis had called Carver at his home in Beaver over the weekend to complain about Cook's insensitive statement. Carver began chewing out Cook as soon as he entered his office. "For god sake, Beano," cried Carver, "the kid's parents were standing right there! They heard what you said!"

Carver continued to read the riot act to Cook for another 10 minutes, telling him to think before he opened his mouth the next time. Cook took his lashes without protest, and looked properly whipped when he went out the door, his tail tucked between his legs.

A minute later, Cook came back into Carver's office and bellowed, "C'mon, Frank, admit it. Better him than Paul Martha!" Then Cook cut out for the safety of his own office.

"There is soccer at Pitt because of Leo Bemis."

Joe Luxbacher has been at the University of Pittsburgh long enough to hear such stories about soccer and Beano Cook and Jerry Yospin and Paul Martha. Luxbacher laughed when I related the above story, one of many legendary stories involving Cook and run-ins with Pitt coaches. He could laugh about Cook's comment now, though he would have been just as hot as Leo Bemis had it been one of his boys.

Luxbacher knows that soccer will always play second fiddle to football as a fall sport at the University of Pittsburgh. That's not always the case at some of the schools he competes against in The Big East Conference. Luxbacher does his best to make sure his soccer team is as competitive as possible. He loves his sport and those who share his passion for the game and its many benefits.

Luxbacher and his boys love their new locker rooms in the refurbished Field House, and believe the best is yet to come. They have been promised a grass field at a yet-to-be-announced site, and would be playing their 2000 schedule at Quaker Valley High School and other Pittsburgh area facilities. The Big East was demanding its soccer teams play on grass fields, and that was cited as another reason that Pitt Stadium and its artificial turf weren't up to snuff anymore.

It's important to be flexible when you're the soccer coach at Pitt.

The Panthers have been at the top and they have been at the bottom in Luxbacher's 16 seasons as soccer coach at his alma mater. It's been a roller coaster ride he has enjoyed for the most part. He's won Coach of the Year awards, the respect of his peers, and struggled to get over .500 at other times. His overall record for those 16 seasons is 136-106-34. He is only the second soccer coach in the school's distinguished history.

Bemis was the founding coach of soccer at Pitt and remained at the helm for 30 years. "There is soccer at Pitt because of Leo Bemis," Luxbacher likes to say.

Luxbacher was a star player for Bemis in the early '70s, setting some scoring records that still stand — he once scored seven goals and had an assist in a game against Edinboro — and later working with Bemis as a graduate assistant while gaining additional degrees. He served as an assistant coach at Pitt during the 1975 and 1983 seasons, and in between he was the head coach for three years at Mt. Union College in Alliance, Ohio.

Luxbacher holds a bachelor's degree in biological science, a master's degree in health, physical education and recreation, and a doctorate in administration of physical education and athletics. He's written a dozen books on soccer and other sundry subjects, and is a frequent guest columnist on sports health issues in the *Pittsburgh Post-Gazette.*

JOE LUXBACHER
Pitt's soccer coach

Young Joe Luxbacher played for Beadling in 1980 National Open Soccer Cup final.

Joe Luxbacher's grandfather, standing at far right, coached Beadling soccer team back in 1915.

When he was in grade school, Luxbacher thought he'd like to work someday in environmental science. He loves the outdoors and welcomes an opportunity to get away in the woods. Soccer grabbed hold of him as a youngster, however, and wouldn't let go. Every time he thought about doing this or that, soccer seized him and presented him with a payday.

"We worry about things that aren't worth worrying about."
—Joe Luxbacher

Soccer was not always No. 1 on his list of favorite sports, either. As a standout athlete at Upper St. Clair High School, his favorite sports, respectively, were football, baseball and soccer. He was a quarterback and a shortstop, which points up his athletic ability, his skills and smarts and leadership qualities. He grew up in a patch on the outskirts of Upper St. Clair called Beadling, a slice of land that has since been absorbed into the township of Upper St. Clair.

I bump into Luxbacher from time to time at the post office in Upper St. Clair. There is a remnant of the front desk of the old Beadling post office on display in the lobby. Beadling has always been a hotbed for soccer. It was a coal mining community and the miners loved playing soccer on weekends.

After a week of dirty and dreary work in cramped and dangerous mine shafts it was a great escape to run free on soccer fields and kick the hell out of a ball and sometimes their opponents.

There are still coal seams evident on cliffs and hillsides around the soccer field that still sits above the Beadling Soccer Club just off Painters Run Road. There are still old-timers living up the hill in Upper St. Clair who once played for national amateur championship soccer teams from Beadling. Luxbacher is a bit of a throwback to that tradition.

Steve Blass, the former ace pitcher of the Pirates who is now part of the Pirates' broadcasting team, lives nearby. Blass once said there was a time in his life when he didn't know whether he was holding the baseball or whether the baseball was holding him. The same could be said of soccer in the life of Luxbacher.

As soon as he graduated from Pitt in 1974, he was offered a contract to play professional soccer, first with the Philadelphia Atoms and then the Pittsburgh Miners, both of the NASL, and then the Pittsburgh Spirit of the Major Indoor Soccer League (MISL), playing for Frank Fuhrer.

His father, Francis, and kid brother, Jerry, both distinguished themselves as soccer players and coaches. Jerry coached WPIAL and PIAA championship teams at Peters Township High School in

Washington County and continues as a teacher there though he gave up coaching a few years back. His grandfather, Joe, was involved with the early soccer and baseball teams in Beadling.

Soccer was a family affair in the Luxbacher home. "I enjoy coaching," allowed Joe Luxbacher. "I love the game. I enjoy the on-the-field stuff. I like to see the kids get better. I love being around the game."

"My dream vacation is Alaska."

Joe Luxbacher is a laidback individual, a lookalike for movie star Mark Harmon, the former UCLA quarterback and son of legendary Michigan All-America Tommy Harmon. Luxbacher was sitting in a high-back chair in a conversation area at the Upper St. Clair Library when we sat down to discuss his career.

He talked for nearly two hours before he had to get home to help his wife, Gail, get the kids, 4-year-old Eliza Gail and 18-month-old Travis Joseph, ready for bed. Luxbacher had turned 49 only the week before. He had been married for eight years. "I've much younger than he is," Gail told me in a telephone conversation when I called to check on something. "We don't talk about Joe's age."

Gail Polkis, 39, comes from the North Hills of Pittsburgh, the Bellevue-Avalon area, according to her husband.

It's no wonder Joe Luxbacher doesn't like to talk about his age anymore. Joe celebrated his 49th birthday on the same Friday in February when former Steelers defensive lineman Steve Furness was on view at the L. Beinhauer Funeral Home in nearby McMurray. Furness was 49 when he had a heart attack and died. Furness had lived in Upper St. Clair most of his professional career and Luxbacher used to bump into him on occasion.

It was something that made you stop and think. Everyone said Furness look physically fit and was excited about his work when he suffered a heart attack.

Luxbacher brought up a similar story that had grabbed his attention.

"I attended the NCAA Coaches Convention in Baltimore from Jan. 12-16," Luxbacher began. "The last meeting I attended was for soccer coaches in The Big East. I sat next to Mike Berticelli, the soccer coach at Notre Dame. He was the last person I spoke to before I left. The meetings ended on Sunday. Mike had a heart attack while sitting in his car in the driveway of his home on Tuesday and died. It brings everything back into perspective.

"We get so upset about some of the things that go on in our lives, losing games, for instance. We get all involved in what we're doing, and worry about things that aren't always worth worrying about. There's no way you expect these things to happen.

"Mike looked like a perfectly healthy guy, just like you're telling me people said about Steve Furness. Then boom. They're gone. Just like that. How many times do we put off to tomorrow something we want to do.

"I have a lot of interests. As I told you, I thought I was going to be a wildlife biologist. I've done some field research projects and enjoyed that. But I put off doing a lot of things and this makes you stop and think about that.

"I went on an elk management program a few years ago. We flew over fields where elk were roaming free and did a census count."

I told Luxbacher about how I'd been stationed for ten months in military service in Alaska. One of the highlights was accompanying pilots in single-engine planes out over fields and glaciers, checking out caribou, moose, mountain goats, buffalo and wolverines.

"My dream vacation is Alaska," said Luxbacher. "That's the last frontier. I better do it."

"Soccer was a family affair."

"We had a real tradition of soccer in our community," said Joe Luxbacher. "Everbody in Beadling played soccer. In 1954 the Beadling Club team won the national amateur soccer championship. They were runner-up in 1958. They played in a regional league with the likes of Dunleavy, Morgan, Heidelberg, Bridgeville, Muse, Cecil and communities like that.

"My dad showed me articles in the newspapers. There'd be box-scores for 30 or 40 games in a weekend. We all grew up playing the game. In the '60s it died down awhile, but when I got to be 11 or 12 they revitalized the soccer programs.

"My dad had played before World War II. He went into the Army and served in Europe. He was on his way to Japan when the war ended. That would have been a nightmare.

"Us kids used to kick a soccer ball around by ourselves. We'd take turns playing goalie and then a few of us would kick the ball around. That's how you really learn how to play soccer, how to get comfortable with the ball. How to move it, how to kick it. You don't learn that playing on teams from the time you are five years old.

"I have run successful soccer camps with Gene Klein for many years in this area, and we get a lot of kids who play on organized teams but have no idea how to move the ball around and they don't really have a feel for the game. Gene was a goal-keeper for some of our Beadling teams that competed in national amateur and open tournaments.

"You have all these age-group community teams with parents lining the sidelines and they're shouting at the kids from one end of the field to the other. The parents usually haven't played soccer and don't know what they're doing. Sometimes that turns the kids off to soccer or to baseball, basketball or football.

"When kids are kids you've got to let them play on their own once in a while."

Luxbacher remembers some of his boyhood coaches fondly. There was Bill Merritt, his football coach at Upper St. Clair High School. He played baseball for Alex Parinus and Erman Hartman. Talking further about Hartman, Luxbacher said, "He was great. He knew the game, and he made it enjoyable for everybody. Of all the coaches I had, I enjoyed him the most."

He said he learned a lot from Bobby Lewis, the baseball coach, and Leo Bemis, the soccer coach, when he was at Pitt.

"Bobby looked forward to so many things," recalled Luxbacher. "He was an optimist. He wanted to win, but he enjoyed the whole process. He knew you didn't always win. Sometimes it gets so out of whack. Winning becomes the only measure of success. You do your best. Bobby taught me the importance of being satisfied to do your best, and to do your best by the kids. Bemis was a true gentleman. We didn't always agree on everything, especially when I was a player. But he was a good man and a true gentleman."

I shared Luxbacher's sentiments about those two guys. Lewis made you feel so good every time you crossed his path. He and Bemis both taught gym classes, as did all the coaches for the minor sports — now called Olympic sports — back in the '60s when I was a student at Pitt.

Bemis recruited me out of a gym class to be a backup goalie on his freshmen soccer team in 1960. I had never played soccer in my life until I came to Pitt that fall — the same fall when the Pirates beat the New York Yankees in the World Series right on the campus — and it was a game that made so much more sense for me than the games I'd played in my youth.

I was small and soccer is a sport where size doesn't matter as much as it does in most other sports. I saw some action in goal for the freshman team that year and it was a great experience. Sports coaches seldom instruct regular students these days. There's been a loss in that respect.

Luxbacher was looking forward to continuing as the coach of the Pitt soccer team, of spending time with his wife and children, of pursuing more writing and environmental-related projects. He said The Big East had one of the strongest soccer conferences in the country, with five of the Top 20 teams last year. "We had three of the teams in the final 16 of the NCAA tournament," pointed out Luxbacher. "So we have quite a challenge ahead of us. Always.

"We have a good bunch of guys. I try to recruit players who are good people. That's the best way. It makes it more enjoyable to coach them. They do a better job of representing the University of Pittsburgh. That's part of my job, I think, that's part of playing for Pitt."

Pittsburgh Proud
Sports Book Series

Here is information relating to the series of books about Pittsburgh sports subjects by Jim O'Brien that are available to you by mail order:

KEEP THE FAITH
The Steelers of Two Different Eras
Interviews with Steelers of the '70s and the '90s to show what they shared in common, and what was different about the challenges they faced. These are the Steelers of Chuck Noll and Bill Cowher, or Art Rooney and Dan Rooney. Going to Ireland in the summer of '97 brought this all home. 448 pages, 200 plus photos. Hardcover: $26.95, plus sales tax and shipping charges. (ISBN # 1-886348-02-2)

DARE TO DREAM
The Steelers of Two Special Seasons
Profiles of the Steelers and their families from the 1994 and 1995 seasons, when the Steelers had two of the best seasons in the team's history, and even got to the Super Bowl under Bill Cowher. Family photographs and stories, especially those offered by their mothers, offer special insights into the Steelers of the modern era. 480 pages, 270 photos. Limited number of books remain. Hardcover: $26.95 (ISBN # 1-886348-00-6). Perfect bound softcover: $16.95, plus charges. (ISBN # 1-886348-03-0).

WE HAD 'EM ALL THE WAY
Bob Prince and His Pittsburgh Pirates
Personal reflections on Bob Prince, who was "The Voice of the Pirates" for 28 seasons (1948-1975), and one of the most talked-about and controversial characters ever to grace the Pittsburgh sports scene. This book also catches you up on what's become of the Pirates of the same era who remained in the Pittsburgh area after they retired from playing the game. 432 pages, over 200 photos. Hardcover: $26.95, plus sales tax and shipping charges. (ISBN # 1-886348-03-0)

DOING IT RIGHT — The Steelers of Three Rivers and Four Super Bowls Share Their Secrets for Success
Tales of the glory days of the Pittsburgh Steelers. Interviews with the stars of the '70s, as well as players from the early days of the franchise, and those who followed the championship seasons. If you've wondered whatever became of some of your favorite Steelers, here are

the answers. 536 pages, with over 250 photos. Hardcover: $24.95, plus sales tax and shipping. (ISBN # 1-916114-09-0)

REMEMBER ROBERTO
Clemente Recalled By Teammates, Family, Friends and Fans
Pirates Hall of Famer recalled by those who knew him best. Interviews with his wife and sons, and his celebrated teammates during his 18 seasons as an All-Star rightfielder at Forbes Field and Three Rivers Stadium. This was the first adult book on Clemente to come out in over 20 years. 448 pages, over 220 photos, many borrowed from players' personal photo albums. Hardcover: $ 24.95, plus sales tax and shipping charges. (ISBN # 0-916114-14-7)

MAZ AND THE '60 BUCS
When Pittsburgh And Its Pirates Went All The Way
Interviews with all the living members of the World Series champion Pirates of the 1960 season, and five of the key members of the New York Yankees. Chapters on every one of the Pirates of that season. An intriguing reminiscence of what Pittsburgh, particularly Oakland, was like in the early '60s. Reproduced autographs of all the players. 512 pages, over 225 photos, many from players' personal family photo albums. Hardcover: $24.95, plus charges. (ISBN # 0-916114-12-0)

PENGUIN PROFILES
Pittsburgh's Boys of Winter
Stories reflecting on the history of hockey in Pittsburgh. Interviews with many of the recent stars, from Mario Lemieux to Jaromir Jagr, to early stars such as Jean Pronovost and Syl Apps. 448 pages, over 200 photos. Hardcover: $24.95, plus charges. (ISBN # 0-916114-12-0)

HOMETOWN HEROES
Profiles in Sports and Spirit
A variety of inspirational stories about men and women from the tri-state area who excelled in some way to become heroes in their hometowns. 432 pages, over 200 photos. Hardcover: $26.95. (ISBN # 1-886348-04-9)

For more information or to place an order please call Jim O'Brien at his home office (412-221-3580). Or write to: James P. O'Brien — Publishing, P.O. Box 12580, Pittsburgh PA 15241. Pennsylvania residents should add 6% sales tax to price of book, and Allegheny County residents should remit *additional* 1% sales tax on price of book, plus $3.50 for postage and handling. Please provide specific signing instructions. Books are mailed the same day the order arrives. You can also contact Mr. O'Brien by e-mail: jpobrien@stargate.net.

Author's Page

Pittsburgh author Jim O'Brien meets another Irish writer, Frank McCourt, the Pulitzer Prize-winning author of *Angela's Ashes* and *'Tis*, when McCourt spoke at Bethel Park High School on October 5, 1999.

"If you're going to be a writer, you have to find the material, and find your own voice. You have to tell your own stories. There's hundreds of thousands of kids in the playgrounds of New York trying to fly high in the air with a basketball the way Michael Jordan does — taking the ball from one hand to the other — and hanging up there for five minutes — floating like an angel. But there's only one Michael Jordan. You have to find your own way to do it."
— Frank McCourt
October 5, 1999

Ron Necciai

Roger Kingdom

Gus Suhr

Herb Douglas

Andy Van Slyke

Michael Mc Geary

Arnie Sowell